Rating von Finanzinstituten

Zafer Diab · Oliver Everling
(Hrsg.)

Rating von Finanzinstituten

Banken und Finanzdienstleister richtig
beurteilen

Herausgeber
Zafer Diab
Capital Intelligence
Agios Athanasios, Limassol
Cyprus

Oliver Everling
RATING EVIDENCE GmbH
Frankfurt
Deutschland

ISBN 978-3-658-04194-6
DOI 10.1007/978-3-658-04195-3

ISBN 978-3-658-04195-3 (eBook)

Die Deutsche Nationalbibliothek verzeichnet diese Publikation in der Deutschen Nationalbibliografie; detaillierte bibliografische Daten sind im Internet über http://dnb.d-nb.de abrufbar.

Springer Gabler

Gedruckt auf säurefreiem und chlorfrei gebleichtem Papier

Springer Fachmedien Wiesbaden ist Teil der Fachverlagsgruppe Springer Science+Business Media
(www.springer.com)

Vorwort

Die Finanzkrise hinterlässt eine völlig veränderte Bankenlandschaft. In kürzester Zeit zerfielen nicht nur einstige Großbanken, sondern es formierten sich auch völlig veränderte Institute aus Fusionen und Übernahmen. Der verschärfte Wettbewerb unter Banken wird nicht nur unter dem Joch einer ungelösten Staatsschuldenkrise ausgetragen, sondern auch unter erhöhtem Druck der Bankenaufsicht und der nächsten Generation von Finanzdienstleistern. Viele Geschäftsmodelle wurden erst durch neue Informations- und Kommunikationstechnologien möglich und harren auf Bewährung in der Praxis. Die Gesetzgebung erfasst inzwischen jedes Finanzinstitut und unterstellt es der Aufsicht. Unser Buch soll daher nicht nur Konsequenzen der Regulierung und des Wettbewerbs für das Credit Rating von Banken aufzeigen, sondern auch Maßstäbe, Kriterien und Verfahren zur Beurteilung des existenziellen Risikos sonstiger Finanzinstitute.

Staatliche Unterstützung für systemrelevante Banken und Einlagensicherungssysteme entbinden nicht von der Verantwortung, das aus jeder Bankverbindung resultierende Risiko eingehend zu analysieren. Galten Banken bis zur Finanzkrise als Risikotransformatoren zum Nutzen der Realwirtschaft, wurden sie in der Krise selbst zum Risiko. Die Risikoproblematik begrenzt sich nicht auf Kreditinstitute, sondern bezieht sich auf jedes Finanzinstitut, also auch solche Dienstleister, die bisher nicht nach dem Gesetz über das Kreditwesen oder sonst der Finanzdienstleistungsaufsicht unterworfen waren.

Mit dem Verlag Springer Gabler wollen wir den Titel daher nicht als theoretisches Werk zur wissenschaftlichen Modellierung von Bankenratings verstanden wissen, sondern eher als Scharnier zwischen Wissenschaft und Praxis. Das Buch zeigt deshalb nicht nur Beurteilungsansätze für die Praxis der Analyse von Finanzinstituten auf, sondern stellt diese auch in den Kontext der neuen Informations- und Kommunikationstechnologien und deren Implikationen auf Arbeitsabläufe, Dienstleistungsprozesse und Effizienzsteigerung.

Indem der Titel auf die Sicht von professionellen Anlegern und Banken bzw. Entscheidern abstellt, soll dem Leser ein Herausgeberwerk geboten werden, das zwar wissenschaftlich fundiert ist, aber eher als praxisorientiertes Kompendium mit konkretem Nutzen für die Betroffenen positioniert ist. Zielgruppe sind demenstprechend Leser aus Banken, Versicherungen und anderen Finanzdienstleistern, Investoren, Consultants, Asset Manager, Vermögensverwalter, Finanzberater, Wissenschaftler, Wirtschaftsjournalisten und Anleger.

Unseren Autoren sind wir für ihre Artikel wie auch darüber hinaus für ihre fachliche Beratung der Inhalte unseres Buches ebenso verbunden wie auch Herrn Guido Notthoff aus dem Lektorat des Verlags für seine höchst professionelle Betreuung unseres neuen Titels. Anregungen und Kommentare unsere Leser nehmen wir gerne auf: post@everling.de.

Frankfurt am Main   Zafer Diab
                                                                            Dr. Oliver Everling

Inhaltsverzeichnis

Mitarbeiterverzeichnis

Bojidar Archinkov Sofia, Bulgarien

Tobias Basse Hannover, Deutschland

Yvette Bellavite-Hövermann Frankfurt am Main, Deutschland

Bernd Lüthje Hamburg, Deutschland

Stefan-Sorin Mureşan Bonn, Deutschland, Bucharest, Romania

Johannes-Jörg Riegler München, Deutschland

Christian Schmid St. Gallen, Schweiz

Götz Schürmann München, Deutschland

Christoph Wegener Hannover, Deutschland

Theodor Weimer München, Deutschland

Norman Weißer Frankfurt am Main, Deutschland

Laura Zdrzalek Frankfurt am Main, Deutschland

Michael Zlotnik Bad Homburg, Deutschland

Die Herausgeber

Zafer Diab ist seit Dezember 2007 Geschäftsführer der Capital Intelligence (www.ci-ratings.com), einer EU-registrierten Ratingagentur (www.esma.europa.eu). Von 2002 bis 2007 war Diab in verschiedenen Führungspositionen innerhalb von Capital Intelligence tätig, so als Business Development Manager und als Senior Credit Analyst. Diab hat einen Bachelor of Science Degree in Computerwissenschaften der Baylor University sowie einen Abschluss als Master of Business Administration mit dem Schwerpunkt Finanzierung von der Lebanese Amercian University.berd.

Dr. Oliver Everling ist seit 1998 selbständig (www.everling.de) und Geschäftsführer der RATING EVIDENCE GmbH (www.rating-evidence.net). Als Mitglied von Rating-kommissionen (www.dvfa.de), Mitherausgeber der Zeitschrift „Kredit & Rating Praxis" (www.krp.ch) oder als Gastprofessor in Peking (www.cueb.edu.cn) ist er aus unterschiedlichen Perspektiven mit Ratings befasst. Zuvor war er sechs Jahre lang Abteilungsdirektor und Referatsleiter einer Großbank und von 1991 bis 1993 Geschäftsführer der Projektgesellschaft Rating mbH (www.boersen-zeitung.de), nachdem er am Banken- und Börsenseminar der Universität zu Köln über Credit Rating promovierte.

Finanzinstitute: Definition und Bedeutung

Yvette Bellavite-Hövermann

1

1.1 Einleitung

Der Begriff Finanzinstitut ist allgegenwärtig, und das nicht nur in der Wirtschafts- und Finanzwelt, sondern auch und gerade in Lehre und Politik. In der Fachsprache kommt ihm seit Inkrafttreten neuer Aufsichtsregeln Anfang 2014 besondere Bedeutung zu. Im allgemeinen Sprachgebrauch wird er eher als Oberbegriff bzw. Synonym für Kreditinstitute, Broker- oder Börsenmaklerfirmen, Banken mit ihren diversen Unterarten wie Handels-, Investment-, Genossenschafts- und Geschäftsbanken, Sparkassen, Investmentfonds oder Finanzdienstleistungsinstitute verwendet. Manche verstehen darunter gar noch umfassender die Finanzbranche oder gleich den gesamten Finanzsektor. Solange die unspezifische Verwendung nicht den Blick auf die enge Definition im regulatorischen Umfeld verstellt, ist sie völlig unschädlich. Aber da sie sogar in Fachkreisen üblich ist, könnte es durchaus zu irrigen Schlussfolgerungen bzw. falschen Verhaltens- oder Handlungsentscheidungen kommen. Um es mit Ludwig Wittgenstein zu fassen: „Die Bedeutung eines Wortes ist sein Gebrauch in der Sprache." Der Gebrauch eines Wortes wird durch Regeln bestimmt, vergleichbar der Verwendung einer Schachfigur. Somit hängt die Bedeutung eines Wortes elementar mit seiner Regelhaftigkeit zusammen: ohne genaue Definition kein Spielverständnis!

Y. Bellavite-Hövermann (✉)
Frankfurt am Main, Deutschland
E-Mail: dr.hoevermann@googlemail.com

© Springer Fachmedien Wiesbaden 2016
Z. Diab, O. Everling (Hrsg.), *Rating von Finanzinstituten*,
DOI 10.1007/978-3-658-04195-3_1

1.2   Was unterscheidet ein Finanzinstitut vom Kreditinstitut?

Seit dem 1.1.2014 hat die Europäische Union ein umfassendes, für alle Mitgliedstaaten verbindliches Regelwerk für die Bankenaufsicht. Die englischen Titel – Capital Requirements Regulation und Capital Requirements Directive – werden sich im deutschen Sprachgebrauch wohl überwiegend als Abkürzungen durchsetzen: CRR und CRD IV. Dabei entfalten die europäischen Regelungen im jeweiligen nationalen Recht mittelbare (durch Umsetzung durch den nationalen Gesetzgeber) oder unmittelbare Wirkung. Im Rahmen dieser Regelungen wurde u. a. der Begriff Finanzinstitut, allerdings mit neuer Funktion, wieder in das KWG aufgenommen bzw. eingefügt.

Der Begriff „Finanzinstitut" wurde mit der 6. KWG-Novelle am 1.1.1998 durch den Begriff „Finanzunternehmen" ersetzt; damit wurde zugleich eine Neuabgrenzung durch Einführung des Institutstypus „Finanzdienstleistunginstitut" vorgenommen. Die Änderungen im KWG waren von der Umsetzung der Wertpapierdienstleistungsrichtlinie veranlasst (vgl. Bellavite-Hövermann u. a. 2001, S. 9,16).

So wie er nunmehr im KWG verwendet wird, hebt er sich deutlich vom Begriff Kreditinstitut ab – und hat es in sich. Denn durch die Anwendung der CRR im KWG werden gleiche Tätigkeiten einerseits dem Kreditinstitut nach § 1 Abs. 1 KWG zugeordnet und andererseits nach Art. 4 Abs. 26 CRR dem Finanzinstitut. Zudem sind Tätigkeiten, die unter den Begriff des Finanzinstituts fallen, weiterhin auf verschiedene Unternehmenstypen, darunter auch Finanzdienstleistungsinstitute und Finanzunternehmen, anwendbar. Diese Parallelstruktur gibt dem Begriff, sagen wir, eine gewisse Komplexität und vereinfacht die Anwendung nicht unbedingt.

Auch wenn einige Tätigkeiten der Finanzinstitute im KWG Kreditinstituten zugeordnet sind – ein Finanzinstitut ist kein Kreditinstitut. Die Unterscheidung ist wichtig, weil die Aufsichtsbehörden an beide „Institutsformen" – Finanzinstitute und Kreditinstitute – unterschiedlich hohe Anforderungen stellen. Doch wie die Begriffe Kreditinstitut und Finanzinstitut voneinander abgegrenzt sind und welche Strukturen sie wiederum verbinden, lässt sich – wie die folgenden Ausführungen zeigen werden – nicht in einem Satz ausführen.

1.2.1   Finanzinstitut

Was Finanzinstitut oder vielleicht genauer CRR-Finanzinstitut bedeutet, wird im KWG nicht definiert, der Begriff wird dort ohnehin kaum direkt verwendet, genauer gesagt: Im ganzen KWG findet er sich an zwei Stellen (direkte Verwendung findet der Begriff nur in § 1 Abs. 17 KWG „Sicherungsgeber" und § 14 KWG „Millionenkredit"). In der Anfang des Jahres 2014 in Kraft getretenen Neufassung wird lediglich auf die CRR verwiesen, eine Methode, die der deutsche Gesetzgeber häufig benutzt, angefangen bei § 1 KWG mit dem Verweis auf „Verordnung (EU) Nr. 575/2013 des Europäischen Parlaments". Das zieht sich dann durch das gesamte KWG, gedeckt von der Tatsache, dass EU-Verordnungen direkte Anwendbarkeit im nationalen Recht genießen.

Nach Art. 4 Abs. 26 CRR besteht der Geschäftszweck eines Finanzinstituts darin, Beteiligungen zu erwerben oder eine der in Anhang I Nr. 2 bis 12 und 15 CRD IV aufgezählten Tätigkeiten auszuführen. Dies schließt Zahlungsinstitute, Kapitalanlagegesellschaften sowie (gemischte) Finanzholdinggesellschaften ein. Damit sind z. B. Versicherungsholdinggesellschaften keine Finanzinstitute i. S. d. CRR.

Welche Art von Beteiligungen ein Unternehmen hält, ist für die Zuordnung zu den Finanzinstituten irrelevant. Es müssen keineswegs Beteiligungen des Finanzsektors sein; reine Industrieholdinggesellschaften fallen b. a. w. nicht hierunter (EBA/Q & A 2014_857)

1.2.2 Kreditinstitut

Was ein Kreditinstitut ist, wird vom KWG unter dem Oberbegriff „Institute" festgelegt. § 1 Abs. 1b KWG unterteilt sie in „Kreditinstitute" und „Finanzdienstleistungsinstitute", wobei Kreditinstitute gemäß § 1 Abs. 1 KWG Institute sind, die ausschließlich und abschließend Bankgeschäfte tätigen, während § 1 Abs. 1a KWG für die Finanzdienstleistungsinstitute statt einer Definition einzeln aufzählt, welche Geschäftsarten diese betreiben dürfen.

Die CRR definieren in Art. 4 „Institut" als Kreditinstitut oder Wertpapierfirma, und das KWG übernimmt diese Definition mit dem Ausdruck CRR-Institute – in Abgrenzung zum Begriff „Institut" i. S. v. § 1 Abs. 1b KWG – wobei der Begriff des Kreditinstituts im Rahmen der CRR wesentlich enger gefasst ist:

Für die Zwecke dieser Verordnung bezeichnet der Ausdruck Kreditinstitut ein Unternehmen, dessen Tätigkeit darin besteht, Einlagen oder andere rückzahlbare Gelder des Publikums entgegenzunehmen und Kredite für eigene Rechnung zu gewähren (Art. 4 Abs. 1 Nr. 1 CRR).

Danach ist ein Finanzinstitut sowohl im Sinn des KWG als auch im Sinn des europäischen Aufsichtsrechts (CRR, CRD IV) kein Kreditinstitut.

1.2.3 Geschäftsfelder und ihre Zuordnung

Was aber ist ein Finanzinstitut dann? Nachfolgende Übersicht zählt die 12 Geschäftstätigkeiten auf, die Art. 4 CRR bzw. Anhang I CRD IV – über den Erwerb von Beteiligungen hinaus – diesem Unternehmenstyp zuweisen:

1. Darlehensgeschäfte, insbesondere Konsumentenkredite, Hypothekendarlehen, Factoring mit und ohne Rückgriff, Handelsfinanzierung (einschließlich Forfaitierung)
2. Finanzierungsleasing

3. Zahlungsdienste i. S. d. Artikels 4 Nr. 3 der Richtlinie 2007/64/EG des Europäischen Parlaments und des Rates vom 13. November 2007 über Zahlungsdienste im Binnenmarkt

4. Ausgabe und Verwaltung anderer Zahlungsmittel (z. B. Reiseschecks und Bankschecks), soweit diese Tätigkeit nicht bereits unter Nr. 3 fällt

5. Garantien und Zusagen

6. Handel für eigene Rechnung oder im Auftrag der Kundschaft mit Geldmarktinstrumenten (Schecks, Wechseln, Depositenzertifikaten usw.), Devisen, Finanzterminkontrakte und Optionen, Wechselkurs- und Zinssatzinstrumenten, Wertpapiere

7. Teilnahme an der Wertpapieremission und den diesbezüglichen Dienstleistungen

8. Beratung von Unternehmen über die Kapitalstruktur, die industrielle Strategie und in damit verbundenen Fragen sowie Beratung und Dienstleistungen auf dem Gebiet der Zusammenschlüsse und Übernahme von Unternehmen

9. Geldmaklergeschäfte

10. Portfolioverwaltung und -beratung

11. Wertpapieraufbewahrung und -verwaltung

12. Ausgabe von E-Geld

Folgende im KWG als Bankgeschäfte definierten Tätigkeiten schreibt die CRR Finanzinstituten zu:

1. Finanzkommissionsgeschäft (§ 1 Abs. 1 S. 2 Nr. 4 KWG)

2. Depotgeschäft (§ 1 Abs. 1 S. 2 Nr. 5 KWG)

3. Garantiegeschäft (§ 1 Abs. 1 S. 2 Nr. 8 KWG)

4. Wechseleinzugsgeschäft (§ 1 Abs. 1 S. 2 Nr. 9 KWG)

5. Reisescheckgeschäft (§ 1 Abs. 1 S. 2 Nr. 9 KWG)

Unternehmen, die diese Tätigkeiten anbieten, fallen im KWG unter die Institutsdefinition und sind Kreditinstitute.

§ 1 Abs. 1a KWG schreibt dem CRR-Finanzinstitut zudem einige Tätigkeiten von Finanzdienstleistungsinstituten zu (wobei es hier noch auf die Ausgestaltung ankommt, im Einzelfall ist auch eine Zuordnung zur CRR-Wertpapierfirma gemäß Art. 4 Abs. 1 Nr. 1 CRR denkbar):

1. Platzierungsgeschäft (§ 1 Abs. 1a Nr. 1c KWG)

2. Abschlussvermittlung (§ 1 Abs. 1a Nr. 2 KWG)

3. Finanzportfolioverwaltung (§ 1 Abs. 1a Nr. 3 KWG)

4. Eigenhandel (§ 1 Abs. 1a Nr. 4d) KWG)

5. Anlageverwaltung (§ 1a Abs. 11 KWG)

Damit nicht genug: Tätigkeiten, die das KWG den Finanzunternehmen zuschreibt, werden im Rahmen der CRR-Finanzinstituten zugeschlagen. Gemäß § 1 Abs. 3 KWG, sind

Finanzunternehmen Unternehmen, die weder Institute noch Kapitalverwaltungsgesell-schaften oder extern verwaltete Investmentgesellschaften sind und deren Haupttätigkeit darin besteht,

1. Beteiligungen zu erwerben und zu halten (vom Wortlaut her ist der Begriff Beteiligung nach KWG nicht deckungsgleich mit dem nach der CRR, der sich nur auf „erwerben" beschränkt, vgl. Luz u. a., KwG-Kommentar, Bd. 1, 2015, KWG § 1 Rn. 87),
2. Geldforderungen entgeltlich zu erwerben,
3. Leasing-Objektgesellschaft i. S. d. § 2 Abs. 6 S. 1 Nr. 17 zu sein,
4. (weggefallen),
5. mit Finanzinstrumenten für eigene Rechnung zu handeln,
6. andere bei der Anlage in Finanzinstrumenten zu beraten,
7. Unternehmen über die Kapitalstruktur, die industrielle Strategie und die damit verbun-denen Fragen zu beraten sowie bei Zusammenschlüssen und Übernahmen von Unter-nehmen diese zu beraten und ihnen Dienstleistungen anzubieten oder
8. Darlehen zwischen Kreditinstituten zu vermitteln (Geldmaklergeschäfte).

Vor allem der erste Punkt zeigt, dass „Finanzunternehmen" nach KWG im Rahmen einer groben Orientierung dem Begriff CRR-Finanzinstitut noch am nächsten kommt.

Last but not least gehören CRR-Zahlungsinstitute und CRR-Kapitalanlagegesellschaf-ten zu den CRR-Finanzinstituten.

Viel mehr, als dass erst der genaue Blick auf die Geschäftätigkeit zeigt, un-ter welchen Begriff nach welchem Regelwerk ein Institut zu subsumieren und welche Aufsichtsbehörde(n) zuständig sind oder nicht, lässt sich angesichts dieser Bestimmungs-vielfalt kaum festhalten. Immerhin: Alles bewegt sich innerhalb der Finanzbranche. Aber auch da kann man von einer gewissen Begriffsunschärfe reden.

1.2.4 Finanzbranche

Zu den Unternehmen der Finanzbranche zählen gem. Art. 4 Nr. 27 CRR:

a) Institute
b) Finanzinstitute
c) in die konsolidierte Finanzlage eines Instituts einbezogener Anbieter von Nebendienstleistungen
d) Versicherungsunternehmen
e) Drittland-Versicherungsunternehmen
f) Rückversicherungsunternehmen
g) Drittland-Rückversicherungsunternehmen
h) Versicherungs-Holdinggesellschaften

k) gemäß Artikel 4 der Richtlinie 2009/138/EG vom Anwendungsbereich jener Richtlinie ausgenommene Unternehmen

l) Drittlandsunternehmen, deren Hauptgeschäftstätigkeit mit der eines Unternehmens unter den Buchstaben a bis j vergleichbar ist.

§ 1 Abs. 19 KWG hingegen unterteilt die Finanzbranche in die beiden großen Bereiche Banken und Versicherungen und differenziert innerhalb beider Sparten:

1. die Banken- und Wertpapierdienstleistungsbranche; dieser gehören Kreditinstitute i. S. d. Abs. 1, Finanzdienstleistungsinstitute i. S. d. Abs. 1a, Kapitalverwaltungsgesell-schaften i. S. d. § 17 des Kapitalanlagegesetzbuchs, extern verwaltete Investmentge-sellschaften i. S. d. § 1 Abs. 13 des Kapitalanlagegesetzbuchs, Finanzunternehmen i. S. d. Abs. 3, Anbieter von Nebendienstleistungen i. S. d. Abs. 3c oder entsprechende Unternehmen mit Sitz im Ausland sowie E-Geld-Institute i. S. d. § 1a Abs. 1 Nr. 5 des Zahlungsdiensteaufsichtsgesetzes sowie Zahlungsinstitute i. S. d. § 1 Abs. 1 Nr. 5 des Zahlungsdiensteaufsichtsgesetzes an;

2. die Versicherungsbranche; dieser gehören Erstversicherungsunternehmen i. S. d. § 104k Nr. 2 Buchstabe a des Versicherungsaufsichtsgesetzes, Rückversicherungsunternehmen i. S. d. § 104a Abs. 2 Nr. 3 des Versicherungsaufsichtsgesetzes, Versicherungs-Hol-dinggesellschaften i. S. d. § 104a Abs. 2 Nr. 4 des Versicherungsaufsichtsgesetzes oder entsprechende Unternehmen mit Sitz im Ausland an.

In der Neufassung des KWG seit Anfang 2014 sind also die alten Begriffsbestimmungen stehen geblieben; die zum Kreis der Finanzbranche gerechneten Unternehmen sind nach KWG und nicht i. S. d. CRR definiert. Auch wenn die Abgrenzung der einzelnen Begriffe in KWG und CRR voneinander abweicht (und das fängt beim Kreditinstitutsbegriff an, den die CRR wesentlich enger fassen als das KWG), ist insgesamt beim Umfang der Tätigkeiten eine Gleichheit gegeben. Im Zusammenhang mit dem Begriff „Unternehmen der Finanzbranche" haben Finanzinstitute substanzielle Auswirkungen auf die Abzüge der regulatorischen Eigenmittel (u. a. Art. 36, 56 CRR, vgl. auch Gendrisch u. a., S. 87).

1.2.5   Noch einmal: Finanzinstitut

Es soll nicht unerwähnt bleiben, dass „Finanzinstitut" u. a. in den Vorschriften zur Rech-nungslegung ebenfalls als Teil resp. als Synonym von „Kreditinstitut" verwendet wird, nachzulesen z. B. in der „Richtlinie 2006/46/EG des Europäischen Parlaments und des Rates vom 14. Juni 2006 zur Änderung der Richtlinien des Rates 78/660/EWG". Dort ist von „anderen Finanzinstituten" die Rede und aus dem Kontext geht eindeutig hervor, dass Banken danach als Finanzinstitute zu sehen sind. Auch die Leitlinie der Europäischen Zentralbank (2011) zur monetären Statistik, zur Statistik über Finanzinstitute und zur Finanzmarktstatistik verwendet „Finanzinstitut" als Oberbegriff für Kreditinstitute, Zentralbank und sonstige Finanzinstitute.

Doch das ist noch immer nicht die letzte relevante Quelle für die Begriffsbestimmung von „Finanzinstitut" – eine weitere findet sich in der „(EU) Verordnung über Ratingagenturen". Dort gelten Kreditinstitute, Wertpapierfirmen, Versicherer, Rückversicherer, Einrichtungen der betrieblichen Altersversorgung, Verwaltungs- und Investmentgesellschaften, Verwalter alternativer Investmentfonds und zentrale Gegenparteien als Finanzinstitute (z. B. Nr. 9, Art. 5a). Der Begriff ist also weiter gefasst als nach CRR, in der u. a. Versicherungen mitgezählt werden, die Tendenz weist damit Richtung „Finanzbrache" i. S. d. CRR und KWG.

Die babylonische Sprachverwirrung ist, das zumindest ist vermutlich aus der vorstehenden Bemühung um Klarheit klar geworden, weit gediehen. Die Begriffe Finanzinstitut und Kreditinstitut sowie Finanzdienstleistungsinstitut oder Finanzunternehmen stehen im aufsichtsrechtlichen Umfeld jeweils für sich, stehen unabhängig nebeneinander, beinhalten aber teilweise gleiche Tätigkeiten. Umso wichtiger ist eine sachgerechte Anwendung des Begriffs „Finanzinstitut" insbesondere im aufsichtsrechtlichen Kontext, damit den regulatorischen Anforderungen die richtige Bedeutung zukommen kann.

Nachfolgende Darstellung gibt eine Übersicht der Tätigkeiten von Finanzinstituten nach Art. 4 Abs. 26 CRR im Vergleich zu entsprechenden Tätigkeiten gemäß § 1 KWG. Sie zeigt zugleich, dass die Geschäftstypen bzw. Tätigkeiten der Finanzinstitute nach CRR im KWG bereits bisher erfasst waren bzw. gegenwärtig auch noch sind (Abb. 1.1).

1.3 Was bedeutet das in der Praxis und für die regulatorischen Perspektiven?

1.3.1 Institutsaufsicht

Nach § 6 Abs. 1 KWG übt die BaFin in Zusammenarbeit mit der Bundesbank (§ 7 Abs. 1 KWG)[1] die Aufsicht über die Institute i. S. d. § 1 Abs. 1b KWG aus – die sog. Institutsaufsicht – und richtet sich dabei neben dem KWG nach den dazu erlassenen Rechtsverordnungen, folglich auch nach CRR und CRD IV. Das bedeutet: die Aufsicht erstreckt sich ausschließlich auf Kredit- und Finanzdienstleistungsinstitute, nicht aber auf Finanzinstitute.

Den Umfang der Aufgaben der BaFin legt insbesondere § 6 Abs. 2 KWG fest. Danach hat die Bankenaufsicht Missständen im Kredit- und Finanzdienstleistungswesen ent-

---

[1] Es bestehen verschiedene Vereinbarungen und Vorgaben zu länderübergreifender Zusammenarbeit und Informationsaustausch auf EU-Ebene (mit der Europäischen Kommission § 7a KWG; mit der Europäischen Bankenaufsichtsbehörde und der Europäischen Wertpapier- und Marktaufsichtsbehörde § 7b KWG; mit dem Europäischen Bankenausschuss § 7c KWG, mit dem Europäischen Ausschuss für Systemrisiken § 7d KWG). § 8 KWG regelt die „Zusammenarbeit mit anderen Stellen".

Finanzinstitute nach Art. 4 Abs. 1 Nr. 26 CRR		Zuordnung der Tätigkeiten im Rahmen § 1 KWG	
Art. CRR	Tätigkeiten	Unternehmen im Sinne § 1 KWG	Tätigkeiten §§ KWG
Art. 4 Abs.1 Nr. 26 CRR	"Finanzinstitut" ein Unternehmen, das kein Institut ist und dessen Haupttätigkeit darin besteht, Beteiligungen zu erwerben oder (....)	Finanzunternehmen	§ 1 Abs. 3 Nr. 1 KWG **Beteiligungen**
Art. 4 Abs.1 Nr. 26 CRR, Anhang 1 Nr. 2 CRD IV	Darlehensgeschäfte, insbesondere Konsumentenkredite, Kreditverträge im Zusammenhang mit Immobilien, Factoring mit und ohne Rückgriff, Handelsfinanzierung (einschließlich Forfaitierung)	Kreditinstitut	§ 1 Abs. 1 S. 2 Nr. 2 KWG **Kreditgeschäft**
Art. 4 Abs.1 Nr. 26 CRR, Anhang 1 Nr. 2 CRD IV	Darlehensgeschäfte, insbesondere Konsumentenkredite, Kreditverträge im Zusammenhang mit Immobilien, Factoring mit und ohne Rückgriff, Handelsfinanzierung (einschließlich Forfaitierung)	Finanzdienstleistungsinstitut	§ 1 Abs. 1a S. 2 Nr. 9 KWG **Factoring**
Art. 4 Abs.1 Nr. 26 CRR, Anhang 1 Nr. 2 CRD IV	Darlehensgeschäfte, insbesondere Konsumentenkredite, Kreditverträge im Zusammenhang mit Immobilien, Factoring mit und ohne Rückgriff, Handelsfinanzierung (einschließlich Forfaitierung)	Finanzunternehmen	§ 1 Abs. 3 Nr. 2 KWG **Geldforderungen**
Art. 4 Abs.1 Nr. 26 CRR, Anhang 1 Nr. 3 CRD IV	Finanzierungsleasing	Finanzdienstleistungsinstitut	§ 1 Abs. 1a S. 2 Nr. 10 KWG **Finanzierungsleasing**
Art. 4 Abs.1 Nr. 26 CRR, Anhang 1 Nr. 5 CRD IV	Ausgabe und Verwaltung anderer Zahlungsmittel (z.B. Reiseschecks und Bankschecks), soweit diese Tätigkeit nicht unter Nummer 4 fällt	Kreditinstitut	§ 1 Abs. 1 Nr. 9 KWG **Reisescheckgeschäft**
Art. 4 Abs.1 Nr. 26 CRR, Anhang 1 Nr. 6 CRD IV	Bürgschaften und Kreditzusagen	Kreditinstitut	§ 1 Abs. 1 S. 2 Nr. 2 KWG / § 1 Abs. 1 Nr. 8 KWG **Garantiegeschäft**
Art. 4 Abs.1 Nr. 26 CRR, Anhang 1 Nr. 7 CRD IV	Handel für eigene Rechnung oder im Kundenauftrag mit: (a) Geldmarktinstrumenten (Schecks, Wechsel, Depositenzertifikate usw.) (b) Devisen (c) Finanzterminkontrakten und Optionen (d) Wechselkurs- und Zinssatzinstrumenten (e) Wertpapieren	Finanzdienstleistungsinstitut / Wertpapierhandelsbank / Wertpapierhandels-unternehmen	§ 1 Abs. 1a S. 2 Nr. 4 KWG **Eigenhandel**
Art. 4 Abs.1 Nr. 26 CRR, Anhang 1 Nr. 7 CRD IV	Handel für eigene Rechnung oder im Kundenauftrag mit: (a) Geldmarktinstrumenten (Schecks, Wechsel, Depositenzertifikate usw.) (b) Devisen (c) Finanzterminkontrakten und Optionen (d) Wechselkurs- und Zinssatzinstrumenten (e) Wertpapieren	Finanzunternehmen	§ 1 Abs. 3 Nr. 5 KWG **Finanzinstrumente**
Art. 4 Abs.1 Nr. 26 CRR, Anhang 1 Nr. 7 CRD IV	Handel für eigene Rechnung oder im Kundenauftrag mit: (a) Geldmarktinstrumenten (Schecks, Wechsel, Depositenzertifikate usw.) (b) Devisen (c) Finanzterminkontrakten und Optionen (d) Wechselkurs- und Zinssatzinstrumenten (e) Wertpapieren	Finanzdienstleistungsinstitut / Wertpapierhandelsbank / Wertpapierhandels unternehmen	§ 1 Abs. 1a Satz 2 Nr. 2 KWG **Abschlussvermittlung**
Art. 4 Abs.1 Nr. 26 CRR, Anhang 1 Nr. 7 CRD IV	Handel für eigene Rechnung oder im Kundenauftrag mit: (a) Geldmarktinstrumenten (Schecks, Wechsel, Depositenzertifikate usw.) (b) Devisen (c) Finanzterminkontrakten und Optionen (d) Wechselkurs- und Zinssatzinstrumenten (e) Wertpapieren	Kreditinstitut / Wertpapier-handelsbank / Wertpapier-handelsunternehmen	§ 1 Abs. 1 Nr. 4 KWG **Finanzkommissionsgeschäft**
Art. 4 Abs.1 Nr. 26 CRR, Anhang 1 Nr. 8 CRD IV	Teilnahme an Wertpapieremissionen und Bereitstellung einschlägiger Dienstleistungen	Finanzdienstleistungsinstitut / Wertpapier-handelsbank / Wertpapierhandels-unternehmen	§ 1 Abs. 1 Nr. 10 KWG **Emissionsgeschäft**

Abb. 1.1 Finanzinstitute nach Art. 4 Abs. 1 Nr. 26 CRR und Zuordnung der Tätigkeiten im Rahmen § 1 KWG

Art. 4 Abs.1 Nr. 26 CRR, Anhang 1 Nr. 8 CRD IV	Teilnahme an Wertpapieremissionen und Bereitstellung einschlägiger Dienstleistungen	Finanzdienstleistungsinstitut / Wertpapierhandelsbank / Wertpapierhandels-unternehmen	§ 1 Abs. 1a S. 2 Nr. 1c KWG **Platzierungsgeschäft**
Art. 4 Abs.1 Nr. 26 CRR, Anhang 1 Nr. 9 CRD IV	Beratung von Unternehmen über Kapitalstruktur, industrielle Strategie und damit verbundene Fragen sowie Beratung und Dienstleistungen im Zusammenhang mit Unternehmens-zusammenschlüssen und -übernahmen	Finanzunternehmen	§ 1 Abs. 3 Nr. 7 KWG **Kapitalstruktur**
Art. 4 Abs.1 Nr. 26 CRR, Anhang 1 Nr. 10 CRD IV	Geldmaklergeschäfte	Finanzunternehmen	§ 1 Abs. 3 Nr. 8 KWG **Geldmaklergeschäfte**
Art. 4 Abs.1 Nr. 26 CRR, Anhang 1 Nr. 11 CRD IV	Portfolioverwaltung und -beratung	Finanzdienstleistungsinstitut / Wertpapierhandelsbank / Wertpapierhandels-unternehmen	§ 1 Abs. 1a S. 2 Nr. 3 KWG **Finanzportfolioverwaltung**
Art. 4 Abs.1 Nr. 26 CRR, Anhang 1 Nr. 11 CRD IV	Portfolioverwaltung und -beratung	Finanzdienstleistungsinstitut	§ 1 Abs. 1a S. 2 Nr. 11 KWG **Anlageverwaltung**
Art. 4 Abs.1 Nr. 26 CRR, Anhang 1 Nr. 12 CRD IV	Wertpapieraufbewahrung und -verwaltung	Kreditinstitut	§ 1 Abs. 1 Nr. 5 KWG **Depotgeschäft**
Art. 4 Abs.1 Nr. 26 CRR, Anhang 1 Nr. 15 CRD IV	Ausgabe von E-Geld	E-Geld-Institut	§ 1 Abs. 1 Nr. 2 ZAG **E-Geld**

Abb. 1.1 (Fortsetzung)

gegenzuwirken, welche die Sicherheit der den Instituten anvertrauten Vermögenswerte gefährden, die ordnungsmäßige Durchführung der Bankgeschäfte oder Finanzdienstleistungen beeinträchtigen oder erhebliche Nachteile für die Gesamtwirtschaft herbeiführen können.

Die Erbringung von Bank- und Finanzdienstleistungen nach § 1 KWG erfordert eine Erlaubnis der BaFin (§§ 32, 33 KWG). Finanzinstitute i. S. d. Art. 4 Abs. 26 CRR sind also zunächst einmal nicht erlaubnispflichtig. Für sie gelten die seit dem 1.1.2014 verschärften „Spielregeln" nicht; sie könnten beispielsweise die Qualifikationsanforderungen an neue und amtierende Vorstandsmitglieder nach § 25c KWG ignorieren. Da jedoch Kredit- und Finanzdienstleistungsinstitute i. S. d. KWG Tätigkeiten der CRR-Finanzinstitute umfassen und als Bankgeschäfte bzw. Finanzdienstleistungsgeschäfte im Rahmen des § 1 KWG bestimmt sind, sind diese Tätigkeiten dann auch erlaubnispflichtig gem. §§ 32, 33 KWG. Tätigkeiten, die nach Art. 4 Abs. 26 CRR dem Finanzinstitut zugeordnet sind und nach § 1 KWG als Bankgeschäfte bzw. Finanzdienstleistungsgeschäfte qualifiziert werden, unterliegen somit hierzulande den aufsichtsrechtlichen und regulatorischen Anforderungen für Kreditinstitute.

Gleichwohl sind Finanzinstitute i. S. d. Art. 4 Abs. 26 CRR auch direkt Anknüpfungspunkt für aufsichtsrechtliche Tatbestände. Vorausgesetzt ist die Zugehörigkeit zu einer Instituts-, Finanzholding- oder gemischten Finanzholding-Gruppe i. S. d. § 10a KWG, deren Mutterunternehmen seinen Sitz in einem EU-Land hat. Als „nachgeordnete Unternehmen" werden sie auf konsolidierter Ebene einbezogen, was gemäß § 8a KWG zur Folge hat, dass die BaFin zuständig ist.

1.3.2   Finanzinstitute als nachgeordnete Unternehmen

Finanzinstitute haben, wie vorstehend erwähnt, nach CRR nur im Rahmen der Instituts-gruppe aufsichtsrechtliche Bedeutung, und zwar als nachgeordnetes Tochterunternehmen. Nachfolgend wird im Wesentlichen nur auf die Institutsgruppe eingegangen, aber Finanz-institute sind auch in Finanzholding- oder gemischte Finanzholding-Gruppen einzubezie-hen.

Der Konsolidierungskreis umfasst Mutterinstitute und die Töchter, die die CRR an-wenden müssen (Art. 11 ff. CRR). Art. 18 Abs. 1 CRR schreibt iVm § 10a KWG für alle Tochterunternehmen, die Institute und Finanzinstitute sind, Vollkonsolidierung vor, d. h. das Mutterinstitut muss seine maßgeblichen Positionen (Eigenmittel, Risikoaktiva, Markt-risikopositionen) mit denen der nachgeordneten Unternehmen zusammenfassen (vgl. zu den einzelnen Voraussetzungen Art. 4 Abs. 16 CRR: ein Tochterunternehmen liegt ins-besondere bei Mehrheitsbeteiligungen (ab 50 %) vor oder wenn die Muttergesellschaft faktisch beherrschenden Einfluss hat).

Von den genannten maßgeblichen Posititonen spielen insbesondere die Eigenmittel aufsichtsrechtlich eine große Rolle. Kreditinstitute müssen ihre Solvabilität nachweisen, d. h. dass sie über eine angemessene Eigenmittelausstattung verfügen (§ 10 KWG, § 3 SolvV iVm Art. 92 bis 386 CRR). Durch § 10a KWG iVm Art. 18 CRR gilt die Eigenmit-telvorschrift auch für Institutsgruppen und damit auf konsolidierter Basis. Als Eigenmittel einer Gruppe gelten dabei die zusammengefassten Eigenmittel der einzelnen Gruppenmit-glieder.

Der aufsichtsrechtliche Konsolidierungskreis i. S. d. Art. 18 CRR bringt keine grund-sätzliche materielle Veränderung bzw. Verschärfung im Vergleich zur bisherigen KWG-Regelung. Wie bisher stellt § 10a KWG bei der Einbeziehung nachgeordneter Unterneh-men auf Institute, Kapitalanlagegesellschaften, Finanzunternehmen, Anbieter von Ne-bendienstleistungen und E-Geldinstitute ab. Die Einstufung der Geschäftätigkeiten ist gleichgeblieben, nur auf Gruppenebene gibt es u. a. bzgl. des Umfangs der Gruppeneigen-mittel Neuerungen (etwa bei den Ausnahmen von der Konsolidierung gemäß § 19 CRR oder beim Abzug von den Eigenmitteln als Beteiligung; der Kapitalabzug nach Art. 36 CRR bezieht sich auf Unternehmen der Finanzbranche („Financial Sector Entities") ge-mäß Art. 4 Abs. 27 CRR, hierunter fallen auch Finanzinstitute).

Von der Einstufung eines Finanzinstituts oder einer Wertpapierfirma als CRR-Institut (Art. 4 Abs. 1 Nr. 2 CRR) hängt nicht zuletzt ab, ob das Unternehmen auch als Mutter-unternehmen einer Institutsgruppe gelten kann und ob Minderheitenanteile dieser Unter-nehmen in der Konsolidierung vollständig berücksichtigt werden dürfen. Nach Art. 81 CRR ist das nur für Minderheitenanteile von Instituten und Unternehmen erlaubt, die gem. nationaler Gesetzgebung unter den Anforderungen der CRR unterliegen. Diese Vorgabe führt zu einer Änderung, welche Unternehmen in die Minderheitenanrechnung einfließen dürfen. Neben der Beschränkung auf Institute im Anwendungsbereich der CRR greift die-se auf die folgenden Unternehmen:

- Kreditinstitute, die gem. § 1a KWG Institute i. S. d. CRR sind
- Finanzdienstleistungsinstitute, die gem. § 1a KWG Institute i. S. d. CRR sind

Für die Angemessenheit der Eigenmittelausstattung der Gruppe verantwortlich ist das übergeordnete Unternehmen, aber es darf auf gruppenangehörige Unternehmen, also auch auf nachgeordnete Finanzinstitute, nur insoweit einwirken, als dem das allgemein geltende Gesellschaftsrecht nicht entgegensteht (§ 10 a Abs. 8 KWG).

Art. 11 CRR richtet sich an alle gruppenangehörigen Unternehmen: Die Mutter und ihre Töchter müssen, soweit sie unter diese Verordnung fallen, über eine angemessene Organisationsstruktur und geeignete interne Kontrollmechanismen sicherstellen, dass die für die Konsolidierung erforderlichen Daten ordnungsgemäß bereitgestellt und weitergeleitet werden. Nachgeordnete Finanzinstitute sind ausdrücklich verpflichtet, dem übergeordneten Unternehmen die für die Ermittlung der Angemessenheit der Eigenmittelausstattung auf Gruppenebene erforderlichen Angaben zu übermitteln. Die gesetzlichen Organisations- und Mitteilungspflichten erstrecken sich damit auch auf die gruppenangehörigen Finanzinstitute, die eigentlich nicht der Aufsicht durch die BaFin unterstellt sind, und die BaFin kann ihnen gegenüber auf die ihr gemäß § 44 Abs. 2 KWG zustehenden Auskunfts- und Prüfungsrechte zurückgreifen.

Neben der Eigenmittelausstattung (§§ 10,10a KWG) sind weitere aufsichtsrechtliche Anforderungen auf der Gruppenebene zu erfüllen. Die wichtigsten Bestimmungen beziehen sich auf:

- Kapitalpuffer (§§ 10c–e KWG)
- Liquidität (§ 11 KWG)
- Großkredite (§ 13 KWG)
- Verwaltungs-oder Aufsichtsorgan (§ 25d KWG)
- Besondere Prüfungspflichten des Prüfers (§ 29 KWG)
- Maßnahmen bei organisatorischen Mängeln (§ 45b KWG)
- Leverage Ratio (Art. 429 Abs. 4 CRR)

1.3.3 Mindestanforderungen an das Risikomanagement

Durch die Finanzmarktkrisen klüger geworden, schenken die Aufsichtsbehörden dem Risikomanagement besonderes Augenmerk. Denn es hat sich gezeigt, dass nicht viel gewonnen ist, wenn Kennziffern wie Solvabilitätskoeffizient oder Großkreditgrenzen eingehalten werden. Die BaFin veröffentlicht deshalb schon seit längerem Regelungswerke – die MaRisk –, um das Risikomanagement der beaufsichtigten Unternehmen qualitativ beurteilen zu können. In Reaktion auf die Finanzmarktkrisen wurden Aktivitäten auf internationaler, europäischer und nationaler Aufsichtsebene vorangetrieben und u. a.die Rahmenbedingungen für das Risikomanagement durch die vom Basler Ausschuss für Bankenaufsicht im Januar 2013 veröffentlichen „Grundsätze für die effektive Aggregation von Risikodaten und die Risikoberichterstattung" neu geordnet. Diese sog. BCBS 239 soll Entscheidungsfindungsprozesse und -systeme soweit verbessern, dass Banken Stress- und Krisensituationen künftig besser bewältigen. Neben Bestimmungen zur Aufbau- und Ablauforganisation der Risikofunktion in Banken stellt sie erstmals konkrete regulatorische Anforderungen an die IT-Architektur und das Datenmanagement von Kreditinstituten bzw. Institutsgruppen. Eine Umsetzung ist in der 5. MaRisk-Novelle vorgesehen. Jedoch ist gemäß MaRisk AT 1 Tz. 2 mit der Novelle 2012 für Institute, die „besonders groß sind oder deren Geschäftsaktivitäten durch besondere Komplexität, Internationalität oder eine besondere Risikoexponierung gekennzeichnet sind" bereits die „auch die Inhalte einschlägiger Veröffentlichungen zum Risikomanagement des Baseler Ausschusses für Bankenaufsicht und des Financial Stability Board in eigenverantwortlicher Weise in ihre Überlegungen zur angemessenen Ausgestaltung des Risikomanagements einzubeziehen".

Die MaRisk konkretisieren § 25aKWG. Sie fordern ein angemessenes und wirksames Risikomanagement unter Berücksichtigung der Risikotragfähigkeit und die Festlegung von Strategien: Institute müssen sich auf die nachhaltige Entwicklung ihrer Geschäftsstrategie konzentrieren und sie mit einer konsistenten Risikostrategie flankieren, sie müssen Prozesse zur Planung, Umsetzung, Beurteilung und Anpassung ihrer Strategien institutionalisieren und nachweisen.

Bereits § 25a Abs. 3 KWG besteht explizit auf der Einrichtung interner Kontrollverfahren. Sie bestehen aus einem internen Kontrollsystem und der Internen Revision. Das interne Kontrollsystem umfasst insbesondere

- Regelungen zur Aufbau- und Ablauforganisation
- Prozesse zur Identifizierung, Beurteilung, Steuerung, Überwachung sowie Kommunikation der Risiken (Risikosteuerungs- und -controllingprozesse)
- Risikocontrolling und Compliance-Funktion

Wie das Risikomanagement ausgestaltet wird, hängt von Art, Umfang, Komplexität und Risikogehalt der Geschäftstätigkeit ab. Es muss nicht zuletzt die Grundlage für die sachgerechte Wahrnehmung der Überwachungsfunktionen des Aufsichtsorgans, also des Aufsichts- oder Verwaltungsrats, schaffen und ihn von daher angemessen in die Abläufe einbinden.

Die Forderung nach einem wirksamen Risikomanagement richtet sich nach dem Wortlaut von § 25a KWG und MaRisk an Institute, betrifft also Kredit- und Finanzdienstleistungsinstitute und nicht CRR-Finanzinstitute. Sie werden (mit derselben Konstruktion wie bei Eigenmittelausstattung und anderen regulatorischen Anforderungen) über die Institutsgruppe „eingefangen": Nach § 25a Abs. 3 KWG haben Geschäftsleiter von übergeordneten Unternehmen für eine ordnungsmäßige Geschäftsorganisation zu sorgen, auch für das Risikomanagement (MaRisk AT 2.1, AT 4.5), was im Wesentlichen folgende Funktionen umfasst:

- angemessenes, wirksames Risikomanagement inkl. angemesser personeller und technisch-organisatorischer Ausstattung und umfassendem Notfallkonzept
- angemessene Regelungen zur jederzeitigen Bestimmung der finanziellen Lage
- vollständige Dokumentation der Geschäfte
- angemessene Sicherungssysteme gegen Geldwäsche und Betrug

Das bedeutet, dass das übergeordnete Unternehmen einer Institutsgruppe nachgeordnete Finanzinstitute (vgl. § 10a KWG: Nachgeordnete Unternehmen sind Unternehmen, die nach Art. 18 CRR zu konsolidieren sind oder freiwillig konsolidiert werden; in diesem Zusammenhang ist § 1a KWG zu beachten) in bestimmten Umfang in das Gruppenrisikomanagement einbeziehen muss. Nachgeordnete Unternehmen müssen gemäß § 25a Abs. 3 KWG in den Risikomanagementprozess des übergeordneten Unternehmens nur dann voll einbezogen werden, wenn von der Waiver-Regelung gemäß § 2a KWG gebraucht gemacht wird (vgl. Luz u. a., KWG-Kommentar, Bd. 1, 2015, KWG § 25a Abs. 1–4 Rn. 28).

Das gilt unabhängig davon, ob das nachgeordnete Unternehmen konsolidiert wird oder nicht (MaRisk AT 4.5), vorausgesetzt, das betreffende nachgeordnete Unternehmen birgt Risiken, die als wesentlich einzustufen sind.

Dem Risikomanagement auf Gruppenebene kommt wegen spezifischen zusätzlichen Risiken besondere Bedeutung zu, u. a. das Risiko von Konflikten zwischen gruppenangehörigen Unternehmen, „Ansteckungseffekte" aus Reputationsrisiken sowie Risiken, die sich aus der Komplexität der Gruppenstruktur oder durch Risikokonzentrationen ergeben können.

Ein „wirksames Risikomanagement" auf Gruppenebene setzt voraus, dass das übergeordnete Unternehmen auf das nachgeordnete Unternehmen einwirken kann. Bis zum 1.1.2014 war das für § 25a KWG/MaRisk wie bei der Eigenmittelausstattung (§ 10a Abs. 12 Satz 2 KWG a.F; § 10a Abs. 6 Satz 2 KWG n. F.) KWG) nur möglich, wenn „das allgemein geltende Gesellschaftsrecht" dem nicht entgegenstand (durch den Verweis in § 25a KWG a. F. auf § 10a Abs. 12 Satz 2 KWG a. F. (ab 1.1.2014: § 10a Abs. 8 Satz 2 KWG n. F.). Das wird nun im Einklang mit CRD IV aufgeweicht: Sofern es sich nicht um Tochtergesellschaften in Drittstatten handelt (anders als bei § 25a Abs. 3 Satz 3 KWG), sollen übergeordnete Unternehmen uneingeschränkte Einwirkungsrechte bekommen, die nicht durch ein „anderweitiges Gesellschaftsrecht beschnitten werden" (vgl. die ausführliche Stellungnahme der Deutschen Kreditwirtschaft vom 11.10.2012, CRD IV-Umsetzungsgesetz, S. 23 f., mit Verweis auf die Regierungsbegründung). Die Regierungsbegründung betont allerdings, dass das nachgeordnete Unternehmen die Weisung des übergeordneten Unternehmens auf deren Rechtsmäßigkeit zu prüfen habe und eine Befolgung insbesondere existenzgefährdender oder anderweitig nachteiliger Maßnahmen verweigern könne. Insofern besteht der Vorrang des Gesellschaftsrechts weiterhin fort.

Die konkrete Ausgestaltung des Risikomanagements liegt beim übergeordneten Unternehmen (siehe auch § 2a KWG bei Anwendung der Waiver-Regelung für das nachgeordnete Unternehmen und das übergeordnete Unternehmen sowie Hannemann et al. 2013, AT 4.5). Durch die Mitwirkungspflicht hat das nachgeordnete Unternehmen dem über-

geordneten die für die Sicherstellung der ordnungsgemäßen Geschäftsorganisation erforderlichen Angaben zu übermitteln (§ 25a Abs. 3 KWG). Dadurch greifen die strengen
aufsichtsrechtlichen Regelungen der MaRisk in gewissem Umfang für Tochter-Finanzinstitute, und aufgrund von Folgewirkungen bei Sicherstellung und Zulieferung an das
Mutterinstitut können durchaus höhere Kosten anfallen.

Die KPMG-Studie „Bankenregulierung entfaltet Wirkung" (2013) veranschlagt den
Gesamtaufwand für die Umsetzung und Anwendung der unterschiedlichen Regulierungs-
maßnahmen für die deutschen Kreditinstitute auf rd. 9 Mrd. € jährlich, davon entfallen
geschätzt 2 Mrd. € auf direkte Kosten für Sach- und Personalaufwand und 7 Mrd. € auf
indirekte Kosten für eine verbesserte Eigenkapital- und Liquiditätsausstattung.

1.4   Fazit

Der 1.1.2014 ist ein Tag, an dem sich viel geändert hat. Wesentliche Teile eines riesi-
gen Regelungspakets sind in Kraft getreten und werden das Bankaufsichtsrecht grundle-
gend verändern und verbessern. In diesem Zusammenhang haben sich nicht zuletzt einige
Sprachregelungen im KWG geändert: Das Finanzinstitut feiert sozusagen sein Comeback,
allerdings nicht als Synonym für das Kreditinstitut, wie der Begriff umgangssprachlich
verwendet wird, sondern in einer insofern problematischen Definition, als diese relativ
unübersichtlich ist.

Wichtig ist die Abgrenzung und Einstufung als „Finanzinstitut" vor allem aus regulatorischer Sicht. Der Begriff kommt insbesondere im Rahmen der Thematik „nachgeordnetes
Unternehmen" zum Tragen, also über das Mutterunternehmen der Institutsgruppe bzw. auf
aufsichtsrechtlicher konsolidierter Basis. Letztlich fallen Tochter-Finanzinstitute damit
unter bestimmte Anforderungen, die wegen der quantitativ und qualitativ steigenden Herausforderungen mit Implementierungsaufwand verbunden sind. Unweigerlich stellt sich
die Frage, wie Risiko- und Managementprozesse und Entscheidungsfindung innerhalb der
Institutsgruppe künftig gestaltet sein müssen, damit Zulieferungsverpflichten der Töchter an die Mutter schnell und präzise erfüllt werden. Bedeutungsvoll sind Finanzinstitute
auch im Kontext der Abzüge von den regulatorischen Eigenmitteln im Wege des Begriffs
„Unternehmen der Finanzbranche".

Insgesamt steht die Bankenwelt vor einem Paradigmenwechsel, der kein einseitig von
den Aufsichtsbehörden ausgehender Prozess sein darf, sondern von den Beaufsichtigten
aktiv mitgestaltet werden muss. Allerdings bestehen nach wie vor viele Unsicherheiten in
der Anwendung, denn zahlreiche EBA-Standards – bzw. ITS oder RTS der EBA – wurden
noch nicht verabschiedet. Hier sind weitere Anpassungen für Kreditinstitute und Institutsgruppen zu erwarten.

Literatur

Bellavite-Hövermann/Hintze/Luz/Scharpf (2001): Handbuch Eigenmittel und Liquidität nach KWG.

Gendrisch/Gruber/Hahn (2014): 2. Aufl., Handbuch Solvabilität, Aufsichtsrechtliche Kapitalanforderungen an Kreditinstitute.

Hannemann/Schneider/Weigl (2013): 4. Aufl., Mindestanforderungen an das Risikomanagement (MaRisk).

Dr. Yvette Bellavite Hövermann ist seit 2008 Unternehmens- und Steuerberaterin mit einem Schwerpunkt im Accounting, Risikocontrolling und Steuern. Davor war Dr. Bellavite-Hövermann über zwei Jahrzehnte in verschiedenen Führungspositionen bei Kreditinstituten insbesondere in den Bereichen Rechnungslegung/Risikocontrolling/Bankenaufsicht tätig. Auf diesen Gebieten hat sie zudem zahlreiche Beiträge veröffentlicht. Dr. Bellavite-Hövermann hat Betriebswirtschaft und Volkswirtschaft studiert, im Versicherungswesen und Steuerrecht promoviert und eine Banklehre absolviert.

Principles, Legislative and Institutional Framework in Which Financial Institutes Operate in Germany's Social Market Economy*

Stefan-Sorin Mureşan

Among its many negative effects, the 2007–2009 economic and financial crisis destroyed large amounts of monetary assets. It also cemented the previously creeping process of decay and dissolution of values, of social consensus and social peace.

Now, while the years long huge quantitative easing programmes worth thousands of billions of US dollars and Euros bought us some time, there is an urgent need of profound reform and restructuring of our systems of national organization in politics and economics. For doing this we need to look into their roots.

When systemic political and economic reform is at stake, such as the case currently is with financial institutes, it is necessary to understand the principles of macroeconomic order, of the legislative, institutional and conceptual context and framework in which all economic agents, banks, insurers, etc. act. Among the good examples in which governments successfully managed to rebuild the framework and make a fast comeback after defeat in war, after material, social and spiritual destruction, is Germany.

Helped by the 50 % war debt cut under the London Debt Agreement of 1953, the then newly introduced ordo-liberal market economy system managed to make the German economy recover and grow for several decades. The country made a comeback (but politically still with somewhat limited access) into the small global leadership team of the West.

This book chapter addresses the core principles which lay at the basis of national legislation and institutions which regulate economic and social life in the functional national

---

* This book chapter is the slightly readapted chapter 4 of the book Muresan, Stefan-Sorin, Social Market Economy. The Case of Germany. Springer International Publishing, 2014

St.-S. Mureşan (✉)
Bonn, Deutschland, Bucharest, Romania
E-Mail: sorin.muresan@gmx.net

© Springer Fachmedien Wiesbaden 2016
Z. Diab, O. Everling (Hrsg.), Rating von Finanzinstituten,
DOI 10.1007/978-3-658-04195-3_2

economy of the Social Market Economy in Germany. Financial institutes are at the core of the national economic order and therefore in order to understand how to restore their credibility, we will look at principles and the regulative context in which they work.

Regulation of financial institutes and banks is sensitive. Blaming the banks for the economic and social crisis of 2007–2009, which had devastating effects on the economies of leading Western countries and a negative impact on some other Western economies, appear legitimate in a more superficial analysis. But if we dig deeper, we realize that the banks and the financial sector in general, did two things, a good one and a bad one: the acceptable one for market economy rules was to use the Schlupfloecher offered by the existing market economy rules and their at that time quite deregulated financial and monetary system in order to generate more turnover and profits. These opportunities for them appeared during the deregulation era of the 1980s and 1990s in the West. This was done not only in the UK where Margaret Thatcher is finally responsible for the deindustrialization of the UK (the country to whom we all due the industrialization) but in the USA too. It was not only the Reagan administration which deregulated, but the atmosphere and general trend were towards it. Former Federal Reserve Chairman Alan Greenspan admitted too that too much deregulation was put in place. He admitted this with respect to the regulation of the monetary sector which was under the supervision of the Federal Reserve and said "we made a mistake" (s. Beattie and Politi 2008). The bad and not really acceptable thing the financial sector did, was to abuse the trust of investors by creating, placing on the market and selling financial products of such a complexity that, as some top manager of such companies themselves gave in, they did not really understand to the full. This is unethical and unmoral, but was still done in spite of the UN Global Compact and globally envisaged principles of ethic rules for business leaders (s. Knoepffler et al. 2011, pp. 42–43). This all took place in the context of advancing globalization and which encompassed increasing geographic world regions and increasing parts of markets. There simply were not enough rules by public supervisory authorities to address and prevent collateral damage done locally by globally acting equity management funds and institutes (banks, insurers, raters). The innovation capacity of the financial and investment sector was higher than the ability of supervisory authorities (both national as well as international) to secure that the effects of bringing on the market new products (stocks, bonds, mortgages, derivatives, investment schemes, et alia) to secure that such products brought on the market was helping maintain the stability of income by individuals or companies. Since income revenue is interdependent with social security and finally with public order, we realize that supervisory agencies were not able to prevent such risks and to stop these from entering the financial market. Then, they also failed to prevent them then enter the economy of production of real goods and services and from being transferred internationally across borders. To illustrate that this crisis is a mixture of the lack of balance of power between the private sector and the public supervisory institutions and lack of applied ethics rules we can think of two things. First is the transmission of toxic assets from the packges of financial products developed by Fanny Mae and Freddie Mac in the USA to the banking sector and to the real economy, first in the USA then across the world. Then also think about the sovereign wealth fund

Abu Dhabi Investment Corp. (Singapore) and its activities. By investing massively into the telecommunication sector of Singapore I 2007 this fund with financial assets valued at several hundred of billion of US dollars, not only destabilized the telecommunication market of Singapore by acting against competition rules, but thereby also posed a question of national security.

This papers attempts to address only the regulatory part of the problem with which the free market economies are confronted as national systems since the onset of the effects of globalization in the 1990s. In this approach, I will be studying the roots of the models of successfully creating, upholding and reforming legislation and institutions in the Social Market Economy of Germany.

Again here, within this national system, the financial institutions move within the same legislative and institutional regulatory framework and environment in which any company or economic agent is moving in. The only difference which might appear is that some or other type of financial institutions have lobbied to pass through special exemption for their area of business. For example, banks succeeded to pursue the German government to exempted them from charging VAT. Of course this is a clever move for the banking sector (not approved for the insurance sector, for example), namely that the borrower does not have to pay VAT on the amount he is borrowing. Other types of financial institutions passed other laws specific to them.

Thus, we will look at political freedom, private property, monetary stability, competition, predictability of economic policy, wages, trade unions, collective wage bargaining and company management.

2.1   The Economic and Monetary Reform of 1948 in Germany[1]

Even though it was not stated this way at the beginning of the post-war period, the Social Market Economy in Germany began with the adoption of the package of legislative measures known as "The Economic and Monetary Reform" of 20 June 1948 (Wirtschafts- und Währungsreform).

This reform was the first legislative pillar of the new economic system in post-war Germany. It reintroduced economic freedom; of course this is to be understood against the status quo in which the economy in Germany had been turned into a centralised war economy. Creating the market economy was the first legislative and institutional step undertaken in order to implement the Ordoliberal and Socio-Liberal ideas that had lain until then in the drawers of the group of professors mentioned above as "Fathers of the Social Market Economy".

---

[1] This book sub-chapter is the only slightly readapted chapter 4.1.1.1 of the book Muresan, Stefan-Sorin, Social Market Economy. The Case of Germany. Springer International Publishing, 2014, p. 167–170

The positive effects of this reform, namely that it brought into movement the energies and initiatives of entrepreneurs, were catalysed and accelerated by the Marshall Plan. Through the US$ 1.3 billion that were made available to Germany between 1948 and 1952 (ca. 10% of the total funds made available by the US under the Marshall Plan for Europe), the Marshall Plan contributed to the financial capital and fixed assets required for recovery (s. the history of the OECD on the internet portal of the OECD on http://www.oecd.org/about/history/).

On the one hand, this decisive step of the Economic and Monetary Reform consisted in the monetary and financial reform and, on the other hand, in another series of liberalisations through the adoption of a set of laws concerning commercial and financial liberalisation.

There were four main laws. The first law, the "Currency Law" (Währungsgesetz) (Military Law no. 61) regulated the replacement of the Reichsmark with a new currency called the "Deutsche Mark" (DM) and the initial supply of the population, the public institutions, businesses and banks with a fixed amount of DM. At the same time, the law decreed the cancellation of the old Reichsmark currency and its withdrawal from the market.

The second law was the "Coinage Law" (Emissionsgesetz) (Military Law no. 62) and was related to the means of issuing, transporting, storing and s. o. of new banknotes and coins as well as withdrawing the old ones from the market. It also established the minimum reserve requirements and created a foreign currency Exchange Department within the Bank of the German States. These two laws both came into force on 20 June 1948.

The third law was the "Conversion Rates Law" (Military Law no. 63) that became effective one week later, on 27 June 1948. It regulated—provisionally—conversion rates from the old currency into the new one for the various types of deposits, securities and other contributions. It also established the modality through which the conversion operation was going to be overseen by the newly created Federal Ministry of Finance.

The forth law was the "Fixed Accounts Law" (Festkontengesetz) that came into force only in October 1948. It established the final value for the level of bank accounts and contributions (for the military laws quoted above s. Wandel 1980, pp. 120–125).

This was a fresh new start. The bright ones seized the opportunity. Many who started new businesses then, are now well established companies on the market.

The Reichsmark (RM) was thus replaced by the Deutsche Mark (DM). Up to 10 billion new banknotes were issued and brought on the market. The amount was calculated so that it maintained economic stability. The new banknotes were made "of simple paper, bearing no watermark. The graphical design of numbers and brochures was similar to the dollar notes. Gears, marble pedestals, titans and women were copied from the American railway company's shares" (s. Wandel 1980, p. 129: "einfaches Papier, ohne Wasserzeichen … Die graphische Gestaltung der Ziffern und Brochüren ähnelte den Dollarnoten. Zahnräder, Marmorsockel, Titanen und Frauengestalten waren den amerikanischen Eisenbahnaktien entliehen"). Every German citizen initially received 40 DM in cash, in exchange for 40 RM. Moreover, each employer received 60 DM in liquid assets for each of his employees. The conversion of the other payment means that exceeded the value of 40 RM was made, initially using the formula 100 RM = 10 DM. During the autumn of 1948 however, as a result of inflationist tendencies, the conversion rate for deposits at that specific moment in personal or business bank accounts was reduced to 100 RM = 6.50 DM (comp. Wandel 1980, p. 124).

The other part of the Economic and Monetary Reform, i.e. the liberalisations, were centred on the "Act on reference interest rates for economic activity and the price policy after the Monetary Reform" (Leitsätze für die Bewirtschaftung und Preispolitik nach der Geldreform). The law concerning reference rates and many other decrees and application norms, adopted under Erhard's lead, brought back freedom into economy. These measures invalidated around 90 % of the prescription ordinances for price levels, blocked since 1936. The limitations on wages and the ban on obtaining a bank loan on the basis of a current account were also lifted. Quotas were established for over 400 products (comp. Wandel 1980, p. 118 ff.).

Among academics and public opinion, this Economic and Monetary Reform was supported through individual actions of the other professors, members of the Freiburg group of the forefathers of the Social Market Economy. They backed Ludwig Erhard, federal minister of the economy (1948–1963) the initiator of this reform with written articles, lobby, interviews and s. o.

With the Economic and Monetary Reform, during the special circumstances created by the London Agreement on German External Debt of 1953, the road had been opened towards the much praised "German Economic Miracle" (Deutsches Wirtschaftswunder). Shelves became filled with products literally overnight, on Monday, 21 June 1948. In fact, these goods already existed in the country, but because of the lack of regulation at a macroeconomic level, they were only available on the black market.

It is important to note that the Economic and Monetary Reform took place before any other political reform was generated through German initiative. The economic reform preceded by almost one year, the adoption of the democratic Constitution. Democratic Germany thus made the first step in the economic field, a fact that proves again that this country is an economic nation. It is also the proof that the Social Market Economy has its roots in the real economy and not in social distributive policies.

The Economic and Monetary Reform opened the way for that new economic model of the Social Market Economy, which was to be implemented on the basis of the free market doctrine. This opening also made way for a national democratic political reform which was at that time still to come.

2.2 The Constitution of 1949 and Political Roots of Democracy[2]

In 1949, a new democracy appeared on the European political stage: the Federal Republic of (Western) Germany. The Constitution was adopted and the first general elections were held during the same year. The Constitution is to be seen as the second foundation of the Social Market Economy, the political foundation.

---

[2] This book sub-chapter is the only slightly readapted chapter 4.1.1.2 of the book Muresan, Stefan-Sorin, Social Market Economy. The Case of Germany. Springer International Publishing, 2014, p. 170–176.

Being the fundamental and first national law with political character of postwar Germany, the Constitution bore an appropriate name: the "Basic Law" (Grundgesetz der Bundesrepublik Deutschland; GG). It was adopted on May 8, 1949 by the Parliamentary Council (Parlamentarischer Rat) gathered in Bonn and came into force on May 23, 1949. After the German Reunification of 1990, the West-German Constitution was modified and completed in 1994 in order to include the five new "Länder" of the former German Democratic Republic. The amendments became effective on November 1st, 1995.

Between the free market economy and the Constitution there was a dynamic and mutually conditional relationship. This relationship was described by former Chancellor Schröder too. The Constitution attempts to exclude extremely bad situations for individuals which appear given the market forces. But it is also provides that a command economy cannot appear in Germany. Thus it is a middle way between the two types of economic policy. Social-democrats thus agree with the Social Market Economy as the "third way", even though the decision for it was mainly done Christian-Democrats (s. Schröder 1999, p. 18).

It should be stated from the very beginning that the form of government of the Federal Republic of Germany, as the Second German Republic, or the Bonn Republic, was that of a federal parliamentary republic. It is hard to say whether this form of government was the choice of Germany alone, free from international influences. The federal form was definitely a local choice, but maybe while looking, again, at the model of US federalism.

Nowadays, the Republic still reminds many people of defeat in World War II, while the Reich and the Monarchy are associated with historical traditions, times of glory, stability and prosperity.

If, in the economic field, Germany opted for the continental model of Rhineland Capitalism, the political field was sown with values inspired from the French Republic and US federalism. The French model was embedded in political elements particular to Germany, which then received North American implementation influences. No political programme and no party, aside from those that came to be perceived as extremist after 1945 (i.e. the Republicans and the NPD) abandoned the values promoted by the French Revolution. There is a consensus among political and constitutional experts who draw parallels between the French "Liberté, Egalité, Fraternité" and the values embedded in the German Constitution. If "Liberté" was translated into German political discourse using the exact equivalent, "Freiheit" (Freedom), the other two virtues were equated according to different local German specificalities. "Egalité" was equated with "Gerechtigkeit" (Justice) and not "Gleichheit" (Equality). "Fraternité" was translated using the word "Solidarität" (Solidarity) instead of "Brüderlichkeit" (s. von Nell-Breuning 1979, pp. 150–151) (Fraternity/Brotherhood). According to Nell-Breuning, and other analysts, it is liked to see it such as is all three core elements of the French Revolution are included as well in the German Constitution as in the contemporary political discourse, the legislation of the socio-economic system and institutional principles (comp. von Nell-Breuning 1979, pp. 150–153).

The French triad is embedded in the German specific concept of the state. This concept has strong medieval (Western and Catholic) roots and is based on the concept of divinity and is explained in one of Pope Leo XIII's (1878–1903) encyclical works. According to that concept, the state is "as an entity endowed with authority directly by God in the person of the Prince, in some ways an incarnated bearer of sovereignty" (s. von Nell-Breu-ning 1979, p. 156: "als unmittelbar von Gott mit Autorität ausgerüsteter, in der Person des 'princeps' gewissermaßen inkarnierter Hoheitsträger"). According to this model, the authority is granted with legitimacy from "above" by the grace of God (Gottesgnaden-tum) and, according to the Catholic Medieval vision, this authority is first received by the Pope of Rome. The Pope then delegates and transmits this authority received from above through the coronation of the Kaiser. The latter then transmits it further "down" by delegating it to local noblemen or princes, dukes, counts, etc. This is the feudal system and was called "the system of the lent right and of vassal support" (Lehnswesen; comp. Lexikon-Institut Bertelsmann 1981, p. 711). It is within this system that principalities, as state entities preceding the contemporary 16 Länder of Germany, appeared during the High Middle Ages. The main idea is that noblemen borrow (leihen) from the Kaiser not only the right to exert power locally, but also the right to use the land over which they rule. In his turn, the Kaiser relies (anlehnen) on his noblemen in the governing process and the wars he might have to lead.

The system is similar to the clerical one. In the case of both the Catholic and the Or-thodox Churches, the priests are the bishops' representatives in the territory, i.e. in the parishes. The sole reason for which priests are needed in parishes is that bishops can not be physically present simultaneously in all the parishes of their diocese. According to Canon Law, the only persons directly authorised by Jesus Christ to preach and to give out the Holy Communion to the people (Church customers, in a more economic and cynical language) would be bishops. This is the reason for which only bishops are entitled to ap-point priests as their delegates.

Therefore, we note that in its exertion, the state authority is a top-to-bottom system and is perceived as coming from above and exercised at the bottom through delegates or commissioning (the subsidiarity principle). This delegation/commissioning is clearly visi-ble in Germany thanks to the existence of the Constitutions of the sixteen federal Länder. However, when central power is elected in the federal system, their authority comes from below and it moves upwards by representative democracy becoming perceivable at the meeting in the Reichstag (Bundestag). In Austria the political system is somewhat similar not only because it belongs culturally to the German language area, but because it also belongs to the area of the Holy Roman Empire of German nation.

The Constitution of Germany is a federal one. According to the subsidiarity principle, it does not affect all spheres of public life. It only sets out the basic principles and the ge-neral organization framework for political life. Within this general framework, the specific fields of public life are regulated, in a detailed manner, in Constitutions of each of the six-teen Länder. The Länder, in their quality of semi-sovereign states decided to freely accept the federal Constitution. At the same time, given the right of subsidiarity they did not de-legate all their competences to the federal authority. For example, policing, education and the tax collecting system are just some of the areas in which competence is exerted mainly by the Länder, however, respecting the general limits imposed by the Federal Constitution.

The ethnic German people's orientation towards work, its quest for harmony and consensus and its specific search for its own national vocation strongly influenced the identity of the Social Market Economy system which appeared within its borders. Often, the national vocation within "the concert of peoples" is connected to the Social Market Economy model as it defines the concept of profession, of work and of community as a vocation from God. Here, the concept of profession (Beruf) is the most important because the individuals are main drivers of any economic activity. In this case, profession becomes synonymous with mission, calling, aptitude, talent. The concept bears the name of "Berufung" or "Beruf", just like we saw in Tomas Aquins and Max Weber and becomes visible in the Constitution for the whole nation and is understood as being in front of the international community: "In awareness of its responsibility in front of God and men, inspired by the will to serve world peace as an equally entitled member of a united Europe, the German people, by virtue of its constituent sovereignty, has enacted upon itself this Basic Law" (s. GG, Präambel: "Im Bewusstsein seiner Verantwortung vor Gott und den Menschen, von dem Willen beseelt, als gleichberechtigtes Glied in einem vereinten Europa dem Frieden der Welt zu dienen, hat sich das Deutsche Volk kraft seiner verfassungsgebenden Gewalt dieses Grundgesetz gegeben."). But what is, more precisely, the type of state and of Constitution which the German people has given itself?

One of the basic rights guaranteed by the Constitution is freedom: "The freedom of the individual person is inviolable" (s. GG Art. 2, Abs. 2: "Die Freiheit der Person ist unverletzlich."). Nevertheless, this disposition appears only in Article 2 and seems to be just a means to achieve the main goal in the German model: human dignity. The fact that freedom is not a goal in itself can be inferred from Article 1 paragraph one of the Constitution which mentions dignity, not freedom: "The dignity of man is intangible" (s. GG Art. 1, Abs. 1: "Die Würde des Menschen ist unantastbar."). The German focus is thus the human being as a whole. The holistic approach was definitely transferred from the political level to the economic level of the Social Market Economy as well. Freedom finds itself among the other social values and has the same importance as any of them, but not more. The elements with individual and private character do not have an absolute, but a relative validity.

Then, the Constitution guarantees private property, but rather in a limited way. It states that "(1) Property and inheritance rights are guaranteed. The content and limitations thereto are established by laws" (s. GG Art. 14 Abs. 1: "Das Eigentum und das Erbrecht werden gewährleistet. Inhalt und Schranken werden durch die Gesetze bestimmt."). Connected to property is the principle of responsibility which is formulated in the very next paragraph and connected to the concept of collective rights and responsibilities: "(2) Property creates obligations. The use of property shall equally serve the common good. (3) An expropriation is admissible only for the common good" (s. GG Art. 14 Abs. 2–3: "Eigentum verpflichtet. Sein Gebrauch soll zugleich dem Wohle de Allgemeinheit dienen (3) Eine Enteignung ist nur zum Wohle der Allgemeinheit zulässig."). So, in theory, if the exercise of property rights obstructs common good, e.g. in the case of war, expropriations would be not inconceivable. This political choice is important since it defines the focus on common wealth interests of the business community, on the interests of social groups. Although this might have its advantages for social cohesion, at times though it seems to be a dangerous path to follow, because it always depends on the interpretation by the decision-making body of what is in the interest of common good and what is not.

Through the provisions of the Constitution, the tutorial effects of the social state model also apply to the economic field. The Constitution "does not make the Social Market Economy compulsory, but limits itself to banning a Market Economy that is not bound to the social dimension, as well as banning a Centralised Administration Economy" (s. Grosser 1988, p. 56: "Da das Grundgesetz aber die Soziale Marktwirtschaft nicht festlegt, sondern lediglich eine sozial nicht gebundene Marktwirtschaft, sowie eine Zentralverwaltungswirtschaft untersagt, …").

Because they are included in the Constitution, elements related to the social order have a significant power over the functioning of the market economy. The statement that "The Federal Republic of Germany is a democratic and social federal state" (s. GG Art. 20 Abs. 1: "Die Bundesrepublik Deutschland ist ein demokratischer und sozialer Bundesstaat.") means that the state automatically has some social responsibilities too. The fact that the state is supposed and expected to orchestrate the social order is not determined only by the Constitution, but also by the German traditional way of perceiving the community and the state. "The State (more precisely the Prince) is just, good and wise; he knows what is best for his subjects and wants only their best; his subjects are not mature and uneducated underaged who need education and, in some cases, to be disciplined by the State who assists them with parental authority" (s. von Nell-Breuning 1979, p. 156: "Der Staat (konkret der 'princeps') ist gerecht, gütig und weise; er weiß, was für die Untertanen gut ist und will nur ihr Bestes; die Untertanen sind unmündig, ungebildet und unerzogen, bedürfen der Erziehung und gegebenenfalls in Zucht gehalten zu werden, durch den mit (landes-) väterlicher Autorität ihnen *gegenüber*stehenden Staat."). Therefore, a tutorial interaction exists between the State and its citizens.

As we are about to see below, the social order really contains two "third level" principles derived from the social tasks delegated to the State by political consensus: "the principle of state care" (staatliches Fürsorgeprinzip) and "the principle of state supply" (staatliches Versorgungsprinzip). Through these, the State accomplishes its missions of orchestrating social order and of tutoring its citizens. These two principles represent the starting point for the creation of laws and social institutions with this specific influence of identity.

The way the Constitution is written proves that the goal of the Social Market Economy is to guarantee common good but also to protect against dictatorial and political abuses. It does not indicate the manner in which to reach these goals. The Constitution allows the implementation of any economic model, provided that the social dimension is maintained. The distinctive feature for Germany and which can be pointed out here, is that historical traditions visibly influence the choice of the type of economy, state model and economic policy style.

The competent institution, responsible for the monitoring of the Constitution is the Federal Constitutional Court of Germany (Bundesverfassungsgericht), located in Karlsruhe.

As long as its judges will succeed to maintain an equidistant character of the decisions, the principles of "social justice" and "common good" shall be properly applied in Germany. Still, with the slow decline of the practice of virtue, a "sine qua non" for the functioning of political democracy, it may be that federal constitutional judges might, at times, heed to political pressure.

The implementation of the Social Market Economy within the current political constitutional framework led, during the first three decades after 1945, to good results. Even though there have been voices advocating the introduction of a model similar to the ordo-liberal theoretical model of Walter Eucken, Franz Böhm and Ludwig Erhard that had produced the German economic miracle of postwar reconstruction within the federal Constitution, such a model was not included into the Constitution. Some analysts believe that it was this decision that allowed a turn towards Keynesianism and Socialism in the 1970s. According to another hypothesis, if the model had been included in the Constitution, there is no guarantee that it could have been adjusted in accordance to the change of political doctrine in successive Governments (comp. Grosser 1988, pp. 35–73). In Great Britain, for instance, a final text in a written form of the British Constitution does not even exist; it is rather a huge collection of common law, case law and experience in the judicial field built up over the centuries, and where the social order and the market economy are to be freely governed by the respective governments. No one thinks of questioning it, but this makes the British system flexible according to the specific need of the respective historical age in order to serve British interest.

To sum up, we could say that the Constitution is the primary largest political framework within which the economic processes take place. It could be considered the "exterior ordering circle" or "the largest circle of the Economic Constitution" of the Social Market Economy as it was developed in Germany.

2.3 Business Organizations (Companies), Profit and Investments[3]

As we have seen, in order for it to be functional, any national economy has to be supported by a minimum number of profitable businesses organizations. Among these are banks too. Without these economic cells, ideally producers of profit, maintained at a self-sufficient level, no social-economic life is possible. Their profitability is the ideal case and is needed at any expense because they are the driving force of physical existence. But things are not ideal any more, ever since the West left in 1971 the classical model of the "savings capitalism" and moved to "debt driven" capitalism. The US Governent's tacit fiscal policy of growth by spending in deficit, pursued after the onset of the free floating system in 1971, allowed for a large number of core companies—mainly those operating on the basis of

---

[3] This book sub-chapter is the only slightly readapted chapter 4.1.2 of the book Muresan, Stefan-Sorin, Social Market Economy. The Case of Germany. Springer International Publishing, 2014, p. 176–184.

public procurement, but also other companies which profited from the artificial market demand created by debt-driven consumption—to appear more profitable and productive than they were in fact if regarded strictly from a free market economics point of view. This artificial and illusionary profitability was still able to move the economic life of capitalist countries forward; at least until the financial crisis proved that such high levels of total debt (public, individual and companies) in the range of ca. 300 % of GDP in the USA, around 500 % of GDP in the UK, over 290 % of GDP in Germany and 230 % of GDP in Spain (s. The Economist 2011, July 9th) are not sustainable. Still, in order to be able to think over a restructuring solution for the productive part of the Social Market Economy, we have to resume the analysis from scratch.

At first, any business organization is built respecting the idea and the goal defined by its founders. The goal of the business is included in its statute and in the contract of association between partners and remains the core idea in all its economic activities, until the dissolution of the company or their modifications.

Like any other of their counterparts in the world, entrepreneurs in the Social Market Economy have the same goals: to make profit, become rich and be their own masters. Nevertheless, a core value in this economic system, and often even in Germany where this system is applied, is unique because most entrepreneurs are expected to attain these goals in a specific way, or style: to try harder, maybe only half-conscious, in order for the profit making activity not to be a strictly selfish one, but to include in it the altruistic component of attending to the needs of their human being fellows, providing them with the products they need.

It is true that the basic idea for the creation of a firm or business belongs to its owner, to the entrepreneur. However, because the specific Catholic and Christian mentalities co-exist in societies (this was such at least at the time of the creation of today's institutions in the 1950s and 1960; it is such probably less now, because European societies are not Christian any more) along with other mentalities, this basic idea can't be entirely covered and fulfilled within that firm only, but rather in the community at large. In such countries, "a business is generally accepted as an association of human beings who collaborate for common achievements" (s. von Nell-Breuning 1979, p. 91: "der Betrieb ist allgemein anerkannt als *Verbund* der zu gemeinsamer Leistungserstellung kooperierenden Menschen") says the influential German Jesuit Professor von Nell-Breuning. It is not specified that the purpose of the association is to create profit or pursue happiness, not even the clients'. Some among these many people who collaborate with each other are the ones who come up with the idea that constitutes the starting point for opening businesses. In 2009 there were a total of 3,598,248 businesses (s. Fig. 2.1) whose juridical for was either based on persons, on physical individuals on capital and on some other combined forms. But coming up with the founding idea doesn't mean at all that these people are going to be perceived as forever detaining exclusive decision capabilities on that business. Therefore, unlike in many other economic models, in Germany and in social market economies, the business entity or association is not perceived as the exclusive property of the owner, but in some ways of the employees as well. Quite the opposite in the Anglo—Saxon model, for instance, the business is exclusively the property of its owner and has nothing to do

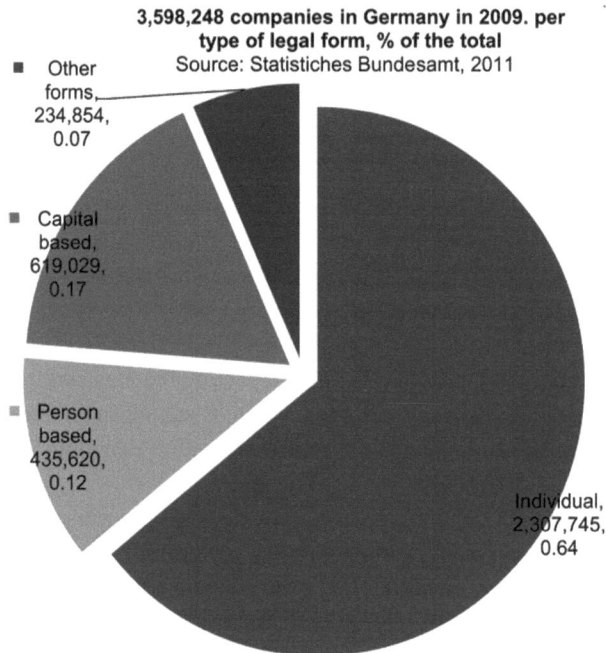

Fig. 2.1 Total number of companies in Germany, classified according to juridical form, 2009

with employees: "the other persons who actively participate in the activities of the respective business, who do not belong to the business, are not its members ... in the sense that citizens belong to a state. From a juridical point of view, they are outsiders for the business in which they actively participate, like suppliers or clients" (s. von Nell-Breuning 1979, p. 123: "die im Unternehmen Tätigen nicht *zum* Unternehmen <gehören>, nicht seine Mitglieder sind [...] wie beispielsweise der Staatsangehörige dem Staat, sondern im Rechtssinn *Außenstehende* sind, die dem Unternehmen wie Zulieferer oder Abnehmer als <Dritte> gegenüberstehen."). Thus, we can see the complete difference between the concept on the business entity in a Social Market Economy country and in a free market neoliberal economy country.

In Germany, the legal form of a company is for the microeconomic activity, what the "Economic Constitution" is for macroeconomics. The law establishes the sharing proportion among the owners' freedom to operate, to administer property and the degree and way in which responsibility is assumed for concluded commercial contracts. It is definitely not easy to create a system, which when implemented, should encourage over 3.6 million. (s. Statistisches Bundesamt 2011) business owners to assume responsibilities.

Several types of company juridical forms will be presented in order to facilitate the understanding of this situation we have in Germany. It has been duly considered that these juridical forms for economic activity via which responsibility is taken on, either by the individual, or by the family association, or by the associates, or shareholders, do cover the whole imaginable range of economic activities: from those of the smallest business, the individual and family, to those of organizations quoted on stock exchanges with hundreds of thousands of shareholders, thousands of employees and which operate globally in dozens pf countries.

First of all, with ca. 2.3 million., the so-called "Einzelunternehmer" (individual entrepreneurs) who basically are to be considered self-employed are by far the largest number of companies from the whole total in Germany. They are the so-called "individual based companies".

Second, are the closed business organizations, which are person-based and are set up either on the basis of the Civil code (Bürgerliches Gesetzbuch; BGB), like "Partnerships under civil law" (Gesellschaft Bürgerlichen Rechts; GBR), or on the basis of the Commercial Code (Handelsgesetzbuch; HGB), such as "Limited partnerships" (Kommanditgesellschaft; KG). "General partnerships" (Offene Handelsgesellschaft; OHG) can also be created on the basis of the Commercial Code (s. HGB §§ 105–160. pp. 53–66 for OHG; then for Kommanditgesellschaft §§ 161–177a, pp. 66–70. The first version of HGB was adopted on May, 10, 1897, one year after the adoption of the German Civil Code (Burgerliches Gesetzbuch; BGB), on August, 18, 1896. They both entered into force on Jan 1, 1900. S. Hefermehl 1993, p. 7).

In what the capital-based business organizations are concerned, a special law exists for "Public companies limited by shares" (Aktiengesellschaft; AG Gesetz) and for "Private Limited Companies by Shares" (Gesellschaft mit beschränkter Haftung; GmbH Gesetz). These capital based companies constitute the backbone of the German economy in what turnover and employees are concerned, even though as a number of the total company registered number they are below 20 %: in 2009, these totalled a number of just over 619,000. Most banks in Germany are AGs.

Saving banks during the crisis of 2007–2009 practically points to an increasing dissolution of the implementation by the judiciary of the basic principle of limitation of, of personal liability and amounts to a de facto abandonment of the principle of responsibility

Other juridical forms than the above comprise combinations of open with closed, of person with capital based companies. As GBR, KG, GmbH and AG are business entities that are relatively well known in most European countries, we shall briefly look at KGaA (Kommanditgesellschaft auf Aktien), GmbH & Co. KG (limited partnership in which one of the partners is a private company limited by shares) and OHG which are less known outside Germany, Austria and Switzerland. Practical details on advantages or disadvantages to these major types of business can be obtained from the Chambers of Commerce and Industry and from "Germany Trade and Invest" (www.gtai.de) which is the government economic development agency dealing with foreign investment too.

Interdependence is more complicated. It is not just managers who have a say in how the company works, it is also the Government, through its economic policy. Company—state interdependence is decisive. The size of the turnover makes big companies who have hundreds and thousands of employees not only subjects, but also actors on the regional and national economic stage. The impact which their managers' decisions have on the related impact on the government's social and financial system is significant. This is how, in the year 2009, the total taxes collected in Germany by the federation, Länder and town councils from all the companies rose to € 524 billion (s. Institut der Deutschen Wirtschaft Köln 2011, p. 68). In that same year, the biggest German industrial companies were Volkswagen with a turnover of € 105,187 billion and E-ON with € 81,817 billion respectively. Together with the other nine following companies Daimler, Siemens, BASF, BMW, RWE, Thyssen Krupp, Robert Bosch, Bayer and Adolf Merckle, they had a higher turnover than the total tax revenue of the combined state budgets of the year (s. Institut der Deutschen Wirtschaft Köln 2011, p. 52). What is socially important, beside the considerable amount the government collected through direct and indirect taxes from these companies, is that each of these had as many employees as several medium-sized towns. In 2009, Volkswagen employed 351,600 people, Siemens 405,000 people and the other nine companies mentioned above registered a cumulated figure of up to 2,023,500 employees. Even if only half of these are employed on German territory and not abroad in the international branches, 1,000,000 employees for ten companies is a high number compared to a total of 38,662,000 employees in the whole of Germany in that year (s. Institut der Deutschen Wirtschaft Köln 2011, p. 13 and 52). Therefore, it can be stated that the executive management of these companies truly deploy social and economic policies, not only at a regional level, but most certainly at a national level, if we take vertical and horizontal interdependence between suppliers and clients into account.

The existence of healthy and stable companies means that individuals can practise their profession within an organised structure. They have the opportunity to grow professionally and personally by answering to their professional calling, as we have seen in the last chapter. While growing personally, in ideal conditions people start to love their country and their society more, thus bringing a new wave of support for the existing economic and social order. This increased support brings extra stability to the act of governing that country. With gained support and credibility, the government is stronger when it comes to correctly implementing economic and social order, collecting taxes and levies that are as low as possible, without giving in to pressure from interest groups. All this boosts the health of the economic environment further.

In other words, a state which is apparently financially poor is, in fact strong, because it normally has healthy companies at its disposal, which, in case of dire need, it can occasionally "skim." This possibility is based on the assumption that politicians have the strength not to let themselves bullied by managers and employers of the huge concentrated economic power bundles, as happened with the financial crisis of 2007–2008. Back then, banks forced the governments, and thus the tax payer, to bail them out of their expected responsibilities and from going bankrupt if they managed wrongly.

The interaction between the business, its management and the government is important. The dynamics of the 'market economy' as part of the Social Market Economy is maintained by keeping businesses, the basic components of them, within a profit zone where, they produce "black figures" (schwarze Zahlen), not in "red figures" (rote Zahlen)—meaning losses, as they say in German—in the balance sheets.

While looking at the principle of the free market economy also from the point of view of producing sustainable growth, we must unfortunately conclude that in the long term, the free market economy seems to be doomed. The reason is simply that its survival depends on more and more consumption and uninterrupted sales and the need for new markets. Well, as the Earth's resources are limited, it is obvious that the free market economy, which otherwise is the instrument for creating fastest growth and alleviating poverty, its applicability is limited in time. It will have to be replaced by another systemic principle which cannot be defined at time point. Of course this does not apply only to the Social Market Economy, but to any national economic system where it is present.

2.4 Competition[4]

Competition is a third "second-level" principle at the basis of a market economy, and thus of the Social Market Economy as we know it in Germany too. Along with freedom and private property, competition can, if applied and supervised correctly create the pre-requisites to lead to a high level of economic productivity. It creates a dynamic between companies. Competition is an impersonal mechanicism, but it makes sure that the price formed at the meeting point between supply and demand, stays functional and becomes credible. It also puts pressure on individual businesses by stimulating them to improve their performance, product quality, innovation and product amounts in order to remain on the market. The reverse of competition is the socio-psychological phenomenon of burn-out of some of the staff who are not able to sustain over long periods of time the high level of productivity required by market survival needs.

One of the explanations of how the principle of competition functions is the observation, from this point of view, of the mechanism of mergers. The motivation companies have to merge, to enter new markets and to adopt a market-oriented behaviour is usually given by the financial advantages resulting from lower costs relating to supply, production and finance. Many economists uphold the view that the most important advantage in a merger is the enlargement of the client base by adding the clients of the merged partner. Up to the crisis of 2007–2008 no government official or minister seemed to have worried that mergers will produce "companies too big to fail". These came, as we have repeatedly seen, into a position to force many governments to bail them out of bankruptcy—and this not with money produced by the neoliberal "self-regulating" free market, but with the loathed taxpayers money. As a result, there has been an increase in the perception among government officials and policy makers around the world about the dangers of mergers and acquisitions which give too much power to companies in general and to certain com-panies in particular. At some point after the crisis, the volume of international mergers and acquisitions dropped quite spectacularly. In only two years, the yearly volume of these international M&A dropped in 2009 to only ca. 37% of its highest ever value of 2007

---

[4] This book sub-chapter is the only slightly readapted chapter 4.1.3 of the book Muresan, Stefan-Sorin, Social Market Economy. The Case of Germany. Springer International Publishing, 2014, p. 184–188.

(s. OECD 2010, Fig. A.8.2). Thus, the social injustice which ensued from the thousands of billions of Euros of taxpayers money used to bail out these inflated merged companies is a price all tax payers had to pay for the governments not having watched over the implementation of the principle of competition and limits to concentration of power in the respective markets.

The legal instrument which is used in Germany against violations of the principle of competition in the Social Market Economy, is the Act Against Restraints on Competition (Gesetz gegen Wettbewerbsbeschränkungen) adopted by the Bundestag in 1957. It is the concrete practical result of Franz Böhm's theoretical but applied work in this direction. This Act came into force on January 1, 1958 and has been amended at least seven times so far, with the last one in 2011. Its purpose is to limit power build-ups in the private sector. In the very first article of this Act, in its amended and republished form, it is stipulated that "Agreements between companies, decisions by associations of companies and concerted practices, which aim at hindering, restriction or distortion of competition, are prohibited" (s. § 1 of the Law against Limitations of Competition (Gesetz gegen Wettbewerbsbeschrankungen; GWB) "Vereinbarungen zwischen Unternehmen, Beschlüsse von Unternehmensvereinigungen und aufeinander abgestimmte Verhaltensweisen, die eine Verhinderung, Einschränkung oder Verfälschung des Wettbewerbs bezwecken oder bewirken, sind verboten."). This prohibition in itself is a good thing. But who, be it person or institution, could interpret and decide impartially on the illegal aspects of cooperation between businesses?

In Germany it is the Federal Cartel Office (Bundeskartellamt) who supervises and should ensure that the law and the principle of competition are respected. In the name of the government, it has the mission of "monitoring abuse" (s. Grosser 1988, p. 43: "eine Missbrachsaufsicht ausübt"). In other words, there is an open and public indirect heed of opinion, that abuse against competition in the market does exist and that it can only partially be eliminated. In order to preserve the balance of power on the market, the government needs to be informed about as many trespasses of competition regulations as possible. Otherwise market mechanisms will not function coherently enough in order to make the system credible to the entrepreneur. The implementation of the Competition Act had positive results: if in 1930, the German Weimar Republic apparently had between 2000 and 3000 cartels for a much smaller economy than that of today`s Federal Republic of Germany. The latter had in 1978 barely over 260 cartels, and the figure went further down to barely above 240 in 1985 (for exact figures here s. Grosser 1988, p. 44).

The Federal Cartel Office systematically monitors market share of companies and the concentration of power in individual product markets at the national level. It groups similar economic branches together according to certain criteria which it considers significant, thereby establishing economic sectors for the purpose of monitoring. There can be differences between various economic sectors as far as the respective market share is concerned. At the beginning of the 1980s, market power concentration (it is usually defined as the cumulated market share of the three largest companies in that sector) was with 75.2 % highest in the national economy in the office supplies and IT sector (s. Grosser 1988, p. 44; other market power concentration was ca. 63 % in mining, ca. 61 % in tobacco, ca.

50 % in lubricants and ca. 49 % in automotive sectors). What follows is a process of complex, interdisciplinary, economic, political and social interpretation of the results in order to establish what the effects of market concentration are on competition in a particular sector. Interpretation is done by the Bundeskartellamt according to certain principles.

There is a high degree of the complexity of this work of supervision. Then, there is to be distinguished between implicit and explicit cartels (comp. Haucap 2014, folie 2) or oligopolistic situations. Discovering overt company mergers is relatively easy because they are explicit cartels. But discovering contracts of association that are sometimes confidential which de facto are implicit cartels (but de iure are not) and may lead to monopolistic or oligopolistic situations on the market is rendered difficult by the fact that companies use the power they already have and withhold the relevant information from the media market. There are procedures in place according to which the Kartellamt should be able to buy information from the market, including from the customs authorities or from the intelligence communities.

Operatively speaking, along with European unification and the creation of the Single Market, as well as the massive globalization process we are in, competition monitoring jurisdiction moved to a large extent to Brussels, to the European Commission. However, given the principle of subsidiarity, this jurisdiction was delegated back to some extent to the national and even local Cartel Offices, in Germany's case to the Bundeskartellamt. Should the focus of supervision be within Land (local state, or regional level. Germany consists of 16 Länder; s. Appendix 9) lines, jurisdiction belongs to the Land Cartel Office (Landeskartellamt). Consequently, as long as the European Union does not get involved, the Office may continue to supervise free competition in Germany, as it did before the creation of the single market.

Since 1999, after successive amendments to the law, the Federal Cartel Office has received in Germany extra competences. As a result, when public works contracts are auctioned, it should make sure that the bidding companies have an equal and fair chance against discrimination in the tender.

The Bundeskartellamt is part of the Federal Ministry of the Economy, is based in Bonn and in December of 2009 it had 320 employees, of which economists and lawyers occupy about half of each of these posts.

2.5 Monetary Stability and Predictability of Economic Policy[5]

We will not get here into the debate about the nature of money nor about the self-awarded monopoly of the State, carried out through the Central Bank, to be the only actor allowed to issue means of payment within its national territory. Thus, we shall start our analysis based on the assumption that a granted legitimacy to this monopoly.

---

[5] This book sub-chapter is the only slightly readapted chapter 4.1.4 of the book Muresan, Stefan-Sorin, Social Market Economy. The Case of Germany. Springer International Publishing, 2014, p. 188–195.

Provided there are sufficient funds available, that there is a stable and efficient banking system which can be bailed out in case of a crisis, we can say there is monetary stability as well as predictability of the economic policy. These are crucial conditions for the competitive functioning of any modern national economy. In Germany's case, these, are the fourth and the fifth "second level" principles of the market economy area in the Social Market Economy.

The most important institution able to ensure these principles during the era when the Deutsche Mark was Germany's currency, was Germany's Central Bank, named the German Bank of the Federation (German Central Bank or Deutsche Bundesbank). The Bundesbank is still located in Frankfurt am Main, and online at www.bundesbank.de. The activity of the civil servants delegated by the Bundesbank to the European Central Bank can be investigated at www.ecb.eu.

After the third step toward the European Monetary Union was completed on June 30, 2002 with the introduction of the Euro banknotes and coins, the Bundesbank could no longer exist independently of the European Central Bank, as it had been introduced in the European System of Central Banks. Still, in order to have a better understanding of the mechanisms of today's Social Market Economy not only in Germany, but all over the Eurozone and the countries depending on this zone, it is necessary to be aware of the evolution, the principles, characteristics and activities of its predecessor, the Bundesbank between 1958–2002 and of the Bank of the German States (Bank Deutscher Länder) between 1948 and 1958.

The main task of the Bundesbank was to ensure the stability of the German currency nationally and internationally. Nationally, it focused on price stability, since it is known that the Germans' high sensitivity towards inflation dates back to the hyperinflation of 1923. (Fig. 2.2)

Price stability is now directly linked to maintaining the value of cumulated capital and especially of savings and economic planning within the businesses.

The key to the Bundesbank's success is attributed by most economists to one of the key elements of its Articles of Association. It could be called a "third level" principle of the Social Market Economy: the independence of the Central Bank's monetary policy from the Federal Government's economic policy (s. § 12 of the Bundesbank Law; Gesetz über die Deutsche Bundesbank). It is a typically German principle, consistently applied over several decades and which has been taken over into the Statutes of the European Central Bank. Certainly, the sovereign debt crisis, which made itself felt over the stability of the Euro at the onset of the Greek crisis in 2010, has severely forced the ECB to undermine this main principle of organization and come to support the anti-crisis quantitative easing measures adopted by the Federal Government.

Returning now to the original state where the theoretical design is to be analysed as the ideal one, as we can see, it is enough to look comparatively at the model applied by the French Central Bank (Banque de France). This has the mission to provide for a great influence of the French Government in establishing monetary policies, leaving the Bank in a position of subordination to it. In Germany, on the other hand, the Bundesbank has never been of part of the Federal Ministry of Finance.

Fig. 2.2 Changes of inflation rate in Germany, 1963–2010 (in %, yoy, Deutsche Mark then Euro. Source: Statistisches Bundesamt (2011) p. 330, Institut der Deutschen Wirtschaft Köln (Hg.) 2011 p. 58, The Inter-agency Group on Economic and Financial Statistics http://www.principalglobalindicators.org)

As a fourth and new instrument of the ECB to promote its policies and which has become known after the economic and financial crisis of 2007–2009 is "quantitative easing". Through this, the Central Banks, not only in the Eurozone, but also the US Federal Reserve and the Bank of England are pumping cash into the market by buying treasury bonds and bank issued bonds from the market. During the four years between 2010 and 2013 the

US Federal Reserve pumped into the dollar market up to US\$ 4000 bn. (s. Vergopoulos 2014, p. 15), which is a stunning ca. 25% of US GDP. Thus the Central Banks are bailing out the "market" part of the free market economy, which by many neoliberal economists is expected to rebalance itself by no outside influence. This is not only incorrect economically, but also an unethical method which is running against the principle of the independence of the Central Banks. The European Central Bank is running quantitative easing programmes similar in size. This is prone to create bubbles and inflation, certainly in the long term and probably even in the medium term. It looks increasingly probable that a bubble which is expected to burst soon will drag most economies into a necessary monetary reset, or monetary reform. Even more draconic measures are expected, namely a full replacement of paper money with electronic money. Rumours among politicians and CEOs of large multinationals circulate saying currently that the new means of payment might be called "Ameron" and it might be a currency common to the euro area and the US dollar area. This would be meant to continue Western leadership at global level, operating in team with the effects of the Transatlantic Trade and Investment Partnership (TTIP).

Let us see how the Bundesbank came to be and how it implements policies and creates a monetary policy adapted to the economic nature of the Central European man where the Social Market Economy resides.

The Bank of the German States (Bank Deutscher Länder) was established in 1948 by an act of the Military Government of the Western Allies. Almost ten years later, in 1957, it was transformed into the Deutsche Bundesbank and it adopted some of the banking policy models of the US Central Bank, the United States Federal Reserve.

The Bundesbank, unlike the Federal Reserve, is a public legal person of the German federation. Its social patrimony belongs to the federal state. It is made up of the main headquarters in Frankfurt, not Berlin, and nine Regional Offices (Landeszentralbank) in the capitals of the former federal states before the reunification of Germany. It is worth mentioning that Saarland only adopted the German Mark in 1959, after the establishment of the Bundesbank. This the reason why Saarbrücken for many years did not have a Landeszentralbank branch.

The bank is ruled by the Executive Board (Zentralbankrat), made up of the bank's executive directors (Vorstand) and the presidents of the Regional Offices.

We can say that the Bundesbank has accomplished its mission successfully. It had a significant contribution to making a name for the Deutsche Mark introduced on June 20, 1948 and replaced fifty years later by the Euro. Figure 2.3 shows that in 1986, the Bundesbank succeeded in having the Deutsche Mark appreciated by 0.1%. Also, it is obvious that the three periods of inflation, when the inflation rate went over 4%, coincided with the necessity of absorbing the shock of the oil crises of 1972–1974, 1979–1981 and of the German reunification.

At a European level, since more than 60% of German exports have gone since memorial times to the European countries, it is clear that Germany has a massive interest in these countries possessing the purchasing power to buy these German goods. After 2000 and until 2010, every year between 60.3 and 64.7% of all German exports went to the EU27 countries (s. Institut der Deutschen Wirtschaft Köln 2011, p. 40). Previously, Germany

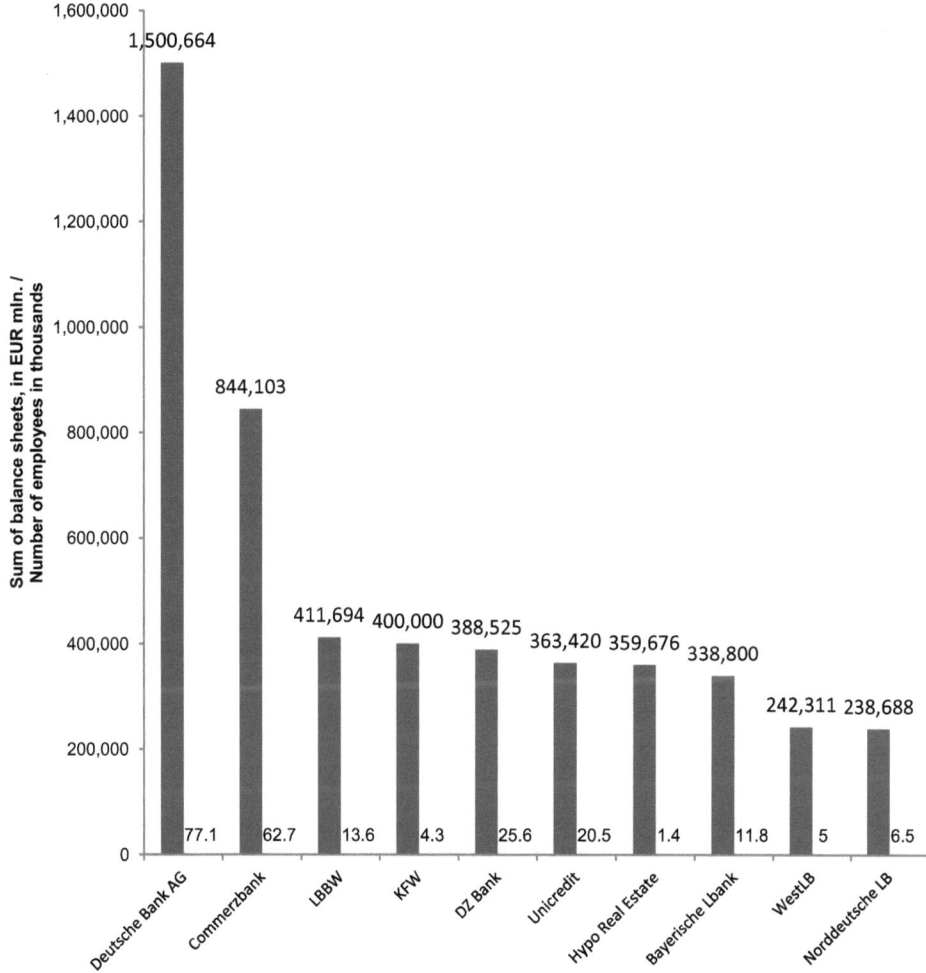

Fig. 2.3 Size of banks, 2009. Balance sheets, EUR mln., employees, thsd (Source: Institut der Deutschen Wirtschaft Köln (2011), p. 52)

exported to the EU less of its total exports, i. e. 39.5% in 1960 and up to 56.5% in 1995 (s. Institut der Deutschen Wirtschaft Köln 2001, p. 42).

Therefore, a joint currency would serve German export interests at least as long as it was kept at a low inflation rate. Thus, once the Treaty on European Union was agreed in the small Dutch town of Maastricht and signed on February 7, 1992, the third stage of the European Economic and Monetary Union commenced. Consequently, the Bundesbank legally became a part of the European System of Central Banks and a founder of the European Monetary Institute. Through this Treaty, the European Central Bank, preceded by the European Monetary Institute, based in Frankfurt am Main, began introducing the common currency between 1999 and 2002. It put in its mission statement the German principle of the independence of the bank from the government's economic policy, the

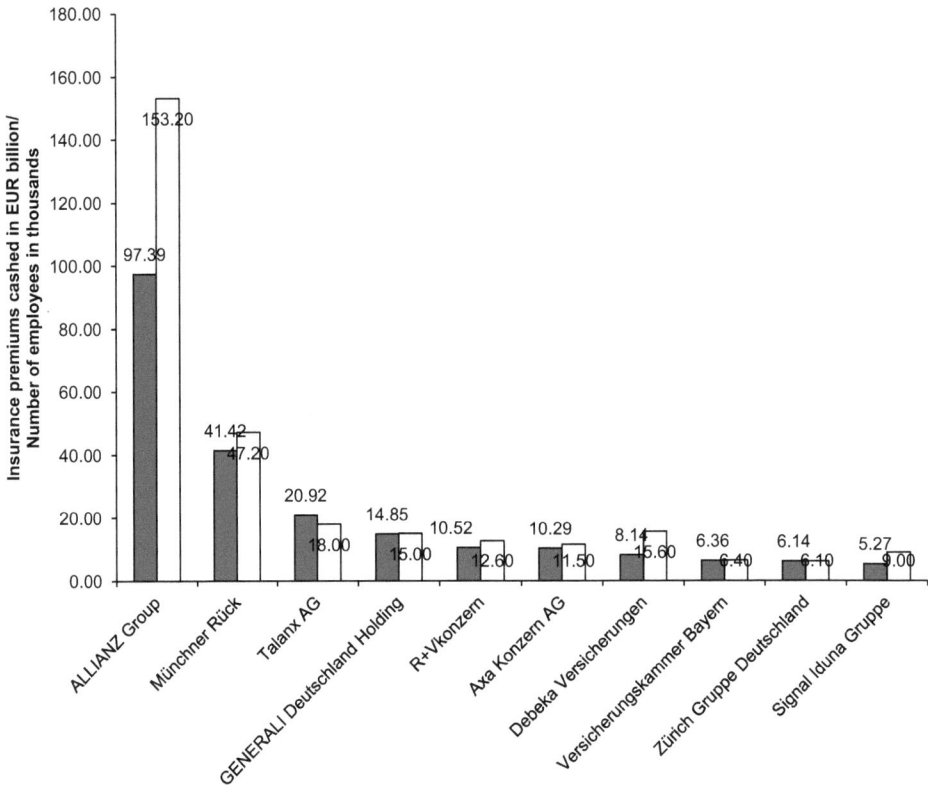

Fig. 2.4 Size of Insurance companies, 2009. Premiums in EUR billions, employees, thsd (Source: Institut der Deutschen Wirtschaft Köln (2011), p. 52)

European Commission's economic policy respectively. This is perhaps the most German contribution to the Social Market Economy model to the European Union: The ECB has, due to its Statutes to focus mainly on the stability of the common currency, the Euro. The common currency used to be named the ECU (European Currency Unit), until the European Council of Madrid in 1995, and was named EURO afterwards. (Fig. 2.4)

As the European legislation integrated these German principles, when the Federal Parliament (Deutscher Bundestag) ratified the Treaty of Maastricht, the Bundesbank Act had to be modified only with respect to its form and not the contents. Article 3 of the amended act reads: "The Deutsche Bundesbank, being the Central Bank of the Federal Republic of Germany, is an integral part of the European System of Central Banks (ESCB). It participates in the performance of the ESCB's tasks with the primary objective of maintaining price stability" (s. Art. 3 of the Bundesbank Act: "Die Deutsche Bundesbank ist als Zentralbank der Bundesrepublik Deutschland integraler Bestandteil des Europäischen Systems der Zentralbanken. Sie wirkt an der Erfüllung seiner Aufgaben mit dem vorrangigen Ziel mit, die Preisstabilität zu gewährleisten.").

Even after becoming part of the ESCB, the Bundesbank continued (at least up to the sovereign debt crisis as of 2010) to abide by the same principle of political independence from the government, as it did before. The difference from the past is that now, this principle is no longer applied in the bank's own name, but indirectly. The Bundesbank underlies, just like any other Central Bank part of the ESCB, to Art. 107 of the Treaty of Maastricht and its subsequent changes under the Treaty revisions. According to this article, neither the ECB nor any other Central Bank of a signatory state of the Treaty and none of the members of its leading bodies are allowed to receive orders during the exercise of duties, or to let themselves be led through any indication from any community, any Government of any signatory state or by any other institution. Just like many others of the principles underlying financial institutions, this principle is under pressure now (2010 and later) from the more political interventionist part of the European economists.

Even if the Bundesbank's activities have a decisive impact on economic life, the Bundesbank and the ECB, respectively, are not the only institutions authorised to supervise and direct the markets and financial systems in Germany. Here, another important authority in the banking system was the Federal Banking Supervisory Authority (Bundesaufsichtsamt für das Kreditwesen BaKred). It originates in 1931 when after the financial crisis and bad experiences registered with banks, it was decided that banking activities should be supervised by the state (s. Bundesministerium der Finanzen 1999, p. 51; the Authority's website was www.bakred.de and was based in Berlin, in the course of time it underwent several reforms and reorganizations. www.bafin.de). Nationally, this Authority has a close collaboration with the Bundesbank, but is subordinated to the Federal Ministry of Finance. The Authority was established after the banking crisis in 1931. It supervised the banks' activities and the way in which they respect banking legislation, especially the Credit Act (Kreditwesengesetz). The Authority also establishes, together with the Bundesbank, the proportion of credit in a bank's assets and liabilities, the amounts credited as compared to the bank's liquid assets. It checks that the banks conform to these rules. In the course of time the supervision of the financial sector underwent several reforms and reorganizations. Now (2013), the Authority is based in Bonn and is called the Bundesamt fur Finanzdienstleistunsaufsicht (s. www.bafin.de). Internationally, the Authority cooperates with the Bank for International Settlement in Basel (s. www.bis.org). Besides being the Bank of the more than 100 Central Banks from across the globe which are its members, the BIS worked, on the New Basel Capital Accords (Basel II and Basel III) and aims at assisting the international financial system to face the demands of globalization. At European level, the European Securities and Markets Authority (ESMA) attempts to supervise financial instruments at European level and related them to the relevance of rating marks (s. Everling and Mureşan 2011). Thereby it is expected that renewed financial crisis like that of 2007–2009 can be avoided and that the euro is not blamed any more in Europe for the crisis. Instead, the blame for the crisis should be attributed to the continuing debt policies, as it is in fact.

As the capital market became more and more developed in the early 2000s (probably driven by fresh Western sovereign and private debt), a new body was needed in order to ensure monetary stability in Germany. So the Federal Securities Supervisory Office (Bundesaufsichtsamt für den Wertpapierhandel BAWE) was created. This Office watched that another "third level" principle is respected so that equality of chances between securities owners is guaranteed: it is forbidden to use information originating from the inside of the financial institution issuing or trading the securities (Insidergeschäfte; comp. Bundesministerium der Finanzen 1999, pp. 54–55) in transactions on the financial market. By using this inside information, the economic actors who have them, even bank employees, could, as soon as new securities are issued, influence their value decisively for their own interest.

BaKred, BaWe and BaV (Federal Office of Supervision of Insurance; Bundesamt für das Versicherungswesen) merged and formed as of May 2002 the national Federal Office for Supervision of the Financial Institutes (Bundesanstalt für Finanzdienstleistungsaufsicht BaFin). It was brought to Bonn as part of the push by the Federal Government to bring national agencies and companies to Bonn to provide for losses of jobs following the move of the federal capital to Berlin in 1999/2000.

The common and generally objective action of these three financial authority institutions is expected to ensure a relatively high degree of equality of chances between the participants in financial life in the Social Market Economy system. This provided, at least until the crisis of 2007–2009 the grounds for a stable, predictable financial system where economic agents can plan their actions years in advance, by taking informed, hence responsible and economically efficient initiatives. A key element here are ratings. Whether they are commercial, sovereign, environmental, issuers etc., rating issuers still have even after the ceconomic and financial crisis a decisive influence on the cost of borrowing or the revenue from crediting (comp. Achleitner and Everling 2004; understanding ratings and their influence on equity price and markets is essential for the finance industry and economics). However, just like many of the federal institutions in the finance and monetary sector BaFin lost a great deal of credibility as it failed to foresee, predict or warn German citizens of the coming financial and monetary crisis of 2007–2009. In other words, the higher monetary stability and economic policy predictability are and the earlier the planning, the lower production costs can be. Consequently, prices will go down making products more competitive on the international market. This (Produktisierung) is crucial for a country as dependent on export and from achieving a current account surplus, i.e. from earning net money from its international economic relations as Germany is. Through monetary stability and tight economic planning, German companies became more competitive on the international market than companies from countries incapable of ensuring the macroeconomic conditions necessary for planning early enough before production. In the current context of expanding globalization, Germany has every interest in signing as many international agreements as possible so that it keeps financial instability shocks from other countries to a minimum, especially shocks from countries from which it imports raw material and countries to which it exports its products. (Fig. 2.5)

But a problem which sprang up across the Western world, including Germany and which became visible especially after the West won the Cold War is the deification of money. "No to the deification of money" (s. Sekretariat der Deutschen Bischofskonferenz (Hg.) 2013. p. 46) appeals the Catholic Church in its internal Evangelii Gaudium of

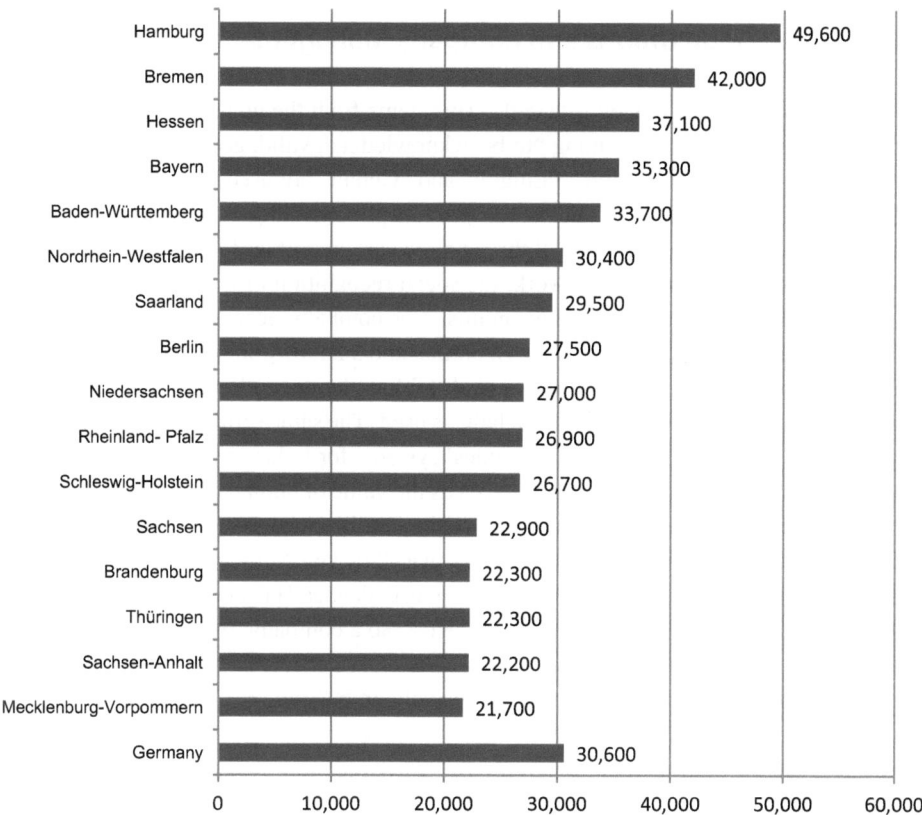

Fig. 2.5 GDP per capita in all Länder Germany's, 2010, EUR (Source: Institut der Deutschen Wirtschaft Köln (2011) p. 123)

November 2013. The other appeal "No to such money which reigns instead of serving" (s. Sekretariat der Deutschen Bischofskonferenz (Hg.) 2013. p. 47) sheds light on the fact that a distortion has appeared in economic life. This distortion consists of a perversion of the treatment and attitude to money. Most Westerners have been treating money not as a means (which it should only be) but as a purpose in itself. This distortion is catalysed by the totalitarian character of money. In its turn, the totalitarian character is due to the monopoly of Central Banks to issue universally valid means of payment. Still, the distortion points to a dangerous voiding of work from meaning and sense. Voiding of meaning equals to loss of direction and of independent thought, even by educated people. I think this status quo could be corrected only via the application of voluntary ethical behaviour and by managers, employees and workers finding the answer to the quest for meaning in everyday life, including by returning to the teachings and doctrines of Christianity.

2.6 Wages, Trade Unions and Company Management[6]

In German, the word for money is "Geld". This stems from the noun "Gold" (for "gold") and from the verb "gelten" meaning "to be acknowledged, valid, accepted." For "salary" on the contrary, the words "Lohn," "Entgelt" and "Gehalt" are used. Each of them means a different thing: "reward," "financial recognition of something valid" and "something to keep you held up" respectively. All three notions are important for shaping a complete image of the relationship between work, the social recognition of the usefulness of work and the reward for working. In the economist's or company accountant's language, for whom the salary is being looked upon as a burden and a liability, more than anything else, the word "Lohn" is used. Whereas in the words of the salaried worker who sees a salary as a positive thing, as income, the word "Gehalt" is used. The same difference in terminology can be observed if we look at the companies' systems for balancing their books. In this case of the companies, salary payment is seen as the value of human contribution, or as re-cognition of "a sacrifice or a load on behalf of the families who send out the labour force, but as a salary cost and the cost with the work place" (s. von Nell-Breuning 1979, p. 130: "*nicht* als Opfer oder Last der die Arbeitskräfte entsendenden Haushalte […] sondern nach Lohnkosten und Lohnnebenkosten veranschlagt"). So a company, from the point of view of it targeting financial efficiency as a profit centre, does not care much for the employee's personal or family life. It tends to focus exclusively on making profit.

It is useful to look at these terminological differences made by German thought, becau-se it shows a kind of separation, or even rivalry, between the social sectors that pay off, as financial resource producers, and the social sectors that consume financial resources. Therefore, it is understandable why trade unions emerged to become powerful and respec-ted groups inside society in Germany and in the Social Market Economy system. They try to protect employees from the employers' abuse, and try to humanise the company by pointing to the value of work as a productive element of the business. The simmering battle between the employers and the interest groups organised by the employees takes place in the realm of salaries, benefits, or that of the rewarding bonuses of the work place. For that reason, it is impossible to understand the system of remuneration, without first looking at the unions.

Throughout decades, unions have been aggressively protecting salary rights. Chart 9 regarding GDP per capita and Table 2.1 regarding companies involved in collective bar-gaining, show how trade union are able to get different results, depending on the Land we are looking at. Even though German trade unions go far back in history, namely before 1914, still they are mainly rooted in the Weimar Republic. They were outlawed by the Nazi regime after 1933, but returned to public life after 1945. The first post-war re-foun-ding of a national union organization took place at the German Trade Union Confedera-

---

[6] This book sub-chapter is the only slightly readapted chapter 4.1.5 of the book Muresan, Stefan-Sorin, Social Market Economy. The Case of Germany. Springer International Publishing, 2014, p. 195–206.

Table 2.1 Degree of wage contract binding of companies and employees, 2000 and (>) 2009, % of total number of companies at national level resp. of employees. (Source: Institut der Deutschen Wirtschaft Köln 2002) p. 110 and Institut der Deutschen Wirtschaft Köln 2011, p. 113)

	D	West	East
	% out of total number of companies		
With			
Sectorial wage contract	41>33	45>36	23>19
Company wage contract	4>3	3>3	4>4
No wage contract	56>64	52>61	73>77
Of which:			
Leaning on a bound wage contract	22>26	20>25	31>31
Without leaning on a bound wage contract	34>38	32>36	42>46
	% of employees, out of total employees		
With			
Sectorial bound wage contract	61>52	63>56	46>38
Company bound wage contract	7>10	7>9	10>13
No bound wage contract	33>39	30>36	45>49
Of which			
Leaning on a bound wage contract	17>20	15>19	24>24
Without leaning on a bound wage contract	16>19	15>17	21>25

tion Congress (Deutscher Gewerkschaftsbund; DGB) in October 1949. Having the SPD stand up for them in federal politics, German unions had considerable strength until the mid-1990s. The highest total number of members was around 1990, when in West Germany, they reached a 9.8 Million. when Federal Republic of Germany had a population of 65 Million. Instead of going up in numbers with at least a 25 %, i.e. the proportion which represents the increase in population from East Germany who was added to West Germany, union membership stagnated. Thus, in 2000 there were 9.732 Million. trade union members in the whole of Germany. By 2010, total membership went down to 7.7 Million., i.e. with ca. 45 %, if we consider the total population of united Germany. The reason is that these trade unions were a mere tool of oppression of the former Communist system and these trade unionists had a totally different style from those in the West.

Currently, the social influence of trade unions is considerably lower than twenty years ago.

Once the "golden generation" of the SPD, with members such as Willy Brandt and Helmut Schmidt, retired from active politics and along with the forced resignation of another leftist, Oskar Lafontaine, from the presidency of the party in March 1999, under the government of Gerhard Schröder, things changed and the SPD was "highjacked" and pushed towards social liberalism.

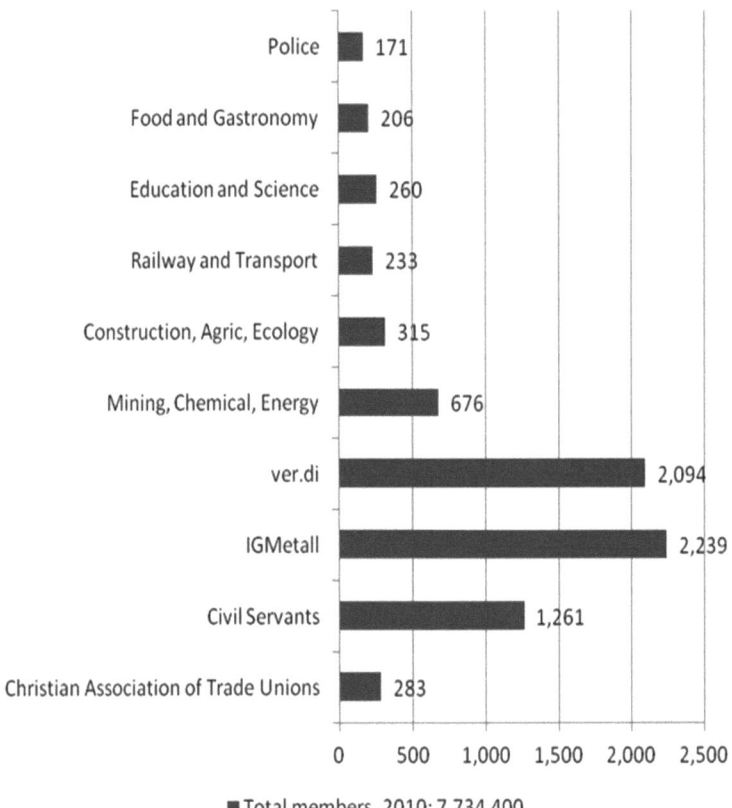

Fig. 2.6 Trade union members, 2010

Returning now to the foundation times of Germany's postwar republic in 1949, we see that initially, the Confederation of German Trade Unions had liberals, social-democrats, communists and Christian-socialists among its members. Each of these groups aspired to be a co-founder of a new economic order in post-war Germany. At that time, unions believed that the best possible system for post-war Germany would be democratic socialism. This opinion brought them in direct collision with Ludwig Erhard and with the ordoliberal market economy he promoted. Still, even if the SPD remained in opposition until 1969, the unions fought the Christian Democrats of the CDU who were in power for all these first twenty years of the democratic West Germany. The result of this fight is the current system of the Social Market Economy, in which "social order" is regarded as a pillar in itself of the whole system. The facts are that "social order" is the second pillar. It is not merely a positive side effect of correctly implementing market economy, as Erhard believed, wished and talked about. (Fig. 2.6)

Thus, the SPD has its own direct contribution to the Social Market Economy, making the model a national one and not only a CDU-driven one.

For example, the adoption of the "Acts on Collective Work Contracts" (Tarifsvertrags-gesetz) and the "Act of co-decision in company management" (Mitbestimmungsgesetz; s. Adam 1995, p. 114–115) of 1976 were a direct result of union pressure. Today they are integral parts of the Social Market Economy system and are only to be found in Germany in this form.

But, in order to gain pressure and negotiation power, unions strove to be economically independent from the employers and the political world. So they built their own econo-mic empire, not just at a regional level, but at federal level, all over West Germany. This empire resisted until the 1980s and is often acknowledged as the union alternative to the market economy and capitalism. This was obvious in the projects "New Homeland" (Neue Heimat) and the "Trade Unions' Bank" (Bank für Gemeinwirtschaft; BfG). Until 1976, the New Homeland built a patrimony of 418,000 dwellings, owned and managed by the trade unions. In those days, the New Homeland was the largest real estate company in Europe. The BfG started as a small bank and moved from a turnover of 133 Million. Deutsche Mark in 1950 to 35 billion Deutsche Mark in 1978 (s. the article Hank 1999, p. W1). Un-fortunately, human nature showed its teeth again, even in West Germany: the trade union empire, with its banking and real estate parts, ended up in a corruption scandal in 1982. The unions' entrepreneurial failure was final in 1986 when most of their businesses had to be sold. Even Ernst Breit, one of the former presidents of the DGB (German Confe-deration of Trade Unions) concluded that "unions are not fit to be private entrepreneurs" (quoted in Hank 1999, p. W1: "Gewerkschaften sind als Unternehmer nicht geeignet"). Nonetheless, for over forty years, the unions succeeded in keeping the employers at bay and put their decisive mark on the Social Market Economy, turning it into an original economic model.

The main aspects with which the unions influenced the model of are in the "Federal Constitution", the "Act of Collective Work Contracts" Tarifvertragsgesetz; comp. Körtgen 1998, p. 18 ff. Körtgen discusses the nature of the collective wage bargaining both from its nature in Germany (pp. 15–32) and its eventual applicability at European level (p. 65– 96) and the "Co-Decision Act" (Mitbestimmungsgesetz; comp. Niedenhoff 1979, p. 12). In order to paint a relatively full picture of their inputs it is enough to examine the "principle of autonomy of collective bargaining" (Tarifautonomie) and the "principle of co-decision" (Mitbestimmung).

Like many other Social Market Economy principles, the principle of autonomy of col-lective bargaining as a "third-level" principle is also rooted in the Federal Constitution. Ar-ticle 9, paragraph three stipulates that any person has the right "to form associations to sa-feguard and improve work- and economic conditions" (s. GG Art 9. Abs. 3: "zur Wahrung und Förderung der Arbeits- und Wirtschaftsbedingungen Vereinigungen zu bilden…"). In concrete economic terms, this means that trade unions and employers' associations have the right to set the level of salaries, of annual increases taking into account the yearly infla-tion rates, through bargaining and common agreement, but with no interference from the state or federal government. Moreover, other benefits relating to working conditions, are also subject to negotiation. These appendages to working benefits are measured in money and are included in the yearly collective bargaining between employers and trade unions.

These comprise collective negotiations on salary levels, working conditions and training in the work place. Unions negotiate in the name of the salaried workers and the employers' associations, in the name of the employers. According to the principle of "Tarif autonomie" and the Collective Work Contract Act (Tarifvertragsgesetz), the parties have negotiate wages and labour conditions (s. Adam 1995, p. 114) and then to sign a collective agreement, usually valid for one year for a certain region and a specified economic sector (e.g. metal processing). Should the unions want improved pay and work conditions, negotiations for the collective agreements normally take place at the beginning of every year, between January and March. The bargaining "technique" goes as far as street protests or strikes, should the need arise. This is the reason that most strikes in Germany take place at the beginning of every year, as we can see from the media. What is original in this system is that the salary level negotiated for that year in an economic sector or in a certain region is usually adopted as reference level by all companies which are members of the trade union associations and in all the regions in Germany where that sector exists. This is how a regional result gets practised throughout the country in collective and also in individual bargaining for that particular economic sector. The federal government's involvement comes down to sometimes requesting that the minimum level of salaries in a particular economic field, in a particular region IS the first negotiation result achieved during a round of bargaining of that year. This declaration is made with the help of the Employment Office in that particular state and is meant to shorten the bargaining period in order to avoid disruption of work due to strikes.

However, not all companies are obliged to be registered into employers' associations, so the negotiated level of payment and benefits will not be compulsory for them. Also, the number of non-member companies not agreeing to enter into these binding negotiations was in 2009 about one third of all companies of a sector or region. Provided they find employees, the non-member companies are able to keep their employees' salaries at a lower level than the reference one for their sector and their region. It was the opposite, until recently, for the Swedish model: there were no salary and benefit levels other than the centralised one. On the other hand, if a company's owners are not part of the employers' associations, but are unfortunate enough to deal with a powerful union inside their own business, in Germany this union may be able to dictate its own level of salaries and benefits to the management, at a higher level even than the one adopted by collective bargaining. It is the other way round for every trade union: they all have the freedom to ponder which situation is more favourable to them—going it alone, or joining the union association in that particular region and economic sector.

Currently, the most powerful trade union association is the Industrial Trade Union in Metal (Industrie Gewerkschaft Metall; IG Metall) of the metal processing industry. The most powerful employers' association is the Federal Association of German Employers (Bundesverband Deutscher Arbeitgeber; BDA). They are mostly responsible for initiating salary indexation or non-indexation talks every year, depending on the lead inflation rate set by the Bundesbank, respectively the European Central Bank for that particular year.

The other third level principle imprinted by the unions into the Social Market Economy in Germany is the principle of co-decision. It refers to the legally guaranteed right of unions and their representatives, respectively, to partake in consultations and sometimes in the making of decisions by the boards of directors and chief executives of companies. The procedure is known as "Mitbestimmung" meaning co-determination, co-decision, co-participation. This is an extension of corporatist beliefs, according to which a company is not just a framework designed to help owners make profit, but also an association where employees have the opportunity to develop their individual personalities, build their own careers, follow the course of their personal evolution and also integrate into a group. "In the Social Market Economy a company is not just a technological and commercial unit, (but, o.n.) is also a community of people, and the relationship between employer and employee is places under the aegis of a social partnership." (s. Müller-Armack 1988, p. 14–15: "Der Betrieb ist nicht nur eine technische und kaufmännische Einheit, sondern eine Personengemeinschaft… (und, o.n.) … das Arbeitgeber–/Arbeitnehmer-Verhältnis in der Sozialen Marktwirtschaft, unter das Leitbild der Sozialpartnerschaft gestellt wird."). As we can see, unity and the social side of any economic activity are expected once again to be the main focus of identity of the Social Market Economy. Co-decision has a supervisory role on the management of the company, but this is only secondary; its primary role is related to social and personnel aspects. "In its widest sense, co-decision is the participation of employees, through their representatives, in collaboration with employers and their representatives, to decision making regarding regulations and measures pertaining first of all to matters of social and personnel aspects, or to the company's economic management" (s. Niedenhoff 1979, p. 5 where the co-decision researcher Weddigen is quoted: "Mitbestimmung im weitesten Sinne ist die Teilnahme der Arbeitnehmer durch ihre Vertretungen in Arbeitsgemeinschaft mit Arbeitgebern und deren Vertretern an Beschlüssen über Regelungen und Maßnahmen, welche Fragen, vor allem sozialpolitischer oder personalpolitischer Art oder Angelegenheiten der Wirtschaftsführung betreffen."). This is the spirit and the purpose of co-decision.

In practical terms, it took decades for the legislative framework on the forms of co-decision between Lands and companies to take a final, somewhat homogenous and consistent shape. Between 1968 and 1976, about sixty practical models of co-decision existed at the same time. Currently, there are three main legally-established models for employee manifestation within company boards: co-participation, co-determination and co-administration.

The specialised body in these matters is the Company Board (Betriebsrat) made of members who are representatives of the employees. The Company Board has been created by the Company Constitution Act (Betriebsverfassungsgesetz), an act dating back to 1920 and 1952 and whose last main renewal was in 1972. Employees have thereby the right to elect their representatives and also to be elected as representatives in the Company Board. This Board is a broader company body, a "people's board" so to speak. The Company

Board defends the interests of the employees in meetings with the Supervisory Board (Aufsichtsrat) and the Board of Directors (Vorstand) regarding either social or personnel issues or even strategic directions to be taken by the company. Calculating the number of members in each group is done according to certain fixed formulas taking into account the number of employees in a company (comp. Halbach et al 1998, pp. 369–484).

Co-participation is the first stage of the co-decision mechanism. It too has, by virtue of the "Co-decision law" several stages of intensity that can be applied. It may take place when the business owner's and the management's obligations are limited to: (1) Simple briefing the Company Board on a decision that was already made by the company executives, but was not yet put into practice (the right to be informed after a take decision) or (2) Hearing the Company Board's opinion on a previously-announced, but not yet implemented decision in one of the company's fields of activity (the right to be heard) or even (3) Consulting by the Company Board before it making a decision (the right to be consulted). In the case of co-participation, the Company Board cannot overrule the top management's decision (comp. Niedenhoff 1979, pp. 7–24).

A deeper level of employee involvement in company management is co-determination. This has profound consequences on the company's development. According to the law, co-determination compels the owner or the management to seek the consent of the Company Board in order to make certain important decisions in the company. Co—determination, has more to do with development strategies and paths, not necessarily common operative decisions of running transactions. In other words, the Company Board has, in this case, a veto over a decision made by the owners or the top management but not yet implemented (comp. Niedenhoff 1979, pp. 7–24).

Further support activities by the Company Board are that it may help the employee in his/her relations with the company's personnel department, helping him/her in obtaining his/her own company file, for example. It is important to note that, in the case of restructuring, the employee benefits automatically from the famous and strict legal right of "protection against (abusive) dismissal" (Kündigungsschutz; comp. Halbach et al. 1998, pp. 190–221) without being tricked out by the personnel department. It is essential to note that, in the case of co-participation and co-determination, the Company Board and the Board of Directors and, respectively, the Supervisory Board face each other as separate legal entities.

There is another level of co-decision: co-administration. In this case, employees co-administrate the company through their Company Board representatives in the company's Board of Directors. While there is a technical and administrative body within the company, the Board of Directors is representative of the entire organization, including members outside the company itself. It is elected and appointed by the General Shareholders' Assembly and controls the activity of the company's upper management, meaning the executives, from a financial and accounting point of view especially. For example, German legislation stipulates that the Boards of Directors of public limited companies and of limited partnerships with shares, have to admit to discussions a certain proportion of employee representatives, depending on the size of the company (more than five but less than 2000 employees, etc.; comp. Niedenhoff 1979, pp. 10–19). For a more liberal business owners of smaller companies a percentage of a third of the seats would be a very high proportion indeed.

That is the reason for which it is more difficult in Germany for speculative businesses to keep afloat and "come in" and "go out" of the country as soon as the profitability rate changes.

The principle of co-administration was also applied to the Privatisation Agency (Treuhandanstalt) for the former East German economy. Trade unions were represented in the Board of Directors of the Treuhandanstalt and had, in certain cases, not only the right to be present at discussions and when decisions were made, but also the right to vote on some of them. This corporatist model was based on the desire to ensure communication with the employees in order to help them understand that privatisation or cut-backs were done for them and not against them.[7] Obviously, this model suits the German consensus based society more than it would suit a free or a more protest based society. In Germany, unions tend to conform or to integrate Board of Directors decisions, rather than try to hinder them. For comparison purposes, we would like to mention that between 1996 and 1999, the Board of Directors of the Romanian State Property Fund acted in a very different way: during that time of fast-paced transition to a free market economy system, there were no union representatives, only political (Parliament and Government) and academic representatives in the Board of Directors. Unions were not permitted first-hand access to information, which is why they began opposing the privatisation policies.

In the Social Market Economy system, mechanisms of controlling private power are strong not only outside the company, but inside it too. Along with co-participation, co-decision and co-administration, there is a fourth principle of socialisation of the economic decision: it is what is known as "three-party talks" between the Government, employer unions and trade unions. But even in Germany this principle is rarely applied, and with varying intensity, depending on the political orientation of the government. Tripartite talks are usually called in the German speaking lands as "Alliance for Labour" (Bündnis für Arbeit) and during the Chancellorship of Gerhard Schröder were meant to create consensus among the three parties to the talks, in order to increase employment levels across society.

Co-decision in private companies employing between 6 and 1,999 permanent staff is based on the Company Constitution Act (Betriebsverfassungsgesetz) of 1952, amended to a considerable extent in 1972 (comp. Halbach et al. 1998, pp. 369–487). Therefore, this law covers most of the companies in Germany. Companies with over 2000 employees as

---

[7] For instance, the German principle of co-decision was recommended by the German federal government to the Ciorbea and Vasile Cabinets of Romania in 1997–1999, once the privatization laws no. 87 of 1997 and 99 of 1999 were adopted. Chancellor Kohl's special envoy for privatization matters was the president of the Board of Directors of the Treuhand, Dr. Joachim Grünewald. He recommended that as much as half of the main union federations in Romania be represented in the Board of Directors of the Romanian State Property Fund (National Privatization Agency), which indeed happened after law no. 99 of 1999 was passed.

permanent staff are also covered by this law and the Co-decision Act (Mitbestimmungsge-setz) of 1976. For the coal and steel industry, there is a special regulation, adopted as early as 1951, called the Mining Co-decision Act (Montan-Mitbestimmungsgesetz) of 1976. For public administration, the Public Employee Representation (Personalvertretungsge-setz) Act of 1955 applies.

The third-level principles of "wage autonomy", "co-decision" and "three-party-talks" provide a number of ways in which employees can participate, from the inside and out-side, to the management of the companies and institutions they work in. Their participati-on, even if this means limitations or at times even hindrances to the business owners, can nevertheless bring more creativity of all participants to the labour market because these principles suit the type of mainstream mentality existing in Central Europe.

These three principles are meant to and can lead to improved, more open and more honest internal organizational communication and to less tense working relations, than there would be if unions did not participate in the management process at all. This applies especially in bad economic times and it is what employees expect from their leaders after all. Nevertheless, more talking is also time consuming and this investment in time has to be recovered by higher productivity in other areas of the business cycle. Participation is expected to lead to more responsibly fulfilled duties and to decisions made for the com-mon good. Still, when unions participate in the economic decision making process, ow-ner-oriented decision fades considerably thereby making the company less dynamic and less able to absorb shocks or adapt to fast change, than purely owner driven companies. I would say, the Social Market Economy style is a more prudent rather than a more dynamic style.

2.7 Conclusion

In order to secure growth in the Western world, more business activities will have to be-come more international, moving out into other areas of the world where the infrastructure is not yet enough built as in the Western world. This means structures and companies based in "the West" will have to become more active in South-America, Africa, Central Asia, Siberia, sound and globally credible finance will be needed. For making finance sound we need action at global institutional and at local business level. The Pontifical Council called for the founding of a global supervisory financial authority "a suprana-tional Authority (…) favourable to the existence of efficient and effective monetary and financial systems …an Authority with a global reach…" (Pontifical Council For Justice and Peace 2011, pp. 21–22). At local business level, for the assessment of the soundness of reformed financial institutes systems, rating of financial institutions will be a useful tool.

It is obvious that in the post 2007–2009 economic crisis world, the banking and mo-netary system has been almost irreversibly discredited in the eyes of public opinion. If one is now walking in German streets adverts calling bankers "banksters" who are to be brought behind bars can be often seen placed in various spots of cities. The need of the public opinion to see justice which is expected to compensate for the abuse of public funds which bailed banks in the crisis is big. Justice is always justified. Only that as long as human nature will have universal needs and will have global trade, we will need a system of payment which can accommodate international functional payment. This is, we are going to need the banking system, even though not necessarily in the form in was before 2007–2009.

Reforming the current system will need at least three lines of action:

Making a comeback to values and ethics, incl. on Christian values which undoubtedly are the basis of the whole Western and Byzantine world. Advertising is distracting people, tempting to disorientation and has a strong power to degrade human beings into consumers. It makes them more superficial and thus easier to disorient and to lose focus on meaning and that which makes sense in life. The contradiction between the quest for meaning in life and advertising is a systemic problem of any market economy. Bringing values to the core of Western people's identities is sine qua non needed in order to overcome the daily psychological pressure from advertising (needed to sell).

Conduct widespread lifelong learning programmes for all parts of the population which is not in education any more. The purpose is to teach issues on economics both national and international in the context of ethics, values and even theology. Thus, more parts of the population will be enabled to follow governmental economic and financial policy.

Governments should make sure their policies are designed in such a way that they take into account the systemic contradiction of any market economy between natural limits (physical time, technology, human energy) to productivity on one hand and the need to growth on the other hand. In order to secure growth, more business activities will have to become more international, moving out into other areas of the world where the infrastructure is not yet enough built as in the Western world.

References

Achleitner KA, Everling O (Hg.) (2004) Handbuch Ratingpraxis. Dr. Th. Gabler, Wiesbaden

Adam, H (1995) Wirtschaftspolitik und Regierungssystem der Bundesrepublik Deutschland. Eine Einführung. Dritte, aktualisierte Auflage. Leske + Budrich, Opladen

Beattie A, Politi J (2008) I made a mistake, admits Greespan. In Financial Times, October 24, 2008. www.ft.com. Accessed May 26, 2014

Bundesministerium der Finanzen (Hrsg) (1999) Unser Bankwesen. Neuausgabe 1999. Referat Öffentlichkeitsarbeit, Bonn

Everling O, Muresan S (2011) ESMA – Autoritatea Europeană a Piețelor și Titlurilor de Valoare îşi începe activitatea la 1 iulie 2011. In EURACTIV online portal, July 1, 2011. http://www.euractiv.ro/uniunea-europeana/articles|displayArticle/articleID_23194

Grosser D (1988) Die Wirklichkeit der Wirtschaftsordnung. In: Grosser D, Lange T, Müller-Armack A, Neuss B (1988) Soziale Marktwirtschaft. Geschichte-Konzept-Leistung. Verlag W. Kohlhammer, Stuttgart, pp 35–73

Halbach G, Paland N, Schwedes R, Wlotzke O (1998) Übersicht über das Arbeitsrecht. 7., durchgesehene Auflage. Bundesministerium für Arbeit und Sozialordnung (Hg.), Bonn

Hank R (1999) Die Gewerkschaften suchen Wege aus der Finanzkrise. Fusionen als Lösungsmög-
    lichkeit. In: Frankfurter Allgemeine Zeitung, Nr. 230, October 10, 1999, p. W1– W2
Haucap J (2014) Wirksamer Wettbewerb und Kartellverbot in der Sozialen Marktwirtschaft. In
    EU-Trust. European Trust Institute, Dusseldorf. Online portal of. http://www.eu-trust.org/down-
    load/2014/140408_haucap_wirksamer_wettbewerb_und_kartellverbot.pdf accessed June 2,
    2014
Hefermehl, W. (1993): Handelsgesetzbuch ohne Seehandelsrecht, mit Wechselgesetz und Scheckge-
    setz. Textausgabe mit ausführlichem Sachregister und eine Einführung von Universitätsprofessor
    Dr.iur. Dr.h.c. Wolfgang Hefermehl. 27. überarbeitete Auflage. Stand 20. Mai 1993. Sonderaus-
    gabe unter redaktioneller Verantwortung des Verlages C.H. Beck, München. Deutscher Taschen-
    buch Verlag, München.
Institut der Deutschen Wirtschaft Köln (Hg.) (2001) Deutschland in Zahlen Ausgabe 2001. Deut-
    scher Instituts Verlag, Köln
Institut der Deutschen Wirtschaft Köln (Hg.) (2002) Deutschland in Zahlen 2002. Deutscher Insti-
    tuts Verlag, Köln
Institut der Deutschen Wirtschaft Köln (Hg.) (2011) Deutschland in Zahlen 2011. Deutscher Insti-
    tuts Verlag, Köln
Knoepffler N, O`Malley M, Reyk A (2011) Global Ethics Charter for Business Leaders. In: Muresan
    S, Preda R (eds.) International Economy and Finance: Whereto? Ethical Inputs. Eikon, Cluj-
    Napoca, p. 41–55
Körtgen A (1998) Der Tarifvertrag im Recht der Europäischen Gemeinschaft – unter besonderer
    Berücksichtigung der Frage betreffend Die Zulässigkeit Europäischer Tarifverträge. Inaugural –
    Dissertation, Westfälische Universität Münster
Lexikon-Institut Bertelsmann (Hg.) (1981) Mosaik Hand-Lexikon. Aktualisierte Neuausgabe. Mo-
    saik Verlag, München
Müller-Armack Andreas (1988) Das Konzept der Sozialen Marktwirtschaft – Grundlagen, Entwick-
    lung, Aktualität. In Grosser D, Lange T, Müller-Armack A, Neuss B (1988) Soziale Marktwirt-
    schaft. Geschichte-Konzept-Leistung. Verlag W. Kohlhammer, Stuttgart–Berlin–Köln–Mainz,
    p. 1–34
Muresan Stefan-Sorin (2014) Social Market Economy. The Case of Germany. Springer International
    Publishing
Von Nell – Breuning S.J. O (1979) Soziale Sicherheit? Zu Grundfragen der Sozialordnung aus
    christlicher Verantwortung. Herder, Freiburg
Niedenhoff HU (1979) Mitbestimmung. Baustein 13. In: Institut der Deutschen Wirtschaft Köln
    (Hg.) (1979) Curriculum Soziale Marktwirtschaft, Bausteine 1–14. Deutscher Instituts Verlag,
    Köln
OECD (2010) Measuring Globalistion. OECD Economic Globalisation Indicators 2010. OECD Pu-
    blishing, Paris http://dx.doi.org/10.1787/9789264084360-en
Pontifical Council for Justice and Peace (2011) Towards reforming the international financial and
    monetary systems in the context of global public authority. Libreria Editrice Vaticana, Città del
    Vaticano
Schröder G (1999) Wettbewerb sichert Wohlstand. Soziale Marktwirtschaft, Demokratie und Wer-
    bung gehören zusammen. In „Vorwärts" Die Zeitung der deutschen Sozialdemokratie. Gegrün-
    det 1876. Regionalausgabe Nordrhein-Westfalen, Juli/August 1999. vorwärts Verlagsgesell-
    schaft mbH
Sekretariat der Deutschen Bischofskonferenz (Hg.) (2013) Apostolisches Schreiben EVANGELII
    GAUDIM des Heiligen Vaters Papst Franziskus an die Bischöfe, an die Priester und Diakone,
    an die Personen geweihten Lebens und an die christgläubigen Laien über die Verkündigung
    des Evangeliums in der Welt von heute. Verlautbarungen des Apostolischen Stuhls Nr. 194. 24.
    November 2013, Bonn

Statistisches Bundesamt (Hg.) (2011) Datenreport 1999. Zahlen und Fakten über die Bundesrepublik Deutschland. Bundeszentrale für politische Bildung, Bonn

The Economist (2011, July 9) Debt Reduction. Handle with care. "Deleveraging" will dominate the rich world's economies for years. Done badly, it could wreck them. Leaders section (with July 7 date in online edition), Print edition, London

Vergopoulos K (2014) Capitalism is going nowhere. In: Le Monde diplomatique. English print edition May 2014 No. 1405, p. 14–15

Wandel E (1980) Die Entstehung der Bank deutscher Lander und die deutsche Währungsreform 1948. Die Rekonstruktion des westdeutschen Geld- und Währungssytems 1945–1949 unter Berücksichtigung der amerikanischen Besatzungspolitik. In: Schriftenreihe des Instituts für bankhistorische Forschung. Band 3. Der Wisseschaftliche Beirat des Instituts für bankhistorische Forschung (Hg). Fritz Knapp Verlag, Frankfurt am Main

Stefan-Sorin Mureşan   was born in Cluj-Napoca in 1965 into a Romanian Transylvanian family with roots in the Bariţiu family of national leaders and founders of the modern Romanian state.

He holds an MA in diplomatic studies from the University of Westminster in London, a PhD in economics from the Faculty of Economic Science of the Babeş-Bolyai University Cluj-Napoca and a mechanical engineering degree from the Polytechnic University of Cluj-Napoca.His postgraduate specializations were at the Research Center of the US Library of Congress in Washington D.C. in 1996 and at the Foreign Affairs Committee of the German Federal Parliament in Bonn from 1996–1997. The author taught as associate professor "Global Economic and Financial System" at the University Babes-Bolyai during 2004–2005 and was affiliated there with the Institute of International Studies. Dr. Mureşan now teaches "economic diplomacy" as Visiting lecturer at the University of Applied Science in Würzburg. He is the holder of the 2010 scientific award "Eudoxiu Hurmuzachi" for history of the Romanian Academy of Science and is affiliated to the "Centre Altiero Spinelli for the Study of European Organization" (CASSOE), Department of International Studies and Contemporary History, University Babes-Bolyai Cluj-Napoca, Romania. Since 2014, Mureşan is a member of the Club of Rome's branch in Romania.

Among his more recent publications are the books "Social Market Economy. The Case of Gemany", Springer Science and Business Media, Berlin—New York, 2014 and "Parliamentary Discourse of a Romanian from Transylvania in Vienna, 1863– 1865. George Baritiu, Member of Parliament in the Austrian Monarchy", Editura Eikon, Cluj—Napoca 2008. More recently published research articles are "A Comparative Study: Challenges and Opportunities for European Union Dual Vocational Training Systems" with Arslan R, et al. in Journal of Co-operative Education and Internships, no. 47 Issue 01, Cincinatti, 2013 and "Die Ökonomische Transformation in Rumänien zwanzig Jahre nach dem Systemwechsel von 1989", in Veen Hans-Joachim/ März Peter/ Schlichting Fanz—Josef, Die Folgen der Revolution. 20 Jahre nach dem Kommunismus, pp. 141–163, Böhlau Verlag, Köln—Weimar—Wien, 2010

Mureşan`s work experience is in Romania and in Germany. He worked for several years as a diplomat (First Secretary) in the Department for Economic Diplomacy of the Ministry of Foreign Affairs in Bucureşti and in the Romanian Embassy in Germany. He also worked for several years as a parliamentary expert for international parliamentary relations for the President of the Parliament of Romania in Bucureşti. In privatization and M&A he worked for the Board of the National State Ownership Fund (Romanian privatization agency).

Mureşan now partly lives in Germany where he works as a business consultant specializing in East—West business development for industry, trade, in international project management for The Diplomatic Economist Ltd, (www.diplomatic-economist.eu) whose director he is. Occasionally he works as an expert for the German Federal Institute for Vocational Education and Training (BIBB) for evaluating EU projects (Lifelong Learning Programme and Erasmus+). Mureşan is also a political consultant and lobbyist accredited by the European Institutions in Brussels.

Rating von Finanzinstituten: Funktion und Performance

Theodor Weimer

3.1 Aufbereiten von Informationen

Ratingagenturen versprechen, die Qualität von Zahlungsversprechen auf einer Rangskala zu ordnen – von A (zweifelsfrei) bis D (ausgefallen). Anfangs beurteilten sie Anleihen von Unternehmen, genauer: von amerikanischen Eisenbahngesellschaften. Mit der Zeit kamen weitere Kreditnehmer, die Anleihen begaben, hinzu. In den 1970ern wurden dann auch Staaten benotet und schließlich, vor einem guten Jahrzehnt, forderungsbesicherte, strukturierte Kreditversprechen. Es waren (und sind) vor allem drei amerikanische Agenturen (Standard & Poor's, Moody's und Fitch), die sich den Markt in einem engen Oligopol praktisch seit den Anfängen aufteilen. Im Mittel genügten die Agenturen im abgelaufenen Vierteljahrhundert den Erwartungen in etwa so gut wie die (mittleren) Alternativen, die ja ein ähnliches Leistungsversprechen geben: Banken, die spätestens seit der zweiten Hälfte der 1990er interne Modelle einsetzten, institutionelle Anleger (Versicherungen, Fondsgesellschaften usw.), die spezialisierte Analyseabteilungen halten oder auch unabhängige Analysten. Aus dem Zusammenspiel all dieser Akteure entstehen am Markt Preise bzw. Zinsen. Deren Differenzen wiederum vermitteln ebenfalls die durch Kauf und Halten bekundete Einschätzung der jeweiligen Kreditwürdigkeit.

Bisweilen, wenn auch selten, lagen die Agenturen allerdings sehr deutlich daneben. Das war, was die Einschätzung von Länderrisiken betraf, etwa bei der Asienkrise der Fall (Ferri et al. 1999). Im Verlauf der *new economy* Blase wurden viele Unternehmenspositionen falsch gewürdigt. Ein besonders eklatantes Beispiel lieferte der Energie-Händler En-

T. Weimer (✉)
München, Deutschland
E-Mail: theodor.weimer@unicredit.de

© Springer Fachmedien Wiesbaden 2016
Z. Diab, O. Everling (Hrsg.), *Rating von Finanzinstituten,*
DOI 10.1007/978-3-658-04195-3_3

ron (Healy und Palepu 2003). Die gravierendsten Fehleinschätzungen betrafen aber die im Sommer 2007 ausbrechende mittlerweile so genannte Große Finanzkrise. In Europa mutierte diese in einer Reihe von Teilnehmerländern der Währungsunion in eine Staatschuldenkrise (Gorton 2009). Diese wiederum wurde für Banken zum Problem und besonders für solche mit Sitz in den Problemländern. Mit Ausnahme der Dotcom-Blase waren stets auch Kreditinstitute in erheblichem Umfang betroffen. Und zwar nicht in einem passiven Sinne, als unschuldige Zuschauer. Sie hatten in allen Fällen zu den nicht-durchhaltbaren Positionen finanzierend beigetragen. Ohne dass dies von den Ratingagenturen im Vorhinein gesehen oder beanstandet worden wäre.

Sei der Großen Finanzkrise ist die zuvor bereits geäußerte Kritik an den Agenturen weit stärker geworden. Sie hat mittlerweile auch zu regulatorischen Konsequenzen geführt. In den USA wurde im Zusammenhang mit dem Dodd-Frank Act bei den Ratingagenturen vor allem eine Trennung von Analyse- und Beratungsgeschäft sowie die Zurücknahme der zur Regel gewordenen Bezugnahme auf Ratings in Gesetzen und Verordnungen verlangt. Das gilt auch für Europa, wo die Agenturen seit 2011 von der ESMA (*European Securities and Markets Authority*) überwacht werden. Im Juni 2013 traten eine Verordnung sowie eine Richtlinie (von Parlament und Rat) für Ratingagenturen in Kraft, die diese strikteren Vorschriften und Rechenschaftspflichten unterwerfen.[1] Das Ziel ist, die Qualität der Urteile der Agenturen zu erhöhen. Auch in Europa wird die Trennung von Beratung und Kreditwürdigkeitseinschätzung umgesetzt. Gleichzeitig soll die Anbindung an Ratings verringert und damit die eigenständige Urteilsfindung gestärkt werden.

Ex post wurde jedenfalls klar, wenn es des Beweises auch nicht bedurft hätte, dass Ratingagenturen Fehler machen. Diese machen sie vor allem bei den besonders unsicheren und undurchsichtigen Fällen. Dieses Schicksal teilen sie allerdings mit ihren unmittelbaren Alternativen. Die Frage ist mithin, welche Lehren daraus zu ziehen sind. In diesem Überblicksaufsatz konzentrieren wir uns auf die Fähigkeit der Agenturen, die Kreditwürdigkeit von Kreditinstituten korrekt einzuschätzen. Zunächst lassen wir die Geschichte der Agenturen knapp Revue passieren. Dabei wird auch deutlich, weshalb Ratingagenturen existieren und welche Funktion sie erfüllen. Anschließend werden die Methoden der Agenturen skizziert und die Verfahren erörtert, die ihrer Urteilsbildung zugrunde liegen. Diese werden am besonderen Fall von Kreditinstituten illustriert. Bei deren Überwachung gab es in den vergangenen Jahren zwei schwerwiegende Fehleinschätzungen. Sie betrafen die Würdigung der Ausfallwahrscheinlichkeit (und des potenzielle Verlustes) bei strukturierten Produkten sowie die Einschätzung von Staatsanleihen. Im abschließenden Teil werden, darauf aufbauend, die gegenwärtig diskutierten Reformvorschläge gewürdigt.

---

[1] Siehe EU COM (2013). Die ESMA hat mittlerweile den 4. Jahresbericht veröffentlicht, der eine Einschätzung der Tätigkeit der von ihr beaufsichtigen Agenturen enthält.

3.2   Geschichte, Funktion und Marktstruktur

John Moody vermochte es als Erster (1909), seine Einschätzung von Eisenbahnanleihen an interessierte Anleger zu verkaufen. Dabei brachte er, so der renommierte Kapitalmarkt-historiker Richard Sylla, drei Funktionen zusammen (Sylla 2002): 1) die Sammlung von Daten über die Kreditwürdigkeit von Eisenbahngesellschaften, also eine Berichterstat-tungsrolle; 2) eine analytische Einschätzung aus der Perspektive der Gläubiger, die zuvor vor allem in der Finanzpresse geschah; sowie 3) die Vermittlung zwischen Anlegern und Schuldnern, eine Rolle, die auch von Investmentbanken wahrgenommen wurde, die ihr Reputations- und Beziehungskapital in diese Relation einbrachten.

Bereits 1868, kurz nach dem amerikanischen Bürgerkrieg, hatte Henry Poor mit der Veröffentlichung eines jährlichen *Manual of the Railroads of the United States* begonnen. Seine Firma, die sich später mit Standard Statistics zusammenschloss, startete allerdings erst 1916 mit der vergleichenden Bewertung von Eisenbahnanleihen. Fitch kam dann in den 1920ern hinzu. Die Rating-Industrie war bis in die 1970er im Wesentlichen ein US-Phänomen. Ihr Gegenstand waren vor allem die Anleihen großer, kapitalmarktfähiger Unternehmen. In den USA spielten Kapitalmärkte, *direkte* Vermittlung also, in der ex-ternen Finanzierung eine stärkere Rolle als Kreditinstitute, die indirekte Intermediation gewährleisteten. Banken unterlagen sowohl regionalen (McFadden Act 1927) als auch Geschäftsfeld-Beschränkungen (Glass-Steagall Act 1933). Moody's benotete zwar bereits seit 1919 Schuldverschreibungen von Bundesstaaten und Kommunen. In diesem Segment gab es aber nur sehr wenige Ausfälle, mithin wenig Analysebedarf. Obwohl es schon in den 1920ern Bewertungen von ausländischen Anleihen gab, startete die eigentliche Inter-nationalisierung in den 1970ern, mit dem Zusammenbruch des Festkurssystems und den anwachsenden grenzüberschreitenden Kapitalströmen, die zu zunehmenden Teilen im Wege verbriefter Instrumente geschah. Zu Anfang der 1970er waren z. B. bei S&P kaum mehr als eine Handvoll Analysten beschäftigt, zehn Jahre später waren es in der Industrie-gruppe 30 und weitere 15 Jahre später rund 800 (Partnoy 1999). Heute arbeiten bei S&P und Moody's mehr als 2600 Analysten.

Dieser Zuwachs an Analysten korreliert (unterdurchschnittlich) mit dem Anstieg der bewerteten Anleihen. 1975 waren es bei Moody's 5500 Anleihen, 15 Jahre später 20.000 und heute sind es gut 2 Mio.. Hinzu kommen die strukturierten Produkte (White 2013).

Was aber ist das Leistungsversprechen der Agenturen? Inwiefern stellen sie eine Dienst-leistung bereit, die für (mindestens) eine der beiden Marktseiten am Kapitalmarkt wertvoll ist? Unternehmen treten an den Kapitalmarkt heran, um Projekte zu finanzieren, deren Ausgang unsicher sind und über die sie gleichzeitig deutlich mehr wissen als die Mittelge-ber (die Sparer oder Investoren), die sie für diese Vorhaben interessieren wollen. Derartige Informationsunvollkommenheiten sind mit Anreizen seitens der Unternehmen (Auftrag-nehmer, Handlungsbevollmächtigten – Agenten) verbunden, die die Sparer (Auftraggeber, Vollmachtgeber – Prinzipale) potenziell beschädigen. Ungleich verteilte Informationen machen die Vermittlung sowohl a) beim Zusammenbringen (Fehlauswahl, *adverse selection*) als auch b) in der Abwicklung (nicht vertragsentsprechendes Verhalten, moralisches Risiko) problematisch. Finanzvermittler, vor allem Banken, sind Institutionen, die diese Probleme vergleichsweise kostengünstig lösen. Sie unterstützen die Auswahl der Projekte, und sie überwachen deren Durchführung. Sie bieten mithin Einschätzungs- bzw. Auswahl- sowie Überwachungsleistungen an, und zwar gleichzeitig mit der Finanzierung, als Kuppelprodukt.

Sparer delegieren mithin beide Aufgaben – die der Auswahl (des screening) und jene der Überwachung (des monitoring) – an Banken, aus Kostengründen. Kreditinstitute nehmen Einlagen herein und reichen sie, gegen einen risikoentsprechenden (und eine Mindestrendite gewährleistenden) Aufschlag, an Schuldner heraus. Kreditinstitute bündeln Ressourcen, streuen Risiken und schaffen Liquidität, in dem sie Fristeninkongruenzen (zwischen beiden Bilanzseiten) eingehen. Im Verfolgen dieses Bündels an Tätigkeiten kontrollieren sie eine Reihe von Risiken. Eines der wichtigsten darunter ist das Kreditrisiko. Da die Einschätzung der Kreditwürdigkeit eine umfangreiche Daten- und Analyseinfrastruktur erfordert, ist sie mit erheblichen Fixkosten und folglich auch mit Losgrößen- und Spezialisierungsvorteilen verbunden. Banken vermögen ihre Leistungen also kostengünstig anzubieten.

Bei den großen, grundsätzlich durchsichtigeren Kreditnehmern stehen Banken bei dieser Aufgabe unter anderem im Wettbewerb mit Ratingagenturen. Im Unterschied zu Agenturen investieren Banken allerdings auch ihr Kapital in ihre Einschätzung. Das ist das Kuppelprodukt-Argument. Deshalb ist mit der Vergabe von Krediten, sobald sie bekannt wird, zumeist auch ein positiver Effekt auf Anleihe- oder Aktienkurse der Unternehmen verbunden, die den Kredit erhielten. Das ist ein Bestätigungseffekt, der diejenigen begünstigt, die als Anleihegläubiger oder Aktionäre im Unternehmen investiert sind.

Ratings sind allerdings auch fehlerbehaftet. Daraus könnte eine Haftungsfrage erwachsen. Ex post unzutreffende Einschätzungen haben etwa bei Banken Auswirkungen auf deren Kreditausfälle und somit auf die Gewinn- und Verlustrechnung. Infolge der Finanzkrise werden die Bonitätseinstufungen der Ratingagenturen inzwischen von Emittenten und Investoren wesentlich kritischer gesehen. Großinvestoren und Geschäftspartner von Kreditinstituten bedienen sich daher verstärkt eigener Risikomodelle, um die Bonität von Wertpapieren und Kontrahenten zu bewerten. Neben den Ergebnissen der eigenen Risikomodelle werden weitere öffentlich beobachtbare Indikatoren in die Entscheidungsfindung verstärkt einbezogen. Insbesondere die Prämien, die für Kreditausfallversicherungen eines Kreditinstituts zu entrichten sind, werden berücksichtigt.

Ratingagenturen bekunden dagegen, worauf sie aus Haftungsgründen Wert legen, Meinungen. Sie geben keine Anlageempfehlungen, für die sie in Anspruch genommen werden könnten. Dennoch reklamieren sie eine unabhängige Urteilsfähigkeit. Sie investieren ihre Glaubwürdigkeit (genauer: ihr Reputationskapital) in ihre Einschätzungen. Das schafft einen erheblichen Anreiz, richtig zu liegen. Denn die Reputation ist wichtig für das Aufrechterhalten und Absichern künftiger Einkommensmöglichkeiten (des franchise).

3.3 Verfahren der Kreditwürdigkeitsprüfung

Ratingagenturen beurteilen sowohl auf der Basis veröffentlichter als auch interner Daten die Wahrscheinlichkeit, dass Schuldner ihren Verpflichtungen entsprechen. Bei der Einschätzung der Kreditwürdigkeit von Unternehmen kommen dabei sowohl daten- oder statistisch basierte (diskriminanzanalytische) Verfahren als auch theoretisch fundierte strukturelle Modelle zum Einsatz. Bei ersteren werden mit Hilfe von Kennziffern der Rechnungslegung (Bilanzrelationen, Renditen usw.) Kreditnehmer Risikokategorien zugeordnet. Die in diesen Scoring-Modellen ermittelten Werte (Z-Scores) lassen sich dann auch in Ratingklassen übertragen. Die strukturellen Modelle analysieren Unternehmen im Lichte der Optionspreistheorie, die die relative Beziehung zwischen Gläubiger- und Anteilsansprüchen an Unternehmen abbildet. Dies ist möglich, da die Auszahlungsfunktion eines Kredites der einer Verkaufsoption ähnelt. Kredite lassen sich damit analog interpretieren und ihre Werthaltigkeit berechnen.

3.3.1 Scoring-Verfahren

Das erste, über die Zeit erheblich weiterentwickelte Klassifizierungsverfahren stammt von Edward Altmann (Altman 1968). Grundsätzlich geht es darum, diejenigen Faktoren empirisch zu ermitteln, die die Ausfallwahrscheinlichkeit von Forderungen möglichst präzise erfassen. Schuldner werden dabei in eine gute oder schlechte Kategorie eingestuft. Für Unternehmen haben sich die Verzinsung der Aktiva (return on assets, RoA), der Verschuldungsgrad (die Relation von Verbindlichkeiten zur Bilanzsumme) sowie die Brutto-Erträge (vor Zinsen, Steuern und Abschreibungen) im Verhältnis zu den Verbindlichkeiten (EBITDA) als besonders zweckmäßig für die Eingruppierung erwiesen. Unternehmen, die weniger rentabel (niedriger RoA) sind, eine höhere Verschuldung aufweisen (hohen leverage) und relativ wenig Cash-flow schaffen (niedrige EBITDA zu Verbindlichkeiten) haben empirisch eine höhere Wahrscheinlichkeit, dass sie ihren Verpflichtungen nicht nachkommen, also zahlungsunfähig werden.

Altman berücksichtigte nicht nur einen Indikator, sondern ein Bündel von Faktoren, die zur Klassifizierung dienten. Genau genommen, stellte er damit auch deren Zusammenwirken in Rechnung. Dazu werden in der Vergangenheit herausgelegte Kredit in zwei Gruppen aufgeteilt: Solche, die vertragsentsprechend bedient wurden und jene, die ausgefallen sind. Auf der Basis einer aufeinander abgestimmten Stichprobe (Erhebungsjahr, Unternehmensgröße und Branche) gruppierte er Unternehmenskredite nach der folgenden Anleitung:

$$Z = 1.2X_1 + 1.4X_2 + 3.3X_3 + 0.6X_4 + 1.0X_5 \qquad (3.1)$$

Dabei stehen:

$$X_1 = \frac{Umlaufverm\ddot{o}gen}{Aktiva} \tag{3.2}$$

$$X_2 = \frac{einbehaltene\ Ertr\ddot{a}ge}{Aktiva} \tag{3.3}$$

$$X_3 = \frac{EBITDA}{Aktiva} \tag{3.4}$$

$$X_4 = \frac{Marktwert}{Buchwert} \tag{3.5}$$

$$X_5 = \frac{Erl\ddot{o}se}{Bilanzsumme} \tag{3.6}$$

Mit Hilfe einer Klassifizierungsregel (lineare Diskriminanzanalyse) errechnete er einen kritischen Z-Wert (cut-off) von 1,81. Unternehmen, die einen niedrigeren Wert aufwiesen, galten als nicht kreditwürdig. Das Ausfallrisiko sinkt folglich mit steigendem Z-Wert (siehe für eine ausführliche, auch die Modellerweiterungen behandelnde Beschreibung Altman und Hotchkiss 2006; Altman ermittelte gleichzeitig einen Unsicherheits- oder Graubereich, der von 1,81 bis 2,99 reichte). Die Koeffizienten der Klassifizierungsvariablen bilden zugleich deren relative Bedeutung (Einfluss) ab.

Seither wurde das Verfahren erheblich weiterentwickelt, insbesondere auch von Altman und seinen Mitautoren. Dabei wurden verschiedene statistische Methoden zur Ermittlung des Trennpunktes angewandt: lineare Wahrscheinlichkeitsmodelle sowie logit- und probit-Modelle. Ziel ist es jeweils einen Trennwert zu wählen, der (für die Stichprobe) möglichst wenige Fehlklassifizierungen produziert. *Ex post* können dabei zwei Fehler auftreten: zahlungsunfähige Kreditnehmer werden im Vorhinein als solvent eingeschätzt (Fehler 1. Art, Alpha-Fehler). Oder zahlungsfähige Schuldner werden als potenziell insolvent abgelehnt (Fehler 2. Art, Beta-Fehler). Beides ist mit Kosten verbunden. Dabei sind die Kosten des Alpha-Fehlers, also Kreditvergabe an insolvent werdende Schuldner deutlich gravierender als die Opportunitätsverluste, die aus dem Abweisen eines ex post zahlungsfähigen Kreditnehmers herrühren. Altmanns Verfahren versucht die Gesamtkosten zu minimieren.

Beaver et al. (2005) haben zum Beispiel ein Ausfallraten-Modell (*harzard rate*) geschätzt, bei dem der Logarithmus der relativen Insolvenzwahrscheinlichkeit (die *odds ratio*) mit der nachstehenden Gleichung erklärt wird:

$$\log(relatives\ Ausfallrisiko) = -6.4 - 1.2(RoA) + 2.3\left(\frac{Schulden}{Bilanz}\right) - 3.7\left(\frac{EBITDA}{Verbindlichkeiten}\right) \tag{3.7}$$

Tab. 3.1 Z-Wert und S&P Rating; Quelle: Altman und Hotchkiss 2006, S. 247–248

S&P-rating	Z-Wert (Ø)	Z-Wert (Standardabw.)
AAA	6,20	2,06
AA	4,73	2,36
A	3,74	2,29
BBB	2,81	1,48
BB	2,38	1,85
B	1,80	1,91
CCC	0,33	1,16
D	−0,20	./.

Das relative Ausfallrisiko ist definiert als Verhältnis von Ausfallwahrscheinlichkeit zu der Wahrscheinlichkeit der vertragsentsprechenden Bedienung des Kredits (also: des Nicht-Ausfalls): $= \frac{p}{1-p}$. Diese Relation wird auch als *odds ratio* bezeichnet. (Eine OR von 1 besagt mithin, das korrekte Kreditbedienung und Ausfall gleichwahrscheinlich sind.) Der p-Wert, die Ausfallwahrscheinlichkeit, ist offenkundig ein wesentlicher Faktor bei der Bepreisung von Krediten.

Lineare Wahrscheinlichkeits- ebenso wie Logit-Modelle dienen der Bestimmung der Ausfallwahrscheinlichkeit im Moment der Kreditvergabe. Das Logit-Modell weist dabei Wahrscheinlichkeitswerte zwischen 0 und 1 aus. Das gilt nicht für das lineare Modell.

Das Z-Wert-Verfahren lässt sich auch in Rating-Skalen (der Agenturen) überführen. Es ist also nicht binär, sondern erlaubt eine Graduierung (siehe Tab. 3.1).

Die Z-Wert-Modelle werden häufig eingesetzt, vor allem auch in Banken (bei Kreditkarten, Kleinkrediten, insbesondere bei strukturell ähnlichen bzw. standardisierbaren Ausleihungen). Gegen sie wird allerdings eine Reihe von Einwänden vorgebracht, insbesondere, dass sie auf Rechnungslegungsdaten basieren, mithin vergangenheitsorientiert sind. Aber auch, dass sie daten-generierende Prozesse, die nicht-linear sind, nicht angemessen abbilden können. Werden die Daten aus unterschiedlichsten Perspektiven analysiert (*data mining*), kann ein vermeintlich robuster Z-Wert herauskommen, der allerdings außerhalb der Stichprobenperiode nicht mehr gilt.

3.3.2 Strukturelle Modelle

Aufbauend auf Arbeiten Fischer Black, Myron Scholes und vor allem Robert Merton wird die Rückzahlwahrscheinlichkeit dadurch bestimmt, dass die Zahlungsverpflichtung als eine Option interpretiert wird (siehe z. B. Hull 2012; Rudolph 2006). Unternehmen, die einen Kredit nehmen (oder eine Anleihe begeben) werden diesen nur bedienen, sofern der Marktwert des Unternehmens den Wert der eingegangenen Schulden übertrifft.

Andernfalls wählen sie die Insolvenz, treten also ihre Eigentumsrechte an die Gläubiger ab. Damit ist eine Auszahlungsfunktion beschrieben, die (aus der Perspektive des sich verschuldenden Unternehmens) jener einer Kaufoption entspricht. Der Verlust ist, bei Haftungsbegrenzung, auf das eingesetzte Eigenkapital beschränkt. Diese gibt allerdings Anrecht, sofern der Marktwert die Schulden übersteigt, auf ein grundsätzlich nicht begrenztes Aufwärtspotenzial.

Der Perspektivenwechsel zeigt, dass die Kreditgeber, dem sich verschuldenden Unternehmen einen Kontrakt gegeben haben, der dem Schreiben (Verkaufen) einer Verkaufsoption auf den Marktwert des Unternehmens entspricht. Diese Konstellation lässt sich damit, das war die enorm wichtige Einsicht von Robert Merton, wie eine Option interpretieren und bepreisen. Der Wert der Schulden entspricht dem Ausübungspreis. Für das Eingehen dieser Position erhält der Gläubiger einen festen Zins (und am Ende den Nominalwert der Schulden), der der Prämie der Verkaufsoption entspricht.

Der Marktwert eines Kredits lässt sich damit analog einer Option bestimmen:

$$F(\tau) = Be^{-i\tau}\left[\left(\frac{1}{d}\right)N(h_1) + N(h_2)\right] \tag{3.8}$$

Die Funktion $F(\tau)$ beschreibt den Marktwert eines risikobehafteten Kredits B. ($N(h)$ steht für die Standard-Normalverteilung.) Die Laufzeit des Kredits (τ) und die Schuldenrelation, der mit dem risikofreien Zins diskontierte Marktwert der Schulden im Verhältnis zu den Aktiva (*leverage ratio*: $d = \dfrac{Be^{-i\tau}}{A}$) sind die entscheidenden Parameter. Dabei legt d auch die Varianz des Marktwertes fest. Aus der Formel kann die gleichgewichtige Risikoprämie *ermittelt werden. Kreditgeber sollten diese ändern, sofern die Schuldenrelation* und die Varianz des Marktwertes sich ändern. Leverage und Volatilität determinieren also die Risikoprämie.

Das Merton-Modell erlaubt, gegeben die Markterwartungen, die Bestimmung der Risikoprämie ebenso wie der erwarteten Ausfallwahrscheinlichkeiten. Es wurde in einer firmeneigenen (proprietären) Variante von KMV, einem von renommierten Akademikern gegründeten Analyseunternehmen umgesetzt. Für börsennotierte Firmen kann man mit zwei Gleichungen, a) für den Firmenwert und b) dessen Volatilität, die Ausfallhäufigkeit (*expected frequency of default*) sowie die Distanz zum Ausfall (*expected distance to default*) ermitteln.

Eine Alternative zu Strukturmodellen sind Ansätze, die von reduzierten Formen ausgehen. Kamakura, ein weiteres, von führenden Theoretikern gegründetes Unternehmen, bietet derart fundierte Risikosteuerungsleistungen an. Hier wird auf der Basis von risikoneutralen Ausfallwahrscheinlichkeiten die Ausfallintensität risikobehafteter Ansprüche bewertet (Chava und Jarrow 2004).

3.3.3   Ratingagenturen

Ratingagenturen benutzen im Kern die gleichen Verfahren, die Unternehmensanalysten verwenden (KMV gehört seit Anfang des Jahrtausends zu Moody's). Während Aktien-analysten die Perspektive der Aktionäre einnehmen, derjenigen, die Ansprüche auf das Residualeinkommen (den Gewinn) haben, nehmen Ratingagenturen allerdings die Sicht von Gläubigern ein. Die eben skizzierten Verfahren sind genau genommen quantifizierte Lesarten dieser Position.

Ratingagenturen sind (aus einsichtigen Gründen) nicht sehr transparent, was ihre Ver-fahren angeht, obwohl die Offenheit, regulierungs- und damit auch krisenbedingt, über die Jahre (nach Enron 2001 und Lehman 2008) deutlich zugenommen hat. Unternehmen werden (siehe etwa Standard & Poor's 2008) im Lichte von Geschäftsrisiken, Sektoren-kennzeichen, Wettbewerbsposition, Management-Qualität, Finanzdaten, Gewinnperspek-tiven, Eigenkapital beurteilt. Dabei kommt dem Sektor- oder Industrierisiko das größte Gewicht zu.

Um die Finanzkraft zu bestimmen, ermitteln die Agenturen eine Vielzahl von Indikato-ren (Schuldendeckung, Leverage, Cash-flow usw.), die sie sowohl über die Zeit als auch die einzelnen Unternehmen verfolgen. Die Agenturen verweisen gleichzeitig darauf, dass die qualitative, analytische Deutung dieser quantitativen Indikatoren ausschlaggebend ist. Die Indikatoren allein sind also, so die Agenturen, nicht ausreichend, um das Urteil, das in den Ratingskalen zum Ausdruck kommt, abzuleiten. Es handelt sich um Expertensysteme, deren Urteilsfindung nicht unmittelbar replizierbar ist.

Dabei geht es den Agenturen um eine Würdigung des Kreditnehmers in der mittleren Frist (*through the cycle*). So soll auch eine Stabilität in der Einschätzung gewährleistet werden. Damit ist naturgemäß eine nur träge, zögerliche Anpassung der Urteile an sich verändernde Bedingungen verbunden(deren Nachhaltigkeit soll sich erst erweisen). Bei der aktuellen Würdigung (*point-in-time*) hinken die Agenturen den Markteinschätzungen, wie sie vor allem in Zinsaufschlägen und Prämien für Kreditausfallversicherungen zum Ausdruck kommen, zwangsläufig hinterher. Das gilt auch für Strukturmodelle nach dem Merton-Ansatz. Auch dies ist naheliegend, da der Merton-Ansatz auf Marktdaten basiert. Marktbasierte Verfahren sind damit bessere, bei weitem aber auch nicht stets korrekte Frühwarnsysteme, im Gegenteil.

3.4   Das Rating von Kreditinstituten

Die bisherige Argumentation bezog sich auf einzelne Kredite. Die Analyse lässt sich aller-dings auch in einen Portfolio-Kontext überführen. Dann ergeben sich, je nach dem Grad des Gleichlaufs der Kredite, Effekte der Risikostreuung. Banken und Finanzintermediäre sind nun Bündel derartiger risikobehafteter Ansprüche. Sie weisen zudem weitere Risiken auf, die aus ihrer Vermittlungsfunktion herrühren: Damit sind Risiken der Fristen-, der Größen- und der Risikotransformation verbunden. Die Bedeutung des Liquiditäts- (oder Anschlussfinanzierungs-)Risiko wurde schlagartig in der Finanzkrise deutlich. Sowohl die

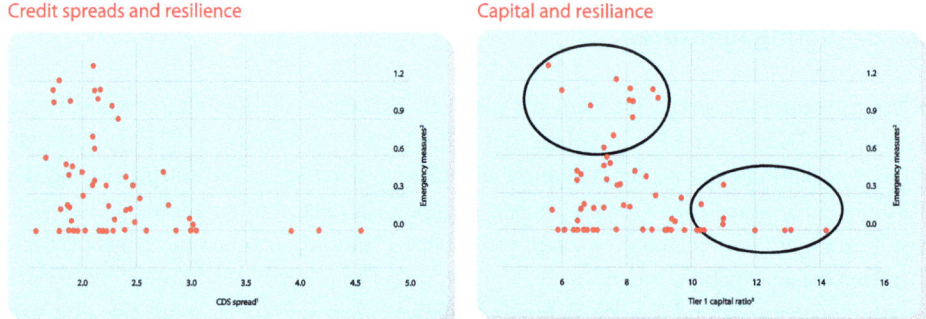

Credit spreads and resilience   Capital and resiliance

¹ On log scale.
² Sum of the values of fixed income, capital an hybrid instrument issued and
  assets sold from mid-2007 to end-2009, divided by total equity in 2006.
³ In per cent.

Abb. 3.1 Pre-crisis characteristics and in-crisis performance of large banks

amerikanische Investmentbank Lehman als auch die britische Hypothekenbank Northern Rock, um zwei besonders prominente Fälle zu nennen, hatten Eigenkapitalquoten deutlich oberhalb der regulatorischen Anforderungen. Northern Rock, mit einem Eigenkapital von 13 % (bezogen auf die risikogewichteten Aktiva) wurde das Verhältnis der durchschnittlichen Bindungsdauer der Aktiva im Vergleich zur mittleren Laufzeit der Finanzierungsseite zum Verhängnis (Shin 2009). Für nahezu die Hälfte der Mittel waren alle zwei Tage eine Anschlussfinanzierung zu finden. Diese stammte zu mehr als zwei Dritteln aus dem Interbankenmarkt, also dem in kritischen Situationen besonders flüchtigen Großhandelsbereich (Abb. 3.1).

Abbildung 3.1 zeigt, dass die Prämien von Kreditausfallversicherungen auf Banken (horizontale Achse) keine Informationen über den Unterstützungsbedarf in der Krise enthielten. Der Zusammenhang ist nur sehr schwach und sogar negativ. Graphik 1b illustriert, dass Banken, die 2006 ein hohes Kernkapital aufwiesen, von Ausnahmen abgesehen, die Krise besser überstanden. Quelle: Packer/Tarashev 2011.

Banken sind nun nicht besonders transparent oder einfach zu durchschauen. Morganbezeichnet sie als opake Industrie – als *black boxes* (Morgan 2002). Die Undurchsichtigkeit rührt daher, dass bestimmte Vermögenswerte, vor allem Kredite und die insbesondere die Werte in den Handelsbüchern, nur schwer (von außen) einzuschätzen und zudem leicht (von innen) zu verändern, also ausgesprochen transitorisch sind. Im Vergleich zu anonymen Kapitalmärkten haben Banken zudem relative, sich mit der Zeit allerdings verändernde Vorteile beim Auswählen und Überwachen von informationsintensiven (sprich: opaken) Unternehmen (Hartmann-Wendels et al. u. a. 2010; Song und Thakor 2010). Das Ausleihen an vergleichsweise weniger durchsichtige Kreditnehmer könnte Banken ebenfalls opaker machen. Damit wäre das Risiko von Banken schwerer einzuschätzen. Der Handel ist dabei die dunkle oder die „Schattenseite der Liquidität" (Myers und Rajan 1998). Diese Undurchsichtigkeit wird grundsätzlich durch einen längeren Schuldenhebel

$\left(d = \dfrac{Be^{-i\tau}}{A} \right)$ verstärkt. Wenn es um Banken geht, stehenRatingagenturen damit vor der Aufgabe, die Überwacher zu überwachen (*monitoring the monitors*).

Daraus gewinnt Morgan seine Hypothese:Ratingagenturen sollten bei der Einschätzung von Banken (und Versicherungen, also Finanzintermediären generell) häufiger zu nicht-übereinstimmenden Urteilen kommen. Eine Hypothese, für die er eine starke empirische Bestätigung findet.

Banken sind also besonders. Sie sind es aber auch, weil sie potenziell auf Unterstützung zurückgreifen können, jedenfalls sofern sie als systemisch gelten. Dann würde ein Ausfall zu Folgen bei unbeteiligten Dritten führen, die mit Ansteckungseffekten und erheblichen sozialen Kosten verbunden wären. Bankinsolvenzen werden also nicht zugelassen, wenn die Institute zu groß, zu vernetzt oder als Gruppe zu erheblich sind (Brunnermeier u. a. 2009). Damit sind die Radien zwischen Haftung und Verantwortung ungleich. Vor allem große Banken, die zu wichtig sind um fallen gelassen zu werden (*too-important-to-fail*, TITF) profitieren davon (IWF 2014).

3.4.1 Ansätze der Ratingagenturen

Grundsätzlich sind die Einschätzungsverfahren für Unternehmen (Forderungen) jedweden Typs identisch. Für Banken und Finanzintermediäre gelten aber eine Reihe von Besonderheiten (siehe Moody's 2013; S&P 2013 und Packer und Tarashev 2011 sowie Tab. 3.2, in Anlehnung an Packer, Tarashev).

Moody's zum Beispiel klassifiziert im Rahmen seines *Bank Financial Strength Ratings* die Finanzstärke eines Instituts mittels einer Skala von 13 Punkten (von A bis E, einschließlich von Graduierungen oder *qualifiers*). Dieser intrinsische Wert wird durch die Marktposition (den *franchise*), die Risikolage, das regulatorische Umfeld, die operative Umgebung und schließlich die finanziellen Ausgangsbedingungen beschrieben. Daraus wird, in einer Gesamtschau, eine erste Form der Kreditwürdigung hergeleitet, das *Baseline Credit Assessment*.

Im Anschluss werden aber auch externe Unterstützungsoptionen in Rechnung gestellt. Diese sind für Anleihezeichner offenkundig von zentralem Interesse, da sie das Kreditrisiko (sowohl die Wahrscheinlichkeit als auch den Verlust im Falle eines Ausfalls) beeinflussen. Dabei werden eventuelle Unterstützung seitens der Anteilseigner (Mütter), genossenschaftliche Nachschusspflichten, lokale oder regionale Regierungen sowie systemische Unterstützung durch Staaten in Rechnung gestellt. Die mit der Richtlinie zur Sanierung und Abwicklung von Banken und Wertpapierfirmen (BRRD) sowie dem Einheitliche Europäische Bankenabwicklungsmechanismus (SRM) angestrebte Entkoppelung von Staats- und Bankinsolvenzen wird im Falle einer systemischen – im Unterschied zu einer bankindividuellen – Krise – kaum durchzusetzen sein. Der Hauptsitz bleibt bis zu einem gewissen Grade belangvoll. Banken mit Zentralen in kreditwürdigeren Sitzländern eine in der Regel höhere Bewertung auf. Hier ist die Wahrscheinlichkeit und die Fähigkeit des Beispringens (*bailing-out*) höher. Ein Ausdruck davon ist, dass die Benotung des Sitzlandes die Basis

Tab. 3.2 Ratingmethoden für Banken; Quelle: Packer und Tarashev 2011

	Fitch	Moody's	Standard & Poor's
Bankindividuelle Einschätzung (intrinsische Finanzkraft)	Fokus: Geschäfte unter dem Bilanzstrich, Refinanzierungs-, Liquiditätsrisiko	Akzent auf zukunftsgerichteter Einschätzung von Kapitaladäquanz, erwarteten Verlusten	Im Fokus: risiko-adjustierte Ergebnisse, Fähigkeit Eigenkapital zu bilden
Würdigung unter Berücksichtigung externer Unterstützung	Eigene Bewertung der Unterstützung des Sitzlandes, Basis der Bewertung	Gemeinsame Ausfallbewertung von Banken und Sitzland	Erwartete Unterstützung wächst mit systemischer Dimension der Bank
System-weite Einschätzung Länderbonität Systemisches Risiko	Makro-Indikatoren Ø-Bankrating Nicht explizit, nimmt mit systemischer Bedeutung der Bank zu	./. Nicht explizit, nimmt mit systemischer Bedeutung der Bank zu	Makro-Indikatoren, Sektor- und Regulierungsumgebung durch Makro-Indikatoren und Sektorbeobachtung
Letzte größere Verfahrensänderung	2005: Systemische Risikoanalyse	2007: Joint-Default Analyse bei Unterstützungswürdigung	2011: Überarbeitung der Methode Systemrisiko Gewinn und Eigenkapitalbildung

für die Einschätzung der Kreditwürdigkeit der jeweiligen Kreditinstitute ist. In aller Regel haben Banken eine niedrigere Bonität als ihre Sitzländer.

Eine Rechtfertigung dafür ist auch, dass Banken bei ihren Anlagedispositionen oft die Anleihen der jeweiligen Sitzländer in ihren Portfolios stärker gewichten. Vor allem in Ländern mit niedrigerer Bonität besteht – wegen des (nicht risikoangepassten) Rendite-vorsprungs – ein Anreiz dazu, da Staatsanleihen (von OECD-Ländern) eine Risikoge-wichtung von null aufweisen.

Einschub: Too important to fail: Finanzinstitute können, relativ zu dem Wirtschafts-potenzial ihres Sitzlandes zu groß, zu kompliziert, zu vernetzt oder kaum ersetzbar sein. Im Nachhinein ist es dann aus einer gesellschaftlichen Sicht kostenminimierend, derartige Institute, die zu wichtig sind, rauszuhauen. Ex ante fördert dies risikobehaftetes Verhalten. Da die Kosten eines Scheiterns von der Allgemeinheit getragen werden, können sich die TITF-Institute auch günstiger refinanzieren. Die Subventionen sind nach Berechnungen schwankend im Zeitablauf, sind während Krisenphasen besonders hoch und vor allem auch substantiell: für die USA belaufen sie sich auf im Mittel mindestens 15 Basispunkte, für Ja-pan auf 20 BP und für Europa auf 60 BP (IWF 2014, S. 104). Im Tiefpunkt der Krise betrug die Subvention 250 BP. In dem Ausmaß, in dem Änderungen bei der Unterstützungsbereit-schaft (bzw. dem Zwang zum Beispringen) vermutet werden, verändern sich die Zinsauf-schläge. Der in Europa auf den Weg gebrachte Restrukturierungs- und Abwicklungsmecha-nismus sollte deshalb, für sich genommen. zu einer Ausweitung der Spreads führen.

Der Nexus von Souverän und Staat wurde im Verlauf der europäischen Staatsschulden-krise zum zentralen Problem (siehe auch Graphik 2a und 2b). Die Mitte 2012 auf die poli-tische Tagesordnung gesetzte Europäische Bankenunion – mit der gemeinsamen Aufsicht für die systemischen Banken ab dem Herbst 2014, dem Restrukturierungs- und Abwick-lungsmechanismus und einer aufeinander abgestimmten Einlagensicherung – soll genau dieses Problem adressieren. Aus der Perspektive der Gläubiger liegt allerdings nur dann eine Entkoppelung vor, die auch einen Niederschlag in der Preisbildung findet, wenn es keinen national differenzierten Zugang zu Unterstützungsoptionen gibt. Genau dies soll, im Verein mit dem europäischen Beihilferecht, die Europäisierung, sprich Ent-Nationali-sierung der Aufsicht, vor allem aber die europäisierte Restrukturierung und Abwicklung von Kreditinstituten leisten. Der Abwicklungsfonds, der auch in der Endstufe einen ver-gleichsweise geringen Umfang haben wird, wird jedoch für die absehbare Zukunft eine überwiegende nationale Komponente aufweisen. Das gilt noch mehr für die Einlagen-sicherung. Im Ausmaß dieser von den Investoren wahrgenommenen Unterschiede dürfte (sollte) es Zinsdifferenzen geben.

3.4.2 Probleme und offene Fragen

Strukturierte Produkte: Ratingagenturen unterliefen die gravierendsten Fehleinschätzun-gen bei der Würdigung von verbrieften Forderungen (forderungsbesicherten Ansprüchen), die auf der Aktivseite von so genannten Zweckgesellschaften (oder *special purpose vehic-les*) verbucht waren. Der Geschäftszweck dieser Gesellschaften war es, von Kreditinstituten vergebene („originierte") Kredite zu kaufen. Das Modell – *originate to distribute* oder Kreditanbahnung und -weitervergabe – war auf die Eigenkapitalentlastung der Banken angelegt. Die SPVs als eigenständige Geschäftseinheiten verblieben unterhalb des Bilanzstriches. Deshalb mussten die kreditvergebenden Banken nur solange Eigenkapital gegen die geschaffenen Kredite halten, wie diese auf ihrer Bilanz waren. Das knappe Eigenkapital konnte deshalb revolvierend zum Kreditschöpfen eingesetzt werden.

Hinzu kam, dass die Zweckgesellschaften in der Haftung waren, die Banken dagegen, die die Kredite ursprünglich herausgelegt hatten, für deren Werthaltigkeit aber keine Verpflichtung mehr hatten. Aus der Sicht der Banken waren die Zweckgesellschaften *bankruptcy remote*. (Bereits zu Beginn der Finanzkrise erwies sich dies allerdings als Illusion. Aus Reputationsgründen nahmen Banken die Forderungen gegen SPVs auf ihre Bilanz. Oder sie standen mit Refinanzierungslinien bereit.) Die Gesellschaften verbrieften die Zins- und Tilgungsleistungen der ihnen übereigneten Forderungen. Die so geschaffenen Wertpapiere waren mithin durch ein Forderungsbündel abgesichert. Für die Akzeptanz dieser Wertpapiere war ihre Einstufung durch Ratingagenturen entscheidend. Deren ausgesprochen hochrangige Bewertungen – mehr als zwei Drittel in der höchsten, also der AAA-Kategorie – waren ausschlaggebend dafür, dass derartige Produkte auf ein so großes Anlegerinteresse (bei institutionellen Investoren, aber auch Banken) stießen.

Länderbewertungen: Bei der Einschätzung der Kreditwürdigkeit haben Agenturen ebenfalls schwerwiegende Fehleinschätzungen zu verantworten (jüngst Vernazza u. a. 2014). Bereits im Nachgang der Asien-Krise wurde den Agenturen vorgehalten, dass sie zunächst die Bonität der Staaten zu hoch eingeschätzt hatten, also besser als es die Daten gerechtfertigt hätten argumentieren (etwa Ferri et al. (1999). Während der Krise seien die Bewertungen dann verschärft worden. Abstufungen führen nahezu zwingend zu Verkaufsdruck bei institutionellen Investoren, etwa weil regulatorische oder statuarische Schwellenwerte übertroffen werden. Dieses hätte die Abwärtsspirale befördert (Abb. 3.2).

Abbildung 3.2a zeigt die Zinsaufschläge, die öffentliche Schuldner zwischen 2007 und heute im Vergleich zu deutschen Bundesanleihen bezahlten. Abbildung 3.2b illustriert die Prämien, die zur Absicherung gegen Bankrisiken bezahlt werden mussten. Deutlich werden der abrupte Anstieg und die Differenzierung im Nachgang der 2010 beginnenden Staatschuldenprobleme in der Peripherie der Währungsunion.

Für die europäische Staatsschuldenprobleme wurden ähnliche Diagnosen gestellt: Die Agenturen liefen den Marktentwicklungen hinterher und kamen zu Einschätzungen, die von den Fundamentaldaten abwichen, jedenfalls in der Lesart der Autoren. Die Tieferstufungen beliefen sich auf 1 bis 1,5 Ratingstufen (Gärtner et al. u. a. 2012). In die gleiche Richtung argumentieren Paul de Grauwe und Yuemei Ji (2012). Sie vermögen mit einem einfachen, mit wenigen unabhängigen Erklärungsgrößen arbeitenden Modell rund 80 % der Streuung der Zinsspreads (relativ zur deutschen Bundesanleihe) in der Eurozone zu erfassen. Das Modell weist für die Eurozonenländer eine Bruchstelle auf, die durch die Griechenland-Krise markiert wird. Für Länder mit eigenständiger Geldpolitik (das Vereinigte Königreich) gibt es diesen Funktionssprung nicht.

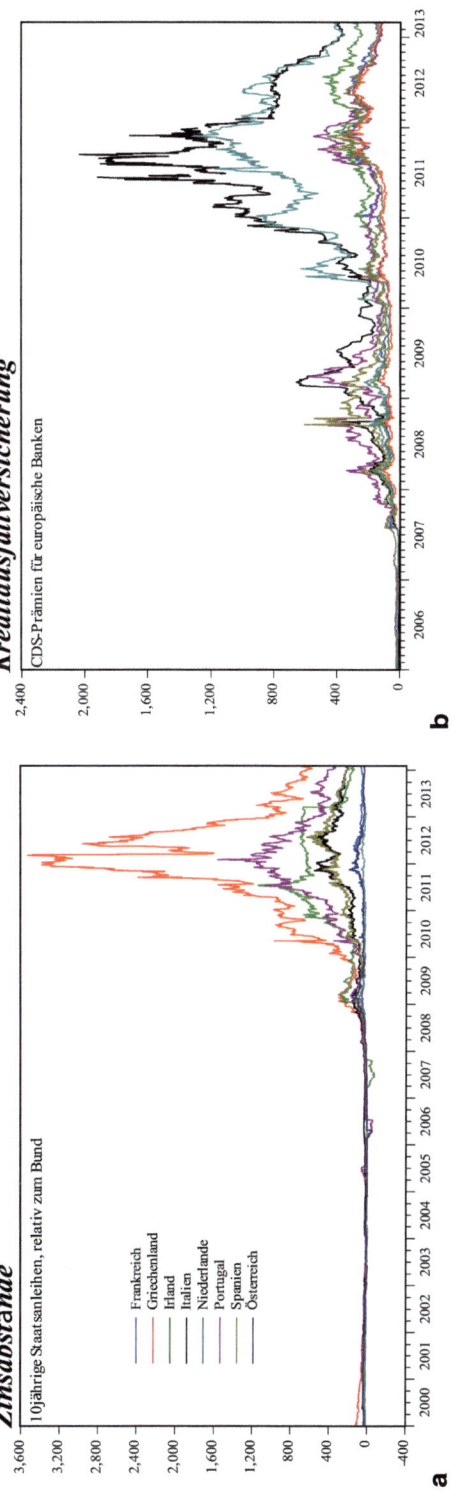

Abb. 3.2 a Zinsabstände **b** Kreditausfallversicherung

Das ist ein eindeutiges Indiz, dass für Eurozonenländer das Anschlussfinanzierungs-risiko potenziell existiert und vom Markt als solches durch höhere Zinsaufschläge ein-kalkuliert wird. Die Teilnehmerländer der Währungsunion sind aus der Sicht der Anleger *Sub*-Souveräne, in etwa wie Bundesstaaten, allerdings *ohne* eine explizite föderale Rü-ckendeckung. Im Gegenteil, aufgrund des expliziten Nicht-Beistands-Gebots (Art. 125 AEUV) des Staatenbundes, stellt die Verfassung der Währungsunion für die Teilnehmer-länder, mit (beschränkter) nationaler Finanzautonomie und ohne einen Ausleiher letzter Zuflucht, eine stärker bindende Restriktion dar. Mit der Ankündigung des *outright mone-tary transactions* Programms der EZB im Sommer 2012, das einen konditionierten Liqui-ditätsbeistand bereitstellt, haben sich die Zinsaufschläge deutlich verengt. De Grauwe und Ji (2014) finden, das gleiche Modell benutzend, aber mit den neuen Daten arbeitend, eine Bestätigung für die These: das Anschlussfinanzierungsrisiko in einem Staatenbund mit *no-bail out* Bindung ist erheblich. Am aktuellen Rand führt die positive, im OMT-begrün-dete Marktstimmung, so ihre Einschätzung, zu einer Risikobepreisung, die nicht durch die Fundamentaldaten gedeckt ist.

Vergütungsmodell: Eine Ursache für die Fehlurteile wird oft in der Art gesehen, in der Ratingagenturen vergütet werden. Banken bezahlen, wie andere Schuldner, ihr eigenes Rating. Das begünstigt mindestens Anreize zu kollusivem Verhalten. Das Argument ist einsichtig. Es ergeben sich offensichtliche Interessenkonflikte. Diese wurden von Jiang et al. (2012) empirisch am Fall der Umstellung des Bezahlmodells durch S&P untersucht. Demnach führte das 1974 von S&P eingeführte Issuer-Pay Vergütungsmodell zu einer Erhöhung der Bonitätseinstufungen und zu einer Verringerung der Ratingherabstufungen. Eine angedrohte Herabstufung könnte einen Kreditnehmer dazu bewegen, die Rating-agentur zu wechseln. Damit wären in einer Umgebung, die die Wahl der Agentur freistellt, Einnahmeverluste unausweichlich. Dieses Problem wird allerdings mit der Anzahl der Kunden und der damit verbundenen geringeren Abhängigkeit von bestimmten Schuldnern gemildert. Umgekehrt gilt ebenso, dass mit steigender Einflussmacht der Emittenten die Abhängigkeit der Agenturen wächst, mindestens implizit. Eine derartige Situation lag bei der Bewertung strukturierter Finanzprodukte vor. Seit etwa 2002 kontrollierten die sechs größten Auftraggeber die Hälfte und die zwölf größten Auftraggeber 80 % dieses Markt-segmentes. In diesem enorm wachsenden Bereich der Verbriefungs-transaktionen war die Verhandlungsposition der Auftraggeber deshalb entsprechend stark. Damit verbunden war zugleich ein Anreiz, den Kunden entgegen zu kommen. Denn die Reputation einer Rating-agentur hängt von ihrem Marktanteil, die gleichzeitig Expertise signalisiert. Der Marktan-teil wächst wiederum mit der Reputation. Obwohl Rating-Inflation zu Reputationsschäden führen kann, kann es, vor dem Hintergrund von Rating-Shopping, dennoch einen Anreiz geben, Schönzufärben. Letzteres ist gleichbedeutend mit dem Ausnutzen (cashing-in) über die Zeit erworbener Reputation (Mathis et al. 2009).

Dieser Interessenkonflikt ist auch deshalb schwerwiegend, da Ratings in der Regel dauerhafte Beziehungen darstellen und mithin der Gebührenverlust ein nachhaltiger ist. Insbesondere bei den strukturierten Produkten, bei denen die Agenturen auf beiden Markt-seiten engagiert waren, scheint dieses Problem relevant gewesen zu sein.

Gegen die darin unterstellte Käuflichkeit der Agentur-Urteile spricht jedoch, dass sie auf ihr Reputationskapital angewiesen sind. Sie verlören an Marktanteilen und Bedeutung, wenn sie systematisch Schönfärben würden.

Eine einfache Lösung scheint darin zu bestehen, die letztlichen Nutzer, die Investoren, zahlen zu lassen. Tatsächlich war dies bis zu Anfang der 1970er auch der Fall. Ratings werden allerdings schnell zu öffentlichem Wissen. Ihr Nutzen nimmt nicht mit der Zahl der davon in Kenntnis gesetzten ab. Sie sind damit im Gebrauch nicht-rivalisierend, auf gewisse Weise öffentliche Güter. Deshalb gibt es für Investoren kaum Anreize, die Ratings zu bezahlen. Sie können sich deren Nutzen nicht aneignen. Nicht-bezahlende Dritte vermögen Trittbrett zu fahren.

Nationalität der Ratingagenturen: In der Vergangenheit wurde immer wieder diskutiert, ob es zweckgerecht sei, eine europäische Ratingagentur als Gegengewicht zu den etablierten U.S. Ratingagenturen zu gründen. Im Unterschied zu den privatwirtschaftlichen U.S. Agenturen sollte diese als eine nicht gewinnorientierte Institution aufgebaut werden. Des Weiteren sollte die europäische Ratingagentur auf Basis eines *Investor-Pay*-Modells, welches bis in die 1970er-Jahre üblich war, ins Leben gerufen werden. Dabei sollten insbesondere europäischen Besonderheiten angemessen Rechnung getragen werden.

Die nationalen Kontexte haben offenkundig einen Einfluss auf die Kreditwürdigkeit von Unternehmen – damit auch Banken. Es gibt vielfältige, in Europa allerdings durch Harmonisierung abnehmende Unterschiede, etwa im Insolvenzrecht. Mit derartigen Besonderheiten sind Folgen für die Zahlungsversprechen und insbesondere deren Sicherheit verbunden. Die Einschätzung solcher nationaler Vielfalt setzt spezifische Kenntnisse voraus. Hinzu kommt, dass es auch unterschiedliche normative Vorstellungen über die angemessene Struktur von Unternehmen (deren Zielfunktion, die beteiligten Interessen – *shareholder* versus *stakeholder* usw.) gibt. Das gilt auch für die Bedeutung des öffentlichen Sektors im Bankwesen.

Insofern bedarf es eines spezifischen Wissens über die Variante des Kapitalismus (so der politikwissenschaftliche Ansatz von Peter Hall und David Soskice), die man würdigt. Am Ende zählt für die Agenturen aber nur, inwieweit den Gläubigeransprüchen genügt wird. Dabei ist ausschlaggebend, ob die Investoren diese Meinung kaufen, im Wortsinne. Europäische Agenturen könnten mehr Wettbewerb in die Rating-Landschaft bringen. Die Regeln würden auch eher in Europa statt bei der amerikanischen Wertpapieraufsicht festgelegt. Tatsächlich ist ja seit 2011 Europa hier mit der ESMA deutlich aktiver. In der Substanz aber sind eher marginale Änderungen zu erwarten. Denn die Nationalität der Agentur dürfte keinen Einfluss auf die Verfahren nehmen. Bereits der Verdacht einer tendenziellen Begünstigung heimischer, europäischer Schuldner würde von den Märkten negativ in Rechnung gestellt. Glaubwürdigkeit setzt Unabhängigkeit im Urteile unabdingbar voraus. Dann aber ist zu bezweifeln, ob europäische Agenturen zu systematisch besseren Urteilen als Agenturen mit nicht-europäischer Eigentümerstruktur kommen.

Dennoch gab es zwei intensive Versuche in dieser Richtung, die aber beide scheiterten. In beiden Fällen gelang es nicht, Finanziers von der Idee zu überzeugen. Ein Grund war die Vermutung, dass Akzeptanz für eine Agentur, die sich vor allem auch regional differenzierte, wohl fehlen würde. Als problematisch wurde unter anderem angesehen, dass eine staatlich angestoßene Ratingagentur andere Maßstäbe als die sachlich gebotenen anlegen könnte, also Rücksicht nehmen müsste. Potenziell stellt sich die Haftungsfrage bei einer, wenn auch nur indirekt öffentlichen Institution (einer Art *government sponsored agency*) noch stärker. Eine stiftungsbasierten europäische Ratingagentur, die dieses Problem gemildert hätte, scheiterte an der fehlenden Finanzierung.

All das spricht nicht prinzipiell gegen eine europäische Agentur. Der wichtigste Grund für eine Zustimmung zu diesem Vorschlag wäre, dass mehr Wettbewerb möglich würde. Dabei ist dieser aber im Rating-Sektor aus strukturellen Gründen beschränkt. Bei einer Vielzahl von Agenturen verlöre deren Urteil seine Eignung als Referenz. Es gibt mithin eine funktionale Begründung für einen Markt mit kleiner Anbieterzahl. Dazu können natürlich auch europäische Agenturen zählen. Und natürlich sind die amerikanischen Anbieter stark begünstigt durch den Franchise, der ihnen mit dem regulierten Marktzutritt geboten wird (White 2013; Partnoy 1999).

Das trendmäßige Verwischen der Grenzen zwischen kapitalmarkt- und bankenorientierter Vermittlung hat zu einem Aufspalten der Wertschöpfungskette des klassischen Bankgeschäftes geführt. Das bedeutet, dass die Bedeutung spezialisierter Anbieter und Märkte entlang der gesamten Angebotspalette wächst. Es gilt auch für die Einschätzung der Kreditwürdigkeit. Hier ist die Nachfrage etwa nach den Produkten, die auf den Märkten für Kreditausfallversicherungen gehandelt oder den Dienstleistungen, die Ratingagenturen anbieten, über die Jahre nachhaltig gewachsen.

3.5 Zusammenfassung und Ausblick

Im Ergebnis der Finanzkrise sind Ratingagenturen (aber auch Regulatoren) – angesichts der sozialen Kosten aus verständlichen Gründen – immer vorsichtiger geworden. Fehler zweiter Art, also das Ablehnen an sich zahlungsfähiger Kunden, werden eher akzeptiert. Das macht die Wirtschaft sicherer. Denn es werden weniger unternehmerische Risiken eingegangen. Es macht sie aber auch weniger innovativ. Chancen werden relativ zu Risiken kritischer, konservativer gewürdigt (Shiller 2012). Damit verringern sich tendenziell die Wachstumsoptionen einer Gesellschaft. Die neue Balance zwischen forsch und langweilig könnte Banken, aufsichts- und rating-bedingt, gesellschaftlich weniger nützlich machen.

Seitdem nicht mehr alle Bankbeziehungen einfach als zweifelsfrei wahrgenommen, vielmehr potenziell sogar als problematisch angesehen werden – eine unmittelbare Folge der großen Finanzkrise sowie des Herausnehmens von staatlichen Sicherungen – verwenden gerade auch Nicht-Finanzunternehmen nicht mehr fraglos die Würdigung von Ratingagenturen. Sie investieren in die eigene Urteilsbildung über die Beziehungen, die sie etablieren. Das führt tendenziell zu einer größeren Differenzierung.

Die veränderte Einschätzung der Kreditwürdigkeit führte in einigen Fällen dazu, dass Banken, obwohl breiter diversifiziert, eine höhere Risikoprämie als zweifelsfreie Nicht-Finanzunternehmen zahlen mussten. Mit den schwindenden (oder verschwundenen) Refinanzierungsvorteilen erodiert zugleich die Geschäftsbasis, mindestens für Beziehungen zu diesen Unternehmen.

Das Setzen auf den Staat (Andrew Haldanes *Banking on the State*) führt zu offenkundigen Wettbewerbsverzerrungen. Es gilt natürlich auch für die implizit abgesicherten, systemischen Banken, ob sie nun durch Größe oder Vernetzung einen relativen Vorteil vor allem in der Refinanzierung haben. Die Verringerung dieser Quersubvention durch Insolvenzfähigmachen (über Testamente zu Lebzeiten oder durch Restrukturierungs- und Abwicklungsmechanismen) ist der gebotene Weg. Es dürfte allerdings nicht gelingen, sich gänzlich aus dem Dilemma zu befreien. Systemische Krisen werden geschehen. Es wäre dann sehr kostenträchtig, Prinzipien bedingungslos aufrechtzuerhalten.

Vor diesem Hintergrund bleibt für Ratingagenturen – ebenso wie ihre Alternativen – eine Rolle. Dabei wird es auch zu institutionellen und methodischen Innovationen, zu Lernen kommen. Das downgrading der Bedeutung von Agenturen – und das gleichzeitige Höhergewichten von Substituten – ist eine zweckgemäße Lehre, die aus der Großen Finanzkrise gezogen wurde. Ergebnisse sind robuster, wenn sie sich im Lichte verschiedener Verfahren bewähren müssen. Unter derartigen Bedingungen macht der Check der Gesundheit von Banken, das *monitoring* der *monitors* durch die Ratingagenturen weiterhin Sinn.

Literatur

Altman, E. (1968): Financial Ratios, Discriminant Analysis and the Prediction of Corporate Bankruptcy, in: *Journal of Finance*, Sept., S. 568–609

Altman, E. und E. Hotchkiss (2006): *Corporate Financial Distress and Bankruptcy*, 3. Aufl., New York: Wiley

Brunnermeier, M. u. a. (2009): *The Fundamental Principles of Financial Regulation*, Genf: Geneva Reports on the World Economy

Chava, S. und J. Jarrow (2004): Bankruptcy prediction with industry effects, *Reviev of Finance*, Nr. 8, S. 537–569

De Grauwe, P. und Y. Li (2012). Mispricing sovereign risk and macroeconomic stability in the Eurozone, in: *Journal of Common Market Studies*, Bd. 50, Nr. 6, S. 866–880.

European Banking Authority (2013), Interim results of the EBA review of the consistency of risk-weighted assets. Top-down assessment of the banking book http://www.eba.europa.eu/documents/10180/15947/Interim-results-EBA-review-consistency-RWAs_1.pdf/ca66e71f-7f91-40ad-9d76-8425fbc73473, abgerufenam 1. Dezember 2013.

European Parliament (2009): Proposal for aREGULATION OF THE EUROPEAN PARLIAMENT AND OF THE COUNCIL amending Regulation (EC) No 1060/2009 on credit rating agencies, http://ec.europa.eu/internal_market/securities/agencies/index_de.htm.

Ferri, G., L.-G. Liu und J. E. Stiglitz (1999): The procyclical role of rating agencies: Evidence from the East Asian crisis, in: *Economic Notes*, Banca Monte deiPaschi di Siena, vol. 28, no. 3, pp. 335–355

Gärtner, M. Griesbach, B. und F. Jung (2012): Die Macht der Meinungsmacher: Ratingagenturen und staatliche Verschuldungsdynamiken, in: *Wirtschaftsdienst*, S. 251–255

Gorton, G. (2009): The Subprime Panic, in: *European Financial Management*, Bd. 15, Nr. 1, S. 10–46

Haldane, A. und P. Alessandri (2009): Banking on the State, Vortrag, Bank von England

Hartmann-Wendels, T., A. Pfingsten und Martin Weber (2010): *Bankbetriebslehre*, Heidelberg: Springer

Healy, P. und K. Palepu (2003): The Fall of Enron, in: *Journal of Economic Perspectives*, Bd. 17, Nr 2, S. 3–26

Hull, J. (2012): *Risk Management and Financial Institutions*, 3. Aufl., New York: Wiley

IWF (2014): *Global Financial Stability Report: Transition Challenges to Stability*, April, Washington, Kap. 3, S. 105 ff

Jiang, J. Harris Stanford, M. and Xie, Y (2012): Does it matter who pays for bond ratings? Historical evidence, in: Journal of Financial Economics, 105, S. 607–621

Mathis, J., McAndrews, J. and Rochet, J.-C. (2009): Rating the raters: Are reputation concerns powerful enough to discipline rating agencies? in: Journal of Monetary Economics, 56, 657–674

Moody's (2013): Rating Methodology. Global Banks, http://www.moodys.com/research/Global-Banks–PBC_154255

Morgan, D (2002): Rating banks: risk and uncertainty in an opaque industry, in:American Economic Review, Bd. 92, S. 874–88

Myers, S. und R. Rajan (1998): The paradox of liquidity, in: *Quarterly Journal of Economics*, Bd. 113, Nr. 3, S. 733–771

Packer, F. und N. Tarashev (2011): Rating methodologies for banks, in: *BIS Quarterly Review*, Juni, S. 39–52

Partnoy, F. (1999): The Siskel and Ebbert of Financial Markets? Two Thumbs Down for Rating Agencies, in: *Washington University Law Quarterly*, Bd. 77, Nr. 3, S. 619–714

Rudolph, B. (2006): *Unternehmensfinanzierung und Kapitalmarkt*, Tübingen: Mohr Siebeck

Shiller, R. (2012): *Finance and the Good Society*, Princeton: Princeton und Oxford UP

Shin, H. S. (2009): Reflections on Northern Rock: The Bank Run That Heralded the Global Financial Crisis, *Journal of Economic Perspectives*, Bd. 23, Nr. 1, S. 101–120

Standard & Poor's (2008): Corporate Criteria: Analytical Methodology, www.standardandpoors.com/

Standard & Poor's (2013): How we rate banks, www.standardandpoors.com/ratingsdirect

Song, F. und A. Thakor (2010): Financial System Architecture and the co-evolution of banks and capital markets, in: *Economic Journal*, Bd. 120, S. 1021–1055

Sylla, R. (2002): A Historical Primer on the Business of Credit Ratings, in: Richard Levich u. a. (Hrsg., 2001): *Ratings, Rating Agencies and the Global Financial System*, Boston: Kluwer Academic Publishers, S. 19–40

Vernazza, D., Nielsen E. und Vasileios Gkionakis: The Damaging Bias of Sovereign Ratings, *UniCredit Global Themes Series*, Nr. 21

White, L. (2013): Credit rating agencies: An overview, in: *Annual Review of Financial Economics*, No. 5, S. 93–122

Theodor Weimer ist seit 2007 bei der UniCredit und verantwortete dort zunächst das Investment Banking. Seit 2009 ist er Vorstandssprecher der HypoVereinsbank – UniCredit Bank AG. Darüber hinaus ist er Country Chairman Germany und Mitglied des Executive Management Committees der UniCredit. Nach seinem Studium in Tübingen/St. Gallen und Promotion an der Universität Bonn arbeitete Weimer von 1988 bis 1995 bei McKinsey, bevor er dann zu Bain & Company wechselte. Dort stieg er zum Mitglied der weltweiten Geschäftsführung auf und spezialisierte sich auf die Beratung von Finanzdienstleistern. Von 2001 bis 2007 war er für Goldman Sachs als Managing Director im Investment Banking, ab 2004 als Partner, tätig.

Role and Regulation of Credit Rating Agencies

4

Zafer Diab

4.1 Introduction

Credit ratings are an integral part of banking and securities markets and their longstanding use by market participants is a testament to their positive value as an input into credit judgements. Credit rating agencies (CRAs) offer investors clear opinions on the creditworthiness of rated entities and financial instruments, set out in detailed research reports and summarised in easy-to-compare rating grades.

Credit ratings are, however, often misunderstood by market participants. Moreover, the embedding of ratings in national and international regulatory architecture, as well as in certain market practices, has had unintended negative consequences both for the functioning of financial systems and the ratings industry itself.

Credit ratings have come under the spotlight in recent years, due to errors that occurred prior to and during the global financial crisis. Those failings were mainly attributable to the three largest international CRAs and mostly confined to one broad asset class, structured finance, and to residential mortgage-backed securities (RMBS) and collateralised debt obligations (CDOs) in particular.

There has been a strong international response over the past 5 years to the perceived deficiencies of CRAs and the risks associated with excessive reliance on credit ratings. Around the world, many laws have been passed to address these concerns and the use of ratings remains a topic of review in several international forums.

In the European Union (EU), as well as in a number of other juri. S. d.ictions, CRAs have been brought within the regulatory perimeter for the first time. The EU's regulatory

Z. Diab (✉)
Limassol, Zypern
e-mail: m.zlotnik@yahoo.de

© Springer Fachmedien Wiesbaden 2016
Z. Diab, O. Everling (Hrsg.), *Rating von Finanzinstituten,*
DOI 10.1007/978-3-658-04195-3_4

regime aims to enhance the integrity, transparency, governance and reliability of activities of CRAs operating in the EU and to ensure that the resulting credit ratings are independent, objective and of high quality. For a number of small- and medium-sized agencies in the EU, such as Capital Intelligence, regulation can serve as a catalyst for raising investor awareness of, and confidence in, the ratings they issue. It also marks the first tangible step towards eroding the oligopolistic structure of the CRA market.

This article provides a brief overview of the uses of credit ratings and of the functions and regulation of CRAs, with particular focus on developments in the EU and on the use of ratings in the banking sector.

4.2 What Are Credit Ratings?

At its simplest, a credit rating is an opinion of the ability and willingness of a debtor to meet its financial commitments, such as payments of interest and principal, in full and on time. CRAs tend to distinguish between two broad types of credit rating: issuer ratings and issue ratings.

Issuer ratings—also known as counterparty ratings—indicate the overall capacity of rated entities (for example banks or corporations) to honour their financial commitments, particularly long-term senior unsecured obligations. Issue ratings—or debt ratings—apply to specific financial obligations and take into account factors such as the terms and conditions of the obligations, as well as their legality and enforceability.

Depending upon the methodological approach of the CRA, a credit rating may indicate the possibility of default or capture expected loss by considering both the likelihood of default and the severity of default (in other words, the rating would take into account the potential for investors to recover at least part of their investment in the event of a default).

Credit ratings are issued using the risk-grading system of the CRA and are usually expressed in terms of alphabetic rating symbols, for example 'AAA' or 'BB'.

4.2.1 Ordinal Not Cardinal

Most types of credit ratings issued by the major CRAs provide an ordinal ranking of default risk among rated entities and obligations. The discussion in this sub-section is applicable to the approach taken by the big three CRAs, Moody's, S&P and Fitch, and also to CRAs such as DBRS and Capital Intelligence. Some small CRAs may follow a different approach.

The ratings capture the relative likelihood of default; they do not provide an absolute (or cardinal) measure of the probability of default over any particular time period. Consequently, and unlike in the internal rating systems of banks, credit ratings are not calibrated to specific default probabilities, that is, CRAs make no explicit attempt to maintain constant default rates for each rating category. For example, when a CRA assigns an issuer rating of 'A' to a bank, it is simply saying that the bank is less likely to default than a bank rated 'BB'—and not that the probability of the bank defaulting is, for example, 0.2%.

Although credit ratings provide only an ordinal ranking of credit quality, most CRAs publish default rate statistics for their rated universes. These may be used to produce an indicative mapping of ratings to default probabilities, provided a sufficient number of cases of non-payment have been observed by the CRA for each rating grade.

The focus on relative credit risk reflects the desire to have a rating system that provides investors with a measure of default risk, but which does not require ratings to be changed en masse in response to movements in the economic cycle. The importance of rating stability is often justified by the aversion of market participants to the potential transaction-related costs that would be triggered by frequent rating changes, as well as by the longer term horizon of many users of ratings.

4.2.2   Credit Rating Not Credit Scoring

The influence of the economic cycle is filtered out to some extent by taking a long-term view of the fundamental strengths and weaknesses of the rated entity, rather than fixating on short-term financial performance. In the context of financial institutions, this focus on long-term creditworthiness requires CRAs to place substantial emphasis on hard-to-quantify factors such as franchise value, market position and management quality. Consequently, the analytical approach of most CRAs includes substantial qualitative analysis in addition to a more quantitative evaluation of financial strength based on metrics derived from financial statements. It is the importance of the qualitative evaluation of key rating factors by experienced analysts, as well as the role of analysts in the determination of the final credit rating (typically through the institution of the rating committee) that distinguishes credit ratings from the more mechanistic, algorithm-based activity of credit scoring.

4.2.3   Limitations of Credit Ratings, Caveat Emptor

Credit ratings focus on one aspect of investment risk—credit (or repayment) risk—and depending on the CRA may or may not explicitly capture loss severity or recovery prospects. All CRAs agree, however, that ratings are not audits or a substitute for due diligence. Nor do they constitute recommendations to purchase, sell, or hold stocks or shares in an institution or particular security. In addition, ratings do not assess or indicate the likelihood of changes in the market price of rated instruments due to market-related factors such as changes in interest rates or liquidity. Finally, ratings do not provide an opinion of the liquidity in the market of an issuer's securities.

4.3 The Role of Credit Rating Agencies

Rating agencies play an important role in banking and securities markets by providing investors with the credit-related information they need to make informed investment decisions and also via credit surveillance activities, which may benefit both investors and rated entities. CRAs also play a so-called 'certification' role owing to the use of ratings—rightly or wrongly—in various rules and regulations.

4.3.1 Narrowing the Information Gap

CRAs help to reduce the information gap that typically exists between investors (lenders) and issuers (borrowers), and to lighten the information-gathering burden for investors.

Issuers, such as banks and corporates, know far more than potential investors about the true condition of their financial health. This situation can give rise to an adverse selection problem in which risk-averse investors are unwilling to provide funding to companies for fear of the financial unknown, or are only willing to do so by charging a high risk premium. This problem can arise in developing or emerging markets in particular, where standards of corporate governance and public financial disclosure sometimes fall short of acceptable levels, or in the case of smaller companies with unfamiliar business profiles.

CRAs contribute to the narrowing of this information gap by providing an independent, third-party opinion of the credit quality of the issuer, which they summarise in a credit rating but justify in a detailed and analytical credit rating report. As part of the rating process, CRAs typically meet with the senior management of the rated entity and discuss factors such as strategic objectives and financing plans, in addition to the entity's financial performance. This interaction with the rated entity affords CRAs a deeper insight into the credit profile of the issuer than would typically be available to an arms-length investor. CRAs may also be trusted with non-public or confidential information, which may be used to guide rating decisions—although the information itself would not be disclosed publicly. From the perspective of the rated entity, the provision of substantial information to the CRA sends a signal to the market that it is open to, and not concerned by, external scrutiny.

4.3.2 Reducing Information Costs

In a world without CRAs, investors and counterparties would have to do their own detailed credit analysis of the instruments and companies they plan to invest in or lend to. Given the sheer number of instruments and entities, as well as the vast amount of information and data available on many issuers, this is an activity that even the largest institutional investors would find burdensome, while smaller investors would likely find the associated research costs to be prohibitively high.

CRAs provide a cost-effective solution to this problem by supplying investors with analysis and key financial metrics for a large number of rated entities and instruments. This does not obviate the need for investors to conduct their own credit analysis, but it does help to lighten the workload and assist investors in taking more informed investment decisions.

By reducing the cost to investors of acquiring information on an entity and of conducting a detailed credit assessment—particularly when the size of the envisaged transaction is small relative to the investor's overall portfolio—credit ratings may also help to lower the cost of capital.

4.3.3   Surveillance: Remaining Alert to Potential Risks

CRAs monitor their ratings on an ongoing basis and in the EU are required by law to formally review and update their ratings at least once annually for corporate ratings (which in the EU means both corporate issuers and financial institutions) and structured finance ratings, and at least every 6 months in the case of sovereign ratings. Surveillance takes time and resources and for investors there are clear economies of scale from, in effect, outsourcing part of the task of monitoring the credit quality of corporates to rating agencies.

4.3.4   Certification Role

In the academic literature, the certification role of CRAs refers to the use of ratings for regulatory purposes and to the use of ratings by institutional investors, such as pension funds and insurance companies, to comply with investment policies. In this context, what economists refer to as "agency costs" can be mitigated by investors limiting the amount of risk that a fund can take on their behalf by mandating that investments be restricted to securities with investment-grade credit ratings.

This certification role is among the most controversial uses of credit ratings since it can contribute to overreliance on ratings and fuel systemic risk in the financial system. The largest CRAs in particular have benefited financially from this role; but they are not entirely to blame for its existence.

4.4   Uses of Credit Ratings

4.4.1   Investors

Investors and counterparties use ratings as a guide to credit quality and, along with the accompanying research, as an input into their investment and financing decision-making processes. Users of ratings appreciate the value of being able to compare to a common methodological standard the credit profile of an issuer in one country with its national peers and counterparts in other countries.

In some markets (notably money markets and OTC derivative markets) ratings may be used by investors to determine acceptable counterparties, as well as collateral requirements. Investors may also establish permissible investment criteria linked to ratings in the mandates they issue to asset managers. Parties to private loan contracts may also choose to incorporate ratings into their financial contracts by setting so-called rating 'triggers' that may, for example, terminate credit availability or accelerate credit obligations in the event of a ratings downgrade.

4.4.2 Issuers

Issuers, or borrowers, use credit ratings to facilitate access to, and improve the terms of, external finance (from home and abroad), as well as to diversify funding sources. Ratings enable issuers to price their issues competitively and make securities issuances more marketable.

Issuers may also seek ratings for their one own internal purposes, including to be able to benchmark creditworthiness against competitors. Some issuers also find the rating process itself to be beneficial, with the level of required information and impartial external analysis helping to promote good governance and foster transparency.

4.4.3 Regulators

The use and influence of credit ratings has increased over time with their incorporation into many national and international regulatory frameworks. An international study (Basel Committee on Banking Supervision 2009) of financial supervisory authorities in the banking, securities and insurance sectors found that credit ratings were used for five main purposes:

1. Determining capital requirements;
2. Identifying or classifying assets, usually in the context of eligible investments or permissible asset concentrations;
3. Providing a credible evaluation of the credit risk associated with assets purchased as part of a securitisation offering or a covered bond offering;
4. Determining disclosure requirements; and
5. Determining prospectus eligibility.

Globally, perhaps the most widespread use of ratings in regulation is in determining capital requirements. In the banking sphere, regulatory reliance on ratings increased significantly with the adoption of the Basel II capital adequacy accord in 2004. Under the "standardized approach" of Basel II, the ratings of what banking authorities call external credit assessment institutions (ECAIs)—in other words, rating agencies—may be used for risk-weighting claims and securitisation exposures.

Central banks also use the credit ratings of CRAs in their rules governing the quality of collateral they will accept from banks and other market participants in exchange for liquidity and also in the valuation of haircuts applied to eligible securities. For example, the European Central Bank (ECB) requires that to be counted as collateral, non asset-backed marketable securities must meet "high credit standards", currently defined as an investment grade rating of at least 'BBB-'.

In the EU, the guidelines on a Common Definition of European Money Market Funds issued by European Securities and Markets Authority (ESMA) require money market funds to invest only in high quality money market instruments. To be deemed "high quality", an instrument must have received one of the two highest available short-term credit ratings by each of the CRAs that have rated it.

4.5   Hardwiring and the Law of Unintended Consequences

Investors' use of credit ratings has increased over the past few decades with the increase in the size, complexity and interconnectedness of financial systems. Sensible usage has given way in some cases to overreliance, due in part to the embedding or "hardwiring" of credit ratings into international banking standards, securities rules and regulations, financial contracts and investment mandates.

The regulatory use of ratings can create the perception that the ratings assigned to an entity or financial instrument have been endorsed or approved by the authorities. It also creates perverse incentives for market participants to simply accept the degree of credit risk implied by the ratings without reading the CRA's supporting analysis, let alone undertaking their own credit analysis.

Overreliance on ratings by investors amounts to poor risk management. The incorporation of ratings in financial regulation—particularly where little discretion is afforded to users of ratings—is tantamount to regulatory authorities abdicating their duty to supervise the adequacy of the credit risk evaluation processes of financial institutions.

For all the hyperbole in recent years, evidence of excessive reliance on ratings by investors is in fact quite limited. Nevertheless, there is certainly the perception, if not the risk, that the hardwiring of ratings in regulations could contribute to less than prudent underwriting and credit assessment practices by financial institutions

Excessive reliance on ratings can cause investors to herd around the risk assessments of CRAs and to react in a similar fashion when ratings or rating outlooks are revised. In particular, the simultaneous reallocation of capital by a large number of investors in response to a ratings downgrade could, in the limit, result in severe liquidity problems for the affected issuer if the rating action triggers collateral calls or access to funding markets is subsequently lost.

4.6   Reducing Reliance

CRAs are perceived to have played a causal role in the recent global financial crisis and policymakers have recognised, somewhat belatedly, that the embedding of ratings in laws, regulations and market practices is a potential source of pro-cyclicality and systemic risk—especially if such hard-wiring contributes to herding behaviour and negative "cliff effects" in prices and spreads. Regulatory authorities around the world are currently seeking to reduce regulatory reliance on credit ratings, but are mindful of the lack of viable alternative standards of creditworthiness in many areas.

In October 2010, the Financial Stability Board (FSB)—which was established by the G-20 countries to coordinate the work of national financial authorities and international standard setting bodies (such as the Basel Committee) in promoting stability in the international financial system—published a set of "Principles for Reducing Reliance on CRA Ratings".

A key aim of the FSB principles is to reduce the mechanistic reliance on credit ratings wherever it exists. Hence, the principles apply not only to regulatory use of ratings but also to a wider range of financial market activities, including investment mandates and private sector margin agreements. The FSB acknowledges, however, that CRAs play an important role in the financial system and that their ratings can appropriately be used as an input into firms' own judgement as part of internal credit assessment processes.

The FSB has also published a roadmap for reducing the reliance on credit ratings. This foresees appropriate revisions to the Basel capital framework and their adoption by jurisdictions from 2016, and the implementation of relevant domestic reforms in member countries by end-2015. However, the pace of regulatory reform has so far been uneven, and implementation dates are likely to be missed in many countries.

The most comprehensive reforms have taken place in the United States and EU. In the US, Sect. 939A of the Dodd-Frank Wall Street Reform and Consumer Protection Act of 2010 ("Dodd-Frank Act") requires each federal agency to "review any regulation issued by such agency that requires the use of an assessment of the credit-worthiness of a security or money market instrument and any references to or requirements in such regulations regarding credit ratings." Federal agencies are also required to amend the relevant regulations to refer to alternative standards of creditworthiness, where appropriate.

4.6.1   State of Play in the EU

The EU supports the FSB principles and has already brought about some changes to sectoral legislation in financial services (partly achieved through amendments to the regulation on CRAs in May 2013) to encourage financial institutions to make their own credit risk assessment and "not to solely or mechanistically rely on credit ratings for assessing the creditworthiness of an entity or financial instrument" (Art. 5a, par. 1 of Regulation (EU) No 462/2013 of the European Parliament and of the Council of 21 May 2013 Amending Regulation (EC) No 1060/2009 on Credit Rating Agencies).

The European Commission has also set 2020 as the target date for removing all remaining references in EU legislation that trigger, or have the potential to trigger, "sole or mechanistic reliance on credit ratings".

The meaning of "mechanistic reliance" has not been defined by the FSB, or in EU legislation. However, in February 2014, the three EU supervisory authorities—ESMA, the European Banking Authority (EBA) and the European Insurance and Occupational Pensions Authority (EIOPA)—offered their definition of "sole or mechanistic reliance". According to the trio:

"It is considered that there is sole or mechanistic reliance on credit ratings (or credit rating outlooks) when an action or omission is the consequence of any type of rule based on credit ratings (or credit rating outlooks) without any discretion" (Paragraph 26 of EBA, EIOPA and ESMA Final Report on Mechanistic references to credit ratings in the ESAs' guidelines and recommendations, February 2014).

4.6.2   Ratings and the Banking Sector

Changes in the use of credit ratings in the banking sector are likely to be incremental rather than radical over the coming years at least, in view of the recent adoption of Basel III.

The EU is implementing Basel III through two pieces of legislation: the Capital Requirements Directive (CRD IV) and the Capital Requirements Regulation (CRR), both of which entered into force at the start of 2014. Under the new framework, larger, more sophisticated banks are encouraged to follow the Internal Ratings-Based (IRB) Approach to capital requirements for credit risk rather than the more CRA-friendly Standardised Approach. Consistent with general policy objectives, this means that banks are being encouraged to develop their own mathematical models to quantify and assign risk parameters (such as the probability of default), rather than derive risk-weights from CRA ratings.

For many banks, however, the modelling route is either not cost-effective or raises too many technical or methodological challenges. Consequently, the less-demanding Standardised Approach—in which CRA ratings are used to quantify capital for credit risk—continues to be widely followed by banks in the EU (and in many other juri. S. d.ictions), either in full or to supplement the IRB approach in certain circumstances, such as when exposures are not material or are challenging to evaluate objectively (securitisations perhaps being the most common example of the latter), or when default data is limited.

This situation is unlikely to change in the near future. As the EBA's Banking Stakeholder Group recently observed: "The small institutions which generally do not have sufficient data or expertise to develop an expected loss model will use the standardised approach and the assessment of the ECAIs [CRAs] in the longer term" (s. EBA Banking Stakeholer Group 2014).

In any case, the extent to which the use of CRA ratings in the context of the standardised approach constitutes "sole and mechanistic reliance" is debatable. The EU supervisory authorities acknowledge that in many cases banks usage falls short of mechanistic reliance due to the existence of some discretionary elements in the standardised approach of CRD IV. In particular, banks have the option of applying higher risk weights than would be required from the mapping of CRA ratings—so conservative banks can effectively break the connection between credit ratings and risk weights.

More fundamentally, there are currently few viable alternatives to the use of CRA ratings. Some of the alternative market-based indicators of credit risk, such as credit default swap (CDS) premia and bond spreads, tend to be pro-cyclical and are more volatile than credit ratings (so there use could result in more volatile capital requirements). Furthermore, CDS premia and bond spreads are often driven by factors unrelated to credit risk and hence changes in their value may not reflect changes in underlying credit quality. Filtering out non-credit related price determinants, such as interest rates and market liquidity, would be highly challenging.

While the Basel Committee is currently in the process of reviewing the standardised approach and the securitisation framework with a view to reducing undue reliance on CRA ratings in the regulatory capital framework, it has already concluded with regards to liquidity standards that it is not possible to only use market-based indicators (the Liquidity Coverage Ratio relies on a combination of qualitative criteria, Basel risk weights and external credit ratings to determine asset class eligibility for the pool of high-quality liquid assets).

Separately, at the central bank level, the ECB has noted that: "Due to the very broad set of collateral which the Eurosystem accepts for credit operations, the elimination of external ratings entirely in the determination of an instrument's eligibility would indeed be very challenging" (ECB 2014).

More broadly, the FSB has cautioned government and regulators to "… guard against the temptation to adopt a small number of alternative measures of assessing creditworthiness in place of CRA ratings, which can result in substituted procyclicality and herd behaviour" (Financial Stability Board 2014, p. 16).

4.7 Regulation of CRAs

For most of its history, the credit rating industry has operated with little or no regulatory oversight throughout most of the world. Initially at least, this may have reflected the view that credit ratings were merely an opinion and should therefore have a limited impact on investor behaviour and financial markets over time. Self-regulation may also have been considered appropriate on the grounds that any CRA publishing inaccurate ratings or pursuing unethical business practices would be quickly disciplined by the market through the loss of business. In short, the reputational and financial risk from systematically issuing low quality ratings would be great enough to ensure that CRAs would work hard to remain relevant and credible.

4.7.1   From Self-Regulation to Official Oversight

The push for greater scrutiny of the activities of CRAs started in response to the growing use of credit ratings in securities markets in the 1990s and the increasing inclusion of ratings in official-sector rules and regulations, including the decision of the Basel Committee on Banking Supervision in 2004 to permit banks to use ratings from CRAs in determining capital requirements. Basel II made it the responsibility of national banking regulators to determine which CRAs banks could rely on for this purpose, but provided no more than a brief set of eligibility criteria for recognising CRAs, with little emphasis on monitoring CRAs on an ongoing basis.

In the US, calls for formal regulation grew louder in response to perceived failings of the largest CRAs in relation to the collapse of Enron in 2001 and Worldcom in 2002. In the EU, similar concerns were expressed following the bankruptcy of Parmalat in 2003 (all of the aforementioned countries received investment grade ratings in the year prior to their default).

Against this backdrop, in 2003 the International Organisation of Securities Commissions (IOSCO) published a "Statement of Principles Regarding the Activities of Credit Rating Agencies". This was followed a year later by the publication of the "Code of Conduct Fundamentals for Credit Rating Agencies" (IOSCO Code), which provided guidance on how the three key principles—quality and integrity of the rating process; CRA independence and the avoidance of conflicts of interest; and responsibilities to the investing public and issuer—could be implemented in practice.

The IOSCO Code was quickly adopted by many CRAs and heralded as a major strengthening of industry self-regulation. CRAs were asked to comply with its provisions—evidenced in part by the publication of their own codes—or to explain publicly where and why their policies and procedures differed from the IOSCO Code, as well as how their practices were nevertheless consistent with the code's provisions.

Implementation of the IOSCO Code was not sufficient to assuage concerns in the US, which in 2006 promulgated the Credit Rating Agency Reform Act, giving the Securities and Exchange Commission (SEC) the authority to regulate CRAs. The EU, which had experienced fewer high-profile rating failures, opted to forgo the regulatory route, arguing in 2006 that the existing financial services directives applicable to credit ratings and the implementation of the IOSCO Code by CRAs covered the most important aspects related to CRA activity.

After assessing the situation the European Commission concluded that "…the case for new legislation in this area remains unproven." However, in summarising the Commission's position the Internal Market and Services Commissioner Charlie McCreevy offered a note of caution, saying: " In short, the rating industry remains 'on watch' and will be monitored. We may need to modify our approach in the light of non-compliance or of changing circumstances" (European Commission 2006).

Circumstances changed profoundly following the collapse of the US sub-prime mortgage market in 2007 and the commencement shortly thereafter of the worst international financial and economic crisis since the 1930s.

The extent to which CRAs were to blame for the global financial crisis is debatable. Much of the industry's failings related to the flaws in the methodologies of the largest agencies for rating mortgage-backed structured credit products, in particular the use of backward-looking models based on historically low mortgage default and delinquency rates and the failure to adequately capture the risk of more adverse economic conditions. Ratings performance in other sectors actually held up fairly well. Nevertheless the poor structured finance assessments of some CRAs were seen as close enough to the origins of the crisis to warrant the re-consideration of existing regulatory approaches.

In April 2009, the G-20 agreed that member countries would introduce a "register and be supervised" model of regulation that would be consistent with the provisions of the IOSCO Code. In the US, the SEC's oversight of CRAs was further strengthened with 2010 Dodd-Frank Act, which established an Office of Credit Ratings to enforce SEC rules and introduced annual examinations of each registered CRA.

4.7.2   EU Regulation on CRAs

The self-regulation of the ratings industry ended in the EU with the approval of the Regulation on Credit Rating Agencies in 2009. Today, any CRA wishing to operate in the EU must be registered in accordance with the regulation and adhere to the provisions of the original law and its subsequent amendments (in 2011 and 2013), as well as to a raft of supplementary regulatory technical standards.

The initial focus of EU regulatory efforts was very much on tackling the problems that arose in the rating of complex structured finance products and on addressing some of the perceived weaknesses in the structure, business model, and internal processes of CRAs. The first set of amendments, passed in 2011, were largely to provide ESMA, as a newly created body, with powers in all matters relating to the registration and ongoing supervision of registered CRAs, including the ability to impose fines. The second set of amendments, in 2013, were more substantial—introducing, among other things, civil liability for CRAs, mandatory rotation for re-securitisations, shareholding restrictions, measures to reduce overreliance on ratings, and some curious rules on the issuing of sovereign ratings.

The principal aims of the EU regulation are to:

- Ensure CRAs avoid or manage appropriately any conflicts of interest;
- Ensure that CRAs remain vigilant on the quality of their ratings and rating methodologies;
- Increase the transparency of CRAs;

- Provide the right of financial redress to users of ratings; and
- Reduce overreliance on CRAs in regulation and financial market practices.

Key provisions to meet regulatory objectives are summarised in Table 4.1.

The size and systemic importance of a credit rating agency within the EU is given short shrift in the regulation. Small credit rating agencies (defined as those with fewer than 50 employees) may apply to be exempt from just four of the numerous requirements, namely those concerning: independent board members, the establishment of independent compliance and internal review functions; and the rotation of rating analysts.

4.7.3   Risk-Based Supervision

ESMA supervises registered CRAs through a combination of desk-based supervision and targeted on-site inspections. Periodic reporting requirements for CRAs are strict and include the following: information on all rating actions (submitted monthly or bi-monthly depending on the size of the CRA); information on financial revenues, costs and staff turnover (reported quarterly); copies of internal methodology reviews, compliance reports, internal audit reports and board minutes (submitted semi-annually); and information on CRA clients and the revenue generated from them, as well as the CRAs financial statements (reported annually). Information on new types of ratings, changes to methodologies and business activities must also be reported.

4.7.4   Regulation: Good, Bad or Indifferent?

The impact of the EU Regulation on the ratings industry has been broadly favourable. The transparency and independence of CRAs has increased significantly, internal control mechanisms have been strengthened and much has been done to manage the conflicts of interest that are inherent in any financial services business model in which one entity is paying to be evaluated by another (the auditing profession is similarly conflicted, for example).

The pace of regulatory change has been relatively fast, however, with the original regulation amended twice within 30 months of taking full effect in December 2010 and several Commission delegated regulations in the form of regulatory technical standards (relating, for example, to credit rating methodologies and periodic data reporting) being issued over the same period. The burden of complying with regulatory requirements has been substantial, especially for smaller CRAs, and medium-term business planning has become more challenging due to the reluctance of lawmakers to allow regulations to bed down before making further changes.

Concerns have also been expressed about the risk of regulatory creep from the use of subordinate legislation and regulatory guidelines. For example, the first regulation ex-

Table 4.1 Key provisions of the EU regulation on CRAs

Managing conflicts of interest and increasing the integrity of the rating process

At least one-third of the members of the administrative or supervisory board of a CRA must be independent and the majority of board members must have sufficient expertise in financial services. CRAs must also establish and maintain an independent compliance function to monitor and report on the CRA's adherence to regulatory requirements

CRAs may not provide consultancy or advisory services to rated entities and are prohibited from issuing ratings in situations that can impair their independence, for example if the CRA has an ownership interest in the rated entity

Rating analysts are subject to a number of restrictions and rules. For example, rating analysts may not participate in discussions regarding fees or payments with rated entities or make proposals or recommendations regarding the design of structured finance products rated by the CRA. In addition, rating analysts should not rate an entity in which he/she has an ownership interest

CRAs must establish a rotation mechanism for rating analysts to mitigate possible risks arising from long-term relationships with rated entities

Enhancing the quality of ratings and methodologies

Credit ratings and methodologies must be monitored on an ongoing-basis and reviewed at least annually reviewed, with the exception of sovereign ratings which must be reviewed every 6 months in accordance with a pre-announced publication calendar

CRAs are required to establish a review function, responsible for reviewing rating methodologies and models and reporting to the independent board members

Rating methodologies used by CRAs must be rigorous, systematic, continuous, and subject to validation based on historical experience, including back-testing. ESMA has the power to verify that this is the case. Any changes to methodologies must be sent out for public consultation for at least 1 month and provided to ESMA before being implemented

Increasing CRA Transparency

CRAs must publish an annual transparency report to include information on the agency's legal structure and ownership, and a description of the internal control mechanisms ensuring quality of their ratings. CRAs must also publish information about their procedures, methodologies, models, and assumptions, as well as disclose actual and potential conflicts of interest

CRAs must provide ESMA with rating performance data, which can be used to compute transition rates and default rates, and which is made accessible to the public by ESMA

Table 4.1 (continued)

When issuing credit ratings, CRAs must explain in press releases or reports the key elements underlying the credit rating and make various disclosures with regard to the rating, including the methodology used and whether the rating was disclosed to the rated entity and subsequently amended prior to publication. CRAs must also provide rated entities with at least one day's advance notice of the rating and rating rationale

CRAs must identify unsolicited ratings and state when issuing such ratings whether or not the rated entity participated in the rating process and whether the CRA had access to the accounts and other relevant internal documents of the rated entity

CRAs have additional obligations in relation to structured finance ratings, including a requirement to inform investors about the loss and cash-flow analysis it has performed

Strengthening accountability through the right of redress

New rules approved in 2013 introduced civil liability of CRAs into EU legislation for the first time. Investors and rated entities are now able to hold CRAs liable for damages caused by an infringement of the EU regulation which impacted a rating action (for example a downgrade), regardless of whether a contractual relationship exists between the parties. (Time will tell whether this change will result in huge legal cost for registered CRAs or deter new CRAs from entering the market) plicitly ruled out official interference in rating methodologies, but subsequent legislation has undermined this principle by providing ESMA with extensive powers to police compliance with methodological requirements, which could potentially be used to judge a methodology. In addition, the third regulation sets out a minimum number of variables that CRAs must describe in sovereign rating reports, regardless of whether these factors are deemed by the CRA to be relevant. Such factors include GDP growth and inflation, but strangely not government debt.

4.7.5 The Need for Greater Choice and Competition in the Credit Rating Market

While increasing choice and competition in the credit rating market is among the stated aims of EU regulatory initiatives, current legal provisions go only a small way towards reducing the market dominance of the three largest agencies and alleviating the concentration risk that can have systemic implications for the financial system. Nevertheless, two of these small steps are particularly important.

Firstly, the CRA regulation requires issuers who intend to appoint at least two CRAs for a particular rating assignment to consider appointing at least one rating agency that has a market share of less than 10%.

Secondly, under the new Capital Requirements Regulation—and in contrast to previous capital rules—all EU-registered CRAs are automatically recognised as ECAIs and their credit ratings are mapped to risk weights (via credit quality steps) by the EBA. The aim is of this 'automatic' recognition process is to open the ECAI market to CRAs other than the three largest.

Stronger measures have been considered, but not yet adopted. For example, the introduction of a rotation rule that would force corporate issuers to switch periodically to a different CRA has been proposed by the European Commission, but so far rules on the maximum duration of contractual relationships between rated entities and CRAs only apply in the highly specialised area of re-securitisations (the limit is 4 years).

4.8 Conclusion

CRAs play an important role in banking and capital markets, perhaps most significantly by mitigating informational asymmetries between investors and issuers. The use of ratings by regulators has, however, shifted perceptions of ratings from an opinion of the credit risk of a rated entity or financial obligation to a semi-official stamp of approval. Regulatory usage has cemented the market dominance of a few CRAs and encouraged overreliance on ratings by users.

Ongoing efforts to end the mechanistic reliance on ratings should help to reduce the potential systemic risk associated with investor "herding" or "cliff effects", as well as to unlock competition in the market for credit risk analysis.

Credit ratings should not be prohibited or replaced by another automatic indicator. Rather, ratings should be among a variety of indicators of creditworthiness available to regulators and market participants. As ratings are one of the more stable, reliable, comparable and economically available measures of credit risk, limitations on their use should be proportionate to the size, complexity and risk profile of the investing institution or lender. Ultimately, however, credit ratings should be regarded as an important analytical input into, but are not a substitute for, investors' own credit risk assessments.

External oversight of CRAs is now stronger than at any time in history, particularly in the EU. Tough regulations combined with the efforts of many CRAs to strengthen internal controls and enhance the quality of methodologies is helping to restore confidence in the industry following the well-documented failings of the largest CRAs in the run-up to the global financial crisis and to increase trust in the ratings issued.

The next challenge is to open up the ratings industry to more competition, to create a level playing field where rating agencies operate under the same conditions. Greater competition and a diversity of rating opinions would offer the prospect of better quality ratings and a reduction in conflicts of interest.

Given the enormous changes in the regulatory landscape over the past 5 years, which CRAs, supervisors and financial institutions are still adapting to, it is essential that future legislative initiatives are truly justifiable and appropriate to the risk posed and that risk of over-regulation in the credit rating sphere is avoided.

References

Basel Committee on Banking Supervision (2009): Stocktaking on the Use of Credit Ratings, June 2009.
EBA Banking Stakeholder Group (2014): Response to the Consultation Paper (JC/CP/2014/01) of EBA, ESMA and EIOPA on the Draft Implementing Technical Standards on the mapping of ECAIs' credit assessments under Article 136(1) and (3) of Regulation (EU) No 575/2013 (Capital Requirements Regulation), June 2014.
ECB (2014): Response to Financial Stability Board (FSB) request for action plans for reducing reliance on Credit Rating Agency (CRA) ratings
European Commission (2006): Press Release, Internal Market: Commission sets out its policy on credit rating agencies European Commission—IP/06/8 09/01/2006
Financial Stability Board (2014): Thematic Review on FSB Principles for Reducing Reliance on CRA Ratings Peer Review Report, May 2014

Zafer Diab ist seit Dezember 2007 Geschäftsführer der Capital Intelligence (www.ciratings.com), einer EU-registrierten Ratingagentur (www.esma.europa.eu). Von 2002 bis 2007 war Diab in verschiedenen Führungspositionen innerhalb von Capital Intelligence tätig, so als Business Development Manager und als Senior Credit Analyst. Diab hat einen Bachelor of Science Degree in Computerwissenschaften der Baylor University sowie einen Abschluss als Master of Business Administration mit dem Schwerpunkt Finanzierung von der Lebanese Amercian University.berd.

Staatsschuldenkrise und europäisches Bankensystem: Deutschland vs. Spanien

Johannes-Jörg Riegler, Tobias Basse und Christoph Wegener

5.1 Vor der Krise: Der Euro führt zu Konvergenz bei den Staatsanleiherenditen

Die Schaffung der neuen europäischen Einheitswährung hatte natürlich Implikationen für die Staatsanleihenmärkte in der Euro-Zone; das Wechselkursänderungsrisiko war nämlich nicht mehr von Relevanz für Anleger, die in Euro denominierte Obligationen anderer Mitgliedsländer investieren wollten. Das Kreditrisiko der Staaten stand vor der aktuellen Krise mit dem Schuldenschnitt Athens zudem kaum im Blick der Märkte. Eine etwas differenzierte Sichtweise der Dinge vertreten an dieser Stelle zwar Geyer et al. (2004), diese Einschätzung kann vor der aktuellen Krise jedoch kaum als herrschende Meinung gelten. Bevor es in Griechenland zum Credit Event kam, wurden Risiken eines Zahlungsausfalles von Staaten in der Tat eher den Kontinenten Südamerika (z. B. Argentinien) oder Afrika (z. B. Elfenbeinküste) zugeordnet oder – mit Blick auf die Industrienationen Europas – aus einem historischen Blickwinkel heraus analysiert (vgl. hierzu vor allem Reinhart und Rogoff 2009 sowie hinsichtlich der historischen Erfahrungen in Europa Dincecco 2009). Reinhart (2002) betont entsprechend die besondere Bedeutung des Ratings von Staaten für die Emerging Markets und sieht weniger Einfluss auf entwickelte Märkte. Damals hat-

J.-J. Riegler (✉)
München, Deutschland
E-Mail: Johannes.Riegler@bayernlb.de

T. Basse · C. Wegener
Hannover, Deutschland
E-Mail: Tobias.Basse@nordlb.de

C. Wegener
E-Mail: cw@kvw-hannover.de

© Springer Fachmedien Wiesbaden 2016
Z. Diab, O. Everling (Hrsg.), *Rating von Finanzinstituten*,
DOI 10.1007/978-3-658-04195-3_5

te der Faktor Sovereign Credit Risk für Industrienationen noch keine größere Relevanz. Dies begann sich erst mit der Krise in Griechenland zu ändern (vgl. Gruppe und Basse 2012). Insofern zeigten sich mit der Einführung der Einheitswährung bei den Zinsen der Staatsanleihen der Mitgliedsländer der Europäischen Wirtschafts- und Währungsunion (EWWU) zunächst klare und nicht zu übersehende Konvergenztendenzen. Lund (1999) zeigt beispielsweise, dass der Rentenmarkt schon 1995 begonnen hatte, die Mitgliedschaft Frankreichs und der Benelux-Staaten einzupreisen, während mit Blick auf Spanien und Portugal noch länger größere Zweifel existiert zu haben scheinen.

5.2   Die Krise löst Verwerfungen am Markt für Staatsanleihen Eurolands aus

Die europäische Staatsschuldenkrise löste dann aber offensichtliche Verwerfungen aus. Diese führten dazu, dass der Faktor Sovereign Credit Risk auch am Markt für die Staatsanleihen der EWU-Mitgliedsländern klar an Bedeutung gewonnen hat. Griechenland musste zunächst von den anderen Mitgliedsländern gestützt werden und hat dann, wie bereits angedeutet, sogar Rückgriff auf offensivere Maßnahmen zur Behebung seiner fiskalischen Probleme genommen. Der Schuldenschnitt in Athen hat den Investoren die Relevanz des Kreditausfallrisikos von Staaten ganz klar vor Augen geführt. Unabhängig von der Laufzeit der Papiere erhielten die Gläubiger für eine Nominale von 100 EUR in alten griechischen Staatsanleihen nur 15 EUR in EFSF-Papieren mit kurzer Laufzeit und 3150 EUR in neuen griechischen Staatsanleihen mit langen Laufzeiten sowie einen an die Wachstumsentwicklung des Landes gekoppelten Besserungsschein (vgl. zum Beispiel Xafa 2013: Waibel 2014). Investoren, die am Schuldenschnitt nicht freiwillig teilnehmen wollten, wurden mittels erst nachträglich eingeführter Collective Actions Clauses – trotz rechtlicher Bedenken (zum Beispiel aufgrund der Umbrella-Klauseln in von Griechenland abgeschlossenen bilateralen Investitionsschutzverträgen) – zur Partizipation gezwungen. Dabei war es nicht möglich, die Aktivierung der Credit Default Swaps zu verhindern (vgl. Waibel 2014). Die Charakteristika der neuen, nach ausländischem Recht begebenen griechischen Staatsanleihen diskutiert beispielsweise Simmons (2013) sehr detailliert. Mit Blick auf die Frage der Markteffizienz ist interessant, dass Sorgen um die griechischen Staatsfinanzen die Risikoprämie des Landes bereits vor dem Schuldenschnitt – um nicht zu sagen sehr frühzeitig – auf ein hohes Niveau hatte steigen lassen.

Dieses veränderte Umfeld mit Blick auf die Einschätzung des Risikos von Investments in Staatsanleihen hatte auch Implikationen für einige andere Länder der Euro-Zone. Die wachsende Furcht vor einem mögliches Auseinanderbrechen der Währungsunion führte am Markt sogar zu recht ausgeprägten Sorgen bezüglich des Vorhandenseins von Redenomination Risk (vgl. Sibbertsen et al. 2014); zudem rückt das Kreditrisiko der EWWU-Staaten nach Athens Schuldenschnitt immer stärker in den Fokus. Das Anziehen der Umlaufrenditen für Staatsanleihen erhöhte die Refinanzierungskosten der Krisenländer und verschärfte die Staatsschuldenkrise somit sogar noch weiter. Insofern erstaunt es natürlich nicht wirklich, dass auch andere Peripherieländer Schwierigkeiten hatten, zumal der Rentenmarkt sich bereits sehr zeitnahe um Griechenland sorgte. Die Refinanzierung der Krisenländer wurde in immer stärkerem Maße zum Problem. Irland musste bereits im Jahr 2010 und Portugal 2011 Mittel aus der zeitlich befristeten Europäischen Finanzstabilisierungsfazilität (EFSF) in Anspruch nehmen. Spanien beantragte 2012 für die Rekapitalisierung seiner Banken Hilfsmittel aus dem Europäischen Stabilitätsmechanismus (ESM), 2013 folgte dann Zypern. Einen guten Überblick geben Moro (2013): Lane (2012).

Das ökonomische Schwergewicht Spanien ist ein gutes Beispiel für das Problem. Das Platzen der Immobilienpreisblase des Landes führte zu massiven realwirtschaftlichen Auswirkungen, was unter anderem einen Anstieg der Arbeitslosenquote von 8,5 % (2007) auf über 25 % (2013) zur Folge hatte. Die spanische Volkswirtschaft ist mit der Krise in die Rezession geraten. Entsprechend zeigte sich ein Zulegen der staatlichen Schuldenstandsquote von 36,3 % in 2007 auf 86,0 % im Jahr 2012 (gemessen am BIP). Zudem brachte die Zunahme notleidender Kredite spanische Banken verstärkt in Bedrängnis und dämpfte die Kreditvergabe – somit zeigt sich eine Art Teufelskreis; die ökonomischen Probleme erhöhten die Sorgen des Rentenmarktes nämlich zusätzlich und erschwerten die Finanzierung des Königreiches Spanien somit noch weiter. Abbildung 5.1, 5.2, 5.3, 5.4, 5.5, 5.6 geben einen Überblick über das herausfordernde makroökonomische Umfeld in Spanien.

Basse et al. (2012) weisen unter Nutzung von Techniken der Kointegrationsanalyse Strukturbrüche im Zusammenhang zwischen den Renditen deutscher und italienischer Staatsanleihen nach und argumentieren, dass die Veränderungen auf die Krise zurückzuführen sind. Gruppe und Lange (2013) präsentieren ähnliche Ergebnisse für Spanien.

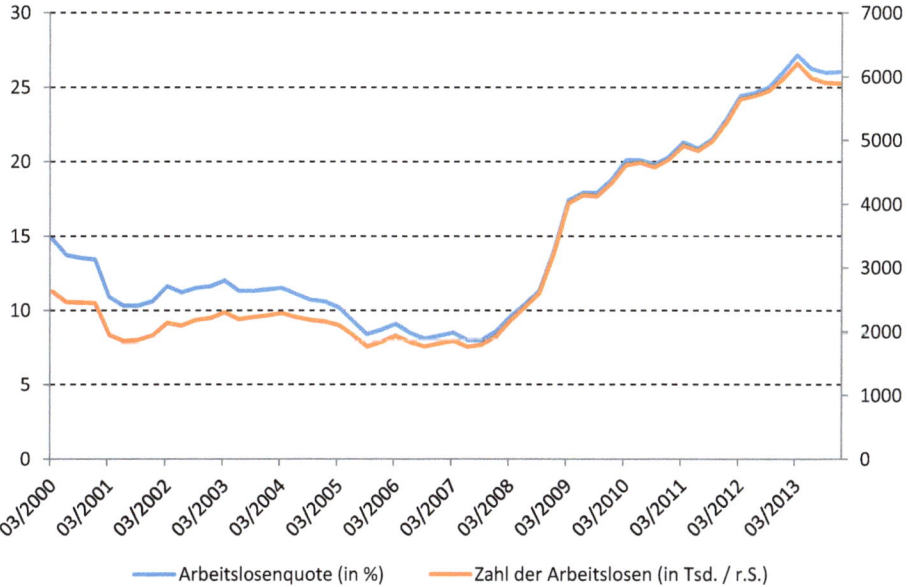

Abb. 5.1 Krise am spanischen Arbeitsmarkt. (Quelle: Instituto Nacional de Estadistica)

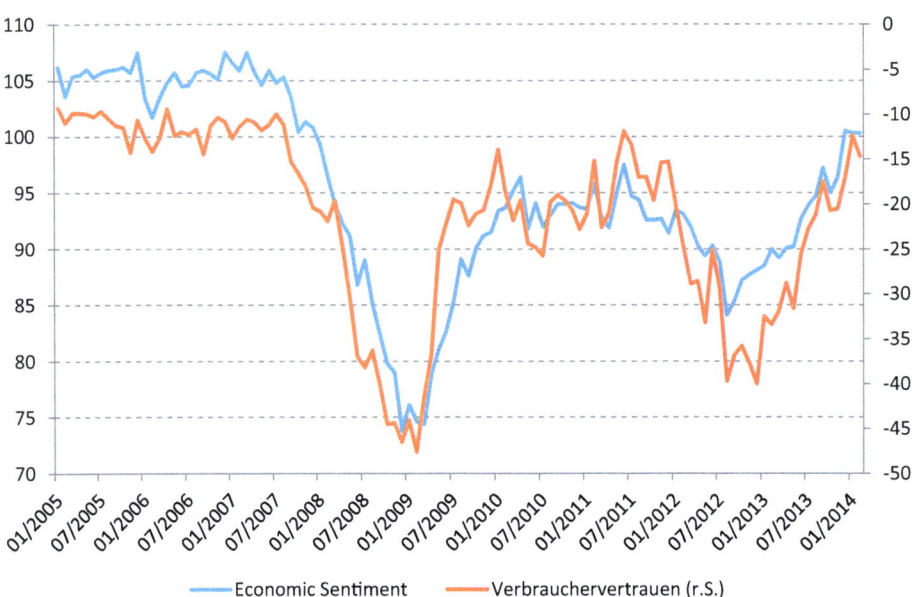

Abb. 5.2 Spanische Stimmungsindikatoren. (Quelle: EU Kommission)

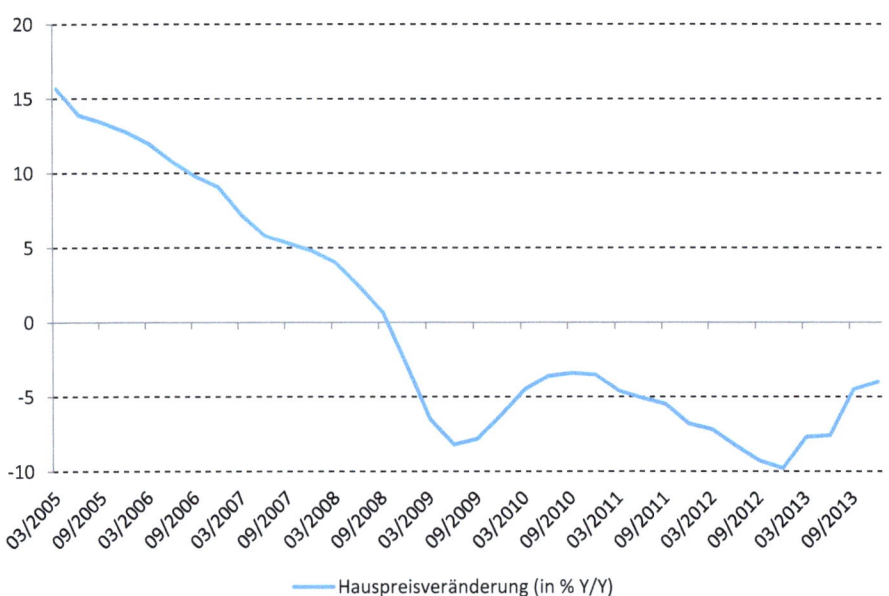

Abb. 5.3 Hauspreise in Spanien unter Druck. (Quelle: Instituto Nacional de Estadistica)

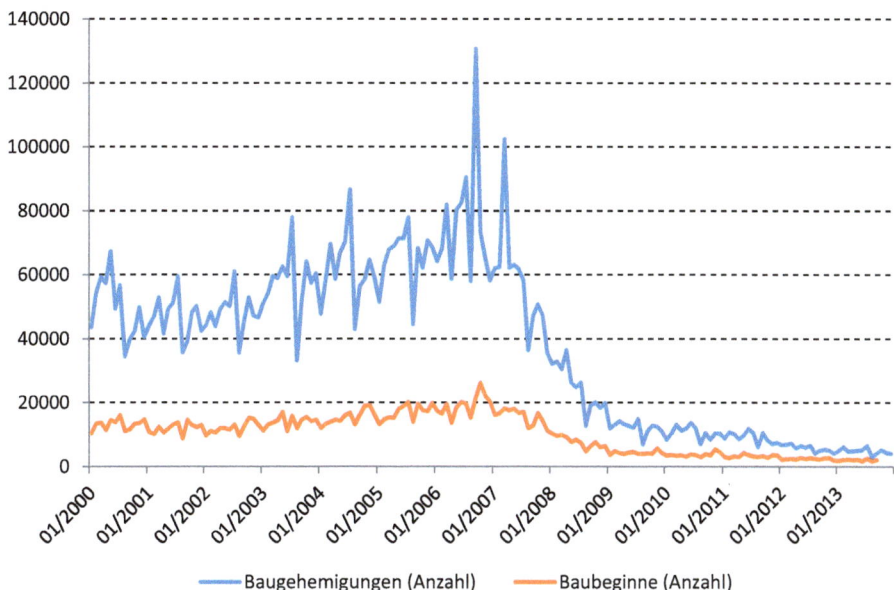

Abb. 5.4 Spanische Bauaktivität leidet. (Quelle: Ministerio de Fomento)

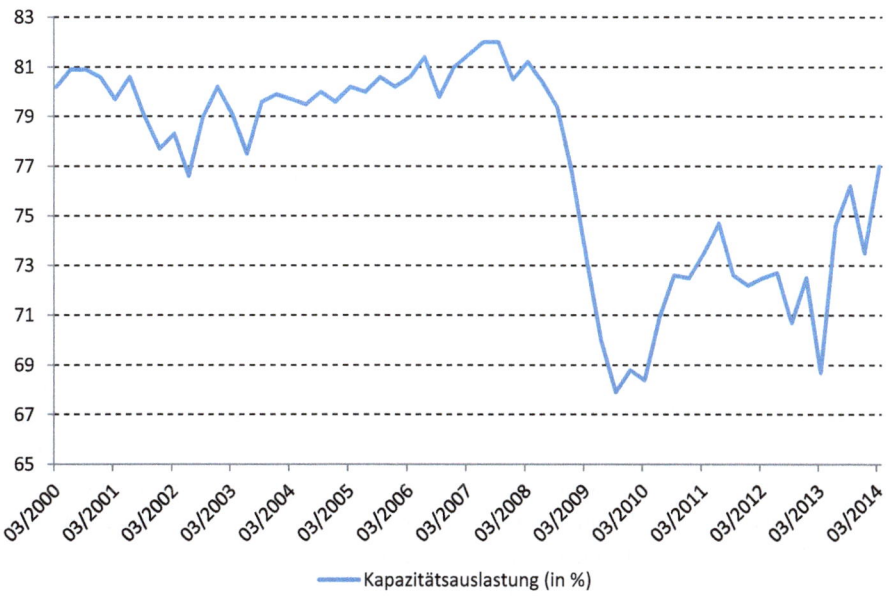

Abb. 5.5 Krise lässt Kapazitätsauslastung fallen. (Quelle: Eurostat)

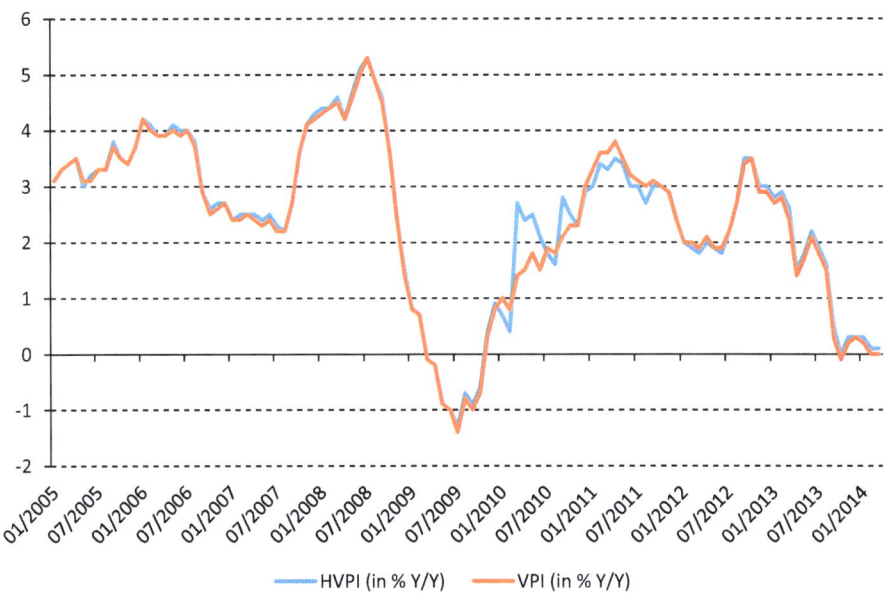

Abb. 5.6 Inflation in Spanien auf dem Rückmarsch. (Quelle: Instituto Nacional de Estadistica)

Diese akademischen Studien haben eine hohe Bedeutung für die Finanzmärkte – die große Wichtigkeit der empirischen Analyse der Zusammenhänge an den Rentenmärkten betonen beispielsweise Abad et al. (2010). Inzwischen liegen einige weitere Studien vor, die in diesem Kontext Testverfahren zur Suche nach strukturellen Veränderungen in den Zusammenhängen nutzen (vgl. zum Beispiel Basse 2013; Sibbertsen et al. 2014 sowie Gómez-Puig und Sosvilla-Rivero 2014). Interessant ist dabei auch eine Untersuchung von Kunze und Gruppe (2014), in welcher mit entsprechenden Methoden Auswirkungen auf die Zinsprognosen von Bankenvolkswirten analysiert werden.

In der Summe scheinen sich damit also klare Signale für eine veränderte Bewertung des Ausfallrisikos von EWWU-Problemstaaten ergeben zu haben. Mit der Krise koinzidierende Strukturbrüche im Spread der Renditen zu deutschen Bundesanleihen sind nämlich in der Tat ein Hinweis für eine veränderte Risikoeinschätzung durch die Marktteilnehmer. Dies deutet auf Veränderungen des Sovereign Credit Risks und eventuell sogar auf Redenomination Risk hin (vgl. z. B. Basse 2013 und Sibbertsen et al. 2014). Abbildung 5.7 illustriert die veränderte Risikoeinschätzung am Markt für EWWU-Staatsanleihen.

Mittlerweile gibt es allerdings schon wieder gewisse Beruhigungstendenzen an den Märkten für EWWU-Staatsanleihen (niedrigere Spreads, Primärüberschuss im griechischen Staatshaushalt). Die Maßnahmen der EZB haben ganz offensichtlich zumindest Zeit erkauft (Liquidität, „Draghi-Put"). Zudem scheinen die Reformen in den Problemländern langsam zu greifen (verbesserte Wettbewerbsfähigkeit, mehr Steuergerechtigkeit, etc.). Der Reformeifer in den Krisenstaaten darf nun aber keinesfalls nachlassen.

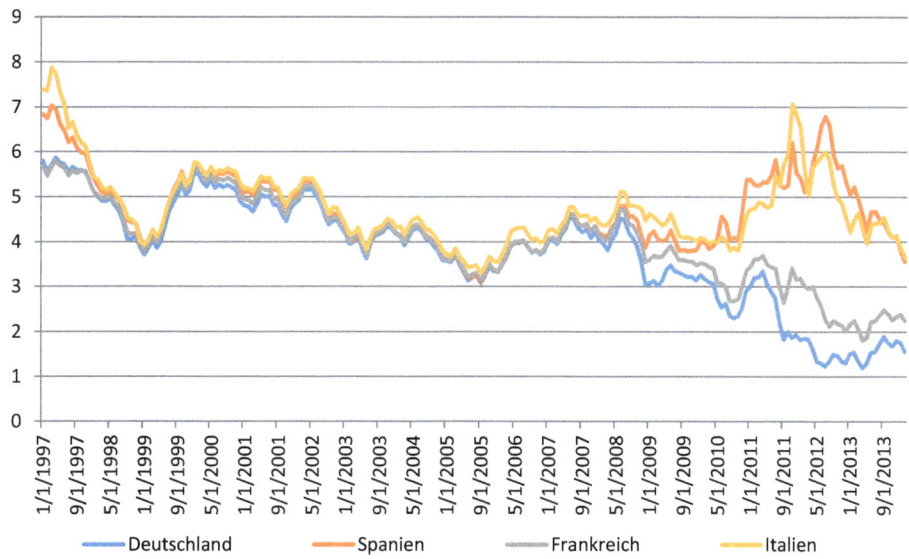

Abb. 5.7 Langfristige Staatsanleiherenditen. (10 J, Quelle: IWF)

5.3   Implikationen für den Bankensektor

Staatsanleihen haben eine hervorgehobene Bedeutung für den Finanzmarkt. Marktbeobachter unterstellen besondere Belastungen für Banken in den Staaten mit Schuldenproblemen. Die Deutsche Bundesbank (2013) fordert auch aufgrund dieser Erfahrungen eine stärkere Entkopplung der Banken vom Staatsanleihenmarkt.

An dieser Stelle wollen wir einen Blick auf den Bankenmarkt (Abb. 5.8) werfen und errechnen die rollierende Renditekorrelation zwischen deutschen und spanischen Banken (jeweils Aktiensektorindizes Total Return). Die rollierende Korrelation (errechnet auf der Basis von jeweils 30 Datenpunkten) ist generell hoch. Es gibt also einen recht ausgeprägten positiven Zusammenhang zwischen den Bankaktien in beiden Ländern, der Korrelationskoeffizient ist aber doch erheblichen Veränderungen im Zeitablauf unterworfen. Er ist ab 2007 zwischenzeitlich geringer (teilweise unter 0,6) und seit 2009 offenbar generell niedriger.

Die Bewegungen der Korrelation lassen sich erklären und interpretieren: Krisen lösen eindeutig Veränderungen von Zusammenhängen aus. Es kann sich hierbei zum Beispiel um Störungen durch veränderte Verhaltensweisen der Marktteilnehmer handeln. Spanische Banken waren weniger stark in US-Hypothekenpapieren investiert, was mit Blick auf die Subprime-Krise half. Die starke Abwärtsbewegung in 2007 war bei den deutschen Banken entsprechen ausgeprägter und die folgende Erholung bei den spanischen Instituten stärker. Dies kann den niedrigeren Korrelationskoeffizienten um das Jahr 2007 herum erklären. Im weiteren Verlauf bekamen die spanischen Banken zunehmend Probleme mit dem heimischen Immobilienmarkt und in der weiteren Folge mit den hohen Exposures in

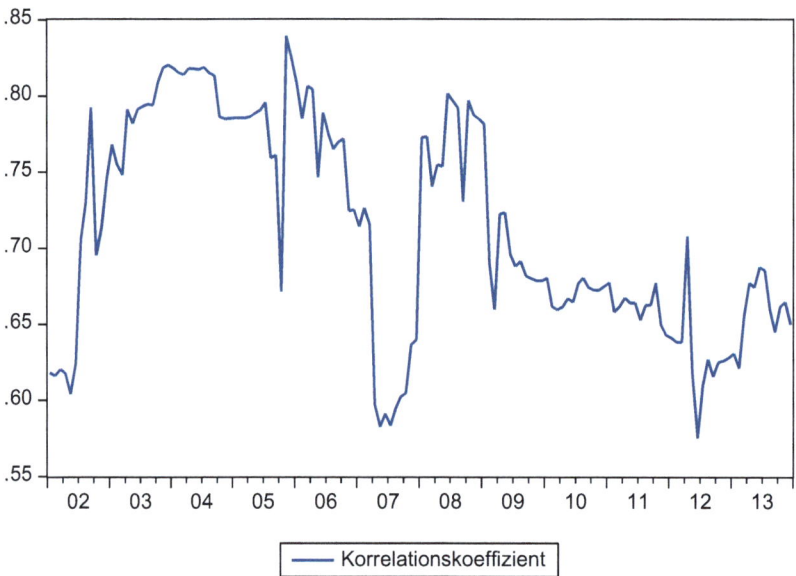

Abb. 5.8 Rollierende Renditekorrelation deutsche und spanische Banken. (Quelle: NORD/LB Research/Volkswirtschaft)

spanischen Staatsanleihen. Hier zeichneten sich für deutsche Banken bereits relative Erholungstendenzen ab. Dieses Faktum kann natürlich die niedrigere Korrelation ab 2009 erklären.

5.4   Staatsschuldenkrise und Auswirkungen auf das Risikomanagement von Banken

Banken sind wichtige Spieler bei der Staatsfinanzierung. Insofern hat das Länderrating eine hohe Bedeutung für den Bankensektor. Im Rahmen des Länderratings muss es in den verantwortlichen Einheiten der Banken zu einer Einschätzung des Transfer- sowie des Staatsausfallrisikos in Fremd- und Eigenwährung und zur Berechnung der Ausfallwahrscheinlichkeit kommen. Relevante Indikatoren sind in diesem Zusammenhang zum Beispiel der Leistungsbilanzsaldo, die Außenverschuldung, das Niveau der Währungsreserven, die Staatsverschuldung und das Haushaltsdefizit. Zentral ist dabei die Größe LGD (Verlustquote). Eine wichtige Frage ist in diesem Kontext natürlich, wie hoch der erwartete Verlust für ein Institut bei Ausfall eines Landes in Relation zum ausstehenden Finanzierungsbetrag wäre.

Auf der Basis von Länderrating und LGD sollte die Berechnung des strategischen Länderlimits erfolgen. Dieses Limit begrenzt die Risiken im Auslandsgeschäft. Alle Geschäfte mit staatlichen und nichtstaatlichen Kunden der Länder werden hierauf angerechnet. Die quartalsmäßige Auslastungsrechnung zeigt frühzeitig Konzentrationsrisiken im Länder-bereich an. Prozesse bei Limitüberschreitungen sind a priori zu definieren. Maßnahmen werden dann eingeleitet, um das Konzentrationsrisiko bei Bedarf in angemessenem Umfang zurückzuführen (zum Beispiel Abbau von Exposure, Kürzung von operativen Limits für Einzeladressen durch das Kreditrisikomanagement).

Ein gutes Risikomanagement hat natürlich frühzeitig Konsequenzen aus der Krise ziehen müssen. Eine geeignete Strategie musste in diesem Kontext auf einer differenzierten Risikobetrachtung aller EU-Länder beruhen. Wichtig war dabei vor allem, zeitnahe eine Neubewertung des Geschäftspotenzials vorzunehmen, wobei aufgrund der engen Verknüpfung zwischen Banken und Staaten nicht nur auf die direkten Risiken der Staatsfinanzierung fokussiert werden durfte (zum Beispiel durch gekürzte Länderlimite und Abbau von Staatsanleihen/Interbankengeschäften in risikoreichen Ländern, Laufzeitbegrenzung dieser Geschäfte in risikoärmeren Ländern). Mit den sich nun abzeichnenden langsamen Entspannungstendenzen am Markt für EWWU-Staatsanleihen sind die neuen Strategien zum Umgang mit Sovereign Credit Risk sinnvoll weiterzuentwickeln.

5.5   Fazit

Hinsichtlich der noch immer zumindest schwelenden Staatsschuldenkrise in Europa bleibt festzuhalten, dass mit Blick auf die Größe Sovereign Credit Risk bekannte und früher stabile Zusammenhänge eindeutig in Bewegung geraten sind. Vor der aktuellen Krise stand das Ausfallrisiko von Staaten nicht sonderlich stark im Fokus. Nun hat sich das Umfeld verändert. In der Tat liegen inzwischen eine Reihe von empirische Studien vor, die die Relevanz von Sovereign Credit Risk nun auch für einige Staaten Eurolands belegen. Diese veränderte Lage ist von zentraler Bedeutung für die Finanzmärkte im Allgemeinen und das Bankwesen im Speziellen. Die Krise hat am Rentenmarkt insbesondere eine ausgeprägte Veränderung der Wahrnehmung des Kreditausfallrisikos von EWWU-Staaten bewirkt. Dieses Faktum schafft große Herausforderungen für das Risikomanagement der Investoren in Staatsanleihen – und damit natürlich auch (um nicht zu sagen vor allem) in den Banken. In einem durch große Verunsicherungen geprägten Umfeld hat das Risikomanagement teilweise ad hoc reagieren müssen, da die Modelle zunächst neu zu kalibrieren waren. Die Weiterentwicklung der Modelle ist nun von zentraler Bedeutung. Hier bietet sich noch ein weites Feld für die Zusammenarbeit von Theorie und Praxis des Risikomanagements.

Literatur

Abad, P., Chuliá, H. & Gómez-Puig, M. (2010), EMU and European government bond market integration. Journal of Banking and Finance 34, 2851–2860.

Basse, T. (2014), Searching for the EMU core member countries. European Journal of Political Economy, 34, 32–S39.

Basse, T., Friedrich, M. & Kleffner, A. (2012), Italian government debt and sovereign credit risk: an empirical exploration and some thoughts about consequences for European insurers. Zeitschrift für die gesamte Versicherungswissenschaft 101, 571–579.

Deutsche Bundesbank (2013), Geldpolitik und Bankgeschäft, Monatsbericht November 65, 25–60.

Dincecco, M. (2009), Political regimes and sovereign credit risk in Europe, 1750–1913, European Review of Economic History 13, 31–63.

Geigant, F. (2002), Stationen und Strukturen: Europas Weg zum Europa, Cunz, R. (Hrsg.): Währungsunionen, Hamburg.

Geyer, A., Kossmeier, S. & Pichler, S. (2004), Measuring systematic risk in EMU government yield spreads. Review of Finance 8, 171–197.

Gómez-Puig, M. & Sosvilla-Rivero, S. (2014), Causality and contagion in EMU sovereign debt markets, International Review of Economics & Finance (in press).

Gruppe, M. & Basse, T. (2012), Die Griechenlandkrise – Credit Risk jetzt auch am europäischen Staatsanleihenmarkt?, in: Schwarzbach, C. et al. (Hrsg.): Die Folgen der Finanzkrise für Regulierung und Eigenkapital – Evolution oder Revolution in der Versicherungsbranche?, Karlsruhe.

Gruppe, M. & Lange, C. (2014), Spain and the European sovereign debt crisis, European Journal of Political Economy, 34, 3–S8.

Kunze, F. & Gruppe, M. (2014), Performance of Survey Forecasts by Professional Analysts: Did the European Debt Crisis Make it Harder or Perhaps Even Easier?, Social Sciences 3, 128–139.

Lane, P. R. (2012), The European Sovereign Debt Crisis, Journal of Economic Perspectives 26, 49–68.

Lund, J. (1999), A model for studying the effect of EMU on European yield curves. European Finance Review 2, 321–363.

Moro, B. (2014), Lessons from the European economic and financial great crisis: A survey, European Journal of Political Economy, 34, 9–S24.

Reinhart, C. M. (2002), Default, Currency Crises, and Sovereign Credit Ratings, World Bank Economic Review 16, 151–170.

Reinhart, C. M. & Rogoff, K. (2009), This time is different: Eight centuries of financial folly. Princeton University Press, Princeton et al.

Sibbertsen, P., Wegener, C. & Basse, T. (2014), Testing for a Break in the Persistence in Yield Spreads of EMU Government Bonds, Journal of Banking and Finance 41, p. 109–118.

Simmons, T. (2013), The new Greek bonds: more than meets the eye, Capital Markets Law Journal 8, p. 319–332.

Waibel, M. (2014), Steering sovereign debt restructurings through the CDS quicksand, Journal of Banking Regulation 15, p. 14–40.

Xafa, M. (2013), Life after Debt – The Greek PSI and its aftermath, World Economics 14, p. 81–102.

Dr. Johannes-Jörg Riegler ist seit dem 1. April 2014 Vorsitzender des Vorstandes der BayernLB. Er hat Rechtswissenschaften studiert und begann seine berufliche Laufbahn bei Kanzleien in Deutschland und den USA. Im Jahr 1993 wechselte er zur Deutschen Bank, wo er über einen Zeitraum von zehn Jahren verschiedene Fach- und Führungsaufgaben im In- und Ausland ausübte. Seine Dissertation in Würzburg absolvierte Herr Dr. Riegler in dieser Zeit berufsbegleitend, ebenso wie den Master of Business Administration (MBA) in London und den Lehrgang zum Fachanwalt für Insolvenzrecht. Im Jahr 2003 übernahm Herr Dr. Riegler die Position des Chief Risk Officer (CRO) bei der Westfalenbank (HVB-Gruppe), in deren Vorstand er im Folgejahr eintrat. 2005 wurde Herr Dr. Riegler ebenfalls als CRO in den Vorstand der NordLB in Hannover berufen. Vom 1. Januar 2013 bis zu seinem Wechsel zur BayernLB war Herr Dr. Riegler bei der Nord LB zudem stellvertretender Vorstandsvorsitzender. Am 1. März 2014 wechselte er in den Vorstand der BayernLB und übernahm zum 1. April 2014 den Vorstandsvorsitz.

Tobias Basse arbeitet seit 2001 in verschiedenen Positionen als Analyst und Volkswirt bei der Norddeutschen Landesbank (NORD/LB) in Hannover und lehrt zudem Corporate Finance am Touro College Berlin. Er hat BWL und VWL in Hannover und Paderborn studiert.

Christoph Wegener, Jahrgang 1986, schloss 2012 sein Studium der Wirtschaftswissenschaften an der Leibniz Universität Hannover ab und begann parallel zu einem Traineeprogramm bei der Norddeutschen Landesbank seine Promotion am Institut für Statistik der Leibniz Universität Hannover bei Professor Philipp Sibbertsen. Im Anschluss an das Traineeprogramm arbeitet Herr Wegener als Analyst in der volkswirtschaftlichen Abteilung der NORD/LB und befasste sich dort mit Modellierungsfragen im Zuge des EZB-Stresstests 2014. Seit Promotionsbeginn forscht er mithilfe der Zeitreihenökonometrie auf dem Gebiet der Finanzwissenschaften. Insbesondere interessieren ihn hier strukturelle Veränderungen im Zuge Finanzmarktkrise und die Implikationen für die Finanz- und Versicherungswirtschaft. Seit Oktober 2014 ist Herr Wegener wissenschaftlicher Mitarbeiter am Kompetenzzentrum Versicherungswissenschaften Hannover.

A Changing Regulatory and Political Environment: What Impact Does it Have on the Analysis of a Financial Institution?

6

Götz Schürmann

6.1 Introduction

About 5 years ago, the way we looked at Financial Institutions, particularly banks, changed abruptly. Until then, the likelihood that a major investment grade rated bank would default and file for bankruptcy within a short period of time was considered extremely low, at a rate of less than 0.5 % within a 12 months period.

The Lehman Case: As we are all aware, Lehman Brothers Holdings Inc. (Lehman) was a well performing, fast growing investment bank (2007 was its fourth consecutive record year). It held a strong franchise and a global reach, conducting investment banking activities not only in the US but also expanding in Europe, the Middle East and Asia … until it filed for bankruptcy on September 15th 2008. This was a major shock for both the financial markets and its participants. A mere 3 months earlier in early June 2008, the Rating Agencies took only minor rating actions downgrading Lehman one notch from 'AA−' to 'A+' with a 'Negative' Outlook (Fitch), from 'A+' to 'A' with a 'Negative' Outlook (S&P's) and affirming the 'A1' rating, but lowering the Outlook to 'Negative' (Moody's). One month later, FitchRatings affirmed the 'A+' long-term issuer Default Ratings and the Individual Rating of B/C of Lehman and its subsidiaries (s. FitchRatings 2008). It also maintained the 'Negative' Outlook. These sound Investment grade ratings indicated a robust bank with an extremely low probability of default. At that time, the equivalent Siemens Financial Services (SFS)-Rating reflected a 5 year Average Cumulative Default Rate of slightly less than 1 %, and only 0.08 % for the 1 year horizon.

G. Schürmann (✉)
München, Deutschland
e-mail: goetz.schuermann@siemens.com

© Springer Fachmedien Wiesbaden 2016
Z. Diab, O. Everling (Hrsg.), *Rating von Finanzinstituten*,
DOI 10.1007/978-3-658-04195-3_6

With the emergence of the financial market crisis in the middle of 2007, which crystallized in increased tightening of market liquidity, rating agencies underlined the growing risk for Lehman—but were of the opinion that the investment firm maintained the necessary liquidity and a solid funding profile to help it weather near-term headwinds. That the financial system was under stress for some months and that the problems banks faced were severe could be seen at Bear Stearns, whose liquidity problems escalated. Nevertheless, Lehman was regarded as one of the top financial institutions in terms of risk management, and was considered able to adequately handle its market and liquidity risks, respectively.

In hindsight, all three agencies highlighted the appropriate risks for Lehman: declining financial flexibility, an inability to reduce exposure to high risk assets through sales or effective hedges, and a lack of investor appetite for additional exposure to financial institutions.

What was not apparent at that time, however, was that Lehman made use of "accounting flexibility" to temporarily remove securities from its balance sheet, rendering it impossible for rating analysts to determine the exact extent of risky assets held by the bank.

Will new regulation prevent such a default in the future and enable analysts to be better equipped in predicting a financial institution's fiscal troubles?

6.2   Regulatory Changes

In the aftermath of the crises, various authorities have developed new regulations designed to avoid further meltdown of financial systems worldwide. Some regulatory changes have already been adopted, while some are due to be implemented in the coming years. Others, meanwhile, have been proposed and are currently still under discussion (s. e.g. IMF Working Paper 2014).

Increasing the stand-alone financial strength of banks—and of important financial institutions in particular—is a central aim of the authorities. Through measures such as higher capital requirements, new liquidity standards and stricter supervision, the risk of one failing financial institution dragging others into a downward spiral that can only be halted by government intervention is thought to be eliminated—or at least substantially reduced. These changes certainly affect the ratings of financial institutions, as they will impact upon their creditworthiness.

Key changes that drive the ratings are explained and discussed in the following:

6.2.1   USA: Dodd-Frank Act

As a consequence of the financial crisis, The Dodd-Frank Wall Street Reform and Consumer Protection Act ("Dodd-Frank Act") was enacted in the US in 2010. It is intended to promote the financial stability of the United States—and therefore avoid bail-outs of failing banks by US-taxpayers—and to protect its consumers. To achieve said stability, "systemic risks" need to be mitigated through stricter oversight by the authorities on the one hand, and require stringent standards, reporting and disclosure requirements on the other.

The higher standards demanded by the Dodd-Frank Act include more prudent risk-based capital and liquidity requirements, as well as leverage limit. The Volker Rule provisions of the Dodd-Frank Act are aimed to avoid speculative activities of banking entities (defined as bank holding companies (BHC), non-US entities treated as BHC, insured depository institutions and affiliates or subsidiaries of them) and prohibit most proprietary trading by US banks and their affiliates, with few exceptions. In addition, the rule restricts Banking entities from owning, sponsoring or investing in hedge funds or private equity funds. Among the permitted activities for banking entities are risk-mitigating hedging activities, which are intended to reduce the risk for the entity. Since July 2015, banking organizations are required to conform with that rule. However, conformity has been extended to 2016 for covered funds and foreign funds that were in place prior to Dec. 2013 (s. Federal Reserve Board 2014).

Dodd-Frank is primarily aimed at the large, interconnected bank holding companies with consolidated assets of more than US$ 50 billion. These institutions are considered systemically important financial institutions (SIFIs). It is the Financial Stability Oversight Council's responsibility to determine those considered to be a SIFI.

In addition, the requirements can also be imposed on Non-Bank Financial Institutions (Sec. 113 of the Dodd-Frank Act) if they are threatened by material financial distress or failure, and therefore pose a risk to the financial stability of the US. These institutions will then be under the supervision of the Federal Reserve. In July and September 2013, the Council voted to designate 3 Non-bank Financial companies as SIFI (American International Group, Inc., GECC, Inc. and Prudential Financial, Inc.) with MetLife, Inc. added in Dec. 2014.

6.2.2   International and UK Regulatory Initiatives

Beyond the US, the Financial Stability Board, a global organization consisting of (among others) national authorities responsible for financial stability and committees of central bank experts, has published an updated list of 30 global systemically important banks (G-SIBs) in Dec. 2014 (s. Attachment 1).

Across the Atlantic, the UK established a new regulatory regime in April 2013, implementing two new regulators, the Prudential Regulatory Authority (PRA) that replaces the Financial Services Authority (FSA), and the Financial Conduct Authority (FCA). One specific aim of the new regulations is to solve the "too-big-to-fail" problem, whereby "the threatened failure of a systemically important financial institution (SIFI)—including non-banks and financial market infrastructures—leaves public authorities with no option but to bail it out to avoid systemic financial instability" (s. Bank of England 2013). In particular, higher capital requirements that are expected to become effective in 2016, and which will increase during a transition period until 2019, will reduce a G-SIB's likelihood of failure and ensuing intervention by the authorities.

Other initiatives, like Denmark's Bank Package III will be discussed later in the section: Likelihood of government support.

6.2.3 Basel III

On a global basis and impacting all banks worldwide, Basel III now sets new, more stringent rules regarding equity and liquidity. Until Jan 2019, capital and liquidity requirements increase during a so called 'phase-in' period.

6.2.3.1 New Basel III Liquidity Standards for Banks

As a consequence of the financial crisis, Basel III proposed internationally harmonized, global liquidity standards, the Liquidity Coverage Ratio (LCR) and the Net Stable Funding Ratio (NSFR).

LCR is defined as:

$$\text{LCR} = \frac{\text{Stock of HQLA}}{\text{Total net cash outflow over the next 30 days}} \geq 100\%$$

HQLA are High Quality Liquid Assets, which must be unencumbered. These assets must be liquid in a market under stress, and the bank must be able to convert them into cash immediately without or only at a small discount.

LCR was introduced in January 2015 with a minimum level of 60%. The ratio will increase each year by an additional 10%, until it eventually reaches 100% in January 2019 (for further details s. Basel Committee on Banking Supervision 2013).

NSFR is defined as:

$$\text{NSFR} = \frac{\text{Available amount of stable funding}}{\text{Required amount of stable funding}} \geq 100\%$$

Available stable funding is defined as the portion of capital and liabilities expected to be reliable over the time horizon, assumed to be 1 year. The required amount is a function of the liquidity characteristics and the residual maturities of the various assets, held by an institution as well as those of off-balance sheet exposures (Basel Committee on Banking Supervision2014).

The Basel III consultation paper on this ratio outlines further details. The complexity of calculating this ratio cannot be overlooked (for details on disclosure requirements see Basel Committee on Banking Supervision 2015). Financial institutions will have to publish these two ratios (NSFR beginning 2018) regularly in their financial statements, thus making them available to rating analysts.

How have these new regulations and requirements impacted the rating approach at Siemens Financial Services? How will they influence future analysis? Will stricter regulations make it easier for an analyst to determine the probability of a Financial Institution's default?

6.2.3.2   New Basel III Capital Requirements for Banks

The new Basel III capital requirements focus on increasing the highest quality component of capital—which is common equity. It is now stipulated that Common Equity Tier 1 needs to be at a minimum 4.5% of risk-weighted assets (compared to 2% previously; for details on the components of capital according to Basel III, s. Basel Committee on Banking Supervision 2011, p. 13). Likewise, Tier 1 Capital needs to be maintained at 6% (up from 4%) of risk-weighted assets at all times. The Total Capital minimum requirement—the sum of Tier 1 Capital plus Tier 2 Capital, also considered as gone-concern capital—will remain unchanged at 8%.

In addition, Basel III introduces a Capital Conservation Buffer. Banks must establish this buffer of 2.5%, using Common Equity Tier 1 only, outside of times of stress and draw on it in the event of an institution making losses. Until this additional buffer has been gradually build up, banks are required to conserve a certain percentage of their earnings in the subsequent financial year. Consequently, dividend payments or share buybacks will be limited in said year.

6.3   Impact of the new Regulatory Environment on SFS's Rating Approach:

Siemens Financial Services has established a specialized and independent rating department that assesses and assigns ratings to all business partners, guarantors or borrowers of SFS, as well as to business partners, customers or suppliers of the Siemens Group. As such, rating methods designed for the analysis of Financial Institutions were developed to evaluate the counterparties of our Treasury (mainly large banks and their subsidiaries), our Trade Finance Advisory Unit (banks in different countries around the globe) and our Commercial Finance/Project and Structured Finance business units (all kinds of Financial Institutions).

To properly assess a Financial Institution and assign the appropriate rating, the analyst must understand the implications of the new regulations. Thus, he/she is required to consider the following:

- To what extent does the enforcement of higher standards protect an institution from insolvency?
- What is the likelihood that a G-SIB or a SIFI will fail in spite of stricter regulations and higher requirements? How will authorities respond in such a situation?
- Do SIFIs automatically deserve a better rating than less important banks that are only required to comply with lower risk-based capital or liquidity requirements, and thus are less protected against unforeseen negative market developments or a deterioration of their asset quality?

- To what extent are specialized subsidiaries of a bank, such as derivative traders outside the US, protected from defaulting through support by their parent company or its authorities, or the local authorities themselves?
- What impact are the new regulations expected to have on independent Hedge Funds?

6.3.1 Financial Institution Analysis: What Did SFS Change in the Most Recent Years?

6.3.1.1 Externally Rated Banks

For banks that are rated by an external rating agency, e.g. Standard & Poor's, Moody's or Fitch, the evaluation begins with a look at the agency's risk assessment and rating outcome. The Senior unsecured Rating (Moody's), the Issuer Credit Rating (S&P's) or the Issuer Default Rating (Fitch) is thereby used as a starting point for the SFS rating. As with all potential or actual borrowers, the analyst will evaluate the bank's business profile and review its risk management, key financial positions and ratios. Since the transparency of how the agencies determine the rating has increased substantially during the last few years, the amount of individual assessment is balanced and focuses on an understanding of the bank's business model (e.g. whether its risk profile is increasing) and the evaluation of the most recent financials and the company's developments that are not addressed by the rating agencies as of yet.

In the past, the final rating by the rating agencies was strongly influenced by expected government support if the stand-alone rating of the financial institution was relatively weaker than the implied support. This approach was applied not only for G-SIBs, but also for domestic financial institutions that were considered to be systemically important in that government's jurisdiction (D-SIFIs). Since the financial crisis and with the enforcement of stricter regulations, the rating agencies have revised their methodologies and a rating uplift has disappeared in many cases. For example, Moody's removed a rating uplift from government support for all US bank holding company debt in November 2013, citing strengthened US bank resolution tools. With regard to large UK bank holding companies, Moody's still assumes some sort of government support resulting in a better rating. For most of the important European banks, Moody's final rating reflects a 1 notch upgrade for government support, while neither S&P's nor Fitch expect government backing, e.g. for Deutsche Bank AG, UniCredit Bank AG or Lloyds Bank plc, in the future.

With the introduction of most of the provisions of the EU Recovery and Resolution Framework for Banks and Investment Firms (Directive 2014/59/EU) in Jan. 2015 – a bail-in mechanism will be imposed beginning 2016 -, the probability of default of a particular instrument rather than the bank itself becomes the center of attention. The question: "What is the probability of default of the bank itself" takes a back seat. Now, the ranking of an instrument within the capital structure of a bank has become more significant. As different instruments could have a different likelihood of default, their ratings will deviate. Senior unsecured bonds have a lower likelihood of being included in a bail-in compared to junior notes. On the other hand, deposits or derivate contracts could get a higher rating uplift from the baseline credit or stand-alone assessment than senior unsecured bonds. As a consequence, the rating methodologies of the 3 major rating agencies have not only been adjusted. They became more complex, but also more transparent. To compare the final rating of the agencies with each other and to use them as the basis for the SFS rating, the analyst has to clearly understand each rating component and their assessment. With regard to government support, the analyst has to form an own opinion and incorporate that into the final SFS rating (see also 6.3.1.2.1 below). Deviations from the rating of the agencies are not uncommon.

6.3.1.2   Not-Externally Rated Banks

The main rating process remains unchanged. Rating criteria such as the Operating Environment, Franchise or Business Model continue to be evaluated, and ratios like Capitalization, Profitability, Impaired loans/Total Gross Loans or Reserves for Impaired Loans/Impaired Loans (trend analysis as well as peer comparison) are assessed. The CAMEL-approach (Capital, Asset Quality, Management, Earnings, Liquidity) is followed. However, more importance is now attached to the following assessment areas:

- Likelihood of government support
- Funding and liquidity
- Capital/Risk-weighted assets ratio

6.3.1.2.1   Likelihood of Government Support

As for all financial institutions, the risk and financial profile needs to be evaluated in detail on a stand-alone basis.

Before the analyst examines the bank's business and risk profile and analyzes the financials, he/she must form a strong opinion as to whether a bank will be considered systemically important by a government or regulator or not. This will not only primarily drive the final rating, but also the institution's risk profile. This appears to be simple task, but merely reviewing the list of D-SIBs (G-SIBs are all covered by the rating agencies) is not sufficient. Not all countries will publish such information, so the analyst is called upon to determine for himself the banks most likely to receive support in case of need. We use the bank's relative size, judged by total assets or market share in deposit taking to determine a bank's importance in a particular country. However, the analyst needs to be aware that governments, although willing to provide support to some banks or the banking sector in general, might not have the financial capability to do so.

In addition, with evolving regulations the names on such lists will change over time and the willingness of a government to provide financial aid to ailing banks will fluctuate with their political focus and pressure from the public. Nevertheless, it is anticipated that governments will continue to reduce their involvement in the banking industry—as the development in Denmark has shown.

In Denmark, which is not part of the EURO-countries, the government has taken the stance already in October 2010 that the taxpayers' money needs to be protected. At that time, Denmark's Bank Package III (Exit package) came into effect. Should a bank be closed due to a failure, a bail-in rather than a bail-out is regarded as the solution. The package introduced Europe's strictest winding-up rules for failed banks. If a failing bank is not taken over, bond holders and depositors must participate and may suffer losses during winding-up of the distressed bank.

The new regulation was enforced for the first time with the collapse of Amagerbanken in February 2011. As a result, the bank's senior unsecured debt holders were forced to take a 41 % haircut on their investment (Financial Times, May, 23rd, 2011).

Whether the Danish government will enforce a bail-in for one of the top 5 banks (Danske Bank A/S, Jystke Bank, Sydbank A/S, Nykredit Realkredit A/S and BRFKredit A/S), in case of need, remains to be seen. Ultimately, the decision depends on whether politicians and their consultants perceive an intervention to be less harmful for the economy than a bank bail-in and all its implications on ratings, funding costs and confidence of the population into the solvency of the remaining banks.

For all 28 EU Member States, the bail-in mechanism of the EU Recovery and Resolution Framework – mentioned earlier – becomes effective January 1st 2016. "Authorities will have a broad range of powers and tools to ensure that any failing bank can be restructured and resolved in a way which preserves financial stability and protects taxpayers".

Nevertheless, uncertainty regarding government support will remain—unless a resolution of an important financial institution has been successfully tested.

If the analyst expects some sort of government support to be given to distressed banks, he also needs to classify the anticipated degree of support—as this will vary depending on the importance of the bank for the economy. With regard to rating, the higher the probability of support, the higher the rating up-lift will be. SFS has set a maximum up-lift of 3 notches (for G-SIB) from the Stand-alone rating. Other important banks judged by their market share in retail deposit taking, or by asset size, can get an uplift of 1 notch. Some banks may not be retail deposit takers, but operate a capital markets financed business that they are dominating, e.g. the mortgage bond market or the financing of governments. Compared to pre-crisis, the likelihood of support has already shrunk and will further decline, thereby reducing the number of banks that are receiving a rating uplift. While ratings of all banks in some countries will be exclusively based on their individual strengths in the future, the author expects that for some countries, such as China, India or the United Arab Emirates to name a few, support will remain likely for the foreseeable future and needs to be factored into the final rating.

On the other hand, with the implementation of stricter capital and liquidity requirements for the systemically important banks, their stand-alone rating is expected to improve.

While evaluating a bank's intrinsic strengths, the analyst is required to keep the following in mind: New regulatory requirements will result in higher capitalization and better liquidity profiles and will thus improve a bank's financial profile. This will come at a cost for the shareholders. The author therefore expects these banks to accept some higher risks to compensate. In addition, if creditors expect to be bailed out, the risks taken by

SIFIs would not be fully reflected in the price of their debt. In turn, this creates incentives for SIFIs to take excessive risks. Consequently, and assuming the analyst has no access to a bank's underwriting standards and risk controlling policies other than what is written in the annual report, he should focus on a bank's asset and loan growth, asset quality and capitalization, as well as funding, liquidity and market risk in particular.

6.3.1.2.2   Funding and Liquidity

A financial institution's funding and liquidity became a major concern after the crisis. Consequently, and as the new Basel III liquidity standards have not yet been fully introduced, the SFS analyst focuses on the following two aspects:

a. Reliance on wholesale funding vs. deposits
b. Liquidity of assets (Level I–III)

Ad a) The ratio customer gross loans/customer deposits is a good indicator for how dependent a bank is on wholesale funding. As wholesale funding can dry up very quickly as the latest crisis has shown, access to customer deposits is a stabilizing factor for a bank. On a generic basis we consider a ratio of no higher than 0.75 as strong, while a ratio of 1 is still satisfactory. Depending on the market, product offering and the bank's overall funding strategy, these thresholds can be set even higher. The analyst must always review the bank's overall funding strategy. Using covered bonds sold to investors is viewed positively, if the particular market has been proven to be resilient in a stress situation.

Ad b) If confidence erodes and markets dry up, a bank might have to liquidate some assets to be able to fulfil its payment obligations. How liquid these assets are depends on how efficient markets function. The value of financial instruments is reflected in their Fair Value assessment. Depending on the transparency of the inputs that are used to determine the value, the financial instruments are classified into 3 levels:

Level I—Inputs are unadjusted, quoted prices in active markets for identical assets or liabilities at the measurement date. Level I assets are highest on the hierarchy, indicating assets/liabilities with the most transparent and tangible valuation techniques, as well as the most verifiable and reliable fair value measurement.

The types of assets and liabilities carried at Level I fair value are generally G-7 government and agency securities or equities listed in active markets.

Level II—Inputs (other than quoted prices included in Level I) are either directly or indirectly observable for the asset or liability through correlation with market data at the measurement date, and for the duration of the instrument's anticipated life. For example, an interest rate swap uses known public data, such as interest rates, and the contract terms can be used to calculate the value of the interest rate swap. The instrument can be valued indirectly using observable data.

Fair valued assets and liabilities that are generally included in this category are non-G-7 government securities, municipal bonds, certain hybrid financial instruments, certain mortgage and asset backed securities, certain corporate debt, certain commitments and guarantees, certain private equity investments and certain derivatives.

Level III—Inputs reflect management's best estimate of what methods market participants would follow in pricing the asset or liability at the measurement date. Consideration is given to the risk inherent in the valuation technique and the risk inherent in the inputs to the model. Level III is the most unobservable of the levels and indicates a use of valuation techniques and data that may not be verifiable. These types of instruments involve a great deal of assumptions and estimates. Examples may include infrequently traded asset backed securities or investments in privately owned companies.

Back to Lehman: In its annual report of November 30 2007, Lehman showed assets at fair market value at Level I of US$ 72.6 bn, at Level II of US$ 176.7 bn and US$ 42.0 bn at Level III. At the same time, Lehman had Total Stockholder's equity of just US$ 22.5 bn. Thus, assets whose value could not be verified were almost double the size of equity.

On the other side, Lehman's Level I assets of US$ 72.6 bn stood against short-term borrowings of US$ 28.1 bn, term deposit liabilities to banks of US$ 29.4 bn and payables to customers of US$ 61.2 bn. With eroding confidence into Lehman's viability, these Level 1 assets considered to be fungible were just not sufficient.

The difficulty of assessing the liquidity of a bank's assets is reflected in a statement in Lehman's 2007 annual report (quote) "During the 2007 fiscal year, our Level III assets increased, ending the year at 13 % of Financial Instruments and other inventory positions owned, measured at fair value and with our derivatives on a net basis. The increase in Level III assets resulted largely from the reclassification of approximately $ 11.4 billion of mortgage and asset-backed securities, including approximately $ 5.3 billion in U.S. subprime residential mortgage-related assets, previously categorized as Level II assets into the Level III category. …This reclassification generally occurred in the second half of 2007, reflecting the reduction of liquidity in the capital markets that resulted in a decrease in the observability of market prices."

Today, the SFS analyst assesses the liquidity of a financial institution by reviewing not only the percentage of Level I assets, but also the Level III assets in relation to shareholder's equity and its development over time. In our view, this ratio should not exceed 1—carefully assuming that the assessment fully depends on the classification by management and the bank's auditors.

Going forward, the new liquidity standards LCR and NSFR will tremendously support the analyst in providing a higher quality assessment of a bank's liquidity situation. These common standards will significantly aid the analyst to use trends as well as peer analyses to compare banks and categorize them into the right rating class.

6.3.1.2.3 New Capital Requirements and Risk-Weighted Assets

One element of assessing a bank's capital ratios is to review its asset portfolio in relation to the required risk-weighting. As banks in Cyprus have demonstrated exceptionally well, meeting the Basel capital requirements does not protect one from defaulting if the asset portfolio consists to a major extent of zero-weighted government bonds from an EU-Country, i.e. Greece. As a result of the Greek crisis, these banks' capital was not sufficient to cover losses from writing down their Greek securities. The SFS analyst thus will not rely on the capital ratio alone, but will undertake a closer examination of the type of securities in a bank's portfolio.

6.3.1.2.4 Market Risk

The Stress Var concept is an appropriate instrument to measure risks inherent in a trading portfolio. We use it in particular for financial institutions with a large trading portfolio. With a simulation of a stress scenario that reflects extreme market developments, the impact on a bank's profit & loss is assessed.

To calculate a Stress Var figure (based on a 99 % confidence level), we use the High Var figure of the published FYE (as required by revised Basel II), which is usually based on a 1-day-holding period, and convert it to a 10-day-holding period as it is more likely that in a market crisis the portfolio can be run down within 10 days as opposed to just 1 day. Assuming a high confidence level, the figure will show the potential loss for the portfolio that then can be compared with the bank's ability to absorb such losses. A value of 15 % for an investment bank as critical.

Again, the trend of this figure over several years will provide a sound indication as to whether the financial institution is adopting further risk with its trading activities, or reducing it.

6.3.1.3 Strategically Important Subsidiaries

Major banks have established specialized subsidiaries for their derivatives and trading activities in particular. Many of them are located in London or other financial centers in the world. Analyzing these entities on a stand-alone basis reveals that their profitability can be extremely volatile and capitalization can be rather thin. The major question to be addressed by the analyst here is: How likely is support by the parent or ultimate parent company and/or is there even the possibility of government support?

There might be smaller operations that are not exactly essential for the whole banking group. However, the vast majority of counterparties we have dealt with maintain a unique selling proposition in the group. They are a vital part of the banking group's overall strategy, are financially integrated into the group and are thus considered at least strategically important. Financial support will come first from the main operating company of the group in form of liquidity or guarantees, should the need arise. In our view, if the operating parent company's capabilities are impaired, support for the group's core or strategically important operating companies will be provided by the bank holding company.

The author maintains that with the implementation of the new regulations in the US and UK, it is highly unlikely that government support would also be provided in such a case where even the bank holding company's resources would not be sufficient to save the specialized subsidiary—unless the financial stability of the US or UK overall are threatened. It is considered unlikely that this would be triggered by a failing subsidiary.

Consequently, the analyst has to first evaluate the ultimate parent company of the group on a consolidated level and assign a rating, followed by an analysis of the stand-alone strength of the subsidiary. The likelihood of support must then be assessed, which will then determine the final rating for the subsidiary.

6.3.1.4   Hedge Funds

Do the new regulations have any major impact on Hedge Funds? The new Dodd-Frank Act requires advisors who manage more than US$ 150 million in assets to register with the Securities Exchange Commission (SEC). Extensive reporting is now required regarding funds activities and positions.

The Volker rule will reduce financial institution's involvement in proprietary trading and excludes them from running their own hedge funds or investing into these funds. Previously, banks could buy and sell securities for their own trading book at their own risk. As these activities are now closed down by the banks, others such as hedge funds will surely step up to gain from this new market opportunity. Consequently, the significance of Hedge Funds will continue to grow as the development in 2013 has already demonstrated. Assets under management have reached a historic high of over US$ 2 trillion (plus 228 bn during 2013), according to the Magazine Futures.

However, with regard to the evaluation of a Hedge Fund's ability to repay its credit obligations, these regulations have little to none impact as transparency continues to be rather limited for the analyst. The rating approach at SFS thus remains unchanged, focusing on evaluating the underlying portfolio, the fund's historic performance, its leverage, liquidity and the fund manager's strategy.

6.4   Conclusion

In general, the new and stricter regulations for financial institutions that are already implemented, or will be introduced in the course of the next 4 years, are assumed to have a positive impact on rating assessments. Further transparency will allow the analyst to better understand a financial institution's risk profile.

However, the more complex regulations are the more it will be a challenge for financial institutions to correctly adhere to them. Thus, only extensive supervision by regulators will create the transparency needed to accurately evaluate a financial institution's risk. With regard to the Volker Rule, it remains to be seen how diligently banks will distinguish between prohibited trade and permitted hedging activities, as well as how effective supervision of that rule can and will be.

Nevertheless, the rating analyst will benefit from the introduction of new ratios, such as the LCR and the NSFR. These ratios will not only allow for an easier peer comparison, they will also increase the accuracy of a financial institution's liquidity evaluation—which was one of the more challenging tasks in the past.

It will become easier to distinguish the good from the bad and the ugly, and the author expects that the higher standards and stricter supervision for the systemically important financial institutions, as well as better transparency, will result in more accurate ratings.

Attachment 1: G-SIBs as of December 2014 according to the Financial Stability Board (FSB) allocated to buckets corresponding to required level of additional loss absorbency

Bucket	Banks	
5 (3.5%)	empty	
4 (2.5%)	HSBC	JP Morgan Chase, US
3 (2.0%)	Barclays, UK	BNP Paribas, FR
	Citigroup, US	Deutsche Bank, DE
2 (1.5%)	Bank of America, US	Credit Suisse, CH
	Goldman Sachs, US	Mitsubishi UFJ FG, JP
	Morgan Stanley, US	Royal Bank of Scotland, UK
1 (1.0%)	Agricultural Bank of China, CN	Bank of China, CN
	Bank of New York Mellon, US	BBVA, ES
	Groupe BPCE, FR	Group Crédit Agricole, FR
	Industrial and Commercial Bank of China Limited, CN	ING Bank, NL
	Mizuho FG, JP	Nordea, SE
	Santander, ES	Société Générale, FR
	Standard Chartered, UK	State Street, US
	Sumitomo Mitsui FG, JP	UBS, CH
	Unicredit Group, IT	Wells Fargo, US

Literatur

Bank of England (2013): Financial Stability Report Nov. 2013.
Basel Committee on Banking Supervision (2011): Basel III: A global regulatory framework for more resilient banks and banking systems: revised 6/2011.
Basel Committee on Banking Supervision (2013): Basel III: The Liquidity Cover Ratio and liquidity risk monitoring tools, Jan 2013
Basel Committee on Banking Supervision (2014): Consultation Document—Basel III: The Net Stable Funding Ratio, Jan 2014.
Basel Committee on Banking Supervision (2015): Net Stable Funding Ratio disclosure standards.
Directive 2014/59/EU of the European Parliament and of the Council of 15 May 2014 establishing a framework for the recovery and resolution of credit institutions and investment firms
Federal Reserve Board (2014): Press release December 18th, 2014.
FitchRatings (2008): Press Release of July, 9th, 2008.
IMF Working Paper (2014): Reconsidering Bank Capital Regulation: A New Combination of Rules, Regulators, and Market Discipline.

Götz Schürmann ist Leiter des Bereichs Risk Controlling – Risk Rating der Siemens Division Financial Services (SFS) in München. Er verantwortete dort neben der Bonitätsanalyse von Kreditnehmern im Finanzierungsgeschäft von SFS auch die im Gesamtkonzern eingesetzten Debitoren-, Lieferanten- und Geschäftspartner-Ratings sowie die Entwicklung von manuellen Ratingverfahren. Nach dem Studium der Volkswirtschaftslehre an der Universität Münster begann er 1989 seine Karriere bei der Bayerischen Landesbank im Kreditbereich und war in München, London und New York tätig. Zwischen 1996 und 1998 führte er bei der Landesbank Hessen-Thüringen ein Team für das internationale Kreditgeschäft. 1999 kam er zur SFS dessen Kredit- bzw. Risikomanagment-Funktion er auf den Gebieten Kreditprozesse und Ratingmethoden maßgeblich mit aufbaute. Die letzten 3 Jahre verbrachte er für Siemens in den USA, von wo aus er den Bereich in globaler Verantwortung weiter führte. Als eine von 9 Divisionen des Siemens-Konzerns bietet Financial Services mit rund 2.900 Mitarbeitern weltweit eine breite Palette von Finanzlösungen an. Diese reicht von der Absatz, Investitions- und Projektfinanzierung über Treasury Services bis hin zum Fondsmanagement und schließt auch Versicherungslösungen mit ein.

Die Finanzwächter und das Bankrating 7

Bernd Lüthje

7.1 Einleitung

Am 5. November 2013 legte Elke König, Präsidentin der Bundesanstalt für Finanzdienstleistungsaufsicht, Bonn-Frankfurt am Main (BaFin), dar, dass „wir auch Verbraucherschutz (treiben), wenn auch indirekt." Diese Feststellung benötigte sie, um sich dann dafür auszusprechen, eine „scharfe Solvenzaufsicht" über Banken auszuüben, dieses auch unter dem Aspekt des Verbraucher- und Gläubigerschutzes (vgl. Dokumentation zum Finanzwächter).

Frau König kündigte an, was inzwischen die amtierende deutsche Bundesregierung mit Unterstützung der sie tragenden Bundestagsfraktionen von Christlichen Demokraten, Sozialdemokraten und Christlichen Sozialen in Bayern der BaFin im Bereich der Bankenaufsicht als neue Aufgabe zugewiesen hat. Ihre bisherigen Kernaufgaben, die Krisenprophylaxe und Solvenz für die ihr unterstellten Institute zu sichern, werden vom Verbraucherschutz, genauer: vom vorrangigen und alleinigen Schutz der Institutskunden, abgelöst.

Im weiteren Gedankengang ist die BaFin immer zusammen mit der Deutschen Bundesbank, Frankfurt am Main, zu sehen, die aus der mitführenden Bankenaufsicht große Betätigungsbereiche für ihre Beschäftigten ableitet. An sich ist die Bundesbank überflüssig. Ihre einzige Aufgabe seit 1948, den Geldwert zu sichern/das Preisniveau stabil zu halten, nimmt heute nur noch allein der Bundesbank-Präsident innerhalb der Europäischen Zentralbank, Frankfurt am Main (EZB), wahr.

In einer konzertiert-anmutenden Aktion wurden nach der Bundestagswahl am 22. September 2013 noch während der Koalitionsverhandlungen und verstärkt danach die neue

B. Lüthje (✉)
Hamburg, Deutschland
E-Mail: dr-bernd.luethje@t-online.de

© Springer Fachmedien Wiesbaden 2016
Z. Diab, O. Everling (Hrsg.), *Rating von Finanzinstituten*,
DOI 10.1007/978-3-658-04195-3_7

Aufsichtsaufgabe der BaFin definiert und unter zwei Gruppen aufgeteilt. Der BaFin wurde der generelle Verbraucherschutz für die Institutskunden zudiktiert. Die staatlich-finanzierte Verbraucherschutz-Organisation mit ihren 16 Zentralen in allen deutschen Bundesländern und eigenem Bundesverband in Berlin erhält als zusätzliche Aufgabe, einzelwirtschaftlicher Finanz(markt)wächter zu sein.

7.2   Kampf um die Hoheit über die Banken

Die nachstehende Untersuchung dient dazu, die ordnungspolitische Frage zu beantworten: Wie wirkt sich die oben skizzierte Entscheidung der Großen Koalition auf die Banken-Steuerung aus? Wer hat zukünftig die Entscheidungen in den Finanzinstituten? Wird damit das Basel-Regime in Deutschland eingeschränkt, gar aufgehoben? Hat das Citibank-Modell als Grundlage von Basel II ausgedient? Welche Schlussfolgerungen ergeben sich aus alledem für das Banken-Rating der weltweit führenden Ratingagenturen? Werden sie zukünftig – zumindest – in Deutschland noch gebraucht?

Es wäre zu einfach, nur den Wegfall von Bankaufsichtsaufgaben der BaFin durch die Koalitionsentscheidung zu untersuchen. Tatsächlich hat sie mit dem Übergang der Bankaufsicht in der Euro-Zone auf die EZB im November 2014 für zunächst 21 deutsche Institute nichts mehr zu sagen. Gleiches gilt für die Bundesbank. Überdies hat die EZB heute schon die Letztzuständigkeit für alle noch nicht von ihr geführten Banken im Euro-Raum. Für die in den anderen EU-Ländern hat die Europäische Bankenaufsicht in London (European Banking Authority, EBA) die Zuständigkeit. Sie hat sich an der EZB-Bankenaufsicht auszurichten.

Die am 16. April 2014 von der EZB beschlossene Regulierung des Zusammenarbeitspapiers (Regulation (EU) Nr. 468/2014 of the ECB/EZB establishing the framework for cooperation within the Single Supervisory Mechanism between the ECB/EZB and national competent authorities and with national designated authorities, kurz: SSM Framework Regulation) legt die Unterordnung von BaFin und Bundesbank fest. Für den EU-Raum organisiert den gleichen Vorgang die EBA. Die Unterordnung wird bestärkt durch die Anweisung, wie die Stresstests auszuführen sind, die die in der ersten Phase von der EZB direkt zu beaufsichtigenden 120 Euro-Institute vor Aufnahme in den Kreis der Auserwählten zu bestehen haben (ECB 2014).

In Zukunft werden BaFin und Bundesbank praktisch in der Bankenaufsicht für die deutschen Institute nicht mehr zuständig sein. Damit ist zugleich ihre Verantwortung beendet. Ein Schelm also ist, der sich dabei denkt: Soll die neue Hauptaufgabe des Verbraucherschutzes für die Bankkunden die Beschäftigung der nicht mehr gebrauchten Aufseher in BaFin und Bundesbank sichern? Wird dafür die Wahrnehmung von Wächter-Aufgaben in den staatlich finanzierten Verbraucherschutz-Agenturen in Kauf genommen? Denn eine Vorgabe ihrer Tätigkeit durch BaFin und Bundesbank, die sie doch wegen ihrer bisherigen alleinigen Zuständigkeit hätten ablehnen müssen, ist nicht bekannt.

7.3   Aufgaben und Zuständigkeiten der Finanzwächter

Aus den Vorarbeiten und ersten Beratungen im Deutschen Bundestag seit 2010 wird deutlich, dass die Finanzwächter zunächst als Entscheider vorgestellt werden, die die Verbraucher vor undurchsichtige Anlageprodukte bewahren sollen. Die politischen Ansätze wurden jedoch allgemeiner formuliert und ließen erweiterte Aufgabenstellungen zu. Der jetzt gültige Koalitionsvertrag hat das erweiterte Aufgabenprofil festgeschrieben.

Die Anträge aus der vorherigen 17. Bundestags-Legislaturperiode, der jetzt gültige Koalitionsvertrag und die Veröffentlichungen verschiedener politischer Mandatsträger, politischer Beamter und Aufsichtsverantwortlicher (vgl. Dokumentation zum Finanzwächter) werden zusammen als Grundlage für die weitere ordnungspolitische Untersuchung genommen. Daraus wird ein Wächtersystem mit Lenkungswirtschaft im deutschen Finanzbereich denk- und sichtbar.

Dagegen kann eingewendet werden, dass die Lobbyinteressen der Verbraucherzentralen und ihrer Verbraucherzentrale Bundesverband in Berlin, zusätzliche Aufgaben vom Staat übertragen zu bekommen, sicherlich auch um eine breitere finanzielle Sicherheit zu erhalten, im Spiel sind. Nicht offenkundig war lange deren Interesse, „strukturell", wie die Lobby formuliert, tätig zu sein, nämlich in die Einzelgeschäfte zwischen Finanzinstitut und Kunden, den Verbrauchern, als letzte Entscheidungsinstanz direkt einzugreifen. Mit dem jetzt gültigen Koalitionsvertrag ist dieses Lobbyanliegen erklärtes Ziel der Bundesregierung und der sie tragenden Bundestags-Fraktionen geworden. Die Oppositionsfraktionen werden bei der Verwirklichung mitmachen, da sie in ihren Anträgen aus der vorigen Legislaturperiode entsprechend votiert haben.

Würden jetzt BaFin und die neuen Finanzwächter ungebremst operieren können, bildete sich schnell ein System heraus, in dem die einzelwirtschaftlichen Entscheidungen aller Finanzinstitute von den Wächtern genehmigt werden müssten. Vordergründig scheint es sich nur um Verbraucherentscheidungen zu gehen. Tatsächlich aber geht es um einen abschließenden Umbau der Finanzwirtschaft, der schon seit längerem stattfindet und die Verantwortungs- und Haftungspyramiden in den Instituten aufhebt. Dieser Umbau beendet die Marktwirtschaft im Finanzbereich.

Die Verlagerung der Aufsichtszuständigkeit zu EZB und EBA wird nicht zu einer grundlegenden Reform der deutschen Aufsichtseinrichtungen führen. Sie haben ihre Aufsichtszuständigkeit abgegeben, bleiben aber über den Geschäftsleitungen rechtlich angesiedelt Letztentscheider im laufenden Bankgeschäft. Dazu gehören gemäß Kreditwesengesetz (KWG) und den auf dem Gesetz beruhenden vielfältigen, ins tiefste Detail gehenden Verordnungen die Letztentscheidungen über Strategien, Geschäftsmodelle, langjährige Wirtschaftspläne, Feststellungen von internen Krisen, Restrukturierungen, Insolvenzen, Vergütungen insgesamt und im einzelnen – die Aufzählung ist nicht vollständig. Was diese Letztentscheidungen mit Aufsicht zu tun hat, erschließt sich weder in langer Praxis noch durch Nachdenken

Im Wesentlichen beruhen Machtfülle und der Machteinsatz der BaFin auf den ins Detail gehenden Regelwerken, die ausgehend vom Basel-Regime über die EU verbindlich durch Bundesregierung und Bundestag für die Finanzinstitute festgelegt worden sind. Eine Abwehr der BaFin dagegen ist nicht bekannt, nur die Verschärfung der Regelwerke aus eigenem Antrieb. Das hat dazu geführt, dass der eigenständige Verantwortungsbereich für Entscheidungen des Managements und der Kontrollorgane heute in einer deutschen Bank nur noch bei 20 % seiner rechtlich gebotenen Aufgaben liegt. So ist die Verantwortungspyramide des Aktienrechts (Vorstand ist oberstes Entscheidungs- und Haftungsorgan) durch das KWG plus Verordnungen weitgehend ausgehöhlt worden. Bei anderen Finanzinstituten, die nicht unter das KWG, aber unter andere Finanzgesetze fallen, sieht es ähnlich aus.

Trotzdem haften die Geschäftsleiter für alles, auch für die Entscheidungen, die die BaFin vorgibt. Beim Wächtersystem ist gleiches zu erwarten. Denn in allen Einrichtungen, die der deutsche Staat betreibt oder an denen er beteiligt ist, haftet für sein Tun im staatlichen Auftrag und für sein eigenes kein Staatsvertreter. Die EZB-Bankenaufsicht haftet überhaupt nicht. Ihre Vertreter haben die Immunität durchgesetzt.

Diese Tatsache haben die Ratingagenturen in ihren Gutachten und Beurteilungen bisher nicht beachtet. Sie gehen für Deutschland von einer Entscheidungs-, Verantwortungs- und Haftungspyramide vergleichbar dem US-amerikanischen Recht und seiner Anwendung aus. Dem entsprechen dem Anschein nach die geltenden deutschen Gesetze, vor allem das Aktienrecht.

Die Ratingagenturen haben auch nicht zur Kenntnis genommen, dass diese Entwicklung ordnungspolitisch dazu beigetragen hat, die Marktwirtschaft im Bankenbereich unumkehrbar abzubauen. Der Vorgang ist nicht allein Folge des Basel-Regimes und der darauf aufbauenden deutschen Aufsichts-Arbeit, sondern eine von der Bundesregierung und vom Bundestag mit Akzeptanz von Basel II 1999 gemeinsam gewollte Veränderung der Wirtschaftsordnung.

7.4   Nur ein Wächtersystem wahrscheinlich

Auf Grund der bekannten Vorstellungen (vgl. Dokumentation Finanzwächter) wird das Wächtersystem, das im Koalitionsvertrag festgeschrieben worden ist, skizziert. Anschließend wird diskutiert, wie es sich zum Basel-Regime und zu der für Deutschland allein wichtigen Bankaufsicht bei der EZB und zur EU-Aufsicht verhält. Und der Frage wird nachgegangen, ob damit nicht die in der augenblicklichen Krise von vielen Politikern verdammte „Herrschaft" der weltweit führenden Ratingagenturen Standard & Poor's und Moody's in deutschen Banken beendet werden wird.

Für die Ausgestaltung des Wächtersystems zeichnen sich zwei Möglichkeiten ab. Die erste Möglichkeit wäre die, die BaFin wandelt sich zur Verbraucherschutzbehörde, wie die Linken sie vorgeschlagen haben. Daneben würden bei den Verbraucherschutzzentralen in den Bundesländern Finanz(markt)wächter aufgebaut. Die Arbeitsteilung könnte über die Schnittstelle Bankleitung zu Kundenbegleitung abgesprochen werden. So würde die BaFin die Bankleitungen einschließlich ihrer Kontrollorgane lenken, während die

Finanz(markt)wächter beim Kundengespräch entscheiden, ob ein Kunde ein Angebot einer Bank annehmen darf oder nicht.

Das bedeutet eine Unmenge von neuen Finanz(markt)wächtern. Kein Kunde aber wird bereit sein, den während seiner Verhandlungen mit der Bank beisitzenden Wächter zu bezahlen. Da die Verbraucherzentralen weitgehend aus staatlichen Mitteln bezahlt werden und ihre sonstigen Träger (so Sparkassen) überwiegend Ziel der Finanzwächter sein werden, bleibt nur eine zusätzliche Staatsfinanzierung für das Wächtersystem als Lösung.

Die zweite Möglichkeit wäre die, dass die BaFin die Kontrolle und Letztentscheidung der Kundengespräche übernimmt. Damit würde sie die Finanz(markt)wächter-Funktion bei sich integrieren. Das hätte den Vorteil, die in den nationalen Einrichtungen nach Abwanderung der Aufsicht zur EZB und EBA freiwerdenden, fachlich gut ausgebildeten Mitarbeiter in neue Aufgaben zu überführen.

Die Wahrscheinlichkeit, dass diese Möglichkeit realisiert werden wird, ist null. Denn die offiziellen Verbraucherberater wollen aus eigenem Antrieb mit den Finanzwächtern die Wirtschaftsordnung im Finanzbereich ändern. Ohne Aufhebens und ohne Beratung des Bundestages wird sie in eine Lenkungswirtschaft überführt. Dabei können sich die Schützer auf die Fraktionen der Sozialdemokraten, Bündnis 90/Die Grünen und Linken stützen. Aus der Fraktion der Christdemokraten und Christsozialen ist Widerstand nicht bekannt.

Das Grundgesetz schreibt keine Wirtschaftsordnung vor, auch nicht die der Sozialen Marktwirtschaft. Aus der Formulierung des Artikel 20, 1. Absatz („Die Bundesrepublik Deutschland ist ein demokratischer und sozialer Bundesstaat."), kann keine bestimmte Ordnung der Wirtschaft abgelesen werden. In weiterer Grundgesetz-Artikeln wird der „soziale Bundesstaat" näher bestimmt. Die verschiedenen Freiheitsrechte, die Eigentumsgarantie und die nur eingeschränkt mögliche Vergesellschaftung (Enteignung nur gegen Entschädigung) von Boden, Naturschätzen und Produktionsmitteln ergeben eine Ordnung, die weder die der staatlichen Zwangswirtschaft noch die der absoluten Bindungslosigkeit erlaubt. Das Pendel der Ordnung kann zwischen den Grenzen hin- und herschwingen, solange die Grundrechte eingehalten werden.

7.5 Im Stillen: Die Lenkungswirtschaft des Bankbereiches

Indem die ordnungspolitische Wirkung der Finanzwächter nicht problematisiert wird, sie über die enge Zusammenarbeit zwischen dem Bundesministerium der Justiz und für Verbraucherschutz und den Verbraucherzentralen, geführt von ihrem Lobby-Bundesverband, eingeführt werden, erfolgt die ordnungspolitische Umschaltung im Finanzbereich im Stillen. Das ist keine Revolution von Bürgern, das ist kein Umsturz durch die Sparer, das ist eine von der Bundesregierung und allen augenblicklich im Bundestag vertretenen Parteien mit ihren Fraktionen gewolltes Hinschwingen der Wirtschaftsordnung auf die staatliche Zwangswirtschaft. Versucht man sie zu erfassen, so ist sie mit der sozialistischen Marktwirtschaft zu vergleichen, die die Volksrepublik China gemäß den Beschlüssen der Kommunistischen Partei Chinas praktiziert.

Die erste Möglichkeit, wie das Wächtersystem ausgestaltet werden wird, ist die allein wahrscheinliche. Die deutsche Finanzwelt wird in Zukunft mit zwei Regulierungen zu tun haben. Sichtbar ist auch, dass es zwei Kreisläufe sein werden. Absehbar ist, dass beide voneinander getrennt werden sollen. Nur so lassen sich die bekannten Äußerungen der Politik zum Wächtersystem und zum Verbraucherschutz als neuer Hauptaufgabe der Bankaufsicht interpretieren.

Die von den Verbraucherschützern entworfene „duale Struktur" (vgl. Dokumentation zum Finanzwächter) ist eine Lobbyformulierung, um vom Kernauftrag für die Wächter abzulenken. Denn die Regulierungen werden in der Aufsichtspraxis von zwei unterschiedlichen Ansätzen ausgehen. Das Wächtersystem wird die einzelgeschäftliche Erlaubnis und das Verbot als Kerntätigkeit ansehen. Ordnungspolitisch wird damit ein Element der Staatlichen Zwangswirtschaft, die Aufhebung der Vertragsfreiheit, realisiert.

Die BaFin dagegen wird den kollektiven (gesellschaftlichen? gesamtwirtschaftlichen?) Verbraucherschutz betreiben und dabei den Vorgaben des Basel-Regimes folgen. Folgte sie Basel nicht, verlöre sie den letzten Teil ihrer früher umfassenden Eigenständigkeit, die nur die Weisung des Bundesfinanzministers einengen konnte.

7.6   Alles beherrschende Großmacht aus Basel

Das Basel-Regime hat das Ziel, nur ein Geschäftsmodell weltweit zu erlauben. Um das zu erreichen, wird seit Basel II eine Steuerung des Eigenkapitalverbrauchs bei Kreditvergaben vorgeschrieben. Das geschieht über die auf dem Ratingsystem von Standard & Poor's beruhende Bonitätsdifferenzierung und daraus abgeleitet der je nach Bonität unterschiedlichen Eigenkapitalanforderungen bei den Banken.

Diese Vorgaben einzuhalten, ist in Zukunft Aufgabe der EZB-Euro- und der EU-Aufsicht. BaFin und Bundesbank haben nur noch Zuarbeiten zu leisten. Die Brücke zum Wächtersystem kann sich aus der gleichen ordnungspolitischen Ausrichtung ergeben: Das Basel-Regime ist ein lenkungswirtschaftliches System wie das der Finanzwächter.

Bisher sind keine Äußerungen bekannt, wie das Wächtersystem seine Verbrauchersteuerung neben der bestehenden des Basel-Regimes begründen will. Wahrscheinlich wird das politisch einfach zu verkaufende Argument zu hören sein, dass das Wächtersystem das bestehende Bankaufsichtssystem ergänzen wird. Sollte es konkreter werden, wird zu hören sein, dass das Wächtersystem den im Basel-System angelegten kollektiven Verbraucherschutz konkretisieren wird.

Abgesehen davon, dass das Regime so etwas will oder betreibt, stimmte das politische Argument nicht. Das Basel-Regime mit seinen für Deutschland wichtigen Trägern EU-Kommission und ihren Aufsichtseinrichtungen sowie die EZB als Bankaufsicht hat Deutschland von seiner Zuständigkeit für die Aufsicht entstaatlicht. Auf Vorschlag der Bundesregierung hat der Bundestag das Vorhaben mit überwältigender Mehrheit gutgeheißen. Im Herbst 2014 wurde es abgeschlossen, da die EZB die Bankenaufsicht an sich gezogen hat.

Das Wächtersystem ist das Gegenteil. Zurzeit gibt es dafür keine Vorgabe des Basel-Regimes oder EU-Kommission. Bundesregierung und Bundestag können also die deutsche Eigenstaatlichkeit für dieses System erhalten. Beim Wächtersystem braucht sich Deutschland überhaupt nicht den EU-Organen unterzuordnen, denn hierfür gelten die Subsidiaritätsvorschriften des gesamten Vertragswerkes für die EU, zurzeit der Lissabon-Vertrag von 2007. Es handelt sich um ein nationales Vorhaben, das den Union-Verträgen nicht entgegensteht. Auch die Beihilfe-Vorschriften des Lissabon-Vertrages bleiben unberührt, weil das Wächtersystem nicht grenzüberschreitend in den internen EU-Wettbewerb eingreift. Das von der EU-Kommission einzuhaltende „level playing field", überall in der Union gleichwertige Wettbewerbsverhältnisse herzustellen und zu sichern, wird nach dem jetzigen Stand des Wächtersystems nicht von diesem eingeschränkt.

7.7 Doppelte Aufsicht: Ordnungspolitik und Rating

Zu untersuchen ist nun, welche Auswirkungen das doppelte Aufsichtssystem hat. Hier interessieren nur zwei – die anderen müssen weiteren Untersuchungen überlassen werden: Die ordnungspolitischen Auswirkungen und die auf die Ratings der Banken sowie auf die künftige Deutschland-Beurteilung.

Der erste Bestimmungsschritt ist eine allgemeine politische Einordnung. Das Wächtersystem ist der direkte vom Staat gewollte Eingriff in die persönliche Vertragshoheit, im Ergebnis ein diktatorischer Akt, auch wenn er vom Bundestag beschlossen worden ist. Das Basel-Regime dagegen will eine von ihm gelenkte Bankwirtschaft weltweit. Im Bereich der EU einschließlich der EZB-Bankenaufsicht hat es sich zur Zentralverwaltungswirtschaft ausgebildet. Aus den unterschiedlichen Ansätzen könnten konkurrierende Entscheidungsstränge folgen. Deren Ergebnis wäre Chaos. Beispiel: Wächtersystem erlaubt Geschäft in bestimmten nachrangigen Schuldverschreibungen – Basel-Regime erhöht für deren Kauf durch Private, wenn diese dafür Kredit benötigen, die Eigenkapitalbindung der finanzierenden Bank auf 150 %.

Ein näherer Blick auf das Basel-Regime macht deutlich, dass es neben sich keine anderen Lenkungssysteme dulden kann, weil sonst sein Herrschaftsanspruch in sich zusammenfällt. Er wird daraus begründet, Bank- und Finanzkrisen im Ansatz zu verhindern. Wenn auch die historische Prüfung dazu geführt hat, dass das Basel-Regime eine über die andere Krise ausgelöst und jeweils verschlimmert hat, beruht seine weltweite Herrschaft (mit Ausnahme in den USA) auf der Krisenprophylaxe. Sie ist nicht demokratisch begründet, aber alle Staaten, ob Demokratien oder nicht, unterwerfen sich den Anweisungen des Regimes.

Das Basel-Regime sitzt unter dem Dach der Bank für Internationalen Zahlungsausgleich in Basel und hat alle Merkmale eines geheimbündlerischen Vereins. Selbst bezeichnet es sich als „Forum". Seine Verabredungen gehen über die EU-Richtlinien nach Deutschland hinein und müssen hier in Gesetze umgewandelt werden. Bekannt sind die „Basel II"-und „Basel III"-Vorgaben.

Mit seiner Entscheidung, aufgrund ratingbasierter Eigenkapitalvorgaben die Bankgeschäfte nach Bonitäten zu differenzieren, hat das Basel-Regime seit Ende der 1980er Jahre ein Wachstum des Finanzgeschäftes angestoßen, das sich von der Realwirtschaft weit entfernt hat. Das Wachstum wurde erleichtert über mathematisch konzipierte Produkte, die nur noch aus sich selbst heraus zu wachsen brauchen. Da der Bezug oder die Grundlage im realwirtschaftlich verankerten Bankgeschäft aufgehoben wurde, verringerten sich die Kapitalbezüge zu den Bonitätseinschätzungen oder fielen ganz weg.

Der Anteil des Eigenkapitals an den stark steigenden Bilanzsummen schrumpfte auf infinitesimale Größen. Beschleunigt wurde dieses immer größer werdende Auseinanderklaffen durch die weder begründete noch bis heute grundsätzlich diskutierte Entscheidungen des Regimes, Banken zu erlauben, Kredite an Staaten ohne Eigenkapital herauszulegen. Selbst in der aktuellen Finanzkrise ist die in jeder Hinsicht falsche Entscheidung vom Regime nicht korrigiert worden. Basel III erlaubt weiterhin die Nullanrechnung, so dass sich Staaten wie der deutsche in 2014 bei steigender Verschuldung insgesamt billiger refinanzieren werden.

Die Verbraucher werden ausgenutzt durch finanzielle Repression des Staates, die persönliche Krisen- und Altersvorsorge wird entwertet. Das ist das Gegenteil von Verbraucherschutz, es ist Enteignung. BaFin und Bundesbank machen dabei voll mit. Schon allein von dieser Tatsachenbeschreibung her gesehen, sind beide ungeeignet, einen kollektiven Verbraucherschutz im Finanzbereich auszuüben.

Wahrscheinlichkeitsrechnung und Mathematisierung der Geschäfte des vom Regime erlaubten und favorisierten Bankmodells wären ohne die Ratings von Standard & Poor's oder Moody's nicht möglich gewesen. Deren Kurzfassung in Buchstaben und Ziffern machten Ableitungen und Berechnungen großer und komplexer Mengen erst möglich. Dabei wurde vergessen, dass Ratings Gutachten und Beurteilungen sind, keine Testate und Noten. Die nach Bonität der Bankkunden erlaubte differenzierte Eigenkapitalausnutzung beruht letztlich auf diesem rechnerischen Trick. Er ist Basis der Derivate, der von irgendetwas „abgeleiteten Geschäfte". Die Banken nahmen dieses Modell begeistert auf, ihre Leitungen trichterten der Öffentlichkeit ein, das Eigenkapital sei der teuerste Kostgänger in einer Bank und nun könnte der Aufwand dafür gesenkt werden. Dieses ist historisch unwahr. Der teuerste Kostgänger sind Wertberichtigungen und Abschreibungen. Allein Bankenleitungen, die die Verluste über die gesamte Existenz des Instituts jedes Jahr unter dem erwirtschafteten Gewinn halten, und dieses ohne Buchhalter- und Bilanztricks, sind erfolgreich.

7.8   Die Baseler Ampel für die US-Ratingagenturen,

Die großen, weltweit führenden Ratingagenturen scheinen sich ein völlig eigenes Geschäftsfeld entwickelt zu haben, das von der US-Verfassung gesichert wird, so könnte man denken. Dem ist nicht so.

Das Basel-Regime hat sich zu einer „Weltregierung" im Bankenbereich entwickelt. Was es an Regeln ausheckt, wird befolgt. Das Regime wird im Innern von den USA beherrscht. Für die US-amerikanische Administration ist das Regime eines unter vielen Mitteln, die eigene Innenpolitik im Finanzbereich global abzusichern. Zu dieser Politik gehört auch, die Beurteilungen der großen Ratingagenturen weltweit durchzusetzen. Es stimmt, dass sie der US-amerikanischen Verfassung von 1788 im I. Zusatzartikel (Amendment) von 1791 unterliegen. Demnach wären die Agenturen in ihren Gutachten/Beurteilungen frei. In der Wirklichkeit jedoch werden sie vom Basel-Regime gesteuert. Damit auch von den USA? Widerspräche das nicht ihrer Verfassung?

Das Basel-Regime hat in Basel II, beibehalten in Basel III, ein Ampelsystem festgelegt, das von allen Staaten übernommen worden ist. Ausgehend von seiner Bonitätsskala gibt es sechs Einteilungen, die in der Wirkung sechs Herrschaftskreise des Regimes sind.

Rot: I. Ramsch (Staaten außerhalb der EU, Unternehmen, Privatpersonen mit schlechter Bonität); Gelb: II. Unternehmen und Privatpersonen mit normaler Bonität (mittleres Eigenkapital oder unbelastetes Vermögen); III. Banken ohne direkte/implizite Staatshaftung; Grün: IV. Unternehmen und Privatpersonen mit bester Bonität (hohes Eigenkapital, mindestens 50 % der Bilanzsumme oder hohes unbelastetes Vermögen); V. Banken und Unternehmen mit direkter/impliziter Staatsgarantie; VI. Staaten (vertreten im Basler Ausschuss für Bankenaufsicht, EU-Mitglieder, Mitglieder der Organisation für wirtschaftliche Zusammenarbeit und Entwicklung/Organization for Economic Co-operation and Development, OECD, Paris).

Über das zentrale Bonitätsschema werden die Herrschaftskreise des Basel-Regimes im einzelnen gesteuert. Der VI. Kreis ist der erste der Wunschkreise. Seine weltweite Bevorzugung durch die Banken wird erreicht, indem diese für Kredite an gut geführte Staaten kein Eigenkapital anzurechnen brauchen. Die Kreise V. und IV. sind auch Wunschkreise, sie werden mit geringer Kapitalunterlegung gefördert. Beim Kreis V. mit direkter/impliziter Staatshaftung kann auch eine Null-Anrechnung zum Zuge kommen. Das entscheidet die Aufsicht.

Die Kreise III. und II. sind Verhinderungskreise. Unter Risikoaspekten sieht das Regime die Geschäfte nicht gern, also wird versucht, sie über hohe Eigenkapitalbindung unwirtschaftlich zu machen. I. ist der Ausschlusskreis. Dazu gehörten einige Mitglieder des Euro-Raumes. Sie wurden durch die Rettungsaktionen der Euro-Länder und der EU, vor allem durch direkte Milliarden-Hilfen und Garantien, sowie durch die künstliche Liquidisierung seitens der EZB, auch durch deren Finanzierung der Target-Salden zwischen den nationalen Euro-Zentralbanken, an den besten Herrschaftskreis herangeführt. Das Basel-Regime hat dieses gefordert und sein Bonitätsschema entsprechend weitherzig interpretiert, um Insolvenzen zu vermeiden. Ramsch bleiben sie so lange, wie keine inneren Reformen vorgenommen werden, sondern diese Staaten sich weiterhin auf den von außen kommenden Geldsegen verlassen (können).

Bisher wurde nicht untersucht, ob die Verhinderungspolitik des Regimes ausschlaggebend für die sogenannte Kreditschwäche in großen Teilen des Euroraumes ist. Die bisherige Feststellung der EZB, die Banken würden zu wenig an Unternehmen ausleihen, beruht auf der Vermutung, dass es für sie einfacher ist, Geld zu wechseln: Geld von der EZB zu extrem niedrigen Zinsen, Ausleihe an EU-Staaten mit hohem Risiko (im begründetem Glauben, dass sie innerhalb der Union immer gestützt werden), keine Anrechnung im Eigenkapital. Dieses einfache und hoch-ertragreiche Geschäft würde das klassische Kreditgeschäft verdrängen. Das kann so sein. Dagegen spricht, dass professionelle Bankleitungen langfristig denken. Ohne treue Kunden in großer Zahl im Passiv- wie im Aktivgeschäft existiert man nicht lange. Macht die Verhinderungspolitik des Regimes also doch das klassische Geschäft nicht nur teuer, sondern sogar und mit Absicht unmöglich?

Von zwei Aufsichtskreisen in Deutschland wurde gesprochen. Sie haben tiefgreifende Auswirkungen. Das Wächtersystem bedeutet für alle Banken in Deutschland die direkte Staatshaftung. Die Anstaltslast/Gewährträgerhaftung für die Förderbanken wird überflüssig. Die Deutsche Bank wie die Sparkasse Holstein haben die volle Staatshaftung der Bundesrepublik Deutschland. Die von der Bankenaufsicht der EZB schon ausgehende, implizite Staatshaftung für die direkt beaufsichtigten Institute wird überflüssig. Die Ratings der Banken werden verbessert, für alle auf das Rating für Deutschland. Das bestehende „AAA" bei Standard & Poor's (gleichlautendes Rating bei Moody's) wäre ein wundervolles Geschenk dafür, dass sich die Banken der einzelgeschäftlichen Diktatur unterwerfen müssen.

Was aber bedeutet dieses Geschenk für Deutschlands Rating selbst? Die deutsche direkte Staatsschuld erhöht sich laufend. Fallen alle Institute infolge des Wächtersystems unter die implizite Staatshaftung, muss diese in der Verschuldung berücksichtigt werden. Allein diese nicht zu quantifizierende Erhöhung müsste Anlass für die Ratingagenturen sein, ihre Gutachten zu Deutschland und seiner zukünftigen finanziellen Belastungsfähigkeit zu überprüfen.

Verstärkt würde der negative Effekt dadurch, dass Deutschland zu einer einzelgeschäftlichen Diktatur zurückkehrt. Sie war zuletzt mit Not- und Preisverordnungen in der Weimarer Republik, verstärkt in der nationalsozialistischen Diktatur eingeführt worden. Auf der Basis der von Edward A. Tenenbaum, Leutnant der US-amerikanischen Besatzungsmacht, konzipierten und vorbereiteten Deutschen Mark, unabhängigen Zentralbank und Währungsreform am 20. Juni 1948 konnte Ludwig Erhard, Chef der Wirtschaftsverwaltung der amerikanischen und britischen Besatzungszonen am selben Tag die Preis-Zwangswirtschaft sprengen.

Jetzt aber wird die für die Finanzinstitute die Marktfreiheit passé sein. In Zukunft werden sie zwei diktatorischen Aufsichtssystemen unterliegen, dem aus Basel und dem aus Berlin, dem deutschen Wächtersystem.

Versucht man beide Auswirkungen – sprunghafte Erhöhung der gesamten deutschen Staatsschuld und Wächtersystem mit einzeldiktatorischer Befugnis – auf das Rating Deutschlands abzuschätzen, wird aus dem derzeitigen „AAA" ein einfaches „A" werden.

7.9 Wie geht es weiter? Fragen und Antworten

Sechs Fragen wurden gestellt und sind zu beantworten:

Wie wirkt sich die Einführung eines Wächtersystems auf die Banksteuerung In Deutschland aus? Wenn auch das Basel-Regime die Befolgung des Citi-Bank-Modells vorgegeben hat, werden die einzelwirtschaftlichen Entscheidungen des Wächtersystems jegliche Geschäftssteuerung unmöglich machen, weil die Institutsleitungen nicht mehr Herr ihrer Tätigkeit sein dürfen.

Wie wird das Finanzwächtersystem aussehen und arbeiten? Es wird eigenständig arbeiten und die Letztentscheidungen im Verkehr zwischen Kunden und ihrem Finanzinstitut treffen, also die Vertragsfreiheit aufheben. Damit ist es die realisierte staatliche Zwangswirtschaft im Finanzbereich, ein klarer Verstoß gegen das Grundgesetz.

Wer hat zukünftig die Entscheidungen in den Finanzinstituten? Die Finanzwächter, nicht die Geschäftsleitungen.

Wie wird sich das Wächtersystem zum Basel-Regime und der Bankaufsicht verhalten? Es wird allein arbeiten. Da die Finanzwächter selbst ein lenkungswirtschaftliches System bilden, wird es mit dem des Basel-Regimes keine Reibungsverluste geben. Beider Einflusssphären werden sauber voneinander getrennt. Das Finanzwächtersystem arbeitet national, das Basel-Regime übernational.

Hat zukünftig das Citibankmodell aus Basel II für Deutschland ausgedient? Nein, solange es darüber zwischen dem Basel-Regime und dem Wächtersystem nicht zum Konflikt kommt.

Wird die aus der Politik behauptete Herrschaft der Ratingagenturen durch das Wächtersystem in Deutschland beendet? In den Banken werden externe Ratings von den Finanzwächtern nicht gebraucht, weil sie einzelwirtschaftliche Entscheidungen auf Grund der Verhandlungsunterlagen zwischen Kunden und Instituten treffen. Das Rating Deutschlands wird weiter bestimmt werden für die Investoren in aller Welt. Durch die Existenz des Wächtersystems (einzelwirtschaftliche Zwangswirtschaft/Aufhebung der Vertragsfreiheit) und infolge der von ihm begründeten impliziten Staatshaftung für alle Finanzinstitute mit der Folge, dass sich die deutsche Staatsschuld im unbekanntem Ausmaß erhöht, wird die Deutschland-Beurteilung auf „A" gesenkt werden. Die jahrzehntelange Triple-A-Stellung wird beendet werden.

Die Formulierungen im Koalitionsvertrag zum Verbraucherschutz im Finanzbereich wurden nicht hinterfragt. Sie sind verbindliche Grundlage der gesetzgeberischen Arbeit in der laufenden Legislaturperiode. Deshalb wurde nicht gefragt, ob das Wächtersystem gebraucht wird. Die Antwort darauf hätte nichts mit Ratingagenturen oder dem Basel-Regime zu tun, allein damit, ob das Volk im Finanzbereich die Lenkungs- oder gar die staatliche Zwangswirtschaft möchte. Dass sich 1989 ein großer Teil dagegen entschieden hat, ist unvergessen.

7.10 Dokumentation zum Finanzwächter

Die Begriffe Finanzwächter, Finanzmarktwächter oder Bankwächter tauchen in der politischen Diskussion verstärkt im Jahr 2011 auf. Sie werden synonym gebraucht. Weder von der Lobby noch in der Politik wird definiert, was diese Wächter ausmacht, auch nicht was sie konkret tun und bewirken sollen. Es wird nur die Forderung erhoben, sie einzurichten und zwar bei den Verbraucherzentralen.

Die Begriffe sind neu und im früheren Sprachgebrauch nicht bekannt. Althergebracht ist ein Wächter: „zunächst eine person, die wache hält, auf der wache ist gegen feinde und drohende gefahren, doch auch bei tage." „Wächter findet sich". auch in der Bedeutung „aufpasser, auflaurer" (vgl. Grimm und Grimm 1922, Spalten 184 und 189). Ein Finanz(markt)wächter wäre jemand, der – passiv – wacht und der – aktiv – aufpasst, den Gefahren auflauert.

Die institutionalisierte Vertretung der Verbraucherinteressen gegenüber Anbietern, Politik und Finanzaufsicht sei unterentwickelt (vgl. o. V. 2012, S. 2). Die Aufgaben der BaFin seien „weitestgehend" auf die Solvenzsicherung der Finanzinstitute beschränkt, wobei eine Vielzahl von Anbietern und Produkten ihrer Aufsicht nicht unterlägen. „Die Berücksichtigung der kollektiven Verbraucherinteressen im Bank- und Anlagebereich ist dagegen weder Ziel noch Aufgabe der Aufsicht" (vgl. o. V. 2012; im Koalitionsvertrag vom 27. November 2013 – s. unten – heißt es auf S. 63, letzter Satz: Die BaFin „erhält den kollektiven Schutz der Verbraucher als wichtiges Ziel ihrer Aufsichtstätigkeit". Die Lobby-Forderung wurde schnellstens erfüllt.).

In der Schrift heißt es weiter: „Der Finanzmarktwächter ist eine … engmaschig aufgebaute Verbrauchervertretung gegenüber Finanzwirtschaft, Aufsicht, Politik und Öffentlichkeit. Er soll aufdecken, wo Verbraucher am Finanzmarkt systematisch kollektiv benachteiligt werden. Das Ziel ist es, die Finanzaufsicht, Landes- und Bundespolitik sowie die Anbieterseite in die Lage zu versetzen, entsprechend ihrer Zuständigkeit und Verantwortung auf diese Missstände zu reagieren. Kern dieser dualen Struktur ist eine präventiv wirkende Marktbeobachtung und -kontrolle, …" „Damit leisten Verbraucherzentralen und der Verbraucherzentrale Bundesverband einen Beitrag zum Schutz und zur Konsolidierung der finanziellen Mittel privater Haushalte, ebenso zur Stärkung des Verbrauchervertrauens in den Finanzmarkt." (o. V. 2012, S. 2).

In diesem Text wird um die kollektive Lenkung und vorausblickenden Bevormundung der Verbraucher überhaupt nicht herumgeredet. Das „duale System" sichere die Lenkungswirtschaft durch die Verbraucherzentralen und ihrem Lobbyverband auf allen Ebenen. Dem entspreche das Ziel, Markt und Marktwirken auszuschalten. „Mit seiner Arbeit sorgt der Verbraucherzentrale Bundesverband für einen Ausgleich zwischen den Interessen der Unternehmen und denen der Verbraucher, denn ohne eine vernünftige Balance zwischen Angebot und Nachfrage kann Wirtschaft nicht funktionieren." (Verbraucherzentrale Bundesverband 2014, S. 2). Weiter heißt es im Text unter der Zwischenüberschrift „Gibt es Alternativen zur Finanzierung durch die öffentliche Hand?", auch die Unternehmen würden davon profitieren, dass „geltendes Recht und die grundlegenden Spielregeln von Markt und Wettbewerb von den Verbraucherverbänden durchgesetzt" würden (Verbraucher-zentrale Bundesverband 2014): „Denn auf komplexen, unübersichtlichen Märkten kön-nen qualitätsorientierte Unternehmen ihre Produkte nur an gut informierte Verbraucher verkaufen, die ihre Rechte kennen und einfordern"(Verbraucherzentrale Bundesverband 2014).

Heike Göbel schreibt, der „Verbraucherschutzminister Heiko Maas" wolle „lückenlos" künftig den Verbraucher schützen. Damit das klappe, sollten etwa mehr Finanzprodukte verboten werden. „Was weg ist, ist weg, da kann sich der Kunde nicht mehr in Gefahr bringen. George Orwell lässt grüßen." (Göbel 2014, S. 20)

Das ist eine milde Wertung. John Orwells unter dem Eindruck der Diktaturen und des II. Weltkrieges seit 1943 geschriebener Roman „Nineteen Eighty-Four" von 1949 (London/ New York) reicht zur Einschätzung dessen, was in Deutschland fast im Stillen geschieht, nicht aus. Bei uns geht es nicht um eine Fiktion, sondern die schon durch die Regula-rien und durch das Basel-Regime eingeschränkte Marktwirtschaft im Bankbereich soll endgültig von einer Lenkungswirtschaft, genau von einer staatlichen Zwangswirtschaft, abgelöst werden. Die Banken werden zu Ausführungshelfern. Gelenkt werden die Banken von der oben angeführten „dualen Struktur" unter Leitung einer „engmaschigen Verbrau-chervertretung", die gesteuert wird vom einem Bundesministerium (der Justiz und) für Verbraucherschutz. Die Beratungen im Bundestag zwischen 2011 und 2013 sowie die Kehrtwendung der CDU-CSU-Fraktion in den Koalitionsverhandlungen des Herbst 2013 haben bewirkt, dass der Bundestag die endgültige Überführung der Bankwirtschaft in die Lenkungswirtschaft mitgetragen hat. Es könnte passieren, dass das Basel-Regime sich querstellt, weil sein eigenes Bestreben, eine globale Lenkungswirtschaft durchzusetzen, gestört werden könnte. Da die BaFin aber Mitträger des „kollektiven Verbraucherschut-zes" im deutschen Finanzbereich geworden ist, bleibt darüber der direkte Einfluss des Regimes gesichert.

Nach Bildung der jetzigen Bundesregierung fällt in den Veröffentlichungen der Bank-wächter weg. Finanzwächter und Finanzmarktwächter werden nunmehr gleichermaßen benutzt. Die Begriffe wurden von den Lobbyisten der Verbraucherzentralen mit ihrem eigenen Verband Verbraucherzentrale Bundesverband e. V., Markgrafenstraße 66, 10969 Berlin, noch in der 17. Legislaturperiode, erstmalig über einen Antrag der Bündnis 90/Die Grünen im Juli 2011 in den Bundestag eingebracht, darüber auch erstmalig in der öffentli-chen Diskussion wahrgenommen. Den Begriffserfindern scheint die Nähe zu der Bezeich-nung der iranischen „Revolutionswächter" verborgen geblieben, nicht aufgegangen zu sein – oder vielleicht doch? Haben sie gewusst, dass die „Wächter" im Iran eine Diktatur sichern? Oder wollen sie auf indirektem Wege eine Diktatur errichten, in der die Verbrau-cherschutz-Zentralen die Kernzellen sind. Wer das Finanzsystem eines Staates lenkt, hat den Staat unter sich und kann seine Ziele verwirklichen. Das „Wächteramt" und das Ziel des „Verbraucherschutzes" verwischen die Diktatur, so dass der Bürger glaubt, geschützt zu werden. Tatsächlich wird er bevormundet und in seinem freien Handel eingeschränkt.

In Deutschland ist es üblich, bei Gesellschaften des öffentlichen Lebens, die im Ein-flussbereich der Bundesregierung und des Bundestages arbeiten, einen Beirat, auch Verwaltungsbeirat einzurichten, dessen Mitglieder vom Bundestag gewählt und von der Bundesregierung ernannt werden. Für das System der Finanz(markt)wächter würde sich nach iranischem Muster als Beiratsbezeichnung schlüssig ein „Wächterrat" anbieten. Bei ihm könnten alle Entscheidungen grundsätzlicher und strittiger Art angesiedelt werden. Auch könnte er Verordnungen erlassen und einzelrechtliche Befugnisse erhalten. Dazu Heiko Maas, Bundesminister der Justiz und für Verbraucherschutz, am 14.März 2014 in Hamburg laut Börsen-Zeitung: Die BaFin solle künftig die Risiken bestimmter Finanzprodukte prüfen und Werbung und Vertrieb beschränken können. Das könne bis zu einem Verbot gehen. (BÖZ, 15.03.2014, S. 3). Dem entsprach der finanzpolitische Sprecher der Bündnis 90/Die Grünen im Bundestag, Dr. Gerhard Schick: Er forderte im Fernsehen am 05.Dezember 2013 mehr juristische Kompetenzen für die BaFin. Die Bankenaufseher müßten nach dem Vorbild der USA ähnliche Eingriffsmöglichkeiten wie die Staatsanwaltschaft erhalten. Begründung: Dann komme es bei Ermittlungen nicht zu Reibungsverlusten (Arbeitsgemeinschaft der öffentlich-rechtlichen Rundfunkanstalten der Bundesrepublik Deutschland 2013).

Bundestags-Erörterung: Antrag der Abgeordneten Kerstin Tack und anderer sowie Fraktion der SPD „Verbraucherschutz stärken – Finanzmarktwächter einführen", Deutscher Bundestag, 17. Wahlperiode, Drucksache 17/8894 vom 06.03.2012. Dieser und der ältere Antrag der Abgeordneten Nicole Maisch und anderer sowie Fraktion Bündnis 90/Die Grünen (Drucksache 17/6503 vom 06.07.2011) hatten den Verbraucherschutz bei Anlageprodukten zum Schwerpunkt. Der Antrag der Abgeordneten Caren Lay und anderer sowie Fraktion Die Linke (Drucksache 17/8764 vom 29.02.2012) ging darüber hinaus und forderte, eine Verbraucherschutzbehörde zur Regulierung der Finanzmärkte zu schaffen, die als Zulassungsstelle „alle Finanzmarktakteure und –instrumente vor ihrer Zulassung auf Verbraucherfreundlichkeit und volkswirtschaftliches Risikopotenzial" zu prüfen hat und „Eingriffsbefugnisse gegenüber den Unternehmen der Finanzbranche erhält". Sie sollte „in ihrer Struktur von der Solvenzaufsicht der BaFin institutionell getrennt" sein, um so unabhängig und gleichberechtigt „zum Schutz" der Verbraucher „zu agieren". Die Anträge wurden von den damaligen Koalitionsfraktionen der CDU/FDP/CSU abgelehnt. Von der jetzigen Koalition aus CDU/SPD/CSU jedoch werden die Elemente aller Anträge, auch die der heutigen Oppositionsfraktionen Bündnis 90/Die Grünen und die Linken, weiterverfolgt.

Während der Koalitionsverhandlungen hat die BaFin selbst die Aufgabe für sich reklamiert: In ihrem Referat „Banken- und Kapitalmarktregulierung: Aktuelle Reformansätze" auf der Kapitalmarktkonferenz des Hamburgischen Weltwirtschaftsinstituts, der Deutschen Bundesbank und des Finanzplatz Hamburg e. V. am 05.November 2013 in der Handelskammer Hamburg führte die BaFin-Präsidentin Elke König aus, in der Bankenaufsicht „treiben wir auch Verbraucherschutz, wenn auch indirekt." Anschließend spricht sie sich für die „scharfe Solvenzaufsicht" über Banken aus, auch unter dem Aspekt des Verbraucher- und Gläubigerschutzes. In der Diskussion fordert Frau König, dass die Aufsicht die Einhaltung einer mikro- und makroprudentiellen Bankenaufsicht mit Regelwerken und Regulierung durchzusetzen habe (aus der persönlichen Aufzeichnung des Verfassers). Damit hebt sie die bisherige Arbeitsteilung zwischen der BaFin (mikroprudentiell) und Bundesbank (makroprudentiell) auf. Das ergibt Sinn, wenn die BaFin ihre Kernaufgabe – wie später im Koalitionsvertrag zwischen der Christlich Demokratischen Union Deutschlands (CDU), der Sozialdemokratischen Partei Deutschlands (SPD) und der Christlich Sozialen Union in Bayern (CSU) für die 18. Legislaturperiode des Deutschen Bundestages vom 27. November 2013, Druckfassung Berlin 27.11.2013, festgeschrieben und vom Bundesminister der Justiz und für Verbraucherschutz Heiko Maas detailliert worden ist – zukünftig im Verbraucherschutz ansehen wird. Daraus ist zu folgern, dass die bisherigen BaFin-Kernaufgaben der Krisenprophylaxe für und Solvenzaufsicht über die Banken aus ihrer Priorität entlassen sind.

Dafür bietet Dorothea Mohn, Teamleiterin Finanzen in der Verbraucherzentrale Bundesverband, den Beweis: „Solange der Anlegerschutz nur als wichtiges, nicht aber als gleichrangiges Aufsichtsziel definiert sei, werde der Anlegerschutz der Sicherstellung der Zahlungs- und Verlusttragfähigkeit (Solvabilität) von Banken, Versicherern und anderen Finanzdienstleistern untergeordnet und der Verbraucherschutz am Finanzmarkt unterrepräsentiert bleiben." (Frühauf 2014, S. 23). Da die amtierende Bundesregierung und zumindest drei Fraktionen des Bundestages alles vollziehen, was die Lobby der Verbraucherzentralen will, wird der Verbraucherschutz von der BaFin „gleichrangig" zu erfüllen sein. Eine Bankenaufsicht kann aber nicht zwei „gleichrangige" Ziele zugleich erfüllen. Ein Ziel muss Priorität haben: Krisenverhinderung oder Verbraucherschutz. Beider Zielerreichung bedürfen völlig unterschiedlicher Maßnahmen. Frau Mohn fordert die Gleichrangigkeit des Verbraucherschutzes. Das bedeutet Zurückdrängung der Krisenverhinderung. Der Verbraucherschutz betrifft Einzelgeschäfte eines Instituts, die Prophylaxe das gesamte Institut mit der Gesamtheit aller Institute. Dieser Konflikt kann nur durch eine Weichenstellung gelöst werden. Die Koalitionsregierung hat es getan. Der Verbraucherschutz steht obenan. Die Entscheidung ist konsequent, da die vorherige Koalitionsregierung mit dem Bundestag die Bankaufsicht für Deutschland auf die EZB verlagert hatte.

Die Formulierungen der Koalitionsvereinbarung vom 27. November 2013 im Einzelnen: Unter „1.5. Regeln für die Finanzmärkte" auf S. 63 der schon erwähnte kollektive Verbraucherschutz als BaFin-Aufgabe. Unter „4. Zusammenhalt der Gesellschaft … 4.2. Lebensqualität in der Stadt und auf dem Land … Verbraucherschutz" auf S. 124: „Wo Verbraucher sich nicht selbst schützen können oder überfordert sind, muss der Staat Schutz und Vorsorge bieten. Zudem muss er die Verbraucher durch gezielte und umfassende Information, Beratung und Bildung unterstützen. Das gilt insbesondere für neue Bereiche wie den Finanzmarkt … Dafür wollen wir die bestehenden Verbraucherorganisationen mit einer speziellen Marktwächterfunktion ,Finanzmarkt' … beauftragen." Wieso ist der Finanzmarkt ein neuer Bereich für die Verbraucher? Schon im Allgemeinen Landrecht für die preußischen Staaten, 1794, werden die Verbraucherrechte abgesichert, davon übergehend im Bürgerlichen Gesetzbuch und im Handelsgesetzbuch.

Weitere Diskussion: „Der Chef des Bundesverbandes der Verbraucherzentralen, Gerd Billen" fordert, „dass die BaFin auch die Geschäftsmodelle von Unternehmen prüfen müsse" (rtr 2013, S. 15). „Ob die Marktwächter die ihnen zugedachten Aufgaben tatsächlich wirksam wahrnehmen können, hängt aber ohne Zweifel in hohem Maße davon ab, wie die Marktbeobachtung konkret durchgeführt werden soll, welche Rechte und Pflichten der Marktwächter bei festgestellten Marktverstößen haben soll, ob es verpflichtende Reaktionen des Gesetzgebers auf beobachtete Marktverstöße geben wird, …"(Bach et al. 2013, S. 40). Das Institut formuliert die Planungsstichworte, um die Lenkungswirtschaft einzuführen. „Wir stehen in den Startlöchern", sagte die Leiterin Verbraucherpolitik beim Verbraucherzentrale Bundesverband, „Helga Springeneer," der dpa (dpa 2014a, S. 28; genauer unter Einbeziehung der BaFin: Drost und Kersting 2014a, S. 8 f.).

Der Staatssekretär für Verbraucherschutz Gerd Billen, vorher Chef der Verbraucherzentrale Bundesverband, führt zur Aufgabe der BaFin aus: Gemeinsam mit dem Bundesfinanzministerium werde geprüft, ob der Vertrieb intransparenter Finanzprodukte beschränkt oder Produkte ganz verboten werden „Es gibt gute Gründe dafür, die Finanzaufsicht Bafin mit diesen Kompetenzen auszustatten." Auf die Frage, ob die BaFin eine „Verbraucherschutzbehörde" werden solle, antwortet der Staatssekretär, dass die Anstalt „künftig mehr Aufgaben im Verbraucherschutz" wird übernehmen können. Dazu brauche sie ein gesetzliches Mandat, so stehe es auch im Koalitionsvertrag. Wörtlich im Koalitionsvertrag auf S. 63: „Die BaFin erhält die Möglichkeit, entsprechend den europäischen Regeln den Vertrieb komplexer und intransparenter Finanzprodukte zu beschränken oder zu verbieten, sofern diese die Finanzmarktstabilität gefährden oder unverhältnismäßige Risiken für Anleger bergen." Ist das ein gesetzlicher Auftrag? Beschließt ihn der Bundestag? Hat das Basel-Regime nicht schon ausreichend Vorarbeit in seinen Werken geleistet, auch den totalen Verbraucherschutz unter seine Lenkung zu nehmen? Wenn ja, braucht man kein neues Gesetz (vgl. Drost und Kersting 2014b, S. 60 f., bestätigt vom Bundesministerium der Justiz und für Verbraucherschutz, www.bmj.de/SharedDocs/-Interviews/DE/PSrBillen/2014/)

Beim Verbraucherzentrale Bundesverband sind Finanzwächter schon tätig. Sie hätten festgestellt, dass vier von zehn Anlageprodukte an den Bedürfnissen der Kunden vorbeigingen (vgl. Sauer 2014, S. 14). Von einer solchen Feststellung bis zum Verbot solcher Produkte ist nunmehr nur noch ein kurzer Weg. Auf die Frage von Markus Zydra, ob Prospekte Anlegern nichts brächten, antwortet Dorothea Mohn, Leiterin Team Finanzen in der Verbraucherzentrale Bundesverband: „Nein, man muss da anders rangehen. Bestimmte Produkte sollten gar nicht für den aktiven Vertrieb an Privatanleger zugelassen werden, weil Anleger bei Zertifikaten, Genussrechten oder geschlossene Fonds keine realistische Chance haben, einzuschätzen, wie das Produkt funktioniert und ob es fair kalkuliert ist. Das Gros der Bevölkerung braucht solche Produkte nicht." (Zydra 2014, S. 26). Das ist eine eindeutig Kette: Verbraucher verstehen nichts, Bevormundung, Verbot, staatliche Zwangswirtschaft.

Die vorsorgende Fürsorge des Bundesministers der Justiz und für Verbraucherschutz denkt schon in diesem Stadium an den Personalausbau der BaFin: „Wenn man die Zuständigkeiten ausweitet, muss man auch die Ressourcen schaffen", sagte (Heiko) Maas (o. V. 2014a, S. 14). Zu fragen ist, ob die Finanzinstitute, die heute rund 90 % des BaFin-Etats bezahlen, weiterhin überhaupt die Anstalt noch alimentieren dürfen. Sie verändert ihre Kernaufgaben. Die neuen zielen einseitig auf die Ausschaltung der Marktwirtschaft im Finanzbereich, somit auf die mögliche und notwendige Ertragserzielung. Die Finanzinstitute würden gegen ihre Eigentümer und ihre Kunden arbeiten, wenn sie weiter die BaFin finanzieren würden. Erschwerend kommt hinzu, dass im Rahmen der vom Basel-Regime angeordneten und von der EU realisierten Maßnahmen die nationalen Bankaufsichten ihre Kompetenzen an EZB und EBA abgeben. Das müsste 1:1 geschehen. Damit würden die Banken keine höheren Aufwendungen für die Aufsicht zu übernehmen haben. Das Gegenteil ist der Fall. Die zentrale Aufsicht durch EZB plus EBA führt schon vorher zu steigenden Aufwendungen. Auf nationaler Ebene kommt es jedoch nicht zum Abbau nun überflüssig werdender Mitarbeiter bei BaFin und Bundesbank. „Im Gegenteil, die Anforderungen wachsen", würden „Aufsichtskreise" sagen. Während die EZB die großen Banken beaufsichtigen werde, würden die nationalen Behörden die kleinen Institute kontrollieren und die EZB obendrein unterstützen. Daher brauche man Mitarbeiter, die sich um die Abstimmung zwischen der Bundesbank (sowie der BaFin) und der EZB kümmern (Heß 2014, S. 5).

Der Graue Kapitalmarkt werde künftig strenger kontrolliert, sagte laut Frankfurter Allgemeiner Zeitung vom 23. Mai 2014, S. 23, Heiko Maas. Darauf hätten sich der Bundesjustiz- und -verbraucherminister Maas mit dem Bundesfinanzminister Schäuble geeinigt. Die Maßnahmen seien insbesondere eine Reaktion auf die Pleite des Windkraftbetreibers Prokon, Itzehoe/Schleswig-Holstein. Die BaFin erhalte nun den „kollektiven Anlegerschutz" als zusätzliche Aufgabe.

Das war aber schon im Vertrag zur Großen Koalition am 27. November 2013, also vor der Prokon-Pleite am 22. Januar 2014, beschlossen worden. Auch die nächste Ankündigung von Maas-Schäuble, als flankierende Maßnahme würden außerdem bestehende Verbraucherzentralen zu offiziellen „Marktwächtern" ernannt, hat nichts mit Prokon zu tun, wie oben in der Dokumentation dargestellt.

Mit dem Wächtersystem wird langsam begonnen. Zunächst sollen Finanzwächter bei fünf Verbraucherzentralen eingerichtet werden: In Baden-Württemberg, Bremen, Hamburg, Hessen und Sachsen (Interview mit Klaus Müller, Vorstand Verbraucherzentrale Bundesverband, in: Focus, 7. Juni 2014, S. 34). Für die Einrichtung des Wächtersystems ist eine Anschubfinanzierung aus dem Bundeshaushalt über 2,5 Mio. € vorgesehen (dpa 2014b, S. 27).

Die CDU/CSU-Bundestagsfraktion möchte den Finanzwächtern keine hoheitlichen Aufgaben übertragen. Die Vorstellung wurde von der Verbraucherzentrale Bundesverband begrüßt. (Reuters Berlin: Union beschränkt Finanzwächter; in: BÖZ, 17. Juli 2014, S. 39. Dazu Billen, Gerd: „Wir brauchen Marktwächter"; in: FAZ, 24. Juli 2014, S. 16. Im Referentenentwurf der Bundesministerien der Finanzen und der Justiz zum Kleinanlegerschutz wird, wie Angela Wefers schreibt, „der «kollektive Verbraucherschutz» als ein Aufsichtsziel der BaFin gesetzlich verankert." (wf Berlin: Noch mehr Schutz für Kleinanleger; in: BÖZ, 30. Juli 2014, S. 6) „Ab Oktober [2014] beginnt der Aufbau des Finanzmarktwächters," teilte Bundesjustizminister Heiko Maas mit. (rtr: Finanzwächter können bald starten; in: Der Tagesspiegel, 06. Oktober 2014, S. 15) Widersprüchlich dazu: Der

Aufbau des Marktwächtersystems solle nach Angabe von Verbraucherzentrale Bundesverband und Bundesjustizministerium im Februar 2015 beginnen. Konkretisiert wird aber dessen Zielsetzung. Es solle zwei Marktwächterprogramme geben: Ein „Frühwarnsystem für den Finanzmarkt und eines für die digitale Welt. Der Finanzmarktwächter soll sich vorrangig um die Bereiche Altersvorsorge, Kredite und Versicherungen sowie den grauen Kapitalmarkt kümmern. Der Marktwächter Digitale Welt soll neben Telekommunikationsdienstleistungen auch den Internethandel sowie die Arbeit von Internetverbraucherportalen unter die Lupe nehmen" (o. V. 2014b, S. 15) Damit verlässt die zukünftige Aufgabenbeschreibung und -stellung für Finanzwächter den ursprünglichen Ansatz. Mit „Unter die Lupe nehmen" erhalten sie direkte Kriminalaufgaben. Diese Ausweitung stimmt nicht mehr überein mit dem geltenden Koalitionsvertrag der Fraktionen von CDU, SPD und CSU. Auch schränkt sie die der BaFin zugeordnete neue Aufgabe, zukünftig den kollektiven Verbraucherschutz wahrzunehmen, entscheidend ein. Denn diese hat keine staatsanwaltschaftliche Befugnis.

In dem „Kleinanlegerschutzgesetz" BGBl I Nr. 28, Bonn 09. Juli 2015, S. 1.114–1.129, wurden die Vereinbarungen im Koalitionsvertrag 2013 realisiert. Damit hat die BaFin den „Schutz der kollektiven Verbraucherinteressen" zu gewährleisten. Das Gesetz enthält keine Hinweise auf Finanz-Markt-Wächter. Die BaFin sei eine Behörde, die Verbraucherzentrale Bundesverband „und die Verbraucherzentralen, die den Finanzmarktwächter bilden, sind privatrechtlich organisierte Akteure ohne hoheitliche Befugnisse. Jede Seite ist und bleibt unabhängig. Wie die Behörde mit den Erkenntnissen des Finanzmarktwächters umgeht, folgt den Regeln Ihres gesetzlichen Handlungsauftrags." (Beecken, Grit: Interview mit Klaus Müller, Vorstand Verbraucherzentrale Bundesverband, Börsen-Zeitung, 09.April 2015, S. 2) Die Finanzwächter werden bis Ende 2017 mit 18,3 Millionen Euro aus dem Bundesministerium der Justiz und für Verbraucherschutz gefördert (Pressemitteilungen der Verbraucher Zentrale Bundesverband, Berlin, 17. Oktober 2014 und 26. März 2015).

Literatur

Arbeitsgemeinschaft der öffentlich-rechtlichen Rundfunkanstalten der Bundesrepublik Deutschland (2013): Erstes Fernsehprogramm, 05. Dezember 2013, www.daserste.de-/information/politikweltgeschehen/morgenmagazin, 08.18 Uhr

Bach, S. et al. (2013): Der Koalitionsvertrag nimmt die Gesellschaft in die Pflicht; in: DIW Wochenberichte, herausgegeben vom Deutschen Institut für Wirtschaftsforschung, Berlin, Nr. 50 vom 09. Dezember 2013

Dpa (2014a): Verbraucherzentralen wollen Finanzmarkt stärker beobachten; in: Handelsblatt, 03. Januar 2014

Dpa (2014b): Finanzwächter ist geplant: in: Frankfurter Allgemeine Zeitung, 7. Juni 2014

Drost, F. M. und Kersting, S. (2014a): Schärfere Instrumente. Der Bund will den Verbraucherschutz stärken. Die Aufsicht soll gefährliche Produkte künftig verbieten dürfen: In: Handelsblatt, 21. Januar 2014

Drost, F. M. und Kersting, S. (2014b): Die Finanzaufsicht ist zersplittert; in: Handelsblatt, 31.01.2014, S. 60 f.

ECB (2014): Official journal of the European Union, 14. Mai 2014, 141/1–141/50

Frühauf, M: (2014): „Der Anlegerschutz ist für die Bafin zweitrangig"; in: Frankfurter Allgemeine Zeitung, 25. März 2014

Göbel, H. (2014): Auf einen Espresso. Abrüsten für Steuerfrieden; in: Frankfurter Allgemeine Zeitung, 15. März 2014, S. 20

Grimm, Jacob und Grimm, Wilhelm: Deutsches Wörterbuch, 13. Bd.; Leipzig 1922, Spalten 184 und 189; Nachdruck durch Deutscher Taschenbuch Verlag; München 1984, Bd. 27.

Heß, D. (2014): Bundesbank. Aufseher verzweifelt gesucht; in: Die Welt, 19. März 2014

Lüthje, B. (2013): Basel Vier. Das Ende des Basel-Regimes; Berlin 2013

O. V. (2012): Druckschrift der Verbraucherzentrale Bundesverband, Berlin 2012

O. V. (2014a): BaFin soll Finanzprodukte verbieten können; in: Die Welt, 17. März 2014

O. V. (2014b): Finanzwächter sollen Anleger besser schützen; in: Die Welt, 18. Oktober 2014

Rtr (2013): Prüfzwang für Bafin; in: Frankfurter Rundschau. 02. Dezember 2013

Sauer, S. (2014): Beratung zum Verkauf. Geldanlage. Verbraucherschützer sehen kaum Verbesserungen beim Finanzvertrieb; in: Frankfurter Rundschau, 25. Februar 2014

Verbraucherzentrale Bundesverband (2014): Häufige Fragen (FAQ); www.vzbv.de-/Haeufige_Fragen.htm, 03/03/2014, 13:13 Uhr

Zydra, M. (2014): „Verbrauchern ist das zu komplex". Warum eine Expertin Vertriebsverbote fordert; in: Süddeutsche Zeitung, 04. März 2014

Bernd Lüthje 1964 Diplom-Volkswirt, 1969 Dr. rer. pol., Universität Hamburg, 1964 bis 2005 Tätigkeiten in Verbänden und Banken, u. a.1974 bis 1989 in der Westdeutschen Landesbank (WestLB), Vorstandsstab und Ressortchef Firmengeschäft, 1990 bis 2002 Hauptgeschäftsführer des Bundesverbandes Öffentlicher Banken Deutschlands, 2002 bis 2005 erster Vorstandsvorsitzender der NRW.BANK, 2002 bis 2004 erster Aufsichtsratsvorsitzender der WestLB AG, 2005 bis 2008 ehrenamtlicher AR-Vorsitzender der Landesentwicklungsgesellschaft Nordrhein-Westfalen mbH (Sanierung und Privatisierung, heute LEG Immobilen AG im M-Dax), seit 2006 autonom, u. a. publizistisch tätig zu finanzwirtschaftlichen Fragen.

Criteria for Rating Financial Institutions

8

Zafer Diab

8.1 Introduction

Assigning a rating to a financial institution, following a detailed and comprehensive analysis of that institution, is both a science and an art. It is a science because there are certain mechanical and mathematical formulae (quantitative factors) which can be applied to the financial profile and which point towards a determination of the overall quality of that institution.[1] It is an art for a number of reasons.

Firstly, there are many qualitative (non-financial) aspects of a bank which must be taken into consideration, but which cannot usually be calculated mathematically.[2] Secondly, even the financial inputs involved in a rating may often lead in conflicting directions. Therefore, an evaluation of how to adequately balance those particular aspects of a bank's financial profile must be made. Moreover, the analysis of a bank cannot be completed in a vacuum. It is only from the experience of extensive reading and preparation of analyses—

---

[1] *'Financial insitution' is a broad term which can be used to include banks, leasing companies, factoring companies, insurance companies, mutual funds, brokerage firms and other firms engaged principally in financial activities. Even the term 'banks' can include commercial banks, savings banks, investment banks, Islamic banks and merchant banks. Since banks account for the overwhelming share of such institutions (both in terms of numbers of institutions and in terms of total assets), the topic here will be limited to banks—typically commercial banks, but reference may occasionally be made to other types of banks.*

[2] *Some of those factors are identified in the sections below and in many cases amount to a series of questions which, when answered, will not provide an immediate answer, but will provide the analyst with the information necessary to come to an informed conclusion.*

Z. Diab (✉)
Limassol, Zypern
e-mail: m.zlotnik@yahoo.de

© Springer Fachmedien Wiesbaden 2016
Z. Diab, O. Everling (Hrsg.), *Rating von Finanzinstituten,*
DOI 10.1007/978-3-658-04195-3_8

thereby obtaining a background against which to rate a particular bank—that an analyst can truly perfect his craft, and fully comprehend where a bank fits on the spectrum of the many thousands of banks worldwide.

A key element to consider is that there is no such thing as a 'perfect bank.' It can safely be said that there is not a bank in existence today which could, with no difficulty, fully meet its obligations to pay back all of its deposits on short notice. A bank able to do so would likely be so liquid as to show very little profitability. More will be said below on some of the trade-offs which banks are required to make among various aspects of its financial profile.

The following discussion approaches the subject of ratings from the point of view of counterparty analysis—that is, to determine the creditworthiness of a bank and its ability to meet its obligations in a timely manner—whether those obligations are funded (repayment of deposit, debt or other on-balance-sheet liabilities) or unfunded (guarantees, commitments or other obligations which are booked off the balance sheet).

8.2 Qualitative Factors

The qualitative factors in a bank's composition include all the factors which make the bank what it is—and which ultimately determine what its financial profile will look like. These factors will be addressed individually, but they ultimately include:

- External factors—the operating environment
  - macro-economic situation
  - regulatory environment
  - auditing and accounting
  - legal system
  - political environment
  - external financial factors
- Internal factors
  - ownership and governance (including history)
  - risk profile
  - management and strategies
  - franchise value

8.2.1 External Factors

8.2.1.1 Macro-Economic Situation

The economy in which a bank operates will be a key determinant of the manner of business it will do and of its financial profile. Factors such as GDP growth, inflation, currency depreciation (or appreciation), and external trade and payments balance will influence a bank's ability to do business and the nature of that business. For example, a bank operating in a country with strong economic fundamentals (such as Saudi Arabia) will be relatively unfettered in its ability to conduct business. Saudi Arabia's most significant economic challenge is how to manage its massive hydrocarbon revenues without creating inflation and de-stabilising the currency. In such an environment, a bank can accept deposits, lend, transfer money and conduct import or export financing with little in the way of macroeconomic factors to restrict its business in that area. There may be prudential regulations governing this or another activity, but that is typical in almost any banking system.

On the other hand, a country such as Turkey must be constantly attentive, in a macroeconomic sense, to the counteracting influences of fiscal policy, monetary policy, GDP growth, inflation and external payments balance. As is frequently the case, monetary authorities may make changes in interest rates which affect GDP growth (and consequently the level of exchange rates and of business activity). In addition, regulatory authorities—which ideally work toward the same objectives as the monetary authorities—may impose or alter regulations encouraging or discouraging certain types of banking activities. Such changes would certainly influence a bank's future business, but may also impact (either positively or negatively) the business the bank already has on its books. For example, increasing required loan-loss provisioning on certain types of loans may discourage a bank from conducting that type of activity in the future, but will also impose a cost on the bank in terms of its existing business of that type.

8.2.1.2   Regulatory Environment

An analyst should assess the quality of the regulatory environment, and can do so by examining several aspects of that environment. Areas requiring examination include:

- Is the regulator independent of political pressures? (Are regulations imposed with the objective of maintaining a sound banking system, or does politics enter into the regulator's actions?)
- Are there prudential requirements of banks and are they evenly enforced?
- Are the regulatory function (creation of regulations) and the supervisory function (enforcement of the regulations) separate? The division of responsibilities not only prevents conflicts of interest, but also contributes to proper enforcement.
- Are there inspections both off-site (online reporting of various prudential requirements on a monthly, weekly, daily or even real-time basis in some cases) and on-site (supervisors visiting the bank—sometimes unannounced—to audit the validity of reporting)?
- Are the supervisors empowered to take action if regulations are not being observed?
- What is the track record of the supervisor? Is there a history of intervening or even closing banks which have demonstrated non-adherence to regulatory requirements?

8.2.1.3   Auditing and Accounting

A bank is only as good as the veracity of the numbers it reports. Left to their own designs, most banks—while not necessarily reporting inaccurate numbers—would give themselves the benefit of any doubt so as to present the most positive picture possible. It is the task of auditors to express an informed opinion, based on their audit, of the management's presentation of the financial statements.

That presentation is made according to the standards operative in that particular country. Those standards are usually a composite of banking law and regulation, and may or may not be similar to international standards. These include International Standards on Auditing (ISA) and International Financial Reporting Standards (IFRS). The use of these standards, or some adaption of them[3], permits the analyst to compare banks within and between countries and banking environments. The requirement for disclosure is paramount among these standards. The international standard governing disclosure[4] is quite thorough, and many countries have adopted a large majority of those requirements. Before initiating an analysis, the analyst concerned should be fully aware of what the disclosure and reporting standards are, and how closely they conform to international standards. In some cases, local standards may actually exceed international standards, but the analyst must still be aware of any key differences or deviations.

A more daunting aspect of examining this factor is a determination of the quality of the accounting profession in a given country. The presence of the major international firms provides a great deal of comfort, but there are often situations where local firms carry a similar or even superior reputation than the global firms. It is often the case that, as opposed to assessing a bank's quality by its auditors, the quality of an auditor can be inferred from the quality of the banks it audits.

8.2.1.4 Legal System

The legal environment plays a vital role in the banking system, particularly in the key area of asset quality. The nature of the legal system becomes important after a loan has become non-performing and a bank wishes to take possession of and/or liquidate the collateral it may have. Does the legal system provide for a bank to perfect its interest in collateral, and thereby prevent the sale of that asset and bar claims from a third party to an interest in that collateral? That perfection could be obtained through notice to the debtor (the least secure method), through registration via land records, a securities exchange or a commercial code registry—or the most secure method (as practiced in many Gulf countries) through actual physical possession of the collateral or its title.

Even if the interest in the collateral can be perfected, there remains the issue of actually foreclosing on the property. Especially in the case of a person's residence, that can be a time-consuming process, and the legal system frequently gives the benefit of the doubt to the borrower—or in some cases actively favours the borrower. However, even in other

---

[3] *ISA and IFRS are suggested standards, but the body responsible for formulating them has no legal authority in any particular country. The standards may be adopted completely, partially or not at all by the banking authorities in a given country.*

[4] *Disclosure referred to here is public disclosure. Regulators, as noted above, usually have even more expansive requirements in respect of disclosure to regulatory authorities.*

instances (such as the foreclosure on commercial property or the liquidation of securities), the nature of the applicable laws, the attitude of the courts and the speed of the process are all aspects to be considered. A lengthy delay can be costly to a bank in terms of continuing to bear the cost of carrying the loan, as well as possible depreciation of the asset. The latter consideration is in addition to the likelihood that the sudden sale of a large quantity of securities or real estate could seriously affect the market—and therefore recoverable value.

8.2.1.5   Political Environment

The political environment includes both domestic and foreign factors. Domestic factors run the gamut from internal political battles to a change in government, to interference in a bank's operation—whether governmental and directed at the banking system as a whole, or political and directed at one or two specific banks. Domestic economic (or more likely, political) considerations may lead to such conditions as directed lending, whereby banks must retain a certain portion of their loan portfolios in a certain economic sector or subsector (or compensate by such means as a fine or increased deposits with the central bank), or the imposition of minimum interest rates payable on deposits or maximum interest rates receivable on loans—rates which may not be in line with the free market.

As might well be expected, foreign factors include border tensions with neighbours, international economic measures—such as sanctions, embargoes, boycotts or blockades engaged in to punish bad behaviour internationally—and ultimately war. In some markets, these factors have existed for such a long period of time that they no longer represent a genuine threat, while in some markets the rise of one or more of these factors may be sudden, and may greatly disrupt business and banking activity. While such future events cannot be accurately predicted, the analyst must remain aware of conditions or situations carrying event risk, potentially leading to drastic upheaval.

8.2.1.6   External Financial Factors

Some of the following factors are a direct result of a country's macroeconomic situation, while some are not. However, in all cases a bank has virtually no control over the extent to which these wider issues may impact upon their business,

In a country where one commodity is crucial to the economy, it is often the price of that commodity which drives the others. A rise in the price of crude oil may cause fiscal difficulties in some countries but will be a windfall in others, and may potentially result in a restrained fiscal policy in order to avoid inflation. In either case, the fiscal policy effects of the commodity price change will have wider ramifications for the government budget and ultimately on the banks, as the state may adjust its tax policy and/or its willingness or ability to expend money on infrastructure projects. Fiscal policy will have an effect on monetary policy and therefore on economic growth. Consequently, banks will also be affected as liquidity rises or falls, as loan demand shifts and as general economic activity rises and falls with the economic tide. As those changes affect the country's external payments balance, the value of the local currency will most likely fluctuate. This change will affect banks both in their own exposure to foreign exchange risk and in that of their borrowing and depositing customers.

8.2.2 Internal Factors

8.2.2.1 Ownership and Governance (Including History)

Studying a bank's history can be very helpful—indeed, essential—to understanding a bank. Did the bank originate as a bank or as something else, such as a money-changing institution, an investment bank or even a depository for public employees' pension funds? The chances are that even if founding took place a quarter-century ago, the bank will have retained many of its lending or deposit preferences and financial characteristics.

Has the bank ever been in severe trouble? How was this resolved? Has the bank acquired other banks over the years? Importantly, has there been a major merger or acquisition in recent years which may have changed the character of the bank and the nature of its business? Are the results of that merger of perhaps a decade ago still being felt? Was the merger a good fit, whereby the two banks provided each other with complementary characteristics which filled gaps each had previously displayed? Was the merger simply another name for a rescue and did the bank seriously impair its asset quality and/or its capital as a result?

Who owns the bank? Perhaps it is the government and if so, does it actively support its existence as a viable bank, or is it used to accomplish social and political objectives? If privately owned, is ownership dominated by one large financial group, one family, or one person?

Judging governance can be difficult. However, it must be determined as to whether the governing body is experienced, professional and independent of political considerations. Are there independent directors who are not involved in the daily management of the bank? Has there been a recent change (or frequent recent changes) in ownership or in the composition of the supervisory board?

8.2.2.2 Risk Profile/Management and Strategies

These areas are closely interrelated and are in fact tied to the bank's history, ownership and governance. In order to correctly analyse a bank, it is important to establish the following:

- What kind of bank is it?
- What kind of bank does it wish to be?
- What are its current objectives?
- Does it have the suitable management, strategies and other resources in place to achieve these objectives?

A bank naturally seeks to maximise its profitability (more on this below), but there are numerous ways of achieving this depending on the business model the bank has adopted or seeks to adopt. Net profit is composed of four basic components: interest income, non-interest income, operating expenses and risk expense. By way of example, a bank which is oriented towards the consumer market will tend to have higher levels of interest income, but also higher operating expenses. This is due to the greater need for an extensive branch system, higher levels of staffing and perhaps more expensive technology. It may also have a higher risk expense in the short term, but depending upon its collection skills may eventually recover greater shares of its non-performing loans than might be the case for a corporate-oriented bank.

A corporate-oriented bank, especially one with expertise in corporate finance, will probably post lower levels of interest income, higher levels of non-interest income (arising from trade finance commissions, advisory fees or capital markets commissions) and lower operating expenses. This is due to the larger average size of its transactions. It will also tend to have lower levels of 'loyal' (i.e. demand) deposits and higher levels of more expensive 'purchased' deposits—such as time deposits or repurchase transactions with customers. Over the short term, risk expense will be lower. However, as history has previously shown, corporate failures can be sudden, large and final, periodically disrupting the bank's asset quality and creating *ad hoc* needs for increased loan-loss provisions.

Comparison of two banks with exceedingly different business models would be roughly the same at the level of the bottom line (net profit), but might be very different in the steps taken to arrive at that bottom line. The analyst needs to take a bank's business model into serious consideration as the various components of profitability are analysed.

The business model of a bank should be consistent with the experience of a bank's management, and strategies undertaken to achieve specific objectives should be consistent with the current or prospective business model. For example, a bank which has made the decision to enter the consumer segment should be organised in such a way as to separate its consumer and corporate lending. It should have also acquired managers experienced in consumer lending (preferably in the geographic market in question), and should be prepared to offer products suitable to the consumer segment. These products might include credit cards (issued by the bank itself or utilising the system of another bank), general purpose consumer loans and housing finance. The bank should also either have—or plan to have—a branch network, as this would promote the growth of such business.

8.2.2.3 Franchise Value

While related to some extent to a bank's history, franchise value refers to the reputation of the bank, especially in the area in which its business model concentrates. It takes into consideration the reputation of its governance and management, as well as its branch system. It is often problematic to assess this value, and it certainly cannot be accurately quantified. However, it is an added value to a bank's rating—although it is also something which a bank can lose quite easily through a one-off scandal or issue of mismanagement, if such matters are not dealt with firmly and efficiently.

8.3   Quantitative Factors

Financial analysis does not ignore the qualitative factors, but rather recognises that it is those qualitative factors which are responsible for the picture the financial statements present. The financial analysis of a bank involves four basic pillars which collectively constitute the basis for assigning a bank's rating. A bank's financial condition can be compared to the construction of a building; the pillars and the corresponding parallels are elaborated on below. The four pillars are:

- Capital adequacy
- Asset quality
- Liquidity
- Profitability

8.3.1   Capital Adequacy

A bank's capital can be equated to the foundation of a structure. It is designed to remain in place regardless of events which may produce damage in other parts of the building. It can usually withstand fire, flood, wind, storms and even earthquakes. Likewise, capital anchors a bank. It is essentially a safety net for the Bank to fall upon when difficult times occur—as they often do.

Total capital includes paid-in capital, share premiums obtained from the sale of shares at more than par value, accumulated reserves which are the result of past earnings which have not been distributed in dividends, and reserves existing because certain assets have been revalued (the latter figure can be negative if net revaluations have been negative). Capital does not include any portion of authorised capital which has not been paid in, or any stock which the bank may have bought back from the market (usually because the bank considered the market price too low). A proper analysis of capital involves the total capital figure; consequently, increases in paid-up capital as the result of bonus shares (stock dividends) or capitalisation of reserves cannot by definition be considered as an increase in capital.

Capital adequacy refers to the extent to which a bank's capital can cover (a) fixed assets, (b) investments in unconsolidated affiliates, (c) any portion of existing non-performing loans (NPLs) which is not covered by loan-loss reserves, (d) future growth in NPLs, (e) future write-offs of NPLs, (f) future net losses and (g) expected future growth. When the first two of these items is deducted from total capital, the result is a figure for free capital—a figure which will be of use in the discussion of asset quality (below).

The use of certain capital ratios provides a tool for examining whether capital is adequate. Key among these is the Capital Adequacy Ratio (CAR), which in most countries is calculated according to standards (often with some adjustment for local conditions) issued by the Basel Committee on Banking Supervision. This ratio, which may be calculated according to Basel II or Basel III standards, expresses the relationship between the bank's eligible capital and its risk-weighted assets (RWA). The figure for risk-weighted assets is calculated by weighting credit risk assets according to their type (cash, government security, loan, etc…) and adding in figures for market RWA and operational RWA. An analysis of a bank's CAR involves comparing the ratio to the mandatory minimum as set by the regulator, to the CAR ratios of the bank's in-country peers, and to the ratios of banks worldwide.

Other key capital ratios include those which prior to the establishment of Basel were the key ratios used to analyse a bank. While Basel ratios have greatly advanced the ability to analyse a bank's capital, the other ratios are still valuable. The principal ratios which fall into this category are the ratios of total capital to gross loans and of total capital to total assets. The latter equates to a traditional leverage ratio, while the former mitigates that ratio and provides some ratings benefit to those banks with smaller shares of their balance sheets accounted for by loan portfolios.

Two other capital ratios are also of value. The rate of internal capital generation measures a bank's ability to generate capital through its profit. While no entity can expect to grow solely from its profit, those institutions with higher ratios—and therefore greater ability in this respect—are less at the mercy of external markets, and therefore have less need to raise capital externally during times of depression in capital markets.

The dividend payout ratio compares cash dividends to net profit. It is related to the rate of internal capital generation in that a high dividend payout ratio reduces that rate. This figure should generally be low for banks whose goals include rapid growth, but this can be problematic in some markets where investors seek regular dividend income. This ratio also has implications for liquidity; if a bank's liquidity is tight, it should display a very low dividend payout ratio in order to conserve cash.

8.3.2   Asset Quality

A bank's asset quality is comparable to the walls of a building. It provides the shape of the building (profile of the bank) and supports the roof. Clearly, walls made of cinder block are stronger than those made of cardboard, even though they can be made to look similar—and under normal circumstances would perform the primary task of defining the bank.

Loans are usually a bank's largest asset class, typically accounting for 60–80% of a bank's assets. In most countries, accounting standards mandate that loans past due more than 90 days be considered 'non-performing,' and that specific provisions be made against them. By the most common standard, that provisioning mandate rises to 50% when the past-due period reaches 180 days, and to 100% at 360 days. In addition, some general or collective provisions must be made against the performing loan book and against off-balance sheet assets. While there have been some actions taken by banks to keep the number reported in the financial statements to a minimum,[5] any analyst can take these into consideration—either by including them in NPLs, or addressing them separately.

The key ratio in respect of asset quality is the non-performing loan (NPL) ratio. This ratio, which relates NPLs to gross loans, provides some insight into a bank's risk management process. A particular bank's business model may dictate a low or a high NPL ratio, as a function of its risk appetite. Clearly, a bank which tolerates a high NPL ratio should also be earning more on its portfolio in general. As with many ratios it is valuable to observe not only the absolute figure and the manner in which it relates to the bank's peers (and banks globally), but also any trends or anomalies. If there has been a sudden upward spike in the number, it is important to identify the reason for it. The sudden appearance of one or two bad loans presents an entirely different picture from a situation of broad-based asset quality decline, which could indicate that risk management has broken down—or that it had never actually been adequate and had just been fortunate up to the current time.

Whether a bank's business model calls for a low or a high NPL ratio, it is to be expected that it will provide for those NPLs. As noted above, accounting requirements dictate certain percentages of coverage depending upon the length of time which a loan is past due. However, since NPLs over 90 days past due tend to stay past due, a conservative assumption is that a bank will have sufficient loan-loss reserves (combining both specific and collective) to cover all—or at least almost all—of its NPLs.

If NPLs are not fully provided, it is useful to compare the portion of NPLs for which provision has not been made to a bank's free capital, as defined above. While there is not necessarily a 'good' number for this ratio, a figure in excess of 100 % indicates insolvency.

Alternatively, and especially if a bank has fully provided for its NPLs, capital adequacy can be measured in a different way. This method compares the bank's NPLs to all of the means it has to cover them. Those means include loan-loss reserves and free capital. In the use of this ratio, a bank does not benefit, nor is it penalised, for its loan-loss provisioning policy. That policy may be influenced by other factors besides asset quality—factors such as regulation, tax law or even a desire to show better earnings (as long as the better earnings are not expended in higher dividends). In other words, whether a bank keeps its earnings in capital reserves or transfers them to loan-loss reserves makes no difference to this ratio. The ratio also establishes a level playing field for comparing banks which have fully covered their NPL portfolios with those which have not. Typically, a bank could be expected to cover its NPL portfolio 3–5 times, but if this multiple is less than 1, it once again indicates insolvency.

Until the economic crisis which began in 2008, asset quality meant loans—but since the losses suffered by many banks as the result of the Lehman Bros bankruptcy and subsequent events, it is important to examine the investment portfolio of a subject bank. Specifically, analysis would include (a) how much of the balance sheet is held in investments

---

[5] *These actions include re-scheduling loans before they become past due and the recent addition of a category of loans termed 'past due but not impaired.' These items could be the subject of an entirely separate discussion.*

(which may be subject to minimum regulatory requirements) so as to avoid overconcentration, (b) the nature of those investments (home government, other governments, private-sector), (c) the quality (investment-grade, speculative grade or unrated), (d) tenor, (e) rate basis (fixed or floating) and (f) the class to which securities have been assigned (available for sale, held to maturity, held at amortised cost, fair value through profit and loss).

8.3.3   Liquidity

Liquidity can be compared to the roof of a building (which ironically keeps 'liquid' (i.e. rain) away from the walls and the remaining interior of the building). Just as protection from the elements in the form of a roof is a necessary cost of protecting the structure's contents, so too is liquidity a necessary cost in maintaining a sound balance sheet.

Liquidity is important because in virtually all cases, banks which have failed have done so because they were unable to meet their obligations *on a particular day*. In other words, a deficiency in liquidity, although that may have been the result of several other factors over a long period of time, was the immediate cause of failure.

For a bank's purposes, the purpose of liquidity (just as it is for individuals and corporations) is to meet three basic needs. Liquidity meets (a) transactional needs (to conduct day-to-day business), (b) emergency needs and (c) opportunity needs (i.e. a chance to acquire an asset at a good price, but where time is of the essence and cash would not only be very helpful but perhaps even be a requirement).

One of the most important aspects of liquidity (for a deposit-taking commercial bank) is a bank's customer deposits—their level, as well as the trend in their movement. That balance-sheet line item figures into three fundamental liquidity ratios. These ratios, all of which involve a comparison to a bank's net loans, are collectively referred to as 'loan-based' ratios. In all cases, the lower the ratio, the better a bank's liquidity is considered to be.

The first of these ratios directly relates a bank's net loans to its customer deposits, and is a traditional ratio used by most banks to review and manage its liquidity. The second adds to the denominator deposits obtained on the interbank market, so that this ratio is usually lower than the first.

The third such ratio includes in the denominator free capital and medium/long-term funding, but does not include interbank borrowings. By this means, a bank which prefers to fund itself through capital rather than customer deposits is not penalised for that policy or practice. In most cases, this is the lowest of the three ratios, and is one key component in understanding a bank's liquidity.

In addition to analysing a bank's liquidity in terms of its deposits, it is also vital to understand its liquidity in terms of total assets. The liquid asset ratio relates a bank's liquid assets (cash, deposits with the central bank, negotiable government securities and deposits with banks) to its total assets. This is a basic measure of asset liquidity, indicating a bank's ability to meet its current obligations in a time of crisis.

It is the composition of the rest of the balance sheet which determines the level of this ratio, which can display a very different picture from that presented by the loan-based ratios. For example, a bank which posts strong loan-based ratios may do so not because of a high level of customer deposits, but rather because of a low stock of loans. For such a bank a large portion of its balance sheet would likely be in liquid assets, resulting in a sound liquid asset ratio. However, examining only the liquid asset ratio could be misleading; conversion of some liquid assets into loans would not be terribly difficult and would not take very long to accomplish. While the result may be a liquid asset ratio which is still sound, the effect on loan-based ratios could be much more dramatic.

In examining the liquid asset ratio, attention should be paid to the nature of a bank's government securities portfolio. In some cases, short-term government obligations may not be readily convertible into cash, especially in times of crisis. In other cases, long-dated securities (which may appear as long-term assets in a maturity mismatch analysis) may actually be very liquid since they may be readily marketable or discountable with the central bank or monetary authority.

The second balance sheet-based ratio provides a determination of how such liquidity is generated. In other words, if the liquid asset component of the balance sheet is artificially inflated through the use of 'purchased funds' as opposed to relationship-generated funds such as customer deposits[6], it reduces the validity of the liquid asset ratio in a stress situation. When the effect of 'purchased funds' is removed from the balance sheet, the result is the bank's net liquid asset ratio.

The objective of an analysis of the net liquid asset ratio is to learn what a bank's liquidity profile would look like if its external short-term lines were completely cut and the bank were not able to replace them. If such an event were to occur, gradually (probably over a period not longer than 90 days), the bank's interbank liabilities and customer repos would shrink to zero—leaving a much lower liquid asset ratio than was the case before.

Not to be overlooked in the analysis of liquidity is the degree of mismatching of assets and liabilities in terms of their maturities. Not to be confused with interest-rate sensitivity, which measures the effects of changes in interest-rate changes on a bank's interest income, maturity analysis is concerned with the effects of differences on a bank's liquidity. It is often said that lending long and borrowing short is a sure formula for profit; however, it is also a recipe for failure. While some mismatching is necessary and prudent—especially in the very short term—a bank must ensure that some of the long-term assets it holds (such as long-dated government securities) are readily marketable or can be discounted to replenish liquidity in the short term.

---

[6] *'Purchased funds' which include interbank liabilities or customer repos, are usually short-term in nature.*

8.3.4 Profitability

Continuing the use of the analogy to a building, profitability represents the finishing touches on that building—the decoration of an otherwise sound structure and renders it attractive. Just as a well-maintained and aesthetically-pleasing structure is attractive to potential buyers, a bank which reinforces sound balance-sheet characteristics in the three areas described earlier is attractive to potential owners (shareholders). The bank will find it easier to raise capital if it is a publicly-owned entity, and will find it easier to convince private-sector or state investors to inject additional capital and/or forego dividends.

The ability to do so is largely influenced by the ratio known as ROAE, or return on average equity. While it is important to potential investors, it is probably the least important to the counterparty analyst. This is usually so because if other profitability ratios are sound, ROAE is likely to be as well, unless the Bank is severely undercapitalised or overcapitalised. Moreover, while ROAE may be valuable as a measure of a bank's profitability, it could be high because of strong profitability or of a low level of capital. Determination of which of these factors is more relevant requires further inspection of a bank's profitability through the use of other ratios.

As referred to previously, profitability can be examined at three levels: gross income, operating profit and net profit. The first, which consists of the total of interest income and non-interest income, can vary between banks due to differences in the business models. Furthermore, the share of each of the two components in gross income may vary according to the business model, as well as to the market in which the bank operates. Generally speaking, banks operating in countries with advanced money and capital markets tend to rely less on interest income and more on fee income—as more sophisticated borrowers may avail themselves of numerous alternate vehicles (beside bank borrowing) for their financing needs. This relationship can be seen in the very simple ratio of non-interest income (or inversely, net interest income) to gross income.

Analysis of net interest income can be somewhat problematic, as it is the product of a bank's net interest margin (NIM)—the difference between the average cost of funds and the average rate of interest earned. Changes in net interest income can be the result of changes in the size of the loan book or of changes in the NIM—which in turn can be the result of a change in one or both of its components.

The step from gross income to operating profit takes into consideration operating expenses (or opex). While banks often include loan-loss or investment provisions in this number, those are not strictly speaking operating expenses. As outlined above, a bank's cost structure is usually heavily influenced by its business model, and an inconsistency between the two would be worthy of note.

Two of the most common cost ratios involve comparing opex to gross income or to a bank's size. In the first instance, the traditional cost/income ratio reports how much of a bank's gross income it keeps and how much it uses up in the factors which generate that income. A commonly accepted principle is that a bank should keep more of its gross income than it expends, so 50 % might be a good benchmark for this ratio. However, there can be justifiable reasons for higher ratios, and lower ratios are common in many markets. The cost structure may be dictated by the degree of use of technology, by prevailing wage levels or by a bank's branch network among other factors. Trends in this ratio should be examined thoroughly to determine if movement is due to changes in the numerator, changes in the denominator or both.

A cost/income ratio which is perceived as high because of a low level of gross income may well indicate that the bank's cost structure is sound, but that improvements are needed in gross income. This hypothesis could be evaluated by a comparison of opex to the bank's balance sheet.[7] If that ratio is low compared to that of its peers, it provides evidence that the bank's gross income is low for its size.

Both operating profit and net profit can be compared to a bank's size and at those levels are universal measures of profitability. In the former case, operating profitability reports how a bank performs in its day-to-day business and is a key yardstick—although the business model of the bank should be taken into consideration at this point.

After allowing for net risk expense (loan-loss provisions, investment provisions, direct write-offs and provision reversals), and after subtracting (or adding) extraordinary items and income taxes, the result is net profit. That figure, when compared to the bank's balance sheet size, indicates how well a bank is making its assets perform and provide benefit to shareholders. Unlike ROAE, which is valuable to a shareholder or potential investor, ROAA measures how a bank performs after all expenses are taken into consideration. It is in the examination of this ratio where banks are most comparable, regardless of their business model.

8.3.5 Concentration

Banks frequently err in 'too much of a good thing.' It is human nature to do so, and it certainly occurs in banking. For example, when a successful product or income source is found, a bank tends to continue to grow that item. Unfortunately, like most good things, it will come to an end. Competition may make the product less profitable, or a bank may relax its standards in its desire to grow that product. The proliferation of providers and users in the market may be such as to attract participants who will find and exploit a flaw in the product. Consequently, a bank should be prepared for that eventuality, and the best way to do that is by controlling growth in that (and any) product through diversification.

Overconcentration in products, such as auto loans or mortgage finance, can create the potential for problems in the future. However, concentration may take other forms. Areas where banks may over concentrate include economic sector, borrower or loan size (especially if the concentration is in large sizes), geography, currency or individual customer.

---

[7] *This could be expressed in terms of beginning total assets, year-end total assets or average total assets (ATA).*

While the latter is usually regulated by banking authorities, all areas of concentration should be examined by the analyst.

Moreover, the issue also arises on the deposit side. Over-reliance on deposits from just a small number of customers may lead to a 'captive' situation on the part of the bank. Liquidity concerns might not allow it to decline renewal of deposits from such customers, forcing the payment of higher interest rates—sometimes with minor differences, but in cases where the depositor is aware of its relative advantage, that cost can become significant.

8.3.6   Related-Party Exposure

Conducting business with a related party can be viewed as helpful to a bank, or in some cases it could be harmful. Clearly, when a shareholding parent seeks to assist its affiliate or subsidiary through deposits or lending business, there is a potential advantage to the bank. The same can be true of other related parties (such as directors, members of management or members of their families) and of other assistance (such as business referrals or assistance in such areas as risk management, technology or human resources). Assistance of the former sort is usually regulated and limited by banking authorities—and for good reason.

The temptation frequently exists for a shareholder to use an affiliate for its own benefit, so that a bank may be called upon to make loans in excessive amounts or under more lenient terms than might be the case in an arm's-length transaction. Usually, regulations limit the amounts of such lending and may require that it be secured with readily realisable collateral. More lenient conditions may also exist on the deposit side, although in that case the only damage a bank might suffer would be to its earnings and not to its asset quality.

In both cases, IFRS requires the disclosure of such related-party business and includes in the definition of related parties a broad array of entities and family members.

8.4   Assigning Ratings

8.4.1   Types of Ratings

A full description of CI's rating scale would be the subject of another document; however, for the current purposes, these ratings can be summarised as:

- Financial Strength Rating (FSR)—a standalone rating of the bank, considering only its financial condition and management, without regard to shareholder support, except through management, credit lines, marketing, synergy, etc.
- Support—a scale of 1 through 5, depending upon the ability and willingness of a support entity to provide support
- Local Currency Rating (LCR) (internal, not published)—may move the FSR down or more likely up because shareholder support is considered

- Foreign Currency Rating (FCR)—considers transfer/convertibility risk; therefore may move the LCR up or down based on the economic environment in which the bank operates. Generally speaking, this rating does not pierce the sovereign rating for the country in question
- FCR is further divided into Long-term and Short-term, indicating the likelihood of default in the long term (the former) or over the 12-month period from the mostly recent statement date (the latter). The two ratings are assigned based on different scales
- Outlook—Positive, Stable or Negative The outlook does not refer to the Bank's earnings or other prospects; rather, it is defined as the most likely course of action to be taken on the rating at the next review cycle—usually based on observable trends during the current year. It is not expressed as a certainty, and very often Positive or Negative outlooks are removed during the subsequent review.

8.4.2   The Rating Process

For the major credit rating agencies, including Capital Intelligence, credit ratings are assigned, and all subsequent rating actions determined, by rating committees and never by an individual analyst. The rating committee serves as the main institutional mechanism for ensuring that methodologies are applied and implemented consistently across credit ratings and regions.

While the analytical process involves consideration of both quantitative and qualitative factors, the variety and range of situations and factors (financial, institutional, economic and political) that can influence counterparty risk is such that there is no algebraic formula by which the ratings of a bank can be predicted. Indeed, comparative analysis of financial strength and default risk is typically complicated by differences in leverage, business mix, and accounting practices between individual banks and across countries. Moreover, even those risk factors that can be quantified need to be interpreted subjectively. Consequently, the distribution of credit ratings across the credit rating scale tends to be based on a blend of numerical analysis, comparative analysis and expert judgement. Since the objective is to provide a relative measure of credit risk by assessing the repayment capacity of one bank compared to another over a long-term horizon, excessively mechanistic or formulaic approaches are best eschewed.

Zafer Diab ist seit Dezember 2007 Geschäftsführer der Capital Intelligence (www.ciratings. com), einer EU-registrierten Ratingagentur (www.esma.europa.eu). Von 2002 bis 2007 war Diab in verschiedenen Führungspositionen innerhalb von Capital Intelligence tätig, so als Business Development Manager und als Senior Credit Analyst. Diab hat einen Bachelor of Science Degree in Computerwissenschaften der Baylor University sowie einen Abschluss als Master of Business Administration mit dem Schwerpunkt Finanzierung von der Lebanese Amercian University.berd

Rating einer Kantonalbank

9

Christian Schmid

9.1 Rating von Finanzinstituten – eine herausfordernde Disziplin

9.1.1 Grenzen öffentlich verfügbarer Informationen

Die Ertrags- und Bonitätsanalyse von Finanzinstituten ist eine herausfordernde Disziplin. Jeder bankinterne Spezialist, welcher je mit einer Benchmarkanalyse seines Instituts betraut worden ist, weiss von den grossen Schwierigkeiten, einzig mit öffentlich zugänglichen Informationen das eigene Institut mit anderen Banken zu vergleichen.

Ertragsanalysen sind ohne Detailkenntnisse über die Zusammensetzung der Kunden- und Produktportfolios, über Laufzeiten und Margen sowie über die Auswirkungen von Sonder- und Einmaleffekten kaum aussagekräftig. Erfahrungsgemäss enden derartige Analysen in Diskussionen über die Anwendbarkeit und Aussagekraft der Vergleiche sowie mit Spekulationen über Marktgegebenheiten und Sonderfaktoren.

Risikoanalysen erleiden trotz der Publikation von gängigen Kennzahlen dasselbe Schicksal. Die Interpretation einer EK-Duration Kennzahl bleibt jedoch im Marktrisikobereich eine vage Vermutung, wenn keine Kenntnisse über Art und Umfang der konkreten Zinsrisikoabsicherungsmaßnahmen, über die Art der Replikation variabel verzinslicher Produkte oder über Laufzeiten und Durchschnittszinssätze pro Laufzeitenband vorliegen. Auch Im Kreditrisikobereich werden allgemein bekannte Maßzahlen wie impaired bzw. non-performing loans sowie Wertberichtigungen/Rückstellungen ausgewiesen. Wie soll jedoch der Aufbau grösserer Risiken in einem Portfolio erkannt werden, ohne dass ein Zugang zu Detailwissen über Kundenzusammensetzung, Konzentrationsrisiken sowie

C. Schmid (✉)
St. Gallen, Schweiz
E-Mail: ch.schmid@sgkb.ch

© Springer Fachmedien Wiesbaden 2016
Z. Diab, O. Everling (Hrsg.), *Rating von Finanzinstituten*,
DOI 10.1007/978-3-658-04195-3_9

Tragbarkeits- und Überbelehnungsmuster im Hypothekargeschäft besteht? Und wie soll aus den zugänglichen Informationenquellen ein relevantes Risikoexposure im Bereich der operationellen Risiken frühzeitig erkannt werden?

Rein auf externen Informationen beruhende (Benchmarking-) Analysen sind daher nur mit viel Vorsicht zu genießen und müssen bzgl. Aussagekraft, insbesondere zur Prognose von Bonitätsrisiken, konsequent hinterfragt werden – ohne Zugang zu zusätzlichen internen Informationsquellen allerdings ein kaum lösbares Unterfangen.

9.1.2   Beginn der Finanzmarktkrise als Beispiel

Die ersten Wochen der Finanzmarktkrise im Herbst 2008 haben zudem eindrücklich aufgezeigt, dass aus einer reinen Außensicht kaum Risikoanalysen möglich sind. Niemandem ist es gelungen, unmittelbar zu erkennen, welche Finanzinstitute in welchem Umfang von den damaligen Risiken betroffen waren. Weltweit versuchten Bankspezialisten verzweifelt, auf Basis von öffentlich zugänglichen Informationen herauszufiltern, wer in welcher Höhe direkt gegenüber Subprime-Papieren und indirekt durch vielfältigste Seiteneffekte exponiert war. Meistens kamen derartige Analysen über die Kenntnis von Differenzen in den Verhältniszahlen von Kundenbeständen, Handelsbeständen und Beständen in den Finanzanlagen nicht hinaus.

Schnell wurde deutlich, dass die Außenbetrachtung keine verwertbaren Erkenntnisse brachte. Auch die Ratingagenturen waren damals nicht in der Lage, in der gebotenen kurzen Zeit neue Bonitätsinformationen zu liefern. Es blieb einzig die Möglichkeit, Bonitätsinformationen aus Marktdaten wie Credit Spreads abzuleiten, nur um festzustellen, dass diese bereits auf blosse Gerüchte reagierten. Die Unsicherheit war damals derart gross, dass alleine vage Gerüchte einzelnen Instituten innert Minuten den Zugang zum Interbankenmarkt verunmöglichten. Nur eine sofortige, international koordinierte staatliche Interventions- und Stützungsaktion konnte die Situation damals beruhigen.

Die Bankenbranche ist aufgrund der herrschenden Informationsasymmetrien und durch ihre wichtige Stellung als volkswirtschaftlicher Finanzintermediär zumindest in westlichen Staaten hochgradig reguliert. Im Rahmen dieser Regulation haben Aufsichtsbehörden und in ihrem Auftrag Revisionsgesellschafen einerseits Zugang zu wichtigen bankinternen Informationsquellen, anderseits liegt ihr Kernauftrag im Gläubigerschutz, d. h. alle Vorkehrungen zu treffen und proaktiv einzugreifen, damit kein Gläubiger Verluste erleidet.

Durch die Tatsache, dass diese Akteure mehr Informationen besitzen und sämtliche Anstrengungen darauf ausgelegt sind, frühzeitig und proaktiv Ausfälle von Banken zu verhindern, beeinflussen sie direkt Ausfallwahrscheinlichkeiten und können daher bei der Bonitätsbeurteilung nicht ignoriert werden. Doch wie soll ihre Tätigkeit in eine Ratingmethodik einfließen?

Die Finanzmarktkrise hat zusätzlich gezeigt, dass trotz einer dichten und proaktiven Regulation Banken in Schieflage geraten können. Aus einer volkswirtschaftlichen Gesamtbeurteilung heraus sehen sich Staaten oftmals gezwungen, zumindest die sogenannt systemrelevanten Banken zu stützen und somit nicht dem Default zu überlassen. Auch dieser Effekt muss mit berücksichtigt werden, da auch er direkt Ausfallwahrscheinlichkeiten von Finanzinstituten beeinflusst.

9.1.3 Erkenntnis

Die geschilderte Ausgangslage zeigt einerseits eine eklatante Informationsasymmetrie und somit das klare Bedürfnis der Marktteilnehmer, Bonitätsinformationen über Finanzinstitute zu erhalten, andererseits die Schwierigkeiten und vielfältigsten Herausforderungen für einen außenstehenden Analysten, diese überhaupt liefern zu können. Am Beispiel der von Moody's mit Aa1 gerateten St. Galler Kantonalbank soll in der Folge betrachtet werden, ob aus Sicht einer Bank einer Ratingagentur diese Herausforderung überhaupt gelingt.

9.2 Das Rating der St. Galler Kantonalbank

Die St. Galler Kantonalbank verfügt über eine Bilanzsumme von rund 24 Mrd. € sowie verwaltete Vermögen von ca. 25 Mrd. €. Sie ist primär im klassischen Finanzintermediärgeschäft (Commercial & Savings) für Privatpersonen und Unternehmen des Schweizer Kantons St. Gallen tätig, ergänzt durch das Anlagegeschäft, ebenfalls in erster Linie für vermögende Einwohner des Kantons St. Gallen. Außerhalb des Kantons ist sie in gewissen Geschäftssparten in der deutschsprachigen Schweiz sowie mit einer Tochterbank in Deutschland tätig. Insgesamt arbeiten rund 1000 Mitarbeiter bei der St. Galler Kantonalbank

Die St. Galler Kantonalbank erhält anfangs 2014 nachfolgende Einschätzung der Rating Agentur Moody's (Tab. 9.1):

Auf den ersten Blick erstaunt die hohe Diskrepanz zwischen dem Rating für die Bank Deposits und das Adjusted Baseline Credit Assessment. Dieses ist auf eine umfassende Staatsgarantie zurückzuführen, welche der Kanton St. Gallen der Bank gewährt. Die sub-

Tab. 9.1 Rating-Einstufung der St. Galler Kantonalbank. (Quelle: Moody's 2014)

Category	Moody's rating
Outlook	Stable (m)
Bank deposits	Aa1/P-1
Bank financial strength	C+
Baseline credit assessment	a2
Adjusted baseline credit assessment	a2
Senior unsecured- Dom Curr	Aa1
Subordinate-Dom Curr	A3

sidiäre Staatsgarantie umfasst sämtliche Verbindlichkeiten der St. Galler Kantonalbank, mit Ausnahme von nachrangigen Darlehen.

Wie kommen diese Ratingeinstufungen nun zu Stande und wie beurteilt die Bank dabei die Moody's Methodik?

9.3 Rating-Methodik von Moody's

Die Ausführungen in diesem Beitrag zur Moody's Methodology entstammen aus den Dokumenten Moody's 2007a, 2007b, 2011, 2014. Zur Gewährleistung der Übersichtlichkeit wird darauf verzichtet, jede Textpassage einzeln zu zitieren. Zudem wurden an gewissen Stellen Vereinfachungen und Verallgemeinerungen vorgenommen.

Die Methodik von Moody's leitet das Kreditrisiko einer Bank aus ihrer intrinsischen Finanzkraft sowie aus der Wahrscheinlichkeit, dass sie von externer Unterstützung profitieren kann, ab. Für die Foreign Currency Ratings wird zudem zusätzlich die Wahrscheinlichkeit, dass die Bank aufgrund von Maßnahmen der Staatsregierung ihren Zahlungsverpflichtungen nicht nachkommen kann, berücksichtigt.

Der mehrstufige Ratingprozess startet mit dem sogenannten Bank-Finanzkraftrating (BFSR) welches als Maß für die Wahrscheinlichkeit verstanden wird, mit der eine Bank Unterstützung durch Dritte in Anspruch nehmen muss, um einen Zahlungsausfall zu vermeiden. Um das BFSR von den Deposit- und Debt Ratings abzugrenzen, werden die Buchstabenratings A-E, wobei A die Bestnote ist, verwendet. Mit dieser Systematik beurteilt Moody's über 1000 Banken in mehr als 90 Länder.

Mittels einer fixen Mapping Tabelle wird die A-E Notation als sogenanntes Baseline Risk Assessment in die gewohnte Moody's Skala transformiert. Ein C + in der BFSR Logik bedeutet als Beispiel ein A2 Baseline Risk Assessment. Kann nun eine Bank keinen externen Support einer Muttergesellschaft, des Staates oder von lokalen Behörden erwarten, ist das Local Currency Deposit Rating identisch mit dem Baseline Risk Assessment. Ist hingegen eine Unterstützung realistisch, so fließt diese über einen Kriterien- und Scoringkatalog als upgrade des Baseline Risk Assessments in das Local Curreny Rating ein. Erhält das Local Currency Rating einen höheren Wert als das Moody's Rating „Foreign Currency Deposit Ceiling" des betroffenen Landes, so reduziert sich der Wert für das Foreign Currency Rating auf diesen tieferen Wert (Abb. 9.1).

Die im nachstehenden Kapitel zu vertiefende BFSR-Scorecard ist als Einstieg in den Rating-Prozess zur Unterstützung von Analysten und Banken gedacht. So soll der Score den Analysten und Ratingkomitees bei der Entscheidung über das BFSR einer Bank einen ersten Anhaltspunkt liefern. Die individuelle Analyse des konkreten Institutes kann bei einem oder mehreren Unterfaktoren der Scorecard zu Anpassungen oder zur Betrachtung zusätzlicher relevanter Kennzahlen führen.

In der publizierten Credit Opinion über das beurteilte Institut wird denn auch sowohl das Resultat des aggregierten BFSR Scores, wie auch das effektiv zugeteilte BSFR-Rating

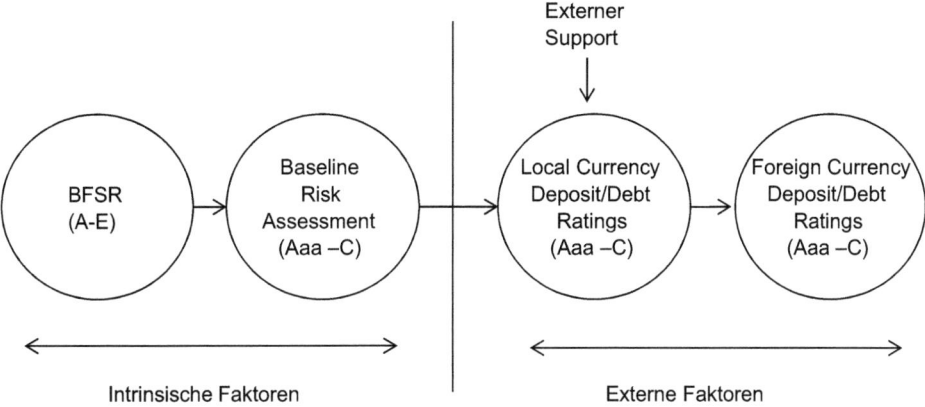

Abb. 9.1 Rating-Systematik von Moody's für Banken

ausgewiesen. Dabei besteht keine Regel, dass das zugeteilte Rating nur gewisse Notches vom berechneten Wert abweichen darf.

Diese Vorgehensweise erlaubt Moody's, Banken weltweit zu vergleichen, der besonderen Risikolage eines einzelnen Institutes jedoch weiterhin Rechnung tragen zu können.

9.4 Die Bank-Finanzkraft Rating (BFSR)-Konzeption aus Sicht der Bank

9.4.1 Systematik

Will eine Ratingagentur vermeiden, Ratings rein auf Basis einer individuellen Betrachtung und Einschätzung des einzelnen Instituts zu vergeben, ist sie gezwungen, weltweit verschiedenste Arten von Bankinstituten in ein einheitliches Ratingschema einzuordnen.

Die geringe Anzahl weltweit effektiv ausgefallener Finanzinstitute verunmöglicht bereits den Versuch, mittels statistischer Methoden aussagekräftige Modelle generieren zu wollen. Dies ist eher ein Glücksfall, denn aufgrund der Diversität der Bankinstitute sowie der weltweiten Unterschiede in den politischen und wirtschaftlichen Rahmenbedingungen würden derartige Modelle ohnehin vielfältigste Angriffspunkte liefern. Ein Ratingschema für Finanzinstitute ist somit zwangsläufig ein Expertensystem, welches bzgl. Faktoren und Gewichtungen in der Lage sein müsste, der enormen Heterogenität der Branche weltweit gerecht zu werden.

Jeder Versuch, diese vielfältigsten Unterschiede in ein Experten-Modell einzubauen, würde jedoch scheitern. Die einzig denkbare Vorgehensweise ist daher, den Ausgangspunkt einer Rating-Einteilung über eine äußerst einfache und transparente Konzeption herzustellen und anschließend individuelle Anpassungen zuzulassen.

Moody's schlägt exakt diesen Weg ein und stellt mit dem sogenannten „Bank Financial Strength Rating" eine einfache und standardisierte Ratingkonzeption an den Ausgangspunkt ihres Ratingprozesses. Die Systematik setzt sich wie folgt aus quantitativen und überwiegend qualitativen Faktoren zusammen:

Quantitative Faktoren

- den finanziellen Fundamentaldaten (50 %)

Qualitative/teils quantitative Faktoren

- dem Wert der Geschäftsposition (20 %)
- der Risikopositionierung (20 %)
- dem aufsichtsrechtlichen und operativen Umfeld (je 5 %)

Die Gewichtungsfaktoren zeigen, dass Einfachheit, Transparenz und Vergleichbarkeit im Zentrum der Überlegungen standen. Die Tatsache, dass Moody's den qualitativen und quantitativen Teil gleich gewichtet und praktisch ohne Ausnahme die (nicht dargestellten) Unterfaktoren, welche zum jeweiligen Faktorwert führen, ebenfalls nahezu ausnahmslos gleichgewichtet, zeigt, dass man eine Diskussion über Gewichtungswerte gar nicht erst aufkommen lassen wollte.

Dieses pragmatische Set-up führt zwangsläufig zum Hauptnachteil, dass ein einzelner oder einzelne hochgradig risikobehaftete Faktorausprägungen im Zuge der generellen Gleichgewichtung keinen genügenden Einfluss auf das Scoreresultat mehr auszuüben vermögen. Dieser Gefahr musste Moody's an diversen Stellen Rechnung tragen:

- Die Faktorgewichte der qualitativen Faktoren zwischen „reifen" und „unreifen" Märkte werden unterschieden, indem in unreifen Märkte für das aufsichtsrechtliche und operative Umfeld das Gesamtgewicht markant von den oben dargestellten je 5 % auf 21 % erhöht wird;
- In den finanziellen Fundamentaldaten erhält der niedrigste Wert des Einzelfaktors eine zusätzliche Gewichtung von 30 % und bestimmt somit fast 50 % des quantitativen und 25 % des Gesamtratings;
- Es wird eine Vielzahl von zusätzlichen Regeln aufgestellt, um risikohaften Konstellationen ein markant höheres Gewicht zu verleihen (so wird bspw. innerhalb der Risikopositionierung dem Unterfaktor „Konzentration der Kreditrisiken" ein zusätzliches Gewicht von 30 % beigemessen, falls der Scorewert tief („D" oder „E") ist.)

9.4.2   Quantitative Komponenten

9.4.2.1   Systematik von Moody's
Bei den finanziellen Kennzahlen greift Moody's wenig überraschend auf folgende generelle, einfache, bekannte und weltweit jederzeit ermittelbare Kennzahlen zurück:

- Rentabilität
- Liquidität
- Kapitalausstattung und
- Effizienz (ausgedrückt als cost/income ratio)

Gemessen wird damit in erster Linie die finanzielle Risikoabsorptionskraft eines Finanzinstitutes: Je höher die Kapitalreserven, je stärker die Ertragskraft, je besser die Effizienz und je umfassender die Liquiditätshaltung einer Bank, desto höher ist ihre Kraft, Verluste auszugleichen, desto ausgeprägter ist die Wettbewerbsfähigkeit und desto geringer die Anfälligkeit auf Vertrauenskrisen. Dies gilt weltweit für alle Finanzinstitute und stellt daher einen guten Ausgangspunkt für eine Ratingvergabe dar.

Erstaunlich ist, dass es Moody's an dieser Stelle nicht dabei belässt, über die finanziellen Fundamentaldaten rein die finanzielle Risikoabsorptionskraft zu messen und die eigentliche Risikoexposition der Bank dem qualitativen Teil zu überlassen. Ergänzt werden die vier erwähnten Faktoren mit einer fünften Kennzahl, der sogenannten

- Aktivaqualität (Problemkredite in % des Gesamtkreditvolumens bzw. in % des Eigenkapitals)

welche einen Teilaspekt des Risikoprofils gleichgewichtet einfließen lässt und damit die ansonsten überzeugende Systematik der Trennung zwischen Risikoabsorption und Risikoprofil verwässert.

Zusätzlich handelt es sich bei der Aktivaqualität um eine Kennzahl, welche dem Nachteil ausgesetzt ist, dass ihre Anreizstruktur in die falsche ökonomische Wirkungswirkung zeigt: Banken, welche eine sehr vorsichtige Rückstellungspolitik praktizieren, proaktiv Rückstellungen bilden und somit die Risikoexposition vermindern, erhalten einen schlechteren Scorewert. In einer Systematik, in welcher zudem die schlechteste Einzel-Ausprägung ein Zusatzgewicht von 30 % erhält und damit das Ergebnis der finanziellen Fundamentaldaten um nahezu 50 % prägen kann, sollte generell auf Kennzahlen mit adversen Anreizstrukturen verzichtet werden. So hatte bspw. die St. Galler Kantonalbank exakt bei dieser Kennzahl im Jahr 2012 den tiefsten Teilfaktorwert und dies noch sehr nahe bei der Trenngrenze. Trotzdem machte es für die Bank selbstredend keinen Sinn, in der Rückstellungspolitik weniger vorsichtig zu fahren, nur um den eigenen BFSR-Score zu verbessern.

9.4.2.2 Vergleich mit Benchmarking der St. Galler Kantonalbank

Die Wahl der finanziellen Kennzahlen durch die internationalen Ratingagenturen können mit den Erkenntnissen aus Benchmarking-Projekten innerhalb der Finanzbranche verglichen werden. Es wurden im Umfeld der Schweizer Kantonalbanken bereits mehrfach Anläufe unternommen, im Kreise dieser Bankengruppe finanzielle Benchmarkings aufzusetzen. Dabei scheint die Aufgabe auf den ersten Blick einfach: Die Kantonalbanken sind betreffend Marktgegebenheiten, Jurisdiktionen und Geschäftsmodellen weit homogener als die Gesamtheit der weltweiten tätigen Banken. Sie agieren im selben rechtlichen Umfeld, mit einem sehr ähnlichen Geschäftsmodell und mit sehr vergleichbaren ökonomischen Rahmenbedingungen Doch selbst unter diesen Voraussetzungen ist bisher jeder Versuch eines sinnvollen Benchmarkings gescheitert: Unkenntnisse über Sonderfaktoren, spezifische Risikoverhaltensweisen, unterschiedliche Definitionen gleichartiger Begriffe sowie differierende Wettbewerbssituationen auf Submärkten verunmöglichen selbst im abgegrenzten Markt der Schweizer Kantonalbanken einen externen Vergleich. Das Dilemma ist offensichtlich: Je sophistizierter Kennzahlenwerte zur Erfassung der Komplexität gebildet werden, desto wichtiger sind internen Kenntnisse, je allgemeiner die Vergleichswerte gehalten werden, desto schwieriger die Ableitung von Erkenntnissen.

Die St. Galler Kantonalbank führt daher vergleichende Analysen der Finanzkraft nur noch mit einigen wenigen Partnerbanken durch, die bereit sind, interne Details auszutauschen. Bei allen übrigen Benchmarks beschränkt sie sich selbst im Kreise vergleichbarer Kantonalbanken analog zu den internationalen Ratingagenturen darauf, die Positionierung mittels nachfolgender Basis-Kennzahlen

- Earnings per Share
- Return on Assets und
- Cost Income Ratio

in einem mittel- bis langfristigen Kontext zu betrachten, um daraus grundsätzliche Schlüsse zur Entwicklung der Wettbewerbsposition und Ertragskraft ziehen zu können (vgl. Abb. 9.2 zur RoA Positionierung).

Zusätzlich werden mit den Net New Money (NNM) und den Net New Loans (NNL)-Wachstumsraten zwei Kennzahlen beachtet, welche insb. auch aktuell aufgrund der Marktbesonderheiten (Tiefzinsphase mit Gefahr zu einem Immobilienboom; internatio-

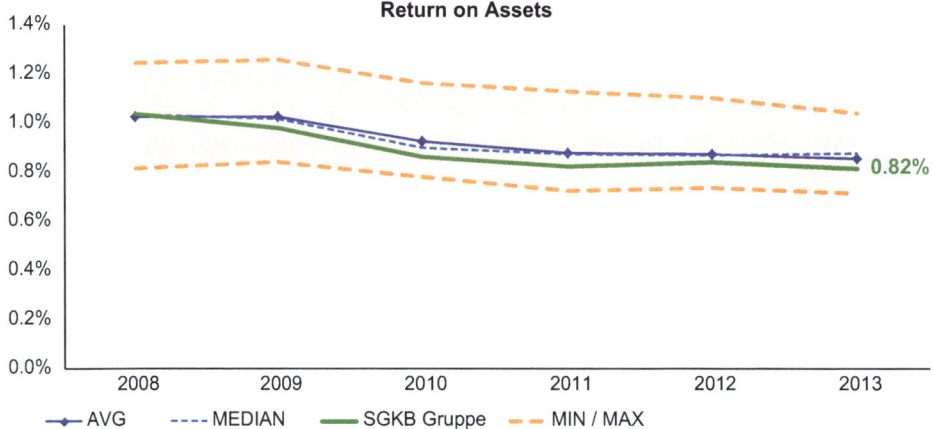

Abb. 9.2 RoA der St. Galler Kantonalbank im Vergleich zu ausgewählten Peers

naler Trend zu einem umfassenden Automatischen Informationsaustauch) besondere Aufmerksamkeit bedürfen.

9.4.2.3 Wertung

Es ist sehr zu begrüssen, dass Moody's bei der Betrachtung der finanziellen Fundamentaldaten den Fokus auf die generelle, internationale Vergleichbarkeit der Risikoabsorptionskraft legt. Durch die Vermeidung, mittels öffentlich zugänglicher Finanzdaten auf die explizite Risikopositionierung schließen zu wollen, wird jede Art von mühseligen, institutsspezifischen Detailkorrekturanforderungen zur Ratingsteuerung ausgeschlossen. Gerade an derartigen Bereinigungswünschen würden sich kaum lösbare Meinungsverschiedenheiten zwischen Ratingagentur und zu ratender Bank entzünden, welche dem erforderlichen konstruktiven Dialog während des übrigen Ratingprozesses nicht dienlich wäre.

Die Erfahrungen der letzten Jahre mit Moody's haben zudem gezeigt, dass ihre Analysten, wie in ihrer Methodology angekündigt, sehr wohl neben den globalen Kennzahlen zusätzliche finanzielle Kennzahlen beiziehen, welche zur Einschätzung des Risikos in einer geographischen Region von Relevanz und somit aussagekräftiger als die generellen Werte sind. So standen in den mit der St. Galler Kantonalbank geführten Ratingdiskussionen der vergangenen Jahre richtigerweise die NNM und die NNL-Wachstumsraten im Zentrum der Gespräche. Unterschiede zwischen den Teilmärkten der Ostschweiz sowie diversen HotSpots wie Zürich und Genf flossen dabei in die Argumentationsketten ein. Diese instituts- und regionenspezifische Sichtweise auf zusätzliche finanzielle Kennzahlen fließt im Dialog über eine allfällige Übersteuerung des BFRS-Scores in die Ratingvergabe ein und wird in den publizierten CreditOpinions textlich ausgeführt.

9.4.3 Qualitative Komponenten

9.4.3.1 Grundsätzliche Überlegungen

Tragen die finanziellen Fundamentaldaten primär zur Beurteilung der relativen Risikoabsorptionskraft sowie zur Einschätzung der generellen Wettbewerbspositionierung bei, so muss das Bild über die Risikonahme und –bereitschaft der Bank insb. über die qualitativen Aspekte entstehen.

Dabei stellt sich die grundsätzliche Frage, ob mittels Analyse und Bewertung einzelner Faktoren eine Außeneinschätzung vorgenommen wird, oder ob man die Informationslücke zur Bank schließt, indem man diese die eigene Risikopositionierung und –einschätzung, welche anschließend verifiziert werden kann, präsentieren lässt. Moody's wählt, wie an nachstehendem Beispiel der Agenda des Jahresmeetings 2013 zu erkennen ist, in erster Linie die zweite Option (Abb. 9.3).

Vor der Betrachtung der einzelnen institutsspezifischen Faktoren gilt es, wie bereits einleitend bemerkt, den Einfluss von Drittorganisationen zu klären. Mit den Bankenaufsichten (und Revisionsgesellschaften) operieren in der Finanzbranche Akteure, welche

Abb. 9.3 Agenda des Jahres-
meetings 2013 zwischen der
St.Galler Kantonalbank und
Moody's

- Jahresabschluss 31.12.2012

  - Konzernabschluss
  - Segmentsberichterstattung
  - Assets under Management
  - Kreditqualität
  - Asset & Liability Management
  - Bilanzqualität/ Eigenmittelausstattung

- Weitere Themen

  - Projekte/ Strategische Herausforderungen
  - Teilprivatisierung/ Staatsgarantie
  - Bedeutende operationelle Risiken

Zugang zu Bankinternas besitzen und zum System- und Gläubigerschutz eigenständige
Risikoanalyse und –begrenzungsmaßnahmen aufgebaut haben. Typischerweise hat die
Bankenaufsicht einen tieferen Einblick in die Risikosituation einer Bank als es Ratingagenturen aufgrund ihrer Tätigkeit je erlangen können. Es gilt daher zu definieren, auf
welche Art diese Erkenntnisse berücksichtigt werden.

Moody's anerkennt in ihrer Ratingsystematik, dass es mit den Aufsichtsbehörden und
Revisionsgesellschaften weitere Akteure gibt, welche Gesamtbankrisikokonzeptionen
überprüfen, Risikomessmethoden und damit verbundene Limiten definieren und deren
Einhaltung auch kontrollieren. Im Falle der Überschreitung einer gewissen Risikotoleranz
haben diese Behörden die Mittel in der Hand, konsequent einzuschreiten und eine Risikoreduktion durchzusetzen.

Moody's beurteilt die Unabhängigkeit der Aufsichtsbehörden, die gesetzten aufsichtsrechtlichen Standards im Bereich der klassischen Risikokategorien, die Professionalität
der Ressourcen der Behörden sowie die Durchsetzungskraft. Die aufsichtsrechtliche Komponente fließt in reifen Märkten mit einem Faktorgewicht von 5 % in den BFSR-Score ein.

Verwandt mit dem Aspekt des Aufsichtsrechts ist die Beurteilung des operativen Um-
feldes, in welchem die wirtschaftliche Stabilität, das Ausmaß von Integrität und Korrup-
tion sowie die Reife und Berechenbarkeit des Rechtssystems beurteilt werden. Auch dieser
Faktor, welcher außerhalb des Einflussbereiches der Bank liegt, wird mit 5 % gewichtet.

9.4.3.2 Ratingfaktor: Risikopositionierung der Bank

Mit diesem Ratingfaktor wird nun die konkrete Risikopositionierung der Bank gemessen.
Diese wird in erster Linie über zwei Wege festgestellt:

- der aktuellen Risikonahme der Bank mittels Kennzahlen und Stresstests zu Kredit-,
  Markt und Liquiditätsrisiken (je ein Faktor für jede Risikokategorie);
- die Wirksamkeit von Risikomanagement und Kontrollmechanismen (ein Faktor).

Der Zugang zu diesen Informationen sowie insb. zu deren Interpretation ist aus einer reinen Außensicht ausgeschlossen. Die Ratinganalysten lassen sich bei einfacheren Werten die dafür notwendigen Datensätze zukommen (zum Beispiel für die Bestimmung von Konzentrationsrisiken im Kreditgeschäft). Bei komplexeren Sachverhalten (wie etwa der Konzeption des Liquiditätsmanagement oder Value-at-Risk und Stresstestberechnungen) werden die bankinternen Werte und Sichtweisen präsentiert und in einem gemeinsamen Dialog plausibilisiert. Auch wenn zuweilen die Unterschiede in den Einschätzungen von Bank und Ratingagentur divergieren und die Agentur Werte übernimmt, mit denen die Bank nicht immer einverstanden ist, so ist zumindest der Dialog rein sachbasiert und daher ausnahmslos konstruktiv.

Eher weniger verständlich ist, weshalb der bedeutende Block der Risikopositionierung mit zwei weiteren, eher unbedeutenden gleichgewichteten Unterfaktoren ergänzt wird, nämlich der

- Corporate Governance und der
- finanziellen Berichterstattung

Der Faktor „Corporate Governance" kommt wohl nur zum Tragen, wenn entweder in der personellen Dominanz von Einzelpersonen, im Geschäftsvolumen an nahestehenden Personen oder in einer komplexen Eigentümerstruktur/Mehrheitseigentümerschaft ein besonderer Risikofaktor besteht. Das offene System von Moody's mit Übersteuerungsmöglichkeit des Rating Scores würde es jedoch erlauben, derartige Aspekte im Rahmen der individuellen Betrachtung in einer Ratingkorrektur zu berücksichtigen. Die Einbindung in die Systematik erlaubt weniger Gestaltungsspielraum, insb. auch bei deren Gewichtung. So erhält bspw. die St.Galler Kantonalbank aufgrund ihrer staatlichen Eigentümerschaft in dieser Position ein tiefes Rating „D", auch wenn nur sehr schwer abzuleiten ist, wie aus der Mehrheitseigentümerschaft des Kantons eine erhöhte Ausfallwahrscheinlichkeit entstehen soll.

Die Art, der Umfang und der qualitative Detaillierungsgrad der Finanzberichterstattung wird stark von Aufsichtsbehörden vorgegeben. So unterscheiden sich denn auch die Finanzberichterstattungen innerhalb desselben aufsichtsrechtlichen Regimes nur marginal. Die Qualität der Aufsichtsbehörden fließt bereits an anderer Stelle in die Ratingkonzeption ein. So verbleibt als eigentliches Differenzierungsmerkmal in dieser Risikokategorie nur die Periodizität der Berichterstattung. Die St.Galler Kantonalbank publiziert ihren Abschluss halbjährlich und erhält daher die eher tiefe Ratingeinteilung „D". Aus einer Kosten-/Nutzenoptik sowie dem geringen Newsflow ist für die Bank eine quartalsweise Offenlegung jedoch nur wenig sinnvoll. Für die Ratingagentur selbst ist dieser Aspekt zudem kaum differenzierend, da sie unabhängig von der Periodizität der Berichterstattung über relevante Risikoereignisse ohnehin umgehend von der Bank informiert wird.

9.4.3.3   Ratingfaktor: Der Wert der Geschäftsposition

Der letzte Faktor, der „Wert der Geschäftsposition", ist für die St.Galler Kantonalbank aus individueller Sicht der Kontroverseste. Mit diesem Faktor misst Moody's

- die geographische Diversifikation,
- die Diversifizierung der Erträge
- die Stabilität der Erträge sowie
- den Marktanteil und die Preisfestsetzungsmacht im relevanten Markt.

Der (zumindest theoretische) Wirkungszusammenhang dieser Faktoren mit einer erhöhten Ausfallwahrscheinlichkeit dürfte wohl argumentativ herzustellen sein und ist daher an dieser Stelle nicht zu hinterfragen.

Für die St.Galler Kantonalbank ist hingegen bedeutend, dass ihr Geschäftsmodell aufgrund ihrer Eigentümerschaft im Wesentlichen auf den Kanton St.Gallen sowie das klassische Finanzintermediationsgeschäft beschränkt ist. Dazu gehört auch, dass nicht nur Privatpersonen und KMU sondern auch mittelgroße Firmen und deren Exponenten zu den Hauptbankkunden gehören.

Nur eine weitere geographische Ausdehnung sowie eine Abkehr vom Firmenkundengeschäft könnten die Einstufungen in den Diversifikations- und Stabilitätskennzahlen verbessern. So müsste bspw. für eine Erhöhung der Einstufung in der geographischen „Diversifizierung" (aktuell „D") die Bank mindestens 25 % der Gewinne außerhalb ihres angestammten Heimmarktes in gering korrelierten Zusatzmärkten erzielen.

Eine derartige Expansion würde aufgrund der fehlenden Marktkenntnisse wohl eher grössere als geringere Risiken mit sich bringen.

Derartige Veränderungen der Geschäftsstrategie sind für die St.Galler Kantonalbank in der aktuellen Governance ausgeschlossen. Es würde bedeuten, Geschäftsrisiken außerhalb des Kantons vermehrt aufzubauen, was wiederum nicht mit der Staatsgarantie des Kantons St.Gallen vereinbar ist. Auch eine bewusste Reduktion des Firmenkundengeschäftes für St.Galler Unternehmen würde das Profil der Bank schwächen, vom Markt kaum verstanden und daher betreffend Stabilität des Unternehmens eher kontraproduktiv wirken. Die Bank wird sich damit abfinden müssen, in dieser Kategorie kaum Spielraum zur Verbesserung ihres „C" Ratings zu besitzen.

9.4.3.4   Fazit

Weit über die Hälfte der Faktorgewichte des qualitativen Teils ist für die St.Galler Kantonalbank faktisch nicht beeinflussbar. Einerseits wird das relevante operative und aufsichtsrechtliche Umfeld beurteilt, andererseits ist es nicht zielführend, das erfolgreiche Geschäftsmodell und die damit verbundene Marktpositionierung an allgemeingültige Risikozusammenhänge (Diversifikation und Stabilität) anzupassen, nur um in einer Rating-ScoreCard einen besseren Wert zu erhalten. Vielmehr müssen Ratingsysteme derart konzipiert sein, dass erfolgreiche Geschäftsmodelle als Konsequenz zu einer besseren Einstufung führen. Eine derartige Konzeption ist zur Abdeckung von weltweit unterschied-lichsten Bankmodellen wiederum nicht möglich.

Auch an dieser Stelle verfolgt daher Moody's den richtigen Weg: Die Scorecard soll den Kunden und Analysten primär zur Unterstützung dienen, in einen gemeinsamen Risi-kodialog über die relevanten Risikofaktoren zu treten. Der Analyst muss die Möglichkeit haben, individuelle Konstellationen argumentativ in einem nicht standardisierten up- und downgrade Anpassungsprozess einfließen zu lassen. Die langjährigen Erfahrungen der St.Galler Kantonalbank mit der Agentur Moody's belegen, dass diese Flexibilität tatsäch-lich auch gelebt wird. Wäre dies nicht der Fall, so wären kontraproduktive Grundsatzdis-kussionen über Faktoren und Faktorgewichtungen unvermeidbar.

9.5 Berücksichtigung staatlicher Interventionen

Die Finanzmarktkrise hat deutlich gemacht, dass in vielen Fällen ein übergeordnetes staat-liches Interesse besteht, das Finanzsystem zu stützen und insbesondere Gläubiger vor Ver-lusten zu schützen. Selbst bei nicht direkt systemrelevanten Banken kann es in bestimmten Phasen grösster Verunsicherung zielführend sein, Schutzmaßnahmen zu beschließen, um die Ansteckungsgefahr einer Vertrauenskrise auf das gesamte Finanzsystem bereits im Keime zu ersticken.

Moody's anerkennt diesen Schutzmechanismus und hat bereits vor der Finanzmarkt-krise im Jahre 2007 empirisch festgestellt, dass die Ausfallraten von Finanzinstituten im Bereich Baa und tiefer unter denjenigen von Corporate Issuers lagen. Dies gilt insbeson-dere für lokale Einlagen.

Zur Anpassung des Baseline Risk Assessments wird in einem ersten Schritt über ein Scoring-System die allgemeine Bereitschaft des jeweiligen Staates zur Intervention beurteilt (Bedeutung der Bankbranche am BSP, historische Bankkonkurse, Stärke des Bankensystems), um anschließend anhand des zu beurteilenden Institutes dessen Bedeu-tung für das Zahlungsverkehrssystem sowie für den nationalen Kredit- und Einlagenmarkt in die Bewertung einfließen zu lassen.

Die St.Galler Kantonalbank verfügt für sämtliche Verpflichtungen (mit Ausnahme nachrangiger Darlehen) über eine subsidiäre Staatsgarantie. Diese gesetzlich veranker-te Staatsgarantie führt gemeinsam mit der Beurteilung der Finanzkapazität des Kantons St.Gallen dazu, dass das a2 Baseline Credit Assessment der Bank um vier Notches auf Aa1 erhöht wird. Basis dieser Bewertung bildet eine eigenständige Zusatzbeurteilung des Kantons durch Moody's und entspricht dem bestehenden AA + Rating des Kantons durch Standard&Poor's.

Tab. 9.2 Aktuelle Ratingstruktur der St.Galler Kantonalbank

Assigning Local & Foreign Currency Deposit Ratings			
BFSR	Baseline Risk Assessment	+ Outside Support = LC Deposit Rating	+ Sovereign Ceiling = Constrained FC Deposit Rating
A	Aaa	Aaa	Aaa
A-	Aa1	**Aa1**	**Aa1**
B+	Aa2	Aa2	Aa2
B	Aa3	Aa3	Aa3
B-	A1	A1	A1
C+	**A2**	A2	A2
C	A3	A3	A3
C-	Baa1	Baa1	Baa1

9.6 Folgerung

Ein zuverlässiges Rating eines Finanzinstitutes ist einzig in Zusammenarbeit und im Dialog mit dem jeweiligen Institut möglich. Eine Einschätzung mittels öffentlich verfügbarer Informationen lässt letztlich nur ein Urteil über die generelle Risikoabsorptionskraft eines Institutes zu. Eine weitergehende Beurteilung benötigt zwingend den Zugang zur gelebten Risikoorganisation und zu Kontrollmechanismen, zu Hintergrundinformationen von Risikokennzahlen sowie zu Annahmen und Resultaten von Stresstests. Auch wenn sich die Offenlegungspflichten der Banken laufend verschärfen, so ist nicht zu erwarten, dass in absehbarer Zeit die für eine fundierte Risikobeurteilung notwendige Transparenz öffentlich vorhanden sein wird.

Soll zudem die Ratingeinschätzung nicht nur die Risikoposition eines einzelnen Institutes ausdrücken, sondern als Basis für effektive Ausfallwahrscheinlichkeiten dienen, so muss die beurteilende Instanz zudem ausgeprägtes Wissen und Fachkenntnisse über das aufsichtsrechtliche und operative Umfeld einer Bank besitzen sowie über Fähigkeiten zur Einschätzung aller Arten von Stützungsmaßnahmen des Finanzsystems verfügen und diese in die Ratingzuteilung auch einfließen lassen.

Die Finanzinstitute werden jedoch nur denjenigen Ratinginstanzen Zugang zu internen Zusatzinformationen gewähren, welche über die ausgewiesene notwendige Professionalität verfügen sowie ihnen einen direkten Nutzen in Form einer vom Kapitalmarkt anerkannten Ratingmethodik bieten. Der Markt wird somit von den traditionellen Ratingagenturen besetzt bleiben, für neue Marktteilnehmer ist ein Markteintritt kaum denkbar.

Im Bereich der konkret angewandten Methodik ist entscheidend, dass sich sowohl die beurteilte Bank wie auch die Ratingagentur über Sinn, Zweck, Aussagekraft und Grenzen der einzelnen Teilschritte der Methodik einig sind. Denn eines ist klar: Der Anspruch eines allgemeinen, weltweit für alle Banken gültigen Ratingsystems führt zum einfachsten und kleinsten gemeinsamen Nenner, welcher einer individuellen Risikoeinschätzung der einzelnen Bank nicht mehr gerecht werden kann. Ratingsysteme von Finanzinstituten sind daher auf einen intensiven Dialog zwischen den Instituten und den Ratingagenturen angewiesen und brauchen in der Anwendung die notwendige Flexibilität, welche verhindert, dass die Methodik selbst zum Gegenstand der Diskussion wird.

Ist das Vertrauensverhältnis zwischen Agentur und Finanzinstitut hergestellt, so wird aus dem Ratingprozess ein Wert resultieren, welcher für außenstehende Dritte ein adäquates Bild der Risikolage der Bank zu vermitteln vermag.

Es gäbe aus einer individuellen Perspektive immer verschiedenste Aspekte, welche an einer Methode kritisiert werden können. Aus Sicht der St. Galler Kantonalbank wäre dies im Kontext der Moody's Systematik der Umstand, dass die stärkstmögliche Profilierung- und Positionierungsstrategie der Bank, nämlich die konsequente Ausrichtung ihres Geschäftsmodells auf Privatpersonen, Gewerbe und Unternehmer des Kantons St. Gallen an verschiedenen Orten der Methodologie (Diversifikation, Risikokonzentration, Governance) zu einer sehr tiefen Einteilung führt, welcher der Gesamtrisikoexposition der Bank eher nicht gerecht werden dürfte.

Die enge Zusammenarbeit und der intensive Austausch mit der Agentur führen jedoch dazu, dass derartige wenig wertschöpfende Diskussionen gar nicht erst geführt werden. Vielmehr konzentriert sich der Dialog darauf, während der einzelnen Teilschritte des standardisierten Prozesses die individuell relevanten Risikofaktoren mit einfließen zu lassen, um in der abschließenden Credit Opinion die individuell bestmögliche Transparenz der effektiven Risikolage darstellen zu können.

Literatur

Moody's (2007a): Globale Methodik für Bank-Finanzkraftratings, Februar 2007;
Moody's (2007b): Incorporation of Joint-Default Analysis into Moody's Bank Ratings: A Refined Methodolgy, March 2007
Moody's (2011): Process Update on Support Provider Inputs for Global Bank Ratings, December 2011
Moody's (2014): Credit Opinion: St. Galler Kantonalbank, 26.02.2014

Dr. Christian Schmid Jahrgang 1969, ist seit August 2008 Mitglied der Geschäftsleitung und Leiter Corporate Center. Zuvor war er seit 2004 Geschäftsführer der RSN Risk Solution Network AG. Von 1999 bis 2003 war Christian Schmid bereits als Leiter Kreditportfoliomanagement sowie als Leiter Bereichsentwicklung in Führungsfunktionen bei der St.Galler Kantonalbank im Bereich Privat- und Geschäftskunden tätig.

Pitch or Ditch for the Bulgarian Credit Ratings?

10

Bojidar Archinkov

10.1 Introduction

Credit rating agencies apply the same set of core principals to analyze banks in Bulgaria, Germany or North America, but the relative importance between factors differs. This article contributes to an understanding of the dynamics in formation of a bank's business franchise, and assessing its performance in one of the European emerging markets. A short review on the recent economic history elucidates constituents of the currency board and current fiscal regime. Bulgaria has still to achieve market maturity, so assignment of higher financial strength ratings is still to come. The unique Bulgarian combination of currency board and a very preferential tax regime, frequently explains the will of local politicians to deviate from the strategic European vision of cohesion, a sense of common purpose, shared identity and unity. Privatization and deregulation in Bulgaria occurred during the period of 1993–2003. Country had chosen centralized method for privatization, entirely focused on selling state-owned banks to foreign strategic partners. Prior privatization there was a demonstrated lack of prudent credit risk models and business-wise decisions. Gradually foreign strategic investors introduced culture of adhering to regulations and professionalism. However post 2004, banks exposed to local use and controls were involved in ensuring financial support to other business endeavors of their owners. The narrow local market and interrelated business environment encouraged all material bank owners to participate in varieties of other financial and non-financial businesses. Retail banking and investment banking overlapped, having no clear borderline between related and non-related businesses. This resulted in the construction of the local financial leaders, possible regulatory imperfections and political crises.

B. Archinkov (✉)
Sofia, Bulgarien
e-mail: bojidar887@gmail.com

© Springer Fachmedien Wiesbaden 2016
Z. Diab, O. Everling (Hrsg.), *Rating von Finanzinstituten*,
DOI 10.1007/978-3-658-04195-3_10

Traditionally, the liquidity profile of the country has a strong positive correlation to bank liquidity. In addition to government, local insurance companies and pension funds are also occupied to provide liquidity to local banks. Forthcoming regulatory revolution designed to reshape the European financial sector may question solvency, elucidate equivocal statuses within portfolios, and clarify a number of large, cross-related credit exposures. The banks' own innovations will be required to preserve the links between banks, citizens and authorities. The involvement of the local banks' owners into non-bank businesses, as well as dynamic interaction with insurance companies and pension funds determined vulnerability to a possible deterioration in economic conditions. These were the major factors intertwisted into second Bulgarian banking crisis occurred in 2014.

Credit ratings agencies should be capable to assess complex interactions between the bank, bank owner and major borrowers. Closer proximity to data sources at home may potentially provide local credit rating agencies with a comparative advantage upon accessing available, but unpublished or confidential information. National level policy-makers must likewise contribute to economic success and financial stability, whilst minding the domestic implications. Credit ratings of the market participants depend on fluctuations of the main inflows of funds to Bulgaria—foreign direct investments, export, tourism and remittances. Finally, the article briefly addresses possible credit rating arbitrage between credit bureaus and regulatory capture.

10.2 Transition from Banking Dirigisme to Franchise Strength

In 1991, Bulgaria was labeled as one of the "Best kept secrets of the Soviet Block". The collapse of a command system revealed genuine achievements in electronics and computer technologies, as well as a piece (?) from complex and deeply concealed trade relations—including innovative export patterns to the Western and Arab worlds. West-East campaigns for privatization and for attracting foreign direct investments exhibited repeated incidences of state-owned enterprises outwitting technology embargos specified by the Coordinating Committee for Multilateral Exports Controls (COCOM). Only then did the scope of the heavy Bulgarian involvement in the design and production of electronic components and computers become clear. This dated back to the earliest days of 1960, including first license agreements for the production of machines such as the Facom-230/231 and others. At its peak, Bulgaria produced 40% of the computers used in the countries of the socialist block. The electronics industry was composed of over 300,000 workers and produced goods worth over US$ 13.3 billion per annum (or at that time, equaling 8 billion exchange-rubles). Further to that, Bulgaria pursued a bilateral clearing trade with the Soviet Union, and surprisingly many analysts reported a rapid mobilization of capital as the primary source of Bulgarian growth (Jerome and Robert 1985). Official statistics declared Bulgarian trade with the Western world to be a mere 11% of the total export-import of the country (the smallest number for an economy in Europe for 1988). However, the complex trade model, including the practice of transfer pricing between local holdings or foreign-trade organizations to their internationally-based subsidiaries, was entirely omitted. Surprisingly enough, Bulgarians were identified as the eighth "most optimistic" people in the world, according to a Gallup survey (Schlack 1993).

Bulgarian Foreign Trade Bank (Bulbank), The State Savings Bank (DSK) and the Bulgarian National Bank were the only three banks comprising the entire Bulgarian banking system. Mineral Bank, which later followed as a fourth, was established in 1981 as a specialized business-oriented bank. Its main purpose was to provide value added expertise in continuing industrialization of the country. Bayerisch-Bulgarische Handelsbank GmbH was established in München in 1987. Gradually, Bulgarian National Bank separated its commercial activities from monetary and supervisory functions. Soon after, a rapid demand for capital and international money transfers caused the number of banks in Bulgaria to increase to 71. In practical terms, this was the largest number of banks the country ever had. The period from 1990 to 1995 witnessed banking prevailing over prudent legislation, compliance and control. Bulgarian First Private Bank was established in 24 July 1990. The respective Banks and Lending Act was not enforced until the end of March 1992 (Minkov 1993).

Transition to the market economy in Bulgaria overlapped with the privatization of formerly public sector organizations in most of the West European countries. The European Union agreed on Maastricht Treaty's convergence criteria, and adopted a series of directives towards liberalization on telecommunications, railways, air transport, energy and postal services. The progress of Economic and Monetary Union encouraged West European governments to sell state assets and stakes in domestic industrial companies. After the pioneering experience of UK, Italy and France in the 1980s, privatization became a distinctive feature of European Union policy for more than a decade—exposing former monopoly markets to competition. These challenging transitional and restructuring reforms domestically absorbed most of the financial and managerial resources of the West European banks and business organizations.

With Western Europe occupied with their home liberalization, Bulgarian professionals perceived it as a divergence in values from social democracy. Distortion of the Eastern Block became transparent for all. Planning, systematic knowledge and coordination were considered both off the agenda and out of fashion. Actions prevailed over accountability and compliance. Experienced bank professionals were frequently distant from the ambitions of the new rich. Incidentally, cases of neglecting professional matters and fear suppressing communication were perceived as achievements in corporate integrity. The transition to a free market engaged most of the country's social energy and vigour.

Bulgarian state-owned enterprises' first wave of bad debts were transformed into the ZUNK-bonds, partially utilized in privatization and then gradually written off. Continuous changes in management of the state-owned giant structures, as well as subsequent restructuring and transformations, diminished the ability to maintain responsibility and control over their representative power. Controversial privatizations, such as cases with BGA Balkan and Balkancar, encouraged the inquiry into missing documentation, in addition to the lost knowledge of foreign ownerships and networks. Bulgarian National Bank was continuously involved in large-scale refinancing of commercial banks, which persistently made "bad" (uncollectable or, at least, uncollected) loans to a number of both state and private enterprises (Wyzan 1998). Crisis in 1994 was demonstrated in a loss of confidence in the domestic currency. The magnitude of the 1996 crisis was substantially amplified by the almost complete loss of public trust in the Bulgarian commercial banks. The run on the currency in 1996 was coupled with a simultaneous run on the banking system, resulting in a massive capital flight and the failure of 15 commercial banks (Dobrinsky 2000). Raiffeisenbank (Bulgaria) EAD, founded in 1994, was the first bank in Bulgaria with 100% foreign ownership—and was fully licensed to operate in the country and abroad. During these periods of economic turmoil and subsequent crises, most affluent Bulgarians chose to bank with Raiffeisenbank, and considered it to be their safest option.

10.3   Currency Board to Ensure Long Lasting Macroeconomic Stability

The introduction of a currency board become effective in July 1997, and was provided at a fixed exchange rate of 1000 Bulgarian Levs to a Deutsche Mark, and automatic fixing of the exchange rate of BGN 1.95583 to € 1 subsequent to 1 January 2002. Bulgarian central bank discontinued direct lending to the budget, refinancing of commercial banks and open market operations. The currency board regulations mandated the central bank to continually maintain domestic base money strictly equivalent to the level of foreign reserves. With memories of past crises still fresh, there is a consensus among the Bulgarian political elite that the currency board enhances national competitiveness. This is one of Bulgaria's justifications for not adopting the Euro, and why its government maintains a distance from the newly- created banking union in Europe.

The Simeon Saxe-Coburg-Gotha liberal government was the first to intently monitor the credit ratings assigned to Bulgaria and its banks (s. Appendix 10.1). Ivo Antonov, Moody's KMV, John Stroughair, Oliver Wyman, Larissa Malycheva, Fitch Ratings, Dr. Oliver Everling, Sharon Yeo, Dun & Bradstreet were among a board of international experts who met with a majority of the executive directors and board members of the Bulgarian banks on April 2004 at Sofia Credit and Risk Management Conference. At that time, Basel II triggered vivid discussion of the design and implementation of new models for credit ratings, in addition to the creation of new businesses devised to assist banks inrisk management. At this point, a Bulgarian company published under the brand INFOSTAT for the first time. This was a highly organized yet compact database, presenting three consecutive years of comprehensive financial data for more than 70,000 local companies (about 35% from the entire business universe of the country).

Between 2002 and 2005, four attempts to establish a credit rating agency in Bulgaria were reported. The first was the Bulgarian Rating Agency, established by a number of bankers. The Bulgarian Export Insurance Agency was also a minor shareholder. Soon after creation, some heavy exposures toward state-owned companies—alongside political tensions—forced owners to cease allcredit rating activities. The second was the Bulgarian Credit Rating Agency, which announced its activities on 23 April 2003. It was established as an entirely private company. The Agency succeeded in signing its first contract with ICRA, India. Targeting international expansion, the agency abandoned geographic affinity, and was remodeled as BCRA—Credit Rating Agency. On 4th April 2011, BCRA became the only Bulgarian and the third European credit rating agency registered in the EU (http://www.esma.europa.eu/page/List-registered-and-certified-CRAs). Amongst other activities, BCRA has proven experience in assigning credit ratings to financial institutions such as banks, insurance companies, leasing companies, pension assurance companies, and bond issues of public and private issuers. The agency recently reported activities in both Romania and Poland, as well as Bulgaria.

ICAP Group, Greece is also registered as a credit rating agency. It is actively involved in credit risk services and credit rating evaluations. Currently, the company predominantly assigns credit ratings to Greek companies. The core business of the company supplies integrated and updated commercial and financial data for companies registered in Greece, Bulgaria, Romania and Serbia. In addition, ICAP announced an exclusive partnership with the Dun & Bradstreet.

The participation of such niche-based credit rating agencies in the economic sector (?) can be viewed as an opportunity to facilitate relations between the banks, governmental, public and private institutions. However, the extent to which credit ratings can contribute to a reduction of the share of grey economy and increased transparency of the economy remains debatable. Most investors will expect niche players to acquire better access to confidential information, but to also make use of such data in their credit rationale—producing adequate and expeditious reports.

International Accounting Standards (IAS) has been mandatory for banks in Bulgaria since 2003, and for bigger companies from 2007. Bulgarian central bank allows local banks to maintain nostro/loro accounts with another local bank in foreign or local currency. The last banking license in the modern history of Bulgaria was given by BNB to the East-West Bank (predecessor of NLB Banka Sofia) at the end of 2003. Privatization of DSK Bank in October 2003 marked the finale in privatization of Bulgarian banks, as well as its expansion into mortgages and consumer lending.

Bulgarian corporate tax was reduced to 15% in 2006 and further to 10% in 2007. Personal income tax rate came to a 10% flat rate, effective from 1st January 2008. A two year VAT exemption was introduced for imports of equipment for investment projects costing at least € 5 million, accompanied by the creation of at least 50 jobs. Foreign direct investments on industrial projects in municipalities with high levels of unemployment are granted a 0% tax rate for over a five year period. Thus Bulgaria, together with Cyprus, came to have the most favorable tax regimes in Europe.

10.4   Does Hot Bank Market for Mortgages Lift Credit Ratings?

International property group Knight Frank named Bulgaria as the second best performing housing market in the world in 2006 (Latvia as number one; Finweek 2006). Bulgaria quickly became a popular choice for the British holiday home buyers, many keen to take advantage of the Bulgarian 'boom time' (Daily Mail 2007). Previously unknown regions such as Bansko and Pamporovo entered into the British consciousness as symbols of vacations, relaxation and escape. While many psychologists and sociologists continued to debate the extrinsic and intrinsic factors regarding the identity of new generations of European youth s, vibrant social media kept their fingers on the pulse. Journalists and business owners alike report the popularity of large gatherings of young people, demonstrated by the enormous number of bars and discotheques where the sale of alcohol and tobacco is cheap. Bulgaria itself has become a common holiday destination for many a Western European youth in search of affordable nightlife. Interestingly, this phenomenon has been exploited in an Ikea advertisement, entitled "We Think You're Too Young To Go To Sunny Beach"—produced by Hjaltelin Stahl & Co., Copenhagen and awarded 'Bronze' at The Cannes Lions International Festival of Creativity 2010 (s. www.peterstrange.com last checked April 2014; Table 10.1).

Prices for newly built homes vary substantially in terms of location, features and the quality of construction. Construction documentation and commercial practices also vary. As a result of this (amongst other factors), the National Statistical Institute of Bulgaria is unable to competently monitor sale prices of new constructions and plots for development. A simple example may better illustrate the market dynamics involved in real estate. A newly built, two bedroom apartment in close proximity to the Doctors' Garden in Sofia was worth (per m^2) about US\$ 350 in 1997; US\$ 1100 in 2001, and around € 1200 in 2003. The sellers shifted prices from USD to EUR, reflecting nominal depreciation of USD below EUR in October 2002. The same apartment was offered at € 3500 in 2008, but was later lowered to approximately € 1700 per m^2 by January 2014. Considering that the average Bulgarian banker's monthly salary is ca. € 740 for 2014, he or she could potentially purchase such an apartment by investing their whole salary for 20 years. Alternatively, many British citizens took the opportunity to spend a mere GBP 2000 or so on an old Bulgarian village house, as opposed to (e.g.) a home cinema package in the UK, which could literally add up to the same amount (Table 10.2).

The Baltic States are similar to Bulgaria and Romania in terms of significant amounts of foreign direct investments related to the banking sector and real estate businesses. This was closely tied to the availability of bank finance, which differentiates the Baltics, Bul-

Table 10.1 The average annual market prices of homes in Bulgaria (excluding newly built homes). Source: National Statistical Institute of Bulgaria

In Bulgarian Leva	1998	2003	2008	2013
Average for 24 biggest cities	266	265	1065	695
Sofia city	504	810	2329	1439
Average annual growth for Sofia		12%	38%	−8%

Table 10.2 Banking indicators and credit ratings in Baltic states, Bulgaria and Romania; Source: Festic 2012

| | Loans to deposits | | | NPL, % of gross loans | | | Loans in FX[a] | Ratings for 2010 | |
	2008	2009	2010	2008	2009	2010	2008	Moody's	S&P
Estonia	199	195	189	1.9	6.5	8.0	85.2	A1 stable	A stable
Latvia	247	250	230	3.6	16.2	19.8	88.4	Baa3 stable	BB stable
Lithuania	196	187	185	4.6	16.1	18.4	64.0	Baa1 stable	BBB stable
Bulgaria	123	121	122	3.2	5.7	10.0	56.7	Baa3 positive	BBB stable
Romania	126	119	116	6.3	16.0	17.5	56.0	Baa3 stable	BB+ stable

[a] Loans denominated in foreign currency as percentage from the total loans

garia and Romania from Central Europe—where most of the capital inflows have been diverted into manufacturing industries.

10.5   Could Remittances Boost Profit and Liquidity?

While no authoritative data on the number of Bulgarian emigrants exists, the Bulgarian Ministry of Foreign Affairs has disclosed estimates for the emigrant population based on information collected from diplomatic missions. According to the Ministry, around 1.6 million. Bulgarians live and work in Europe. Some extreme bloggers, online journalists and publicists fancifully declare that the number of working or self-employed Bulgarians abroad extends to 2.5 million—which is highly improbable considering that there are an estimated 2.2 million employed workers within Bulgaria itself. It is widely acknowledged that wages in Bulgaria are among the lowest in Europe. Most of the Bulgarian emigrants in Europe are concentrated in the UK and Mediterranean countries. Anecdotal evidence suggests that certain emigrants remain unbanked, as they lack the necessary documents to open accounts. Therefore, credit and payment options including online shopping and remittances to and from families in Bulgaria are restricted and/or expensive. Based on the World Bank remittance prices database for 2012 Q2, the cost of sending € 140 from Spain to Bulgaria accounts € 7 (or 5 %) if remitted through a bank, or € 14.00–14.50 (or about 10 %) if remitted through a money transfer organization. Nevertheless, remittances are the most quickly growing item with a material effect for the Bulgarian current account.

Surprisingly enough, European politicians and demagogues are very active in contacting Bulgarian and Romanian emigrants. On 1st January 2014, "bleary-eyed passengers on the 6.30 am flight from the Transylvanian city of Targu Mures arrived at Luton on New Year's day and stepped immediately into the glare of political controversy, as work restrictions on Romanians and Bulgarians were finally lifted" (Parker and Warrell 2014). How many of us will object to the assumption that a qualified eye of a high-ranked political figure is professionally trained to see what it is willing to see?

10.6   Core Principals are the Same, but Relative Factor Weight Differs

Credit rating agencies use similar techniques and methodologies to analyze banks. The core principals, models and technical ratios are very transferable across geographic locations and different stages of development of banking systems. At the beginning of the privatization process, local Bulgarian banks had a decisive role in determining who could purchase what. At the present time, bank managers still retain the ability to provide or withhold funding for an acquisition, and may consider issues outside of typical credit models or conservative banking practices. The local bank owners' strong appetite for acquiring side businesses may be a significant factor in identifying the primary

Table 10.3 Average annual change in total assets and profit or loss calculated between 2008 and 2013 for Bulgarian banks grouped by beneficial owner, use and control (s. Appendix 10.2)

Average change in thousands BGN	Total assets	Profit or loss
Banking industry in Bulgaria	3,239,045	− 160,585
Bulgarian use and control	2,546,631	− 20,334
Beneficial owner linked to Greece	− 9372	− 59,224
Beneficial owner in Austria or Germany	− 62,292	− 35,690

difference between domestic banks and other groups presented in Table 10.3. Tourism, tobacco, wine and alcohol production, telecommunications, pension funds, airlines are just some of the industries where Bulgarian banks owners have heavy involvement. Neither confirmed nor objected publications in the local media imply that owners of the First Investment Bank had a longstanding interest in obtaining VMZ Sopot. It appears that their target was completed in 2013 with the acquisition of MKB Unionbank, held by Bayern LB via Hungarian MKB bank. VMZ Sopot is one of the largest military industrial plants in Bulgaria, producing anti-tank guided and unguided missiles, aviation unguided missiles, artillery ammunition, fuses and other items. Acquiring such a company as part of the non-performing loan portfolio frequently brings extremely positive material rewards for the buyer. However, how many have the nerve and fortitude for such a challenge/activity? Although most of the top level bank managers are Bulgarian citizens with skills, knowledge, r and connections, the bank performance varies widely. To some extent, strategic business decisions implemented by local banks suggest they are better in jockeying for position. This is the main factor behind the later bank ranking in Appendix 10.2.

Until the end of 2013, the Bulgarian banking sector enjoyed a sustained stability, despite the adverse effects of the financial and sovereign debt crises. The Bulgarian National Bank requires a capital adequacy ratio of 12%, well-above the European target of 8%. As of December 2013, the banking sector assets amounted to around € 43.8 billion, with an average annual growth rate of above 7% year-to-year for the last decade. The loans are in the range of 75% from assets, while domestically attracted household and corporate deposits are at 83% from liabilities. As of December 2013, the provision ratio (measured as the sum of IFRS and specific provisions balance over gross book value) amounted to 11%, compared to 10.4% as of December 2012. Non-performing loans of the banking sector (excluding loans to banks) have grown by an average of 1.9% of gross loans per annum between 2010 and 2013. Within non-performing loans, two types of credits are peaking. Bad consumer loans reached 20% of gross loans at the end of 2011, whereas corporate credits peaked in 2012 and have been improving since then. Residential mortgage loans are still at their highest levels of non-performance—although increase stalled, and one could consider it to be a positive sign for future improvement of credit portfolios.

The return on equity, calculated by the aggregate data of Bulgarian banks, hardly chan-ged during the years: The ratio for 2013 dropped to 5% from 28% 15 years ago—and below the average of 17% in period 2003–2008.

Net interest income is decreasing prior to the crisis from 1.5% annually to 0.7%. This is a large decline! Banks are attempting to compensate by endeavouring to increase in-come from fees and commissions. However, high income from companies who easily ac-cept fee increase frequently disintegrate with money laundering investigations. Suffering a continuous burden of slow economic growth, banks would attempt to compensate e by trying to attract customers with the value added services on offer, as a means of gradually increasing the fees and commissions on selected services. This should be a signal of po-licy change toward better profitability, followed by an increase in interest rates. Possible increase of interest rates in Bulgaria will to some extent contrast with overall stabilization and decreased interest rates in Europe. This may result in repeating the cycle of foreign banks financing Bulgarian projects for substantially higher interest income as compared with their home markets.

Bulgarian insurance industry is relatively small and fundamentally different from ban-king in terms of posing a systemic threat to financial stability. Local insurance companies are frequently positioned within bank dominated ambiences, as insurance is an important source of funds and liquidity. In 2013, the industry consisted of 27 general insurance companies—with a total premium income of € 881 million, an increase of 7.7% on an annual basis—as well as 16 life insurance companies with a total premium income of € 157 million, but an increase of 14% on an annual basis. The diminishing interest of foreign investors in owning and managing banks in Bulgaria provides opportunities for insurance companies to cheaply acquire a bank. However, we have yet to see whether a local insurance company's rating would experience a down-grade following the acquisi-tion of a bank.

10.7   Second Post-Communist Crisis in Bulgarian Banking

Bank Leumi Le-Israel Ltd decision to exit Bulgaria on July 2009 became a symbol for the real economic slowdown in local banking. Israel's biggest bank expanded in Romania and Bulgaria in 2006 to make up from regulatory limits on domestic growth, plus to utilize the large number of Israeli businesses active in the local markets. However deteriorating real estate market, lack of political vision and local market imperfections, make bank to change its strategy.

The crisis exploded with publications in the media on 18 June 2014 that Tsvetan Gunev, Deputy Governor of BNB, in charge of Banks' Supervision, is being investigated by the prosecution and is on leave "until the conclusion of the proceedings". Charges have been pressed against Gunev under the Criminal code for criminal abuse of power as related to default loans in Corporate Commercial Bank AD (CCB or KTB). The panic started and people run to CCB offices to withdraw their deposits! 20 June 2014 at 11.40 am, the Bulgarian National Bank received a written notice from the management of Corporate Commercial Bank AD (CCB) that CCB's liquidity had been depleted and the bank had suspended making payments and conducting all types of banking transactions. On these grounds Corporate Commercial Bank AD has been placed under conservatorship and the same measure applied to its subsidiary the former Credit Agricole Bulgaria EAD. Although Central bank declared that the liquidity shortage in the CCB group is an isolated case and is not connected with the rest of the banking system, depositors withdraw € 400 million in cash just on Friday, 27 June 2014 from the First Investment Bank AD. Then, the European Union gave Bulgaria authority to provide BGN 3.3 billion (€ 1.67 billion) in state aid for banks, so within one weekend the tensions have been overcome and the banking sector has returned to its normal functioning.

On 29 October 2008 Moody's Investors Service assigns Ba3 long-term and Not Prime short-term foreign and local currency deposit ratings and a D-bank financial strength rating to Corporate Commercial Bank AD. The ratings reflected CCB small presence in Bulgaria as the country's tenth-largest locally owned bank with a market share of around 3 % in banking assets. It was for the first time CCB received a credit rating. On 16 April 2013 Moody's changes the outlook to negative the bank's standalone bank financial strength rating was lowered to E+, equivalent to a baseline credit assessment of b1 and further downgraded to b2 on 11 September 2013. Despite the lowering of the bank's standalone rating, Moody's affirms the bank's deposit ratings at Ba3/NP, as they incorporate one notch of systemic support uplift, based on Moody's assumptions of the likelihood of systemic support. The uplift reflects Moody's view of the bank's increasing systemic importance as the fifth largest deposit-taking institution in Bulgaria, with a 7.3 % market share in retail deposits as of December 2012. Surprisingly enough Bulgarian political system lacked understanding in providing systemic support to the bank when it overpass 8 % market share in May 2014.

Given the dynamics in relations with Moody's, Corporate Commercial Bank AD asked credit rating to be assigned also by the BCRA—Credit Rating Agency AD (BCRA) in March 2012. BCRA assigned to CCB for the first time credit rating of BBB—and slightly adjusted it to BB+ level until 26 May 2014.

Appendix 10.3 exhibits main developments in the Corporate Commercial Bank AD as a case for dynamic interaction between state institutions, political forces, the media and the credit rating agencies. Future analyses would be needed to investigate possible regulatory capture or arbitrage related to using one or another credit rating agency.

10.8 Bulgaria and the Single Supervisory Mechanism in Europe

During positive economic cycle, most of the banks in Bulgaria had solid profitability levels, elevated business volumes, healthy interest margins and comfortable capital levels. Many banks successfully tap the combination of high operational margins and minute taxes, reporting a remarkable yield. During the booming years, banks overcame limited amounts of local funds by the use of subordinated loan capital or hybrid capital loans via their parent banks and/or financial institutions from abroad. The subordinated loan or hybrid capital instruments are regulated with Directive 2006/49/EC of the EU Parliament of 14 June 2006 for the capital adequacy of investment firms and credit institutions. When subordinated capital should be up to 50 % of the registered capital, the annual interest rate a local bank pays to its mother bank may be as high as 10 % or more.

Local regulation prescribes methods for the evaluation and classification of risk exposures. It required banks to establish specific provisions for credit risk, based on the period of delay of amounts due. Banks had limited flexibility, to assess the financial situation of the debtor and sources for repayment of its debts. The classification criteria positions debtors in four groups: standard exposures, exposures under surveillance, non-performing exposures and loss. Exposures can be assessed either individually, or on a portfolio basis such as buckets. Specific provisions for general credit risk represent the excess of the carrying amount of the specific exposure calculated under applicable accounting standards over the risk value. The carrying value of these exposures is determined according to the provisions of IAS 39 Financial Instruments Recognition and Measurement.

With the beginning of 2014, Bulgarian legislation introduces the European Capital Requirements Directive and the Capital Requirements Regulation. Statutory minimum capital adequacy ratio will be reduced from the current 12–8 %. However, this will be offset by the introduction of several capital buffers. The total capital adequacy ratio of the banking system will exceed the current level.

Bulgaria is debating the possibility of postponing implementation of the new counter-cyclical buffer. A ratio of up to 2.5 % can impose significant challenges. Instead of previously allocated specific provisions, banks are expected to perform additional accounting provisions under International Financial Reporting Standards—aimed at reduction of the carrying value of loans in arrears over 90 days. Assuming all other conditions remain the same, this will affect a relative decrease in liabilities, but heavier pressure to the income statements. Profitability will continue to be the top priority. Banks need to improve confidence among borrowers in the country, ideally by enhancing transparency and assuring greater dialogue on the part of banks when negotiating or repricing.

10.9   Conclusion

Banks usually operate under substantial operational inertia. It is not easy for these "mammoths" to launch up a product, to adjust it or to stop participating in a project. While the Bulgarian manufacturing industry may never reach its historical highs, remittances could have an increasing importance. Many believe that the home mortgages have the optimal risk-to-value, outperforming other elements in the portfolio of a retail bank. Dynamics in Bulgarian lending prove that the value of homes is strongly correlated with the banks' appetite in funding construction industry—but fails to accelerate into the pure asset-based lending. The initial upgrade and subsequent downgrade of the Bulgarian banks' credit ratings further widened amplitudes within the cycle of the real estate market. Although land developers around the globe are normally experiencing severe cash flow problems, neither banks nor government had the motivation to implement a stabilization program. In addition to high economic and social costs, such instability shifts the power to some rich becoming richer than before. Homebuyers in Bulgaria continue to suffer an increased cost of living, lower salaries and higher interest rates on loans. The progress of Solvency II for the insurance industry and Single Supervisory Mechanism for banks will trigger a substantial amount of new regulations affecting the Bulgarian financial sector. The central regulatory handbook will eventually replace the majority of the local regulations. We have reason to suspect that net interest margins will be stabilized at the current levels, but increased costs in reporting and compliance are likely to result downtrend in banks profitability. New market conditions will challenge the professionalism of the credit rating agencies. Hopefully, current bank managers are more highly qualified and have a greater degree of experience than the previous learning-by-doing bankers, who achieved rapid increase in personal wealth in 1987/1997 chaotic transition to market economy. One might hopefully suggest that Bulgaria is reaching a new level of maturity which will provide more opportunities for the banks' to adjust to new market conditions; assuming the bankers do not neglect the new regulatory procedures and responsibilities, and communication remains transparent and concise.

10.10   Appendices

Dynamics of Credit Ratings and Outlooks Assigned to Bulgaria (Table 10.4)
Banks in Bulgaria Ranked by Total Assets as of Year-end 2013 (Table 10.5)
Boom and bust of the Group of Corporate Commercial Bank AD (CCB) (Tables 10.6 and 10.7)

Table 10.4 Dynamics of credit ratings and outlooks assigned to Bulgaria

S&P[a]		Moody's[b]		Fitch[c]		Assigned	Prime minister	European affiliation
BBB	–	Baa2	=	BBB	=	Jan. 2014	Plamen Oresharski May 2013–present	Party of European Socialists
BBB	–	Baa2	=	BBB	=	Dec. 2013		
BBB	=	Baa2	=	BBB	=	Dec. 2012	Boyko Borisov July 2009/ March 2013	European People's Party
BBB	=	Baa2	=	BBB	+	July 2011		
BBB	=	Baa3	+	BBB	–	Aug. 2010		
BBB	=	Baa3	+	BBB	–	Jan. 2010		
BBB	=	Baa3	=	BBB	–	Dec. 2009		
BBB	–	Baa3	=	BBB	=	Oct. 2008	Sergei Stanishev August 2005/ July 2009	Local coalition rooted to: Party of European Socialists and Alliance of Liberals and Democrats for Europe
BBB+	=	Baa3	+	BBB+	–	June 2008		
BBB+	+	Baa3	=	BBB+	=	Mar. 2006		
BBB+	+	Ba1	+	BBB+	=	Oct. 2005		
BBB	+	Ba1	+	BBB+	=	Feb. 2005	Simeon Saxe-Coburg-Gotha July 2001/August 2005	Alliance of Liberals and Democrats for Europe
BBB	=	Ba1	+	BBB	=	June. 2004		
BBB-	=	Ba3	=	BBB-	+	May 2003		
BB+	+	B2	+	BB+	+	Oct. 2002		
BB	=	B2	=	BB	=	Nov. 2001		

Table 10.4 (continued)

S&Pᵃ		Moody'sᵇ		Fitchᶜ		Assigned	Prime minister	European affiliation
BB-	+	B3	=	BB	+	May 2000	Ivan Kostov May 1997/July 2001	European People's Party
B	+	B3	+	BB		Feb. 1999		
B	+	B3	+	BB		Nov. 1998		
		B3	=	BB		April 1998		
		B3	=			Dec. 1997		
		Caa1	+			July 1997		
		Caa	=			Sep. 1996	Zhan Videnov January 1995/February 1997	Party of European Socialists

(−) negative, (=) stable, (+) positive

[a] Standard poor's ratings services—Short term credit rating in local currency

[b] Moody's—long term bank deposits in foreign currency

[c] FitchRatings—long term credit rating in local currency

Table 10.5 Year-end 2013 ranking of Bulgarian banks by total assets. Source BNB

Rank	Name	Total assets December 2013[a]	Growth[b] total assets	Growth[c] profit/loss	Main shareholder[c] origin of the beneficial owner
1	UniCredit Bulbank	12,728,118	16	−30	UniCredit Group, Italy
2	DSK Bank	8,882,401	2	−27	OTP Group, Hungary
3	First Investment Bank	7,445,943	75	−49	Use and control linked to Bulgaria
4	Corporate Commercial Bank	6,740,298	220	77	Use and control linked to Bulgaria 70%, S.A.R.L., Oman—30%
5	United Bulgarian Bank	6,715,118	−13	−92	National Bank of Greece, Greece
6	Raiffeisenbank Bulgaria	5,959,551	−13	−133	Raiffeisenbank, Austria
7	Postbank (Eurobank Bulgaria)	5,697,515	5	−74	EFG New Europe Holding, Greece
8	Central Cooperative Bank	3,746,278	125	−50	Use and control linked to Bulgaria
9	Societe Generale Expressbank	3,664,575	46	−37	Société Générale, France
10	Alpha Bank	3,655,242	70	−101	Alpha Bank AE, Greece
11	Piraeus Bank Bulgaria	3,355,817	−19	−94	Piraeus Bank Group, Greece
12	Economic and Invest-ment Bank	2,187,645	19	−27	KBC BANK N.V., Belgium
13	Allianz Bank Bulgaria	1,977,359	21	−17	Allianz Bulgaria Holding, Germany—80%
14	Bulgarian Develop-ment Bank	1,781,290	314	59	Ministry of Finance, Bulgaria
15	Investbank Bulgaria	1,676,365	50	−96	Use and control linked to Bulgaria
16	MKB Unionbank	1,449,234	−6	−47	Sold by MKB Bank, Hungary on March 2013 to First Investment Bank, Bulgaria

Table 10.5 (continued)

Rank	Name	Total assets December 2013[a]	Growth[b] total assets	Growth[c] profit/loss	Main shareholder[c] origin of the beneficial owner
17	ProCredit Bank (Bulgaria)	1,351,127	34	57	ProCredit Holding AG, Germany—80%, Commerzbank AG, Germany—20%
18	Municipal Bank	1,155,551	16	−42	Sofia Municipality, Bulgaria—67%
19	International Asset Bank	971,641	71	−81	Use and control linked to Bulgaria
20	Bulgarian American Credit Bank	777,729	−5	−130	Sold by Allied Irish Bank on June 2011, so present use and control linked to Bulgaria
21	D Commerce Bank	703,834	139	−91	Fuat Gyuven (Fuat Hyusniev Osmanov), Bulgaria—100%
22	CITI—Branch	635,428	64	−35	Citibank N.A., USA
23	ING—Branch	611,960	28	−102	ING Group N. V., Netherlands
24	BNP Paribas—Branch	453,332	−39	−99	BNP Paribas S.A., France
25	Tokuda Bank	417,440	23	−208	International Hospital Services, Japan 91%
26	TBI Bank (ex—NLB Bank Sofia)	408,025	87	36	Sold by NLB dd Slovenia on April 2011 to TBIF Financial Services (Kardan), Netherlands
27	Crédit Agricole	407,207	−13	299	Crédit Agricole S.A., France (ex-owner Emporiki, Greece)
28	Texim Bank	123,219	139	−91	Use and control linked to Bulgaria
29	T. C. Ziraat Bankası, Sofia Branch	53,751	12	−189	T. C. Ziraat Bankası, Turkey
30	İŞBANK—Branch	13,677	–	–	İŞBANK GmbH, Germany/Turkey
Total		85,746,670	23	−58	

[a] Banks' total assets in Bulgarian Leva '000

[b] Growth rate in percentage calculated between 2008 and 2013

[c] Last available data to exhibit the trend, but having no legal or binding force

Table 10.6 Main business and political developments as related to the group of Corporate Commercial Bank AD. Sources BNB, "Capital" and "Banker" newspapers

1994	Corporate Commercial Bank AD (CCB) was founded as a joint venture between the Bulgarian Foreign Trade Bank and the Soviet Vneshekonombank
2000	Group of investors, including Mr. Tsvetan Vassilev as shareholder, acquired the Bank and starts massive restructuring and reorganization
18 June 2007	IPO—CCB shares publicly traded on the Bulgarian Stock Exchange and included in calculating SOFIX and BG40 indexes
31 December 2007	CCB Annual report: Balance Sheet Net Profit Employees 340
29 October 2008	First-time rated by Moody's Investors Services initial rating Ba3/Stable D-
2009	The State General Reserve Fund (SGRV) of the Sultanate of Oman acquires 30% of the Bank's existing shares
4 November 2011	CCB involved in acquisition of Bulgartabak Holding AD (the biggest tobacco processing and manufacturing Group in Bulgaria)
13 March 2012	BCRA—Credit Rating Agency initial rating BBB-/stable/A-3
14 February 2013	CCB involved in acquisition of K & K Electronics and Technomarket (one of the biggest retail groups for home appliances and electronics in Bulgaria)
16 April 2013	Moody's Investors Services rating changed to B1/Stable E+
27 May 2013	BCRA—Credit Rating Agency rating BB+/stable/B
11 September 2013	Moody's Investors Services rating changed to B2/Negative E+
9 July 2013	CCB involved in acquisition of Bulgarian Telecommunication Company AD and VIVA Telecom Bulgaria AD (the biggest telecommunication group in Bulgaria)
26 May 2014	BCRA—Credit Rating Agency confirms rating BB+/stable/B
12 June 2014	CCB acquires 100% in Credit Agricole Bulgaria EAD
20 June 2014	Management of CCB advises in written the Bulgarian National Bank (BNB) that bank's liquidity had been depleted and the bank had suspended making payments. BNB places CCB under conservatorship for the period of 3 months
22 June 2014	BNB places Crédit Agricole Bulgaria EAD (CAB) under conservatorship for the period of 3 months. BNB orders Deloitte Audit, Ernst & Young and AFA to audit CCB and CAB
11 July 2014	BNB announces the results of the review of CAB confirm it is a well-managed bank. The results of the audit of CCB shows significant parts of credit files for a loan portfolio of BGN 3.5 billion, out of the total BGN 5.4 billion loan portfolio, are missing, most probably destroyed during the days before the conservatorship was placed, a very large connectedness between borrowers and the majority shareholder of the bank, Mr. Tsvetan Vassilev. A cash amount equivalent to BGN 205 887 223, was drawn by a third person, and against a receipt delivered to Mr. Tsvetan Vassilev on 19 June 2014
6 August 2014	President dissolves parliament and calls elections for 5th October
15 September 2014	Conservatorship period is extended for CAB till 25 November for CCB till 25 December 2014

Table 10.7 Main data from consolidated and audited financial statements published in respective annual reports of the Corporate Commercial Bank AD

BGN thousands	2013	2011	2009	2007
Balance sum	6,740,296	4,043,060	2,035,883	1,771,306
Equity	605,563	383,098	275,864	156,083
Net Profit	71,195	60,951	60,350	23,148

Literatur

Daily Mail 2007, Buying a piece of the Bulgarian boom time. Daily Mail September, 2, 2007

Dobrinsky, R. 2000 The transition crisis in Bulgaria. Cambridge Journal of Economics. Sep.2000, Vol. 24 Issue 5

Festic, M. 2012, The Role of the Foreign Banks in the 5 EU Member States, Journal of Business Economics and Management, February 2012, Vol. 13, Issue 1

Finweek 2006, Some markets still steaming ahead. Denmark, Belgium, Bulgaria and Latvia now outperform South Africa. August 24, 2006

Jerome Jr., Robert T. 1985, Estimates of sources of growth in Bulgaria, Greece and Yugoslavia, 1950–1980. Comparative Economic Studies (Association for Comparative Economic Studies). Fall85, Vol. 27 Issue 3

Mason R. 2014 David Cameron: Romania and Bulgaria immigration levels 'reasonable' The Guardian, Monday 27 January 2014

Minkov, Pl. 1993 Banks and Banking Reform in Bulgarian Russia, East European Finance and Trade Coverage: 1992–2002 (Vols. 28–38) Published by: M.E. Sharpe, Inc. ISSN: 10612009

Parker G. Warrell H. 2014 Romanians step on to UK soil into glare of political controversy Financial times, Politics and Policy, January 1, 2014

Schlack, R. F. 1993 Going to Market in Bulgaria: Uphill on a Knife Edge. Journal of Economic Issues (Association for Evolutionary Economics). Jun93, Vol. 27 Issue 2

Wyzan, M.L. 1998 The political economy of Bulgaria's peculiar post-communist business cycle. Comparative Economic Studies (Association for Comparative Economic Studies). Spring98, Vol. 40 Issue 1

Bojidar Archinkov, PhD candidate UNI BIT, Sofia, MBA University of Sheffield, CAMS/AML, was a credit correspondent for 8 years at The Dun & Bradstreet, including the role of business supervisor for Bulgaria, Albania, Belarus, Kazakhstan, Macedonia and Serbia. Archinkov was also Country Manager in Bank Leumi, Romania appointed to establish a bank branch in Sofia utilizing the principle of a "single bank passport". From 2009 till 2014 he was involved in completing NLB dd, Slovenia divestment strategy as related to Bulgaria and the establishment of TBI Bank, where he was promoted to Chairman of the Management Board and Executive Director.

Rating Advisory für Finanzinstitute 11

Michael Zlotnik

11.1 Einleitung

Ratings bleiben für eine wachsende Anzahl von Unternehmen aus dem Finanzsektor weiterhin von großer Bedeutung. Aber das Ratingumfeld und die Zusammenarbeit mit den großen US-Ratingagenturen sind seit Ausbruch der Finanzkrise deutlich schwieriger geworden. Trotz zahlreicher Herabstufungen in den letzten Jahren bleiben die Ratings vieler Institute weiterhin unter Druck. Gleichzeitig ist Ratingverfahren deutlich komplexer und zeitintensiver geworden, und die Ratingagenturen haben ihre Informationsanforderungen drastisch erhöht. Darüber hinaus versuchen in Europa neue Ratinganbieter die dominante Marktposition von Moody's, Standard & Poor's und Fitch anzugreifen, indem sie um die Gunst neuer Kunden und lukrative Ratingmandate buhlen.

Angesichts knapper interner Ressourcen, aber auch oftmals fehlender spezifischer Ratingexpertise, stellt sich für viele Unternehmen aus dem Finanzsektor zunehmend die Frage, inwieweit sie mit Unterstützung durch einen externen Rating Advisor die Zusammenarbeit mit Ratingagenturen verbessern und effizienter gestalten und somit letztendlich ihr Ratingergebnis optimieren können.

11.2 Definition Rating Advisory

Rating Advisory umfasst alle beratenden und unterstützenden Beratungsdienstleitungen im Rahmen einer erstmaligen oder fortlaufenden Ratingbewertung eines Finanzinstituts und dessen zu bewertenden Finanzinstrumente durch eine externe Ratingagentur.

M. Zlotnik (✉)
Bad Homburg, Deutschland
E-Mail: michael@zlotnik-ratingadvisory.com

© Springer Fachmedien Wiesbaden 2016
Z. Diab, O. Everling (Hrsg.), *Rating von Finanzinstituten*,
DOI 10.1007/978-3-658-04195-3_11

Vorrangige Ziele einer kompetenten Ratingberatung sind hierbei sowohl das Erreichen eines optimalen Ratingergebnisses, als auch die effiziente Gestaltung des Ratingverfahrens zur Schonung der unternehmensinternen Managementkapazitäten.

11.3   Ratingumfeld für Finanzinstitute

Ratingagenturen spielen auf den globalen Wertpapier- und Bankenmärkten weiterhin eine wichtige Rolle, da Anleger, Kreditnehmer, Emittenten und Regierungen unter anderem die Ratings dieser Agenturen nutzen, um fundierte Anlage-und Finanzentscheidungen zu treffen.

Dieses Zitat stammt nicht, wie man vermuten könnte, aus einer Marketingbroschüre einer Ratingagentur, sondern aus der entsprechenden europäischen Verordnung über die Regulierung von Ratingagenturen.

Trotz politischer Bestrebungen, die Abhängigkeit der Finanzmärkte von Ratings zu verringern, spielt das externe Rating einer etablierten Ratingagentur für Finanzinstitute weiterhin eine wichtige Rolle.

Neben der Erschließung zusätzlicher Anlegerkreise im In- und Ausland, sind die Nutzung zusätzlicher langfristiger Refinanzierungsmittel (z. B. Covered Bonds, Verbriefungen, hybride Kapitalinstrumente) und die Verringerung der Abhängigkeit von kurzfristigen Zentralbank- und Interbankengeldern treibende Faktoren für die Nachfrage nach Ratings.

Gleichzeitig befinden sich aber die Ratings für Institute, des Finanzsektors und die Zusammenarbeit mit Moody's, Standard & Poor's, Fitch & Co. seit Ausbruch der Finanzkrise in einem anhaltenden „Stresstest".

Ein labiles makroökonomisches Umfeld, steigende Kreditausfälle, gekoppelt mit einem historisch niedrigen Zinsniveau, sowie verschärfte regulatorische Anforderungen führen zu starkem Druck auf Geschäftsmodelle und belasten die Ertragskraft der Finanzbranche massiv. Im Gegenzug haben die Ratingagenturen als Antwort auf während der Finanzkrise erkannte interne Defizite und Versäumnisse ihre Ratingkriterien und Informationsanforderungen in vielen Bereichen drastisch verschärft. Und es drohen, ungeachtet bereits erfolgter massiver Ratingherabstufungen in den letzten Jahren, vor dem Hintergrund der sich abzeichnenden Beteiligung von Anleihegläubigern („Bail-in") bei künftigen Bankenkrisen weitere Ratingverschlechterungen.

11.4   Herausforderungen in der Zusammenarbeit mit Ratingagenturen

Neben weiter drohenden Ratingherabstufungen sind viele Unternehmen aus dem Finanzsektor mit zusätzlichen Herausforderungen in der Zusammenarbeit mit Ratingagenturen konfrontiert.

So mehren sich die Klagen hinsichtlich

- der Häufigkeit, des Ausmaßes, der Vorhersehbarkeit, sowie der Transparenz von Kriterien- und Ratingänderungen
- der zunehmenden Komplexität von Ratingkriterien, aber auch mangelnden Vergleichbarkeit zwischen verschiedenen Ratingagenturen
- der Nachvollziehbarkeit und Vergleichbarkeit von Ratings
- einer deutlich reduzierten Bereitschaft der Agenturen, Ansatzpunkte für künftige Ratingverbesserungen zu diskutieren
- eines mangelnden Verständnis für oder einer fehlenden Bereitschaft zur ernsthaften Auseinandersetzung mit dem jeweiligen Geschäftsmodell, der strategischen Ausrichtung, sowie der potenziellen Unterstützung durch die Eigentümer
- der Sorge vor negativen Ratingreaktionen bei der Kommunikation von (möglichen) strategischen Initiativen oder von „bad news"
- einer zunehmend mangelnden Erfahrung und Seniorität der zuständigen Analysten
- einer ausgeprägten Silo-Mentalität und mangelhaften internen Abstimmung innerhalb den Ratingagenturen, z. B. zwischen Banken-, Covered Bond, Structured Finance und Sovereign Teams
- steigender Ratinggebühren bei gleichzeitig schlechterem Kundenservice.

11.5   Zielgruppe

Die meisten europäischen Banken mit einer hohen Kapitalmarktabhängigkeit, darunter auch die Mehrzahl der großen deutschen Institute wie z. B. Deutsche Bank, Commerzbank, DZ-Bank, Landesbanken, aber auch öffentliche-rechtliche Institute wie die KfW oder die Landwirtschaftliche Rentenbank verfügen seit vielen Jahren über externe Ratings der global agierenden Ratingagenturen Moody's, Standard & Poor's oder Fitch.

Neben dem klassischen Rating für Anleihen, nutzen diese Banken inzwischen vermehrt Ratings für eine große Palette von Refinanzierungsprodukten, wie z. B. Hybridanleihen oder Verbriefungen. Hinzu kommt eine weiter wachsende Schar von neuen Emittenten im Zuge der Einführung von Covered Bond Gesetzgebungen in vielen europäischen, aber auch außereuropäischen Ländern.

Zunehmend interessieren sich aber auch Finanzinstitute außerhalb des klassischen Bankensektors in Deutschland und Europa für externe Ratings.

Hauptantriebsfeder sind hier oft die Überlegungen der Unternehmen, die Abhängigkeit vom klassischen Bankkredit zu reduzieren, ihre Refinanzierungspalette zu erweitern und sich neue, auch internationale, Investorenkreise oder Gegenparteien (z. B. Swapgeschäft) zu erschließen.

Die großen Ratingagenturen haben auf die zunehmende Erweiterung der Ratingnachfrage mit der Entwicklung von zusätzlichen Ratingkriterien für spezielle Segmente des Finanzsektors und für verschiedene Ratingprodukte reagiert. Hierzu gehören u. a. spe-nach Art des Finanzinstitutes

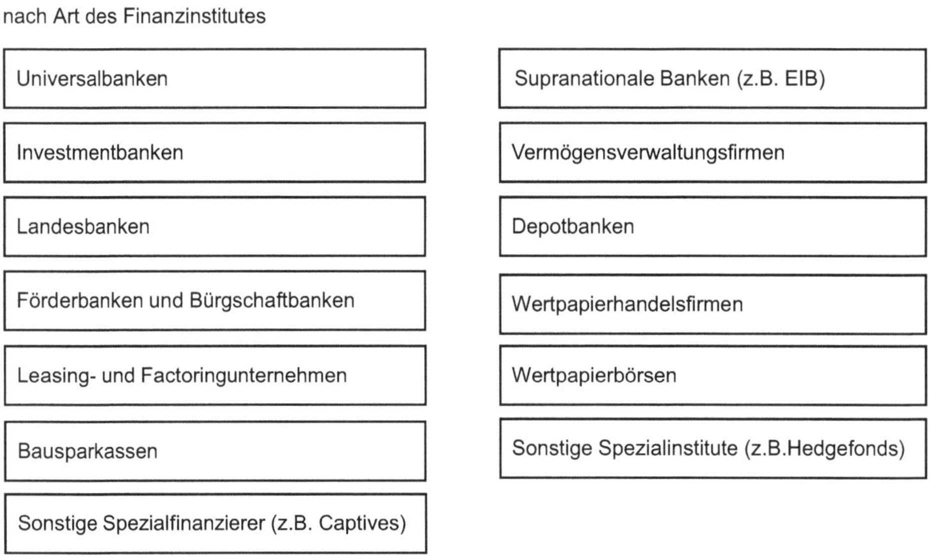

Universalbanken	Supranationale Banken (z.B. EIB)
Investmentbanken	Vermögensverwaltungsfirmen
Landesbanken	Depotbanken
Förderbanken und Bürgschaftbanken	Wertpapierhandelsfirmen
Leasing- und Factoringunternehmen	Wertpapierbörsen
Bausparkassen	Sonstige Spezialinstitute (z.B.Hedgefonds)
Sonstige Spezialfinanzierer (z.B. Captives)	

Abb. 11.1 Zielgruppe Rating Advisory

zielle Ratingkriterien für Leasingfirmen, herstellerabhängige Spezialfinanzierungsinstitute (Captives), Asset Management Firmen, Wertpapierbörsen, aber auch Hedgefonds (s. Abb. 11.1).

11.6   Zielsetzung und Leistungsspektrum

Die Ratingoptimierung, eine erhöhte Effizienz des Ratingverfahrens und eine verbesserte Kommunikation mit den Ratingagenturen sind die Hauptziele beim Einsatz eines externen Rating Advisors.

Bei der Ratingoptimierung geht es dabei nicht immer – wie man auf den ersten Blick meinen könnte – um Ratingverbesserungen.

Zum einen stehen die Bankenratings seit dem Ausbruch der Finanzkrise unter starkem Druck und weitere Herabstufungen drohen. Somit sind die Verteidigung der bestehenden Ratings und das Vermeiden weiterer Herabstufungen bei der Ratingberatung zunehmend in den Vordergrund gerückt.

Zum anderen spielen Kosten-Nutzen Aspekte eine zunehmend wichtige Rolle bei der Definition eines optimalen Ratings. Selbst wenn ein „AAA" gemäß den Ratingkriterien der Ratingagentur theoretisch möglich wäre, wird ein solches Rating für ein Institut unter Umständen gar nicht mehr angestrebt. Man denke hier nur an die deutlich gestiegenen Übersicherungsanforderungen und zahlreichen kostentreibenden strukturellen Sicherheitsmaßnahmen für AAA Ratings von deutschen und europäischen Pfandbriefemittenten.

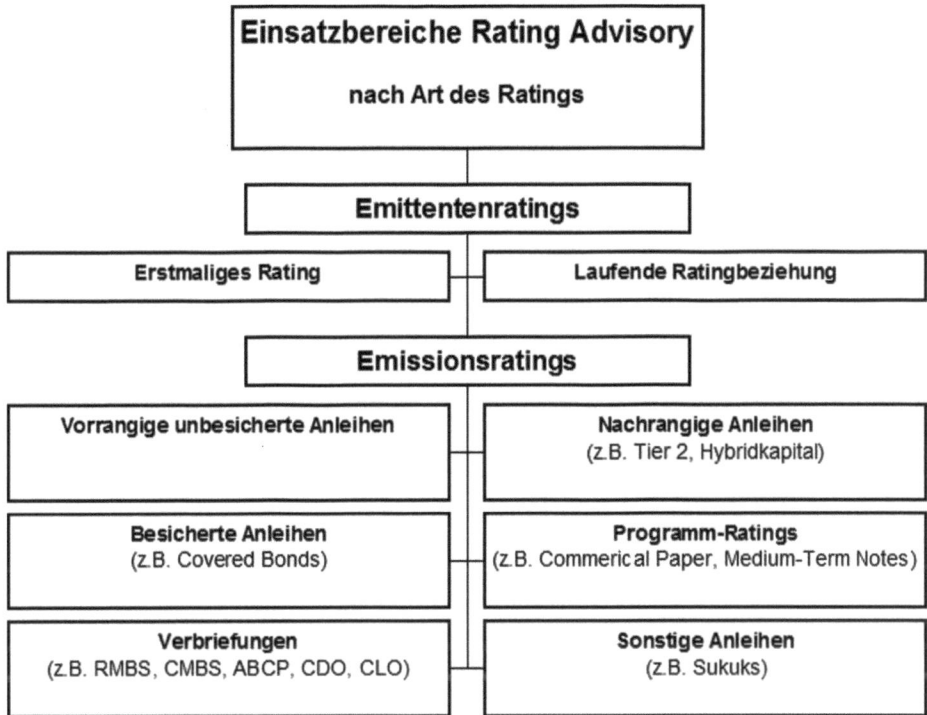

Abb. 11.2 Einsatzbereiche Rating Advisory

Darüber hinaus stellt der Rating Advisor einen effizienten und reibungslosen Ablauf des Ratingverfahrens sicher, der den Ressourcenaufwand für alle am Ratingverfahren Beteiligten, inklusive der Führungskräfte, minimiert.

Eine erste Grobeinteilung des Leistungsspektrums eines Rating Advisors lässt sich folgendermaßen treffen (s. Abb. 11.2):

- Beratungsleistungen können im Zusammenhang mit einem Emittentenrating, d. h. im Rahmen eines erstmaligen Ratings, aber auch einer bereits bestehenden Ratingbeziehung stehen.
- Ergänzend hierzu stehen die Beratungsleistungen im Zusammenhang mit Emissionsratings, d. h. bei der Vergabe von Ratings für einzelne Schuldverschreibungen, aber auch Covered Bond oder Verbriefungen.

Anhand eines typisierten Ablaufs eines Ratingverfahrens sollen die verschiedenen Aufgabenbereiche eines Rating Advisors dargestellt werden: (s. Abb. 11.3)

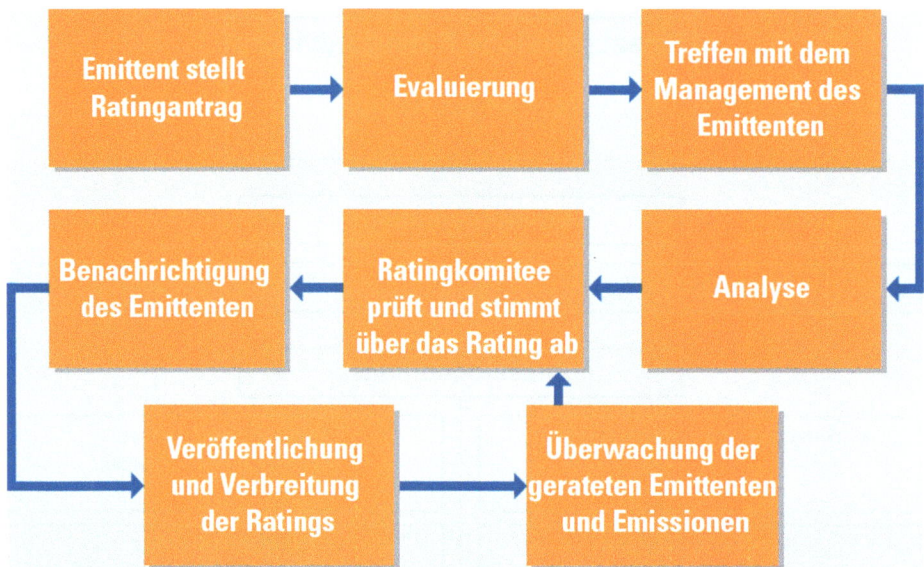

Abb. 11.3 Ablauf eines Ratingverfahrens

11.6.1 Mandatierung einer Ratingagentur

Zwar bedeutet das Eingehen einer Vertragsbeziehung mit einer Ratingagentur keinen ewigen Treueschwur. Doch angesichts der typischerweise langfristig angelegten und kostenintensiven Vertragsbeziehung will die Wahl der richtigen Ratingagentur wohl überlegt sein. Hierbei kann der Rating Advisor bereits im Vorfeld des eigentlichen Ratingverfahrens wertvolle Entscheidungsunterstützung liefern. Hierzu gehören Aspekte wie der möglichen Mehrwert und Nutzen eines Ratings, der Ablauf des Ratingverfahrens, die relevanten Ratingkriterien und Unterschiede zwischen den verschiedenen Agenturen, sowie der mit dem Rating verbundene einmalige und fortlaufende Zeit- und Ressourcenaufwand.

Darüber hinaus kann die Erstellung eines indikativen Ratings und der Vergleich mit bereits gerateten Mitbewerben aufschlussreiche Hinweise über das mögliche erreichbare Rating liefern.

Wertvollen Input kann der Rating Advisor auch bei der Entscheidungsfindung liefern, mit welcher und mit wie vielen Ratingagenturen zusammengearbeitet werden soll. Diese Thematik betrifft nicht nur neue Ratings, sondern zunehmend auch bestehende Ratingverbindungen. Während in der Vergangenheit die meisten großen europäischen Finanzinstitute von den drei großen Agenturen bewertet wurden, ist hier eine deutliche Trendwende zu erkennen.

Die Beratung hinsichtlich der Frage und der möglichen Auswirkungen, ob und mit welchen Ratingagenturen die Vertragsbeziehungen beendet werden sollen, gewinnt vor dem Hintergrund weiter steigender Ratinggebühren, divergierender Ratingkriterien und Ratingergebnisse, sowie neuer Wettbewerber zunehmend an Bedeutung.

Aufgrund der in den vergangenen Jahren stark angestiegenen Ratinggebühren, sowie der mangelnden Transparenz und Vergleichbarkeit von Ratinggebühren und anderer wesentlicher Vertragsbedingungen kann die Einbeziehung eines erfahrenen Rating Advisors in die Vertragsverhandlungen teilweise deutliche Ersparnisse für den Emittenten bedeuten.

11.6.2   Vorbereitung auf das Ratinggespräch

In dieser Phase geht es vorrangig um die Unterstützung bei der Erstellung der Ratingdokumentation und der Schärfung der „Credit Story" als Grundlage für das Managementgespräch mit dem Analystenteam der mandatierten Ratingagentur. Ebenso wichtig ist die professionelle Vorbereitung der involvierten Führungskräfte auf die Ratinggespräche.

Dies kann im Rahmen eines erstmaligen Ratings sein, aber auch im Rahmen der regelmäßigen Überwachung eines bestehenden Ratings.

Ausgangspunkt ist in der Regel ein von der Agentur zur Verfügung gestellter Anforderungs- und Fragenkatalog. In der Ratingpraxis hat sich hier eine enge Zusammenarbeit zwischen dem Rating Advisor und dem vom Unternehmen bestimmten Ratingkoordinator bewährt. Der Ratingkoordinator, in der Regel auch direkter Ansprechpartner der Ratingagenturen, gewährleistet den Zugang zu den relevanten internen Ansprechpartnern in den verschiedenen Abteilungen, den effizienten Zugriff und die Aufbereitung der für das Ratingverfahren benötigten Daten, sowie die Zusammenstellung der Ratingdokumentation.

Jedoch ist es mit einer reinen Abarbeitung des Fragenkatalogs bei weitem nicht getan. Ein solches Vorgehen würde das Risiko beinhalten, wesentliche ratingrelevante Faktoren aus Sicht des Unternehmens nicht optimal umzusetzen. Der Schwerpunkt des Rating Advisors liegt vorrangig auf dem strategischen Input, u. a. der Entwicklung bzw. Schärfung der sogenannten „Credit Story" durch die Brille einer Ratingagentur. Dies beinhaltet zunächst die Identifikation und die Analyse der wesentlichen Einflussfaktoren auf das Rating des Finanzinstituts und Ansatzpunkte für Maßnahmen zur gezielten Verbesserung des Ratings. Darauf aufbauend erfolgen Vorschläge zur umfassenden und überzeugenden Darstellung des Instituts unter Berücksichtigung der aus Sicht der Ratingagentur relevanten Ratingfaktoren und Ratingtreiber, der Stärken und Schwächen, sowie dem (Rating-) Vergleich mit relevanten Wettbewerbern (s. Abb. 11.4).

Ein weiterer wesentlicher Einsatzbereich des Rating Advisors liegt in der Vorbereitung der Führungskräfte auf die regelmäßig stattfindenden Ratinggespräche mit dem Analystenteam der Ratingagentur.

Diese Ratinggespräche werden von vielen Vorständen oft als einseitig negativ empfunden. Vor allem der stark ausgeprägte kritische Fokus der Ratinggespräche und bohrende Fragen zu akuten und potenzielle Risiken, Schwächen und Herausforderungen eines Instituts sind für viele Führungskräfte oft ungewohnt.

Die Rolle des Rating Advisors ist demzufolge, die Führungskräfte für den Ablauf der Gespräche, die Sichtweise der Ratingagenturen und Analysten, die relevanten Ratingtrei-

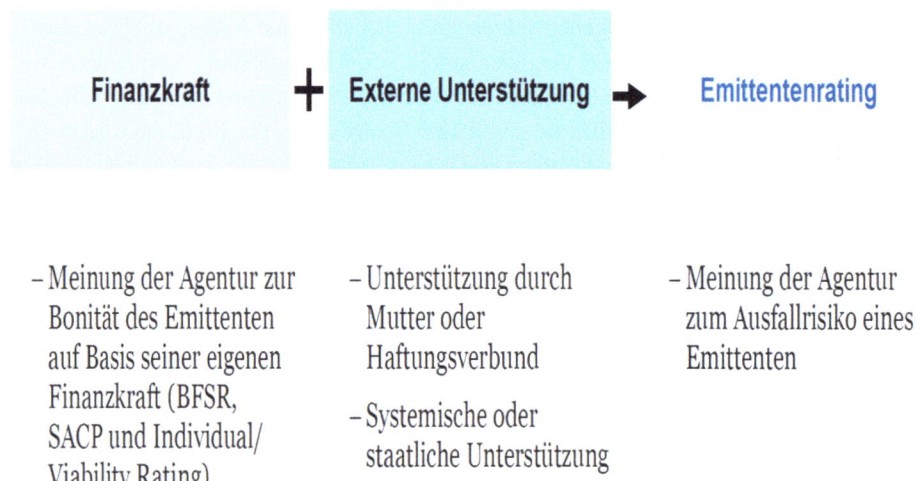

Abb. 11.4 Analytische Komponenten des Bankenratings

ber, sowie die zu erwartenden Fragen der Analysten zu sensibilisieren und entsprechend vorzubereiten.

Eine überzeugende, konsistente und glaubwürdige Präsentation seitens des Managementteams gegenüber den Ratinganalysten kann im späteren Ratingkomitee „das Zünglein an der Waage spielen", um ein optimales Ratingergebnis zu erzielen.

11.6.3 Ratinggespräche

Die regelmäßigen Ratinggespräche mit dem Management des zu bewertenden Unternehmens („Management Meeting"), sowie die subjektive Einschätzung des Managementteams, sind zentrale Element im Ratingverfahren. Hier bietet sich die Möglichkeit, dem Analystenteam ein umfassendes und überzeugendes Bild des Unternehmens und seines Topmanagements zu präsentieren.

Nach einer professionellen Vorbereitung der Ratinggespräche und der Teilnehmer ist eine persönliche Teilnahme des Rating Advisors an den Ratinggesprächen nicht unbedingt zwingend notwendig. Allerdings kann eine Teilnahme in bestimmten Fällen von Vorteil sein. So kann der Rating Advisor aus dem Verlauf der Gespräche und der Fragen der Analysten oft wichtige Schlussfolgerungen für die Nachbereitung der Gespräche ziehen. Bei einer Teilnahme des Rating Advisors, sollte jedoch die Maxime sein, dass er nicht aktiv in die Ratinggespräche eingreift.

11.6.4   Ratingentscheidung und Ratingveröffentlichung

Auch nach den Ratinggesprächen ist die regelmäßige Kommunikation mit der Ratingagentur weiterhin wichtig. So bleibt bis zum Ratingkomitee die Möglichkeit, noch offene
Punkte aus den Ratinggesprächen mit dem Analystenteam zu klären, etwaige Missver-
ständnisse aufzuklären, neue Entwicklungen zu kommentieren, und zusätzliche Informationen zur Verfügung zu stellen.

Nachdem die Ratingentscheidung gefallen ist, unterstützt der Rating Advisor das Institut bei der Analyse und Interpretation der Ratingentscheidung, den möglichen Handlungs-
alternativen und deren Konsequenzen:

- Soll bei einem erstmaligen Rating das Ergebnis akzeptiert werden und der Veröffentlichung des Ratings zugestimmt werden oder soll das Rating vorläufig vertraulich bleiben?
- Sofern seit der Ratingentscheidung neue ratingrelevante Informationen vorliegen bzw.
Ereignisse stattgefunden haben, die aus Sicht der Agentur voraussichtlich zu einer ver-
änderten Ratingeinschätzung führen könnten, ist zu erwägen, ob gegen das Ratingergebnis in Form eines Rating Appeals Einspruch erhoben werden soll.
- Kritische Analyse der Ratingveröffentlichungen und Überprüfung auf faktische Fehler, den Einschluss von vertraulichen Informationen oder missverständlicher Formulierungen.

11.6.5   Regelmäßige Überwachung und Surveillance

„Vor dem Rating ist nach dem Rating". Im Rahmen der von der Ratingagentur regelmäßig vorgenommenen Überwachung (Surveillance) des Ratings ergeben sich zwangsläufig
zahlreiche Anknüpfungspunkte für eine Beratung durch den Rating Advisors, u. a. bei

- der Erstellung eines Maßnahmenplans zur Beseitigung der von der Ratingagentur kri-
tisierten Schwächen und die nachhaltige Beibehaltung bzw. weiteren Verbesserung der
Stärken
- der Kommunikation (u. a. Details, Timing) gegenüber der Agentur bei möglichen ra-
tingrelevanten Entwicklungen, wie z. B. einer möglichen M&A-Transkation, Restrukturierungen, Gewinnwarnungen, Auswirkungen regulatorischer Anforderungen (z. B.
Bail-in, Basel III, Asset Encumbrance)
- der Analyse der Auswirkungen von Kriterienänderungen und deren Wechselwirkun-
gen, z. B. zwischen Banken- und Covered Bond Ratings, oder den Abhängigkeiten
zwischen Länder- und Bankenratings
- der Beratung hinsichtlich der potenziellen Ratingkonsequenzen bestimmter unterneh-
menspolitischer Entscheidungen, wie z. B. Restrukturierungen, Etablierung einer Bad
Bank, Veräußerung von Tochtergesellschaften oder Unternehmensteilen, Akquisitionen
etc.)

- der Optimierung der Überdeckungsanforderungen und Transaktionenstrukturen bei Covered Bonds und Verbriefungen
- der Kommentierung von geplanten Kriterienänderungen (Request for Comments)
- der Analyse von möglichen Ratingauswirkungen von geplanten Kriterienänderungen und darauf basierender Handlungsempfehlungen
- der Analyse veränderter regulatorischer Anforderungen an Ratingagenturen und der Konsequenzen für das Ratingverfahren und die unternehmensinternen Prozesse.

11.7 Anbieter von Rating Advisory Dienstleistungen

Vielen Unternehmen stellt sich angesichts knapper interner Ressourcen und fehlender spezifischer Ratingexpertise die Frage, inwieweit die Einbeziehung externer Expertise einer besseren Erreichung der jeweiligen Ratingziele dienen kann.

Die Hilfe der Ratingagenturen selbst ist hier naturgemäß sehr begrenzt, nicht zuletzt aufgrund expliziter regulatorischer Vorgaben, die eine Beratung des zu bewertenden Unternehmens ausschließen. Somit reduziert sich die Unterstützung der Ratinganalysten zunehmend auf mehr oder weniger hilfreiche Erläuterungen der spezifischen Ratingkriterien und Ratingprozesse, sowie Verweise auf sonstige Researchveröffentlichungen.

Wertvolle Unterstützung im Ratingverfahren kann dahingegen ein Rating Advisor bieten.

Der Anbietermarkt für Rating Advisor lässt sich grob in drei Kategorien einteilen:

- Angelsächsische Investmentbanken bzw. europäische Universalbanken
- Große Wirtschaftsprüfungs- und Beratungsgesellschaften
- Unabhängige Rating Advisor

Traditionell war Rating Advisory ein komplementäres Geschäftsfeld, welches in der Regel in die Bond-Origination-Teams von angelsächsischen Investmentbanken oder in Corporate-Finance Abteilungen von europäischen Universalbanken integriert war. Dabei stand (und steht heute noch) Rating Advisory oft unmittelbar im Zusammenhang mit Kapitalmarkttransaktionen, wie z. B. der Auflegung eines neuen Commerical Paper oder Medium-Term-Note-Programmes eines bislang noch nicht gerateten Emittenten, bzw. der Emission von Hybridkapital oder strukturierten Finanzierungen.

In ähnlicher Weise haben die großen Wirtschaftsprüfungsgesellschaften im Bereich Corporate Finance ihr Beratungsgeschäft um Rating Advisory Dienstleistungen ergänzt. Auch hier liegt der Fokus sehr stark auf Beratungsleistungen im engen Zusammenhang mit spezifischen Kapitalmarkttransaktionen.

Daneben haben sich in den vergangenen Jahren unabhängige Rating Advisor etabliert, die ihre Dienstleistungen nicht zwangsläufig im Zusammenhang mit einer Kapitalmarkttransaktion anbieten. Zielrichtung ist hier vielmehr, sich durch einen umfassenderen Beratungsansatz, sowie spezifische Branchenkenntnisse und relevante Ratingpraxiserfahrung von den „großen" Konkurrenten abzuheben.

Während sich auf dem Beratungsmarkt für Industrieunternehmen eine große Anzahl von Ratingberatern aus allen drei Bereichen tummeln, ist das Angebot an spezialisierten Ratingberatern für Finanzinstitute aufgrund der notwendigen Kenntnisse und Erfahrungen vor allem im deutschsprachigen Raum deutlich kleiner.

11.8   Anforderungsprofil

Eine Aussage, ob das Institut einen Rating Advisor benötigt und wer der optimale Rating-berater für ein Finanzinstitut ist, lässt sich nicht pauschal treffen. Vielmehr hängt dies von der spezifischen Beratungssituation ab, so u. a. von

- den Ratingzielen des Auftraggebers
- den intern verfügbaren Kapazitäten und deren ratingspezifischen Know-Hows
- der Erfahrung und Expertise des jeweiligen Beraters
- den möglichen Interessenkonflikten bzw. der Konkurrenzsituation zwischen Auftrag-geber und Advisor.

Bei der Wahl eines geeigneten Rating Advisors sollten aus Sicht des Auftraggebers folgen-de Anforderungskriterien im Vordergrund stehen:

- Relevante Ratingerfahrung
- (Aktuelle) Expertise
- Track record
- Neutralität und Unabhängigkeit

Unabdingbar für den erfolgreichen Einsatz eines Rating Advisors sind dessen berufliche Qualifikation und Historie (Track record). Langjährige und relevante Erfahrung im Be-reich Ratinganalyse von europäischen Banken und Finanzinstituten sind hierbei unabding-bare Voraussetzungen. Idealerweise hat der Advisor mehrere Jahre als Senior Analyst und Mitglied des Ratingkomitees bei einer der großen Ratingagenturen gewirkt und verfügt somit über hervorragende Kenntnisse über die Ratings und relevanten Ratingtreiber- und Ratingkriterien im jeweiligen Marktsektor, aber auch die Sichtweisen, Präferenzen und Vorurteile und internen Abläufe bei den verschiedenen Agenturen. Soll der Berater auch zu kommerziellen Themen wie Vertrags- und Gebührenverhandlungen hinzugezogen wer-den, ist dessen praktische Erfahrung aus früheren entsprechenden Managementpositionen bei einer Agentur hilfreich.

Angesichts der sich rapide verändernden Banken- und Ratinglandschaft ist es ebenso unabdingbar, dass der Rating Advisor stets auf dem aktuellen Stand der Entwicklungen (z. B. regulatorische Anforderungen, Bilanzierung, Kriterienänderungen, neue Wettbe-werber etc.) bleibt, um seine Kunden stets professionell beraten zu können.

Die Erfüllung hoher Standards an Expertise, Erfahrung, Glaubwürdigkeit und Seniorität sind auch Grundvoraussetzung dafür, dass die in das Ratingverfahren involvierten Führungskräfte den Rating Advisor als kompetenten Sparringpartner akzeptieren, mit dem sie strategische und oft sensible Themen offen und kompetent auf Augenhöhe diskutieren können.

Für viele Institute spielt die Unabhängigkeit und Vertraulichkeit bei der Auswahl eines des Rating Advisors eine entscheidende Rolle. Zwar bieten viele Anbieter ihre Rating Advisory Dienstleistungen stark subventioniert oder sogar „umsonst" im Paket mit entsprechend nachgelagerten Produkte (z. B. Emission von Anleihen) an.

Doch zum einen scheuen sich Unternehmen, strategische bzw. vertrauliche Themen mit einem Rating Advisor Team zu diskutieren, der letztendlich für ein Konkurrenzinstitut arbeitet. Zum anderen präferieren viele Emittenten eine Entkopplung von Rating Advisory und Produkt-Dienstleistungen, um jeweils die beste Leistung unabhängig wählen zu können.

Last, but not least, sollte der Berater bereits in der Vergangenheit bewiesen haben, dass er ähnlich komplexe Ratingmandate erfolgreich bewältigt hat. Wie so oft, können Empfehlungen von befreundeten Instituten auch bei der Auswahl eines Rating Advisors von Vorteil sein.

11.9   Nutzen aus Sicht des Finanzinstituts

Da letztendlich das Ratingkomitee der Agentur über das Rating entscheidet, bietet die Einbindung eines Rating Advisors im Ratingverfahren (leider) keine Garantie für die Erreichung der Ratingziele eines Finanzinstituts,

Allerdings kann die Ratingbegleitung durch einen erfahrenen und kritischen Rating Advisor einen wesentlichen Beitrag dazu leisten, dass die Ratinganalysten und letztendlich das Ratingkomitee sich ein umfassendes Bild über das Risikoprofil eines Institutes bilden können. Dies wiederum führt dazu, dass das Ratingurteil nicht durch unzureichende Kenntnisse über das zu bewertende Unternehmen, oder aufgrund übertrieben konservativer Annahmen, negativ beeinträchtigt wird.

Von entscheidender Bedeutung ist hierbei, dass der Rating Advisor die Sichtweise durch die Brille einer Ratingagentur einnimmt, und ratingkritische Themen offen anspricht (und ansprechen kann).

Im Vordergrund steht hierbei der Fokus auf die quantitativen und qualitativen Ratingfaktoren und Ratingtreiber, die für die Ratingagentur wesentlich sind. Dazu liefert der Rating Advisor wertvollen Input bei der überzeugenden Darstellung der „Credit Story", sowie der zielgerichteten und effizienten Aufbereitung der im Ratingverfahren benötigten Daten und Unterlagen.

Eine kritische Rolle spielt der Rating Advisor vor allem bei der Vorbereitung der Ratinggespräche, wo es um die Sensibilisierung der Führungskräfte für ratingrelevante und sensible Themen geht.

In Zeiten, in denen viele Finanzinstitute vor signifikanten strategischen Herausforderungen stehen, ist für viele Unternehmen der Rating Advisor auch ein gefragter Sparringspartner, mit dem Führungskräfte kritisch die eigene Positionierung, Risikofelder und Verbesserungspotenziale, sowie mögliche Ratingauswirkungen diskutieren. Ein solcher Meinungsaustausch mit den Ratingagenturen ist heute nur noch sehr eingeschränkt möglich, und oftmals auch nicht gewünscht. Dies liegt zum einen an den verschärften regulatorischen Anforderungen an die Ratingagenturen (Stichwort: Beratungsverbot), die zu einer deutlich eingeschränkten Kommunikation zwischen Analystenteam und Emittent geführt haben. Zum anderen besteht bei vielen Emittenten die Sorge, dass eine zu offene Kommunikation mit den Agenturen, z. B. hinsichtlich möglicher strategischer Planungen, zu ungerechtfertigten negativen Ratingreaktionen führen könnte.

Eine solche professionelle und zielgerichtete Begleitung im Ratingverfahren sichert somit den effizienten und kostensparenden Einsatz von knappen Unternehmens- und Managementressourcen.

Nicht unerwähnt sollte bleiben, dass auch die Ratinganalysten von einem Rating Advisor profitieren: Der reibungslose Ablauf des Ratingverfahrens und einer umfassenden Darstellung und der wesentlichen Ratingfaktoren sollte es ihnen leichter machen, das Ratingkomitee vom „richtigen" Rating zu überzeugen.

11.10   Schlussbetrachtung

Ursprünglich konzentrierte sich das „klassische" Rating Advisory auf die Begleitung von Finanzinstituten bei deren erstmaligen Rating, oft im Rahmen der internationalen Platzierung von Kapitalmarktprodukten wie Commerical Paper oder Medium-Term Note Programmen. Zunehmend hat sich in den letzten Jahren der Fokus verstärkt auf die Beratung von Finanzinstituten mit bestehenden Ratings verlagert. Für diese Unternehmen sind im Zuge der Finanzkrise die Vermeidung weiterer Herabstufungen und die Optimierung des Ratings unter Kosten-Nutzen-Aspekten in den Vordergrund gerückt. Heute ist der Rating Advisor zunehmend als strategischer Sparringpartner und Ratingcoach während des gesamten Ratingprozesses und über die gesamte Refinanzierungspalette hinweg gefragt.

Michael Zlotnik ist seit Anfang 2015 als Geschäftsführer von Capital Intelligence (Germany) für den Ausbau der Ratingaktivitäten in Deutschland, Österreich und der Schweiz (D-A-CH) zuständig. Capital Intelligence (www.ciratings.com) ist eine von der ESMA registrierte EU-Ratingagentur (www.esma.europa.eu) mit ECAI-Status. Davor hat er als unabhängiger Rating Advisor Banken, Unternehmen und Regierungen beraten. Bis Ende 2010 war er 17 Jahre bei Standard & Poor's in verschiedenen Führungspositionen tätig, unter anderem als Leiter des Bankenteams für die Region Europa, Naher Osten und Afrika (EMEA). Vor seinem Wechsel in die Ratingwelt war er als Aktienanalyst für Banken tätig. Michael Zlotnik hat einen Abschluss als Diplom-Betriebswirt (BA) – Fachrichtung Bank der DHBW Stuttgart.

Banking 2020: Nur neue Wege sichern neue Erfolge

12

Norman Weißer und Laura Zdrzalek

12.1 Einleitung

Die Gewinne der Banken sind am Boden. Zinsen nahe der Nulllinie lassen die Zinserträge schmelzen. Die Regulatorik wirkt zudem nachhaltig negativ auf der Kostenseite. Die Projektportfolios beinhalten zu 70 % regulatorische Umsetzungsthemen. Der Großteil des restlichen Budgets wird für die Aufrechterhaltung der operativen Systeme benötigt. Nur wenig bleibt für Innovationen.

Alle Indizien sprechen dafür, dass sich die Lage, im Gegensatz zu früheren Tiefs, in naher Zukunft nicht entspannen wird und die Gewinne automatisch wieder sprudeln. Ganz im Gegenteil kann damit gerechnet werden, dass diese Phase noch Jahre andauern wird.

Einzelne Ertragsteigerungs- oder Kostensenkungsprogramme werden den Banken nicht helfen; es sind überproportionale Anstrengungen notwendig, um zumindest den Status Quo zu erhalten. Eine Reihe von Stellhebeln müssen angegangen werden, um die Herausforderungen der kommenden Jahre zu bewältigen. Zuvor muss jedoch eine wesentliche Erkenntnis reifen – Menschen machen den Unterschied. In Zukunft wird es nur durch die Mobilisierung der eigenen Mitarbeiter möglich sein, gemeinsam die Herausforderungen zu bewältigen. Dies gilt in allen Bereichen, vom Vertrieb bis ins Back-Office.

N. Weißer (✉) · L. Zdrzalek
Frankfurt am Main, Deutschland
E-Mail: karim.schaefer@faktenkontor.de

© Springer Fachmedien Wiesbaden 2016
Z. Diab, O. Everling (Hrsg.), *Rating von Finanzinstituten*,
DOI 10.1007/978-3-658-04195-3_12

12.2 Wachstum ist kein Selbstläufer mehr

12.2.1 Makroökonomische und regulatorische Veränderungen

Die Finanz- und Wirtschaftskrise hat die Phase expandierender Financial Services Anbieter und deren über die Maßen gewachsene Bilanzen abrupt beendet. Der gesamte Finanzsektor – Banken, Finanzdienstleister, Versicherungen – hat in den letzten fünf Jahren massive Anstrengungen unternommen, um das Überleben des eigenen Geschäftsmodells im Nachgang der Krise zu sichern. Nachdem Wachstums- und Expansionsziele damit unfreiwillig ad acta gelegt werden mussten, wurde der Fokus zunächst auf die Regulatorik gelegt. Die erwartete Markterholung ist bis dato leider nur teilweise und deutlich langsamer eingetreten als erwartet. Eine Rückkehr zum Vorkrisenzustand scheint in den kommenden Jahren immer unwahrscheinlicher. Die Branche, die in den letzten zehn bis 15 Jahren ein beeindruckendes Wachstum vorweisen konnte, kämpft heute darum profitabel zu bleiben.

Diese Entwicklungen, die die gesamte Finanzwelt in Atem gehalten haben, sind nicht ohne Folgen geblieben. Regierungen, supranationale Institutionen und Behörden reagierten und verschärften die Regulierungen:

- Durch Basel III wurde die Kapital-Anspruchs-Direktive in die nationale Gesetzgebung aufgenommen und Minimalanforderungen für Banken festgelegt. Darunter die ‚leverage-ratio‘, welche von 2018 an die maximale Schuldenlast der Finanzdienstleister regulieren wird, und komplementär zur bereits bestehenden CRD agiert.
- Solvency II wird ab 2016 die Regulierung der Versicherungsbranche reformieren.
- Die Dodd-Frank Wall Street Reform wurde als direkte Reaktion auf die amerikanische Finanzkrise eingeführt, ihr folgend wurden verschiedene Gesetze im Bereich des Verbraucherschutzes, des Arbeitsschutzes und anderer verwandter Gebiete erlassen.

Insgesamt zielen die neuen Regulierungen auf eine Risikoreduktion ab. Sie sollen die Position der Konsumenten gegenüber den Banken stärken. Die Auswirkungen auf die Banken sind enorm. Es müssen nicht nur vereinzelt Produkte zurückgezogen, sondern auch ganze Geschäftsmodelle umstrukturiert werden.

Es ist zu beobachten, dass ein grundlegender, allumfassender Strukturwandel nötig ist. Dies muss auch freiwillige Restrukturierungen in der Firmenstrategie, Shareholder Struktur und Finanzierung nach sich ziehen. Im neuen Status Quo ist das Wachstum signifikant niedriger und schwerer zu erreichen. So sind zum Beispiel RoEs (Return on Equity) um zehn Prozentpunkte gefallen. Obwohl die Lage weiterhin angespannt ist, hat sich innerhalb der Eurozone eine spürbare Stabilisierung vollzogen. Der Bankensektor ist heute zu einem hohen Grad von Zentralbanken und politisch ausgelösten Stimuli abhängig.

12.2.2   Mehr als nur regulatorische Veränderungen

Neben den engmaschigen Regulierungen sind die Banken mit weiteren Herausforderungen konfrontiert:

- Auch Banken erreichen nun das digitale Zeitalter, in welchem Internet und mobile Anwendungen die Norm sind.
- Im Rahmen der Digitalisierung sind weitere Konkurrenten auf den Markt getreten. So nehmen Unternehmen wie Amazon und Google Bereiche des traditionellen Kerngeschäftes der Banken ein, letzterer Konzern hat darüber hinaus kürzlich eine Banklizenz in Luxemburg erworben.
- Die niedrigen Zinsraten stellen ebenfalls ein Problem für die Banken dar, da sie für geringere Margen im Geldverleih sorgen.
- Diese Faktoren werden noch verstärkt durch einen allgemeinen Vertrauensverlust der Kunden in den gesamten Finanzsektor. Dies führt zum einen zu dem Wunsch nach mehr Transparenz, zum anderen aber auch zu einer geringeren Kundenloyalität.

Obwohl an dieser Stelle nur einige Faktoren, welche die Erholung der Wirtschaftslage negativ beeinflussen genannt werden können, ist die generelle Tendenz klar: Die derzeitige Situation europäischer Banken ist immer noch weit von der Normalität entfernt. Dies muss zwangsläufig zu weiteren strukturellen Umstellungen führen, um die Konkurrenzfähigkeit langfristig sicherzustellen.

12.2.3   Ein Blick in die wirtschaftliche Zukunft für Finanzdienstleister

In Anbetracht der derzeitigen Bemühungen zur Regulierung des Finanzmarktes ist von einer bereits jetzt zu beobachtenden, verstärkten Konsolidierung auszugehen. Unter anderem ist dies auf die steigenden Kosten, bedingt durch die regulatorischen Maßnahmen, zurückzuführen. Die Konsolidierung wirkt gerade im Lichte der fortschreitenden Regulierung, deren erklärtes Ziel das Verhindern eines Unternehmenswachstums einzelner Konzerne zu sog. „too-big-to-fail" Organisationen ist, paradox.

Begleitet wird dieser Prozess von einer starken Zurückhaltung und mangelndem Vertrauen, sowohl von Firmen als auch Privatkunden. Dies führt zwangsläufig zu einer geringeren Nachfrage und geringeren Umsätzen und Gewinnen.

Um die Folgen der oben beschriebenen Umstände auf den Finanzmarkt zu verstehen, haben wir eine vereinfachende Modellrechnung erstellt. Diese macht deutlich in welch dramatischen Ausmaßen Banken ihre Strategien verändern müssten, um im neuen Status Quo zu bestehen.

Es müssen tief greifende Veränderungen an der Umsatz- und Kostenbasis vorgenommen werden, um die Cost-Income-Ratio stabil zu halten oder einen angemessenen RoE an die Shareholder ausschütten zu können. Derzeit haben die meisten europäischen Banken einen RoE von ca. 7%. Da die Kapitalkosten jedoch bei 11% liegen schaffen die Banken es nicht, Gewinne für ihre Shareholder zu generieren.

Zur Veranschaulichung der Beziehung zwischen Cost-Income-Ratio und Return on Equity, sowie deren Abhängigkeit von Kapitalvorschriften, haben wir verschiedene Beispiele erstellt.

Zur Vereinfachung wird davon ausgegangen, dass alle Banken über dieselbe Bilanzsumme, dieselbe Debt/Equity Struktur und dieselben Kapitalkosten verfügen. Sie unterscheiden sich jedoch in Bezug auf Ihren Erfolg, welcher durch das CIR und RoE gemessen wird (siehe Abb. 12.1). Unter diesen Voraussetzungen wurden drei Modelle hypothetischer Banken erstellt.

Aufgrund der makroökonomischen Situation und des verringerten Vertrauens der Kunden, prognostizieren wir bis 2020 einen Umsatzrückgang und eine gleichzeitige Steigerung der Kosten für Banken. Die Situation wird weiterhin verschärft durch angekündigte, teils bereits spürbare Forderungen nach einer breiteren Kapitalbasis für die kommenden Jahre. Strengere Regulierungen sind angestoßen und es wird über eine Deckelung des Leverage nachgedacht – einigen Schätzungen zufolge bedeutet das eine Erhöhung der Kapitalbasis von über € 250 Mrd. für europäische Banken.

Obwohl relevant, gehen wir an dieser Stelle nicht darauf ein, wie ein Ansteigen/Fallen der Mindestkapitalanforderungen den RoE beeinflusst – dies hängt maßgeblich von der Quelle des Kapitals, der Möglichkeit jeder einzelnen Institution ihr Fremd- und Eigenkapital auszubalancieren und der Bilanzstruktur selbst ab und würde den Rahmen der Modellrechnung sprengen.

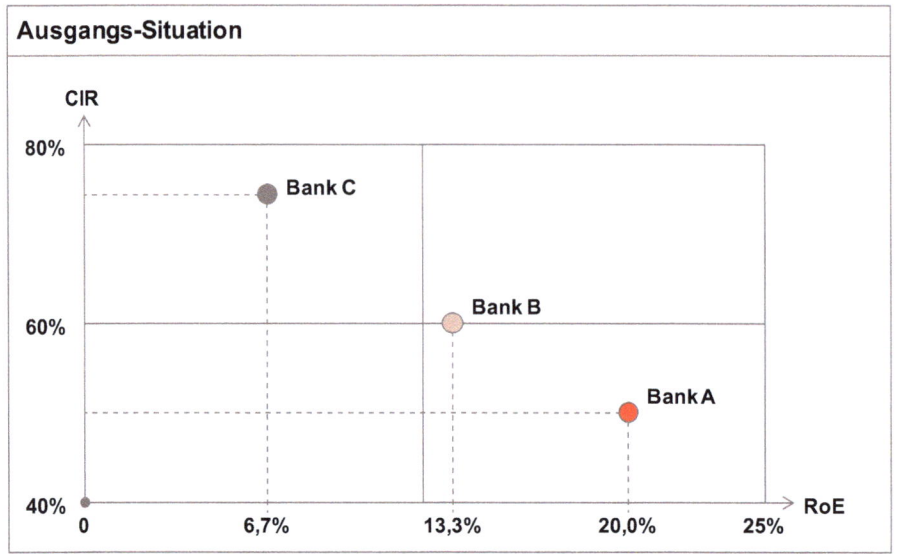

Abb. 12.1 Ausgangs-Situation

Nichtsdestotrotz würde ein 10 %iger Anstieg der Mindestkapitalanforderungen – der uns sehr realistisch und eher am unteren Ende des Möglichen erscheint – die notwendigen Kosteneinsparungen, um den RoE stabil zu halten, noch einmal drastisch erhöhen.

Um einem 10 %igen Umsatzrückgang und einen 10 %igen Kostenanstieg begleitet von einem 10 %igen Anstieg der Mindestkapitalanforderungen bis 2020 entgegenzuwirken, müsste Bank A ihre Kosten laut der Modellrechnung tatsächlich um über 35 % senken, Banken B und C um je 30 und 24 %. Diese Beispielrechnung gefährdet effektiv das Überleben der Banken. Alternativ könnte Bank A sich natürlich auf eine Umsatzstrategie fokussieren, das würde bedeuten, dass die Bank ihre Umsätze um über 22 % anheben müsste, um die oben genannten Effekte auszugleichen und den RoE stabil bei 15 % zu halten.

Im Einklang mit den neuen Regulierungen erscheint eine Kombination beider Strategien, in der sowohl Umsatz- als auch Kostenfaktoren berücksichtigt werden, als die beste Lösung. Dazu müsste allerdings das gesamte Geschäftsmodell der Bank umstrukturiert werden. Massive Kosteneinsparungen bei gleichzeitiger Umsatzsteigerung durch neue Produkte und/oder Kunden wären von Nöten.

12.2.4   Die zukünftigen Herausforderungen

Die Kalkulationen bieten Anlass zur Sorge und geben einen guten Einblick in die Herausforderungen, mit denen Banken im derzeitigen Markt konfrontiert werden. Die Stabilisierung oder gar der Ausbau der Gewinne unter gleichzeitiger Kostenkontrolle, um einen positives RoE zu erhalten, ist äußerst wichtig aber stellt auch hohe Anforderungen an die Unternehmen. Es gibt zahlreiche Stellhebel, durch deren konzertierten Einsatz Banken wieder auf einen Wachstumspfad gelangen können. Voraussetzung ist jedoch die Unterstützung durch mobilisierte Mitarbeiter.

Die Bedeutung der Mobilisierung wird im Folgenden für drei Stellhebel beispielhaft dargestellt. Generell sollte das Konzept der Mobilisierung als Philosophie aufgefasst werden, durch dessen Anwendung in den meisten Bereichen (nicht nur den beschriebenen) deutlich nachhaltigere Wirkungen entfaltet werden können.

12.3   Die Bedeutung der Mobilisierung

Banken haben in der Vergangenheit unzählige Optimierungsinitiativen durchgeführt, von denen viele nie zum gewünschten Erfolg geführt haben. Ein wesentlicher Faktor, der oft nicht oder nicht genug berücksichtigt worden ist, ist das sich ändernde Verhalten von Mitarbeitern und Kunden (Abb. 12.2).

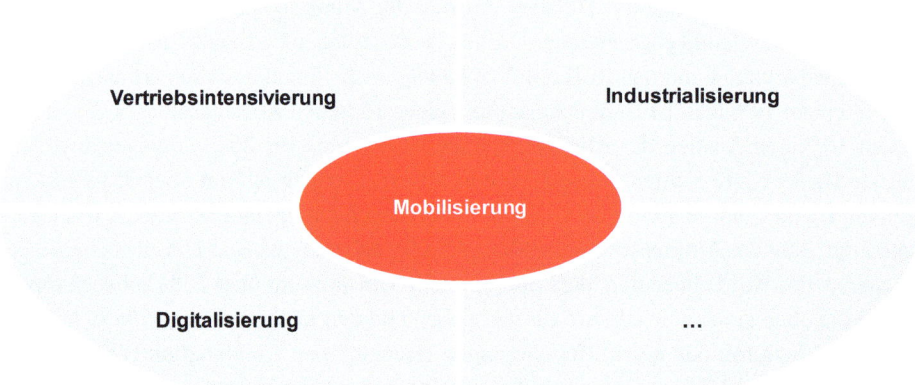

Abb. 12.2 Mobilisierung

Mitarbeiter haben steigende Erwartungen in Bezug auf ihren Arbeitsplatz:

1. Mehr Freiheit bei der täglichen Arbeit, Raum für ihre Ideen und deren Anerkennung
2. Höhere Verantwortung und ein vertrauensvolles und unterstützendes Management. Diese Erwartungen sind sogar noch ausgeprägter in Organisationen mit einem hohen Grad an Zentralisierung und/oder stark zentralisierten Prozessen.

Auf der anderen Seite haben sich die ändernden Kundenerwartungen und Verhaltensweisen massiv auf die Verkaufszahlen der Banken ausgewirkt. Kunden werden stetig preisempfindlicher, während gleichzeitig der Anspruch an Beratung und Produktqualität steigt.

So hat eine Studie (Kundenbankstudie 2013, EUROGROUP, 2013) kürzlich gezeigt, dass "schwindendes Vertrauen, gefühlt starke Vernachlässigung und eine hohe Veränderungsbereitschaft die Bankkunden von heute charakterisieren". Vertrauen und persönliche Beziehungen sind entscheidend für eine dauerhaft starke Kundenbeziehung. Banken scheinen hier jedoch einen klaren Rückstand aufzuweisen, insbesondere in Bezug auf Vertrauen und Aufbau von Kunden/Berater-Beziehungen.

Banken und Finanzinstitute haben versucht, ihre Prozesse, Strukturen und IT-Systeme in den letzten zwei Jahrzehnten zu optimieren. Dies hat sich zwar als hilfreich erwiesen, zeigt jedoch auch Folgen: eine branchenweite Konvergenz hat stattgefunden. Diese hat dazu geführt, dass Geschäftsmodelle, Prozesse und Produkte, um nur einige zu nennen, immer homogener geworden sind und damit eine echte Differenzierung zunehmend schwerer wird. In einem derartigen Umfeld sind Mitarbeiter zu einem der wichtigsten Unterscheidungsfaktoren geworden.

12.4   Menschen als Erfolgsfaktoren

Wenn reine Optimierungsstrategien nicht mehr ausreichen, um profitabel zu bleiben und die Menschen einen entscheidenden Erfolgsfaktor der Zukunft darstellen, kann Mobilisierung eine strategische Rolle spielen. Durch Förderung der vorhandenen Talente im Unternehmen können lang-anhaltende Erfolge erzielt werden. Mobilisierung hilft dabei ein Umfeld zu schaffen, welches die Mitarbeiter stärkt und ermutigt gemeinsame Ziele zu erreichen.

Das bedeutet, die Mitarbeiter in den Prozess der Definition von Unternehmensphilosophie und -werten einzubeziehen. Von Beginn an eingebundene Mitarbeiter werden die erarbeiteten Prinzipien konsequenter (vor-)leben als Mitarbeiter, denen alles von „oben" vorgegeben wird. Strategie darf nicht eine reine top-down Initiative bleiben, sondern muss ebenso unterfüttert sein durch bottom-up Ideen.

Absoluter Fokus auf den Kunden und hohe Qualität können nur erreicht werden, wenn Mitarbeitern mit Kundenkontakt ermöglicht wird, ihre eigenen Ideen einzubringen. Schnellere Reaktionszeiten auf Veränderungen am Markt sind die Folge.

Die Teilnahme an der Strategieentwicklung ist jedoch nur der erste Schritt in der Verlagerung von zentraler zu dezentraler Verantwortung. Die Mitarbeiter benötigen auch mehr Freiheit in ihrer täglichen Arbeit im Allgemeinen, sei es die Vertriebsplanung, Organisation von Back-Office-Aufgaben oder andere Aktivitäten.

An dieser Stelle könnte der Eindruck entstehen, dass gründliche Optimierungsstrategien und Prozess-automatisierungen genau das Gegenteil des oben Beschriebenen bewirken: Einerseits wird der Mensch als der entscheidende Erfolgsfaktor beschrieben, andererseits mündet eine höhere Automatisierung in der Regel in einen geringerem Bedarf an Mitarbeitern (ein Trend der durch Digitalisierung und Industrialisierung noch verstärkt zu werden scheint).

Diese Feststellung erscheint jedoch kurzsichtig. Wir sind der Meinung, dass Mitarbeiter in dieser Gleichung an Bedeutung noch zulegen werden. Eine hoch automatisierte Umgebung erhöht den Bedarf nach noch besser ausgebildeten Mitarbeitern.

Mitarbeiter in einem hoch automatisierten Prozess müssen flexibler, qualifizierter und kundenorientierter sein, z. B. bei der Beseitigung von Fehlern. Sie müssen eine steuernde Funktion einnehmen, die deutlich komplexer ist als die einfache Abarbeitung manueller Tätigkeiten. Der Arbeitnehmer bleibt weiterhin ein entscheidender Faktor in der Gleichung.

Wie entscheidend zeigen wir in den nachfolgenden Kapiteln, die sich jeweils mit den Themen „Vertriebsmobilisierung", „Industrialisierung" und „Digitalisierung" beschäftigen. Alle diese Hebel sind Antworten auf die oben beschriebene, makroökonomische Situation der Banken und können zum Strukturwandel beitragen. Natürlich lassen sich die Hebel ebenso ohne einen Fokus auf Mobilisierung anwenden, wir sind jedoch der Ansicht, dass sich nachhaltige Erfolge nur dann einstellen, wenn Mitarbeiter und Kunden im Fokus der Strategie stehen.

12.5 Vertriebsintensivierung

12.5.1 Aktuelle Entwicklungen und Problemstellungen – Top down Vertriebsinitiativen versagen

Top-down Vertriebsinitiativen durchlaufen oftmals eine sehr typische Entwicklung. Anfangs beobachtet man zwar steigende Verkaufszahlen, nach einer Weile fallen diese jedoch zurück auf das alte Niveau. In der Vertriebsleitung herrscht häufig Ratlosigkeit über den nur kurzfristigen Erfolg. Zwar wurde die Vertriebsinitiative in sämtlichen vertriebsnahen Bereichen ausgerufen (z. B. Vertriebsprozesse, Vertriebstraining, CRM, zentrale Vertriebsunterstützung), ein wirklicher Wandel der Vertriebskultur hat unter den Mitarbeitern jedoch nicht stattgefunden.

In einer Vertriebsstudie (Kundenbankstudie 2013, EUROGROUP 2013) stellte sich heraus, dass durchschnittlich jeder fünfte Kunde, insbesondere im mittleren Einkommensbereich, nie von seiner Bank kontaktiert wird. Eine höhere Kontaktfrequenz der Vertriebsmitarbeiter, auch unter bestehenden Kunden, könnte die Einkommenserosion der Banken bereits deutlich abfedern.

12.5.2 Zukunftsmusik – Mitarbeiterpotenziale voll ausschöpfen

Top-down Initiativen oder solche, die auf eine Zentralisierung des Vertriebs-Know-hows in den Vertriebsunterstützungsbereichen ausgelegt sind, lassen das Potenzial der eigentlichen Vertriebsmitarbeiter, die in ständigem Kundenkontakt sind, vollkommen ungenutzt. In dieser Konstellation arbeitet die Organisation letztlich gegen sich. Der Standardansatz, Menschen dazu zu bringen ihr Verhalten zu ändern, involviert häufig das Einführen neuer Prozesse und einer forcierten Nutzung derselben. Dieser Ansatz ist für gewöhnlich zum Scheitern verurteilt. Der Effekt ist meist sehr gering und schnell wieder umgekehrt. Nur durch eine echte Befähigung der Mitarbeiter können diese ihr volles Potenzial ausschöpfen und ihre beste Performance bringen.

12.5.3 Drei Schritte, um nachhaltig verbesserte Vertriebszahlen zu erreichen

Um Vertriebszahlen nachhaltig zu steigern und einen Rückfall zu alten Vertriebsniveaus erfolgreich zu verhindern, ist ein Vorgehen in drei Schritten erforderlich:

Verantwortung für den Vertriebsprozess teilen, d. h. beispielsweise die Mitarbeiter in den Filialen selbst entscheiden lassen, welche Vertriebsaktivitäten auf welche Art und Weise durchgeführt werden sollen

1. Förderung eines gesunden Wettbewerbs durch
   a. Relative Erfolgsmessung – Erfolg wird beispielsweise am Erfolg anderer Teams gemessen
   b. Wöchentliche Kommunikation, um sicherzustellen, dass Erfolgsstories bekannt und direktes Feedback eingeholt werden kann
   c. Überführung der häufig existierenden "Listenlogik" in eine so genannte "Ligalogik", um Anonymität so weit wie möglich zu unterbinden
2. Einführung eines Team-Ansatzes durch
   d. strenge Teamorientierung – es wird kein Einzelerfolg/-misserfolg mehr gemessen
   e. Anpassung der internen Arbeitsorganisation nach Stärken/Schwächen und Präferenzen im Team anstelle der Optimierung von Einzelzielen
   f. Team-orientiertes Belohnungssystem – das Team entscheidet, wer in welcher Höhe honoriert wird

Die Motivation, die die Mitarbeiter durch die oben genannten Konzepte und deren konsequente Einhaltung entwickelt, birgt das Potenzial, die Vertriebsperformance nachhaltig zu steigern.

Verkehrskreuzungen bieten ein interessantes Studienobjekt, um zu untersuchen, wie eine Verlagerung von zentraler zu dezentraler Verantwortung auf die Performance wirken kann (Abb. 12.3).

Entgegen der landläufigen Meinung, dass durch Ampelschaltung zentral kontrollierte Kreuzungen deutlich effizienter sind als Kreisverkehre, in welchen die Autofahrer selbst und ohne vorgegebene Führung handeln müssen, ist das Gegenteil der Fall. Kreisverkehre sorgen statistisch gesehen für einen 30 % effizienteren Verkehrsfluss, gleichzeitig vermindern sie die Anzahl von Verkehrsunfällen ebenfalls um 30 %.

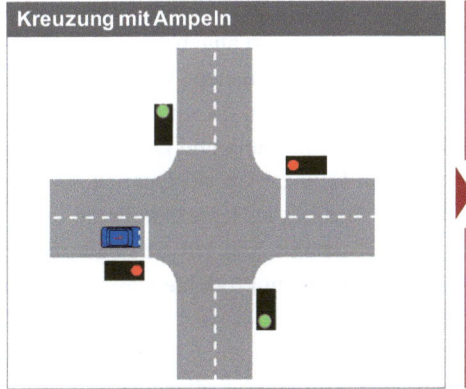 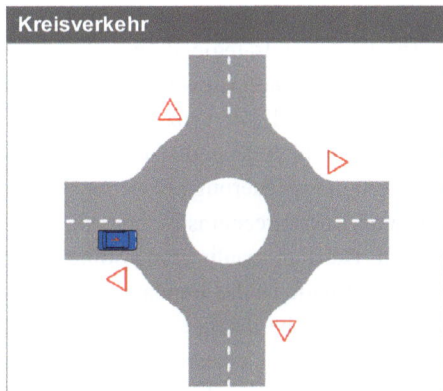

Abb. 12.3 Verkehrskreuzungen

12.6   Industrialisierung

Aktuelle Entwicklungen und Problemstellungen – bisher kein konsequentes Durchhalten der Industrialisierung bei Finanzdienstleistern

Viele Finanzdienstleister nehmen für sich in Anspruch, Industrialisierungsansätze bereits implementiert zu haben. Doch bislang blieben solche Initiativen Stückwerk und dienten oft nur dazu, kurzfristig Kosten zu senken. Ein Blick auf die Automobilbranche zeigt, dass Industrialisierung vielmehr ein Prozess ist, der Hartnäckigkeit erfordert und nur langfristig zum Erfolg führt.

12.7   Zukunftsmusik – Schritt für Schritt zu mehr Effizienz

Ein Modell, um diesen Prozess abzubilden, besteht aus vier Bausteinen und einer übergeordneten Philosophie:

- Industrialisierungsphilosophie
- Produktstrategie
- Wertschöpfungsstrategie
- Prozessstrategie
- Steuerungsstrategie

Die Industrialisierungsphilosophie legt die Ziele der Implementierung fest, etwa stärkere Kundenorientierung, mehr Flexibilität und eine höhere Qualität. Der eigentliche Industrialisierungsprozess setzt bei der Produktstrategie an. Die Verantwortlichen prüfen beispielsweise, ob und wie sich das Portfolio sinnvoll reduzieren lässt. Ein modulares Produktdesign hilft, das Produktportfoliomanagement zu vereinfachen. Der zweite Baustein, die Wertschöpfungsstrategie, definiert, welche Produkte standardisiert angeboten werden und wo eine Individualfertigung erfolgt. In diesem Zuge wird auch festgelegt, welche Prozesse auszulagern sind. Die Prozessstrategie definiert darauf aufbauend die unternehmensweite Prozessarchitektur und standardisierte Verfahren für Optimierung und Dokumentation. Die Fertigungssteuerung als vierter Baustein basiert auf Kennzahlen, die Qualität, Durchsatz und Ressourceneinsatz messen, um den Betrieb flexibel an Kundenaufträge anzupassen. Die Industrialisierung sollte aufbauen auf IT-Strategie und HR-Strategie. Denn die IT-Strategie ist das Fundament für Finanzdienstleister, deren Produkte wesentlich aus Informationen bestehen.

Die Einführung eines industriellen Geschäftsmodells erfordert einen langen Atem und bedeutet viel Aufwand, der sich jedoch auszahlt. Er verhilft Finanzdienstleistern dazu, Kundenbedürfnisse langfristig zu befriedigen. Trotz allen technischen Fortschritts bleiben letztendlich die Mitarbeiter diejenigen, die die bereitgestellten Instrumente zum Klingen bringen. Sie geben zudem Anstöße dafür, Produkte und Technologien kontinuierlich zu verbessern.

So bedarf es in einer industrialisierten Welt mehr Mitarbeiter, welche mehr Verantwortung und Kreativität in den Prozess einbringen möchten. Es bedarf mehr Mitarbeiter, welche Prozesse von Beginn bis Ende gesamtheitlich verstehen und fähig sind, wertschaffende Analysen zu liefern und weniger mit der Ausübung kleinteiliger Aufgaben beschäftigt sind. Dies kann beispielsweise in Risikoabteilungen der Fall sein: weg vom erstellen automatisierter Reports per Knopfdruck aus dem System, hin zur Analyse zugrundeliegender Daten und Diskussion der Erkenntnisse auf Augenhöhe mit dem Front-Office.

12.8   Digitalisierung

12.8.1   Aktuelle Entwicklungen und Problemstellungen – Die Digitalisierung verändert das Geschäftsmodell von Banken nachhaltig

Digitalisierung bedeutet den Einzug digitaler Technologie in den Alltag der Menschen und damit auch der Bankkunden. Dies ermöglicht Kunden, zum Schaden der Institute, viele Finanztransaktionen ohne Zutun der Banken selbst bzw. über neue Spezialanbieter abzuwickeln, Zum Beispiel bei Zahlungen über Paypal oder NFC über das neue iPhone 6. Den Banken werden damit wichtige Teile der Wertschöpfungskette genommen. Nach und nach gelingt es branchenfremden Anbietern durch die Digitalisierung sogar auch komplexere Produkte, wie zum Beispiel Peer-to-Peer-Kredite, anzubieten und den Finanzinstituten damit weitere Umsätze abzunehmen.

Prozesse werden durch neue Identifikationsverfahren in nahezu sämtlichen Branchen immer stärker entmaterialisiert (z. B. digitale Signatur), der Kunde muss also nicht mehr vor Ort sein, um Geschäfte zu tätigen. Die rechtlichen Rahmenbedingungen der Digitalisierung passen sich hingegen nur langsam an.

Banken müssen sich sowohl im Backoffice als auch im Frontoffice mit diesen neuen Gegebenheiten auseinandersetzen:

Im Backoffice werden manuelle, einfache Tätigkeiten immer weniger an der Tagesordnung sein. Papierlose Prozesse können die Effizienz deutlich erhöhen und Abläufe verschlanken. Da die Transaktionsvolumina nicht oder nur sehr gering ansteigen, wird immer mehr Personal auf Grund der steigenden Produktivität durch Digitalisierung überflüssig werden.

Digitalisierung führt auch insgesamt zu deutlich weniger Laufkundschaft in Filialen, so dass sich diese immer mehr zu Kostenstellen anstatt zu Umsatzbringern entwickeln.

Blick in die Zukunft – das Aussterben von nachgelagerten Funktionen und der Filialen wie wir sie kennen

Nachgelagerte Funktionen werden in ihrer jetzigen Art und Funktionsweise nicht mehr länger bestehen bleiben, das Personal wird drastisch gekürzt werden. Prozesse, die schon heute zu den klassischen, entmaterialisierten Abläufen gehören, wie zum Beispiel das

Scannen, werden durch die Digitalisierung noch weiter optimiert. Im Ergebnis wird ein Rückgang von nicht weniger als 25 % des Personals bis 2020 projiziert.

Damit nicht genug – sämtliche „klassischen" Transaktionen werden zukünftig nicht mehr als Kerngeschäft gesehen und in sogenannten „Fabriken" abgewickelt (entweder intern, gemeinsam mit anderen Banken oder als Outsourcing Service).

Schon jetzt lässt sich beobachten, dass etliche Banken ihre Filialnetze verkleinern – dieser Trend wird sich weiter fortsetzen. Die Anzahl an Filialmitarbeitern wird sich voraussichtlich noch weiter verringern als die Anzahl der Filialen selbst, auch hier prognostizieren wir einen Rückgang von ca. 15 bis 30 %. Doch auch verbleibende Filialen werden sich nachhaltig verändern müssen, um in Zukunft bestehen zu können.

12.8.2 Neugestaltung unumgänglich

Die nachgelagerten Funktionen müssen im Zeitalter der Digitalisierung ihre Rolle neu erfinden. Zunächst sollte das Filialnetz auf eine kritische Masse bzgl. Kosten, Kompetenzen und Präsenz vor Ort reduziert werden. Zusätzlich können virtuelle Fabriken zum Beispiel durch joint ventures, outsourcing oder near-shoring eine Reihe von Filialaufgaben übernehmen.

Backoffices sollten in skalierbare middleoffices mit hoch qualifizierten Ressourcen umgewandelt werden. Silostrukturen zwischen Marktbereichen und Backoffice sollten möglichst zerschlagen und der Fokus stattdessen auf den Kunden gelegt werden. Die gesamte Organisation sollte überdacht und nahtlose Übergänge vom Vertrieb bis in die Abwicklung sichergestellt werden.

Die Personalstrategie spielt in dieser Hinsicht eine wichtige Rolle: Mitarbeiterprofile, Karriere- und Trainingspläne sowie das Management der verbleibendem Backoffices müssen organisiert werden.

Mitarbeiter in den Filialen müssen sich auf die neue Situation einstellen, da das klassische Filialgeschäft in seiner ursprünglichen Form nicht mehr existieren wird.

Der Abbau von Mitarbeitern im Zuge der Digitalisierung und die gleichzeitige Mobilisierung der verbleibenden Arbeitnehmerschaft ist eine große Herausforderung. Nichtsdestotrotz kann eine frühzeitige Einbindung und das gemeinsame Formulieren der neuen Strategie eine solide Basis für das Vorangehen im digitalisierten Zeitalter schaffen.

Die Institute müssen sich mit geringeren Personalkapazitäten neu erfinden und die Kompetenzen ihrer Mitarbeiter dabei so effizient wie möglich einsetzen. Der Fokus sollte zwecks Differenzierung dabei auf wertschöpfenden Tätigkeiten liegen (z. B. Beratung). Ein geschulteres, besser qualifiziertes und mobilisierteres Personal ist die Voraussetzung.

12.9   Fazit

Statische Umsätze und steigende Kosten, unter anderem durch neue regulatorische Vorgaben, sowie verändertes Kunden- und Mitarbeiterverhalten stellen die Finanzbranche vor große Herausforderungen. In vielen Fällen steht ein struktureller Wandel bevor, der, wie die Modellrechnung zeigt, Maßnahmen sowohl auf der Kosten- als auch der Ertragsseite erfordert. Um diesen Wandel zu schaffen, müssen die Mitarbeiter in den Mittelpunkt gestellt werden. Mobilisierte Mitarbeiter erleichtern die Implementierung der beschriebenen Stellhebel Vertriebsintensivierung, Industrialisierung und Digitalisierung und sind der Schlüssel zu nachhaltigem Erfolg.

Norman Weißer ist seit elf Jahren Unternehmensberater im Bankensektor und derzeit Senior Manager bei Eurogroup Consulting (www.eurogroupconsulting.de), einer in Frankfurt ansässigen Unternehmensberatung für Finanzdienstleister. Seine Fokusgebiete sind die Entwicklung von IT- und Sourcing Strategien sowie die Front-to-Back Organisation und Prozesse insbesondere bei Asset Managern. Weißer hat einen Abschluss als Diplomkaufmann der Universität Mannheim.

Laura Zdrzalek ist seit über sieben Jahren Unternehmensberaterin im Bankensektor und derzeit Managerin bei Eurogroup Consulting (www.eurogroupconsulting.de), einer in Frankfurt ansässigen Unternehmensberatung für Finanzdienstleister. Ihre Fokusgebiete sind der Wertpapierservicebereich, sowie die umfassende Prüfung laufender (Groß-)Projekte. Zdrzalek hat einen Abschluss als Master of International Business von der Grande École Audencia in Nantes (Frankreich).

FSC
www.fsc.org

MIX
Papier aus verantwortungsvollen Quellen
Paper from responsible sources
FSC® C105338

If you have any concerns about our products,
you can contact us on
ProductSafety@springernature.com

In case Publisher is established outside the EU,
the EU authorized representative is:
**Springer Nature Customer Service Center GmbH
Europaplatz 3, 69115 Heidelberg, Germany**

Printed by Libri Plureos GmbH
in Hamburg, Germany